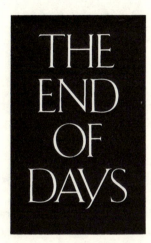

THE
END
OF
DAYS

Advance Praise for *The End of Days*

"This is a history in the tradition of Barbara Tuchman and Simon Schama—full of vivid human detail with a driving narrative power. It is also a profound reminder that to learn from the past we must not repeat the mistakes of the past."

—Phyllis Grosskurth, author of *The Secret Ring:
Freud's Inner Circle and the Politics of Psychoanalysis*

"Erna Paris's *The End of Days* puts together a very large amount of material about what happened in Spain over a 1,000-year period into a well-focused and exciting presentation. . . . The story of Spanish history up to 1492 is presented both as narrative and as drama. . . . Paris . . . leads the reader to see the sad story of what happened in Spain over 500 years ago as a most important object lesson for 20th-century readers. . . . An exciting and tragic story."

—Richard H. Popkin, Professor Emeritus,
Washington University, Adjunct Professor, UCLA

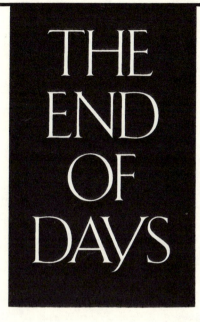

THE END OF DAYS

A STORY OF TOLERANCE, TYRANNY, AND
THE EXPULSION OF THE JEWS FROM SPAIN

ERNA PARIS

Prometheus Books
59 John Glenn Drive
Amherst, New York 14228-2197

Illustrations in insert courtesy
Ampliaciones y Reproducciones MAS, Barcelona, Spain.

Published 1995 by Prometheus Books

99 98 97 96 95   5 4 3 2 1

Library of Congress Cataloging-in-Publication Data

Paris, Erna [date]
    The end of days : a story of tolerance, tyranny, and the expulsion of the Jews from Spain / Erna Paris.
        p.   cm.
    Includes bibliographical references and index.
    ISBN 1-57392-017-7 (hardback : alk. paper)
    1. Jews—Spain—History. 2. Marranos—Spain—History. 3. Inquisition—Spain. 4. Religious tolerance—Spain—History. 5. Spain—Ethnic relations. 6. Spain—History—711–1516. I. Title.
DS135.S7P34   1995
946'.004924—dc20   95-24016
                                                                          CIP

Printed in the United States of America on acid-free paper

For Tom, Michelle, and Roland—always,

and for David Lewis Stein, my friend since childhood,
who first encouraged me to write

"And history with all her volumes vast
hath but one page."

—Lord Byron, *Childe Harold's Pilgrimage*

Contents

9

Part Two: Epilogue

Acknowledgments

Dozens of people assisted me in this long and passionate journey of five years. Some directed me to specific materials, or took time from their schedules to read sections of the manuscript; others helped with research and translations; still others were willing to discuss ideas as they developed, or to offer much appreciated emotional support when my resolve flagged. To name all of these people would require a book in itself, but as they read this story, each will recognize his or her essential contribution.

I would like to express special thanks to the following people: Lynn Cunningham, Marcella Durán, Claudio Durán, Isolda Dyson, Bernice Eisenstein, Jane Gelfman, Mark G. Hall, Jacques Kornberg, Myrna Kostash, Michelle Lapautre, Malcolm Lester, Ruth Miller, Eric Miller, Steven L. Mitchell, Peter R. Newman, Michelle Paris, Roland Paris, Richard H. Popkin, Julie Popkin, David Lewis Stein, Lucinda Vardey, Gail Weber, and Bruce Westwood. As always my deepest appreciation goes to my husband, Tom Robinson, for his unfailing support and love.

I would also like to thank the Canada Council, the Ontario Arts Council, and the Toronto Arts Council for their generous financial assistance.

Chronological List of Rulers and Monarchs of Spain Mentioned in Text

Visigothic Rulers:

Athanagild:	551–567
Leovigild:	572–586
Reccared:	586–601
Wamba:	672–680
Rodrigo:	710–711

Muslim Spain:

Tariq ben Ziyad:	710–712
Abdur Rahman I:	756–788
Hisham I:	788–796
Abdur Rahman III:	912–961
Hakam II:	961–976

The Nasrid Kingdom of Granada:

Muhammed XI (Boabdil):	1486–1492

Christian Spain: Castile and León:

Alfonso VI of León:	1065–1109
and Castile:	1072–1109
Alfonso X (The Wise):	1252–1284
Pedro I:	1350–1369
Enrique II:	1369–1379
Enrique III:	1390–1406
Juan II:	1406–1454
Enrique IV:	1454–1474
Isabel I (Isabella, wife of Ferdinand II of Aragon):	1474–1504

Aragon:

Jaime (James) II	1291–1327
Pedro IV:	1336–1387
Juan I:	1387–1395
Fernando (Ferdinand) I:	1412–1416
Juan II:	1458–1479
Fernando II (Ferdinand, husband of Isabella I of Castile):	1479–1516

Modern Spain:

General Francisco Franco:	1936–1975
Juan Carlos I:	1975–

Chronology of Major Events in Spain with References to Events Elsewhere in the World

B.C.E.

133——Fall of Numantia: the last opposition by indigenous Celtiberians to Roman rule in the Iberian Peninsula.

——About this time, Simon Maccabeus expels the Syrians from Jerusalem.

——The Roman politician and orator Cicero is born.

C.E.

409——The Visigoths invade Hispania.

——The beginnings of alchemy with the search for the Philosopher's Stone and the Elixir of Life.

587——King Reccared of the Visigoths converts to Roman Catholicism and declares it to be the state religion.

——Around this time, the first plans for the Vatican Palace are drawn up in Rome.

——Venice is founded by refugees from Attila's Huns.

711——Tariq the Moor reaches the Peninsula and routs the Visigoth king Rodrigo.

——Dagobert III is king of the Franks.

718——Pelayo defeats the Moors in battle initiating the Christian Reconquest of Spain.

——The Benedictine monastery at Montserrat is already in existence.

——The first copper coinage is struck in Japan.

785——Construction begins on the great mosque of Cordoba.
——Charlemagne takes Gerona.
——Tuma of al-Ruba, translator of the *Illiad* into Arabic, dies.

1085——The Muslim kingdom of Toledo is reconquered by the Christians.
——In England, the following year, William the Conqueror has the *Doomsday Book* compiled: an assessment for tax purposes.

1147——Fanatic Almohads from North Africa end multireligious tolerance in Andalusia. Many Arabized Christians and Jews move north to the Christian territories.
——The Second Crusade is led by Conrad III of Germany and Louis VII of France.
——The cultivation of silk is introduced into Sicily.

1238——Construction of the Alhambra Palace in Granada.
——Moscow is sacked by the Mongol army.

1348–53——The Black Death sweeps Europe provoking anti-Jewish pogroms.
——Boccaccio writes the *Decameron*.
——The English philosopher William of Ockham dies.
——Florentine bankers establish banks in France, England, Italy, and Constantinople.

1391——Massacres of Jews across Spain.
——Charles VI of France is asked to intervene to end the Great Schism.
——Kanejeje, King of Kano, introduces quilted armor and iron helmets.

1414——Opening of the Disputation of Tortosa.
——The Medici of Florence become bankers to the papacy.
——Council of Constance. John Huss is arrested.
——Henry V of England demands all lands held by the Plantagenets.

1449——A rebellion against Jewish converts (*conversos*) in Toledo and the introduction of purity of blood statutes.
——Lorenzo de Medici (The Magnificent), future ruler of Florence, is born.
——War between England and France.

1479——Union of Castile and Aragon under Isabella of Castile and Ferdinand of Aragon.
——Brussels emerges as the center of the European tapestry industry.
——Copenhagen University is founded.

1481——The Holy Inquisition against Depraved Heresy is established in Castile.
——Botticelli and Ghirlandaio paint frescoes in the Sistine Chapel in Rome.

1485——The Holy Inquisition against Depraved Heresy is established in Aragon. Inquisitor Pedro de Arbués is assassinated by conversos.
——Henry Tudor, Earl of Richmond, defeats and kills Richard III at Bosworth and succeeds as Henry VII.
——First printing of the Quran in Arabic.
——Establishment of the Yeomen of the Guard in England.

1491——The Holy Child of La Guardia trial and auto de fe* takes place in Avila.
——Copernicus studies at Cracow University.

1492——The expulsion of the Jews from Spain.
——Christopher Columbus sails from Palos, Spain, and reaches Cuba two months later.
——The Christian Reconquest comes to an end with the capture of the last Arab kingdom of Granada.
——Elio Antonio de Nebrija publishes the first Castilian grammar.
——Roderigo Borgia becomes Pope Alexander VI.
——The first terrestrial globe is constructed by Nuremberg geographer Martin Behaim.
——Leonardo da Vinci draws a flying machine.

---

*The Spanish auto de fe will be used throughout the text instead of its Portuguese equivalent, auto-da-fé (ed. note).

Abbreviations

AHR	*American Historical Review*
BAE	*Biblioteca de Autores Españoles*
BAH	*Boletín de la Real Academia de la Historia*
EHR	*English Historical Review*
JQR	*Jewish Quarterly Review*
RABM	*Revista de Archivos, Bibliotecas y Museos*
RAH	*Real Academia de la Historia, Madrid*
REJ	*Revue des Etudes Juives*
RH	*Revue Historique*

Introduction

Celts, Romans, Visigoths, and Moors; pagans, Christians, Jews, and Muslims. It was a rich, multicultural stew that bubbled and simmered over the Iberian Peninsula for more than a thousand years producing a unique, pluralistic society. In spite of the dictates of religion and politics—an Inquisition to rid the Catholic Church of "Judaizing" heretics, and the ultimate expulsion from the country of both the Jews and the Moors— this underlying crucible of race and culture remains visible five hundred years after the tolerant attitudes it reflected were formally crushed. A woman's voice wails in melancholy Arabic cadences from behind a window thrown open in a narrow Tarragona street; Christian churches tower over the foundation stones of ancient synagogues; and in the faces of many Spaniards one glimpses a distinct reminder of Semitic ancestry. Fortress castles that once delineated the battle lines of the Holy Reconquest against the infidel Moors continue to dominate the mountaintops in a still lonely terrain. In Spain the sharply restrained passion of a lone voice and guitar and the sensuality of tambourine rhythm and flamenco have survived for hundreds of years in unlikely partnership with the most pervasive, watchful, Catholic power in Europe.

That Spain was, for centuries, the most tolerant nation in Europe, and subsequently became the most zealously *in*tolerant, is the heart of this book. What actually happened, and how, and why? And is there anything to learn from the cataclysmic upheaval of a distant age as the violent, tortured twentieth century draws to a close? As human beings we seem to change little from one epoch to the next, in spite of the strangeness of past eras which have included, along with eccentricities of style, the varying fanaticisms of religious absolutists, political extremists of left and right, and a myriad of other forgotten utopians who have tried to codify, clas-

19

sify, and force upon us their respective visions of the world. We are, it seems, a stubbornly anarchic breed, and it is likely that all we can hope to alter is our awareness of the natural, economic, social, and psychological conditions that are likely to produce tragedy.

The subject of cultural and political transformation has intrigued me since I first lived in France in the early 1960s. It was a time when the French were determined to forget the war and the German Occupation. Everyone had been a hero of the Resistance. No one had collaborated with the Nazis, except a few certified monsters who were tried in a frenzy of rough justice after the Liberation. No one had actually wanted to deport the Jews to Auschwitz. To talk about such things was embarrassing, in bad taste. Because I needed to see for myself, I visited Struthof, a Nazi concentration camp in the Vosges Mountains. There I saw the crematorium and the large table used for dissections with its channels for run-off blood.

The shock of that visit lasted for many years, and in retrospect it was probably the defining experience of my young adult life. I am not a survivor of the Holocaust, nor did I personally know any member of my extended family who may have died in Europe. I believe the shock came from the terrible contrast between the comfortable family life I had left behind in Toronto, including my youthful vision of the world as a rational place, and the horror I was forced to confront. This eventually was transformed into a need to understand what combination of event and circumstance had led to a human catastrophe of this order, a need that has underscored much of my work over two decades and is the genesis for this book.

*   *   *

To enter the Middle Ages is to step into a God-drenched world where every natural event is a sign or threat from above, and every human act has divinely ordained consequences. It is to step into a world that is beset with conflicts and contradictions—just as ours is. The long Holy Reconquest to recapture the Iberian Peninsula from the Moors, who had occupied most of Spain since the eighth century, was marked by powerful myths about presumed hostilities between Christians and "infidels"; however, reality was quite the opposite: Christians, Moors, and Jews actually lived together in comparative harmony. Ideals of chivalry exalted women, but a society infused with Christian misogynism reviled them as descendants of Eve and dangerous despoilers; the Spanish Church preached against usury, but members of the clergy engaged in money-lending at interest just like everyone else; and from the pulpits of Castile and Aragon preachers threatened excommunication to those who broke faith while the Church itself had never been so divided or corrupt.

The conflict between faith and reason had particularly far-reaching consequences, for the same era that placed God at the core of existence and the Catholic Church at the center of every life also fostered early glimmerings of rationalism, of a sort that bypassed religion altogether. Such thinking, which grew from the rediscovery of the philosophical works of Aristotle, heralded a distinctly "modern" mind-set, which did not come into general focus until the Enlightenment of the eighteenth century. Budding secularism was nothing short of dangerous, yet many intellectuals were edging in that direction, creating a small vanguard of an era yet to come.

Although I am writing about a world that identified itself religiously, this is not a book about religion. It is, rather, about a common outcome of religion, which was true in the Middle Ages and is still much with us: the exclusiveness that so often characterizes belief and other ideologies, and the consequences of that exclusiveness.

Us and Them. The in-group and the outsider. The Other. Twentieth-century psychology has identified differentiation as the earliest awareness of self; the infant who grows to distinguish herself from her parent, or to recognize that the foot she so enthusiastically directs toward her mouth belongs to her body and is separate from the world outside, has taken a step toward human self-consciousness. But if separateness is an ingredient of being human, it also nurtures a dangerous core. Distrust of the Other seems to slumber within us, ready to erupt under certain conditions into xenophobia and violence. Exclusion is expressed through hundreds of familiar unities—from the self, to the family, to the neighborhood, to the tribe (be it national or religious), to the state. Tolerance of difference may be less "natural"—an attitude we learn (or do not learn) in our families or society—and it appears always to be vulnerable to the effects of propaganda.

More than a thousand years ago in what is now Spain, the ruling Visigoths accused the minority Jews living in their midst of plotting to take over the kingdom and murder the Christians—namely, themselves, the power-holding majority. The Visigoths had made Christianity the ideological center of their political state (a premise that was naturally rejected by the Jews), and the distrust and suspicion subsequently directed toward the newly defined Other pinpoints the conflict living at the heart of every regime that makes conformity a condition for membership. Following their definition of nationhood, the Visigoths quite logically declared that "only Catholics can live in Spain." Centuries later, King Ferdinand and Queen Isabella agreed, on identical grounds, and expelled the Jews.

In the twentieth century, national obsessions delineating Us and Them reached fantastic proportions. Nazi criteria for group belonging bypassed the sphere of religion altogether, but like their spiritual forebears in Spain they, too, decided that "only Aryans can live in Germany." Before long, this was converted to "only Aryans can live." The Nazis had unparalleled modern technology and went infinitely further than the fifteenth-century Spanish Inquisition or the Expulsion. But persecution based on criteria of conformity, and the creation of an impersonal bureaucracy capable of effecting mass genocide, found a common ancestor in inquisitorial Spain. With historical distance the markers foreshadowing future upheaval assume more recognizable patterns. From a modern perspective the transformation of medieval Spain from tolerance to religious inquisition offers a startling paradigm for events closer to our time.

There were unavoidable difficulties to researching a book such as this about a time so long ago, including the foreignness of a remote world in which religion was the organizing feature of society and infinitely more central to people's lives than it is today. Yet it is transparently true that when the outside skin of cultural difference is peeled away, we are left with whatever remains unchanged in the human condition. To discover recognizable human beings struggling with familiar dilemmas is a profoundly moving experience. To glimpse the universality of human emotion, desire, and also vice across the centuries is to link the past and the future, like the generations of a family. There is nothing like the study of history to help one understand that humankind is not, and never will be, perfectible.

Another concern was the thinness of sources in some places. The Spanish Inquisition kept scrupulously detailed records of its activities, just like the Nazis, but other eras were less well documented. Certain events, like the assassination of Inquisitor Pedro de Arbués by convert Jews in the cathedral of Saragossa, were sensational enough to be recorded in detail by chroniclers, but elsewhere there were inevitable lacunae. An additional problem was the impossibility of identifying the hard data of dates and numbers. Chroniclers exaggerated notoriously, sometimes using large numbers to make the literary point that there were a lot of people involved. I have adopted generally accepted figures, but they are all estimates based on extrapolation and averaging. I have also used contemporary terminology such as multiculturalism, racism, pogrom, etc. to describe conditions and events that occurred before any of these words were voiced; and with the exception of individuals such as King Ferdinand and Queen Isabella, who are well known to us in the twentieth century, I have used Spanish name spellings.

The minefield of historical fashion over the centuries was tricky since propaganda and ideology have played a central role in the study of Jewish and Moorish history in Spain, and in writings on the Inquisition. The latter was a religious battleground for centuries, defended by Catholics and attacked by Protestants. As for the Jews, for hundreds of years after their expulsion in 1492 the presence of "Jewish blood" in the population was a negative measure of religious purity. There were no Jews in Spain, but their supposed "treachery" continued to inform school history books and is still routinely evoked to explain the Expulsion. As for the Moors, if today we know so little about their civilization, it is because they were defeated in "Holy Reconquest," then subsequently denigrated for centuries. Although modern archival scholarship has been the norm for a long time now, it would be a mistake to think that ideology has entirely disappeared from the field.

Contemporary scholarship is highly focused and detailed (much of it consists of doctoral-thesis investigations into local archives) and I refer to it often. But I have also returned to primary sources wherever possible, that is, to the early chronicles of Spain. Chronicles are currently out of fashion as source material because their authors were biased; however, the argument of complete objectivity in history (or anywhere else) is, or ought to be, outdated. Chronicles remain indispensable because they contain narratives of people and events that expose the texture of another time, and because they help us to uncover motivation. In the nineteenth and early twentieth centuries, Spanish scholars annotated and edited these ancient works, providing a basis for writers like myself who have followed. In 1887, Fidel Fita found and published the Inquisition trial of Yucé Franco, a young boy who was charged in the infamous Holy Child of La Guardia affair, about which I write at length. In 1875, the great José Amador de los Rios did the same for the lost *Libro Verde de Aragón* (The Green Book of Aragon), which brought to light the sensational assassination of Inquisitor Pedro de Arbués by convert Jews in 1485. Juan de Mata Carriazo has edited a number of chronicles from the period, as has A. Paz y Mélia. I am deeply indebted to these dedicated scholars and to many others who uncovered material and made it accessible.

Part One of this book is the story of Spain's transformation from religious pluralism to religious tyranny. In keeping with my theme of the political consequences of exclusiveness, it is a tale of influential people and key events that effectively altered the general attitude toward minorities. The spotlight is on individuals who set cultural and ideological agendas and changed the direction of society, which means, unfortunately, that there are few women in this story, just as there are few "ordinary" men.

Part Two is an extended essay in which I suggest parallels and draw conclusions. The research suggested to me that trigger events leading to tyranny are often variations on familiar themes. Although many of us may sense this intuitively, I hope I have been successful in exposing some of the interconnecting threads of the process in a visible, useful way. My own bias on behalf of pluralist, multicultural society, in spite of its inherent tensions, will be more than evident throughout. I make no apologies for this view of the world, which writing this book has reinforced beyond measure.

Although the body of the book takes place during the fifteenth century, I ask the reader to accompany me on a journey through earlier days. With the exception of the Columbus expeditions, Spanish history is little known outside Spain, and for the reader who is starting from scratch the dramatic transformations of the country, and the fate of its minorities, must be understood against a backdrop of the events and myths that precipitated change. The Muslim occupation was crucial. As the historian Américo Castro put it, "Christian Spain came into being" through its interaction with the Muslim world "and found its soul in the Reconquest," the winning back of the country from the Moors. A more contemporary word for "soul" in this context might be "national consensus," and it was this transformed agreement about the nation and its definition that underscored the shift to tyranny.

The transition from inclusion to exclusion slammed the door on a rich and complex Arab civilization, marked one of the saddest chapters in Jewish history, and ultimately reduced the Iberian Peninsula to a stagnant backwater sealed off from Europe for hundreds of years. Spain did not rejoin the contemporary world in any real sense until 1975. That was the year Generalissimo Francisco Franco died and democracy crossed the Pyrenees.

A Word about the Title

The End of Days struck me as a resonant evocation of medieval thinking since people living then conceived of time as a linear process leading to an end point that had been prophesied. For Jews, "the end of days" represented that longed-for moment when the Messiah would appear to lead the righteous back to the Promised Land. There they would live in a kingdom of peace and all humankind would be redeemed. For Christians, the Hebrew messianic prophecies had already been fulfilled in the incarnate life and work of Jesus. What remained unfulfilled was the *second* appearance of the Messiah, which would happen on the Day of Judgment. At that moment "history" would end and a new era of salvation begin.[1]

More specifically, the title invokes the end of time for Spanish Jews, who had lived in the Iberian Peninsula for more than a millennium.

Because of the abruptness of the expulsion and its devastating effects, some rabbis believed the end of the world was at hand, and that the suffering of the Jews signaled the "birth pangs of the Messiah." This was also the end of an era for Spain itself. At the close of the fifteenth century (and this book), Columbus sails off to the "Indies" opening a new epoch of European colonialism. That age is ending only now.

Sources

Readers will find source material listed in the bibliography, and throughout the book I have footnoted what I believe to be the most important references. I have also included a separate English-language bibliography for readers who might wish to pursue the issues raised. Unfortunately, Dr. B. Netanyahu's recent, comprehensive book on the Spanish Inquisition appeared too late for me to use in the preparation of this work.

A Word About Currencies

The names of the currencies changed often during the Spanish Middle Ages, and the reader will come across at least half a dozen types. The thirteenth century tried standardization with the florin (3.5 grams of gold, minted in Florence) and the ducat, which was minted in Venice. This was only partially successful. In general, money called "gold" was a true coin. Other coins had a variable weight and gold content.

Wherever possible I have tried to indicate what the purchasing power might have been, but given the difficulties, my advice to the reader is to ignore the name of the currency and think of the amount simply as a large or small sum of money.

Note

1. Christian eschatólogy derives directly from Jewish sources. For further reading see *The Interpreter's Dictionary of the Bible* (Abingdon Press, 1962).

Part One

The Story

1

1391

A white-hot midday sun is boring into the tile roofs and cobbled paving stones of Valencia, a prosperous city tucked into a cove along the Mediterranean coast. It is June 9 in the year 1391, a Sunday, as it happens—an easy, lazy day of rest. Not much to do today but attend mass (making sure the neighbors take appropriate note). Not much to do but sit in the shade of one's patio and enjoy the meal that is being prepared at this very moment by wives or servants busy in the kitchen. A delicious aroma of roasting meat wafts from open windows all over the city. Sunday is the best day and lunch the best time to exchange gossip and information over the favorite dish of the era, pork loin accompanied by a bottle or two of hearty red wine from the local vineyards shimmering in the sun just outside the city walls.

On this particular Sunday the talk is the same at every table in Valencia, from the hovels of street cleaners to the villa of Prince Martin, the king's brother, who is in town preparing an expeditionary fleet to Sicily—the same at the tables of Christians, Jews, and Moors who make up the population of the city, each in their separate quarters. Disturbing news has just arrived of a vicious massacre in the southern city of Seville, brought by dusty, road-weary couriers. Everyone now knows that just three days ago a frenzied mob attacked and destroyed the Jewish quarter, urged on by a local archdeacon, Ferrán Martínez. More than a thousand people are rumored dead. Thousands more are said to have been baptized at sword point.

The Jews of Valencia have asked for and received a promise of protection from their local authorities should the violence spread to their city, but all the same the stillness of this Sunday noon harbors a watchful edge of dread. Jews have lived here in Valencia since the time of the Romans, coexisting peacefully with Christians and Moors. But for the past year or so a local Dominican priest named Vicente Ferrer has been persistently calling for their conversion and the destruction of Judaism itself, just like Ferrán Martínez in Seville. Ferrer has a captivating tongue, in fact he is held in universal awe. Wherever he goes crowds gather to listen to him preach, and it is said that although he speaks in Catalan, *everyone* can understand him, whether they are French, Italian, or German. Vicente Ferrer is so holy he can cure the sick, and there are people who swear he has brought the dead back to life.

So far there have been no attacks. Old traditions of tolerance continue to run deep in Valencia. But in recent months the king of Aragon has grown concerned enough over Friar Vicente's preaching to fortify the Jewish quarter with a wall three palms thick, and the Jews themselves have blocked the entrance to their quarter with wooden doors strengthened with iron bars.

While adults talk in hushed tones over their midday meal, forty or fifty young people begin to gather in the sun-scorched central marketplace. These are bored children with nothing to do on a Sunday noon. Like their parents they have heard what happened in Seville, and, being children, they are excited by the prospect of a little action.

They amuse themselves by tearing up a few pieces of cloth for a make-shift processional banner. This might be fun. They look around; stalks of sugar cane left lying on the ground after market day will serve as impro-vised crosses. Everyone is in high spirits as they begin to march toward the main entrance of the *judería,* or Jewish quarter, at the Figuera Gate, shouting at bystanders to join them.

Within minutes the swollen procession has reached the main entrance to the quarter. The young people shriek goading insults at the tops of their voices. "The archdeacon of Seville is coming to baptize you!" they shout mockingly as a few of their leaders push their way through the gate.

Hearing the shouting, the Jews leave their tables abruptly. Quickly they lock the gates to the *judería,* but—God help them—a few of the young ringleaders are accidentally shut inside. One of these is struck dur-ing the commotion.

"Help! They're murdering me!" he screams.

Word spreads through the city like fire. A Christian child is being mur-dered by the Jews! Unemployed drifters and freed galley slaves (of whom there are many in the city) are the first to answer the call. They gleefully prepare themselves for the welcome distraction of a riot by blackening their faces and pulling up the hoods from their cloaks. The entire popu-lation of Valencia runs to the Figuera Gate: the knights and the bour-geoisie, direct from their Sunday roasts; mendicant priests; police; members of the Order of the Knights of Montesa; and hundreds of peasants who happen to be in town that day. All of Prince Martin's soldiers who are just about to leave for Sicily also rush to the Jewish quarter.

The city notables try desperately to restore order. They push their way to the front of the crowd and command the Jews to open the gate, but the terrified Jews refuse. The mob heaves against the barred, wooden door and batters at the gate with clubs. For several minutes the locks hold; then there is a break. The crowd surges forward, swords and daggers in hand. The defending Jews are trampled underfoot or impaled on the spot, and in the confusion a young Christian is killed.

The boy's body is carried out of the *judería* and displayed. His parents scream. The mob explodes in rage. Several men push through a weak link in the wall surrounding the quarter. Others climb onto the roofs of neighboring houses and leap into the narrow streets of the *judería*.

Inside the quarter men, women, and children cower in hidden corners of their houses; others rush through back alleyways to take refuge in the synagogue. It is almost impossible to see for the dust in the air, impossible to know where one's family might be, impossible to hear for the terrified cries of the dying and the shouts of rioters who have fanned across the length and breadth of every street. The Jews shoot crossbows from behind the peristyle columns of their houses, but they are vastly outnumbered, and now it seems that nothing will stop this madness. People are dragged out of their homes regardless of age and slaughtered. Their blood reddens the drain channels that run down the center of every narrow street. Women are raped beside the bodies of the dead, houses are looted and burned.

"Convert to the Holy Faith or die!" cry the priests over the din. Conversion is the single key to survival, if one is lucky enough not to be stabbed on the spot. Some Jews will choose to die rather than accept baptism, but most want desperately to live. Thousands flee from the *judería* to the cathedral and the baptismal font.

Moving about through the heat and dust is the outline of a familiar figure: Vicente Ferrer. Friar Vicente has never been a man of overt violence; he is subtler by far than Ferrán Martínez, his counterpart in Seville. But this is Ferrer's day, his glorious hour. Vicente Ferrer calms the rioting mob and invites the terrified Jews to accept Jesus as the rightful Messiah. He is saving their lives. The Jews throw themselves at his feet and he baptizes them, one after the other. "He is like Christ's apostle," murmur the amazed Valencians.

Suddenly miracles are proclaimed. Four notaries swear that in the parish of St. Andrés the empty baptismal vessels fill of their own accord as they are needed for the conversions of thousands of Jews.[1] Clearly this is God's work. Before the day is out the massacre in the Jewish quarter is being hailed as divine. The End of Days seems imminent: the day of the Second Coming of Christ which will happen only when the Jews have accepted Christianity.

At sundown an eerie quiet blankets the blood-stained streets of the *judería*. Wary survivors creep cautiously from cellars and secret recesses to collect the bodies of mothers, fathers, children, and friends. They meet in the half light of dusk and cling to each other wordlessly. But it is too soon to grieve; another procession is coming toward them. Rhythms of drums, tambourines, and the high-pitched notes of piccolos announce the approach of bare-footed friars, church canons, and bishops dressed in full regalia. They have raised great, jewelled crosses to the glory of God. They are singing joyously and the rich notes of the ancient Latin hymn *Te Deum* swell through the streets.

The procession enters the Jewish quarter two abreast, the width of the street itself. Still singing, the priests pass the smoldering shells of houses, stepping over torn clothing and household possessions lying broken on the cobblestones. They do not stop until they reach the doors of the main synagogue. There they triumphantly reconsecrate the ancient house of Jewish prayer to Christ and Saint Christopher.[2]

On June 14, 1391, a report from the municipality of Valencia confirms that every survivor of the pogrom has been baptized—except those who are still in hiding.[3] By August the flames of pogrom have spread across all of Castile and Aragon. Thousands of Jews are dead. Their communities are destroyed entirely.

They will never recover.

The Jews of Spain did not forget Friar Vicente Ferrer or the preparatory role he played during the year preceding the massacre of Valencia. In his post-Expulsion chronicles, Rabbi Joseph ben Joshua ben Meir speaks of "Friar Vincent from the city of Valencia of the sect of Baal Dominic. . . ."

> He was unto them [the Jews] a Satan and stirred up against them all the inhabitants of the country, and they rose to swallow them alive, and slew many with the edge of the sword, and many were burned with fire, and many were turned away with the power of the sword from the Lord, the God of Israel. And they burned the books of the Law of our God, and trampled upon them as upon the mire in the streets; and the mother they dashed in pieces upon her children in the day of the Lord's wrath. . . . And some of them [the Jews] killed their sons and daughters that they might not be defiled. . . . Those who were baptized became numerous in the land of Sefarad [Spain] and they put upon them a mark of distinction unto this day. . . .
>
> And this Belial was in their sight a saint; and the Pope Calixtus wrote

his memory among the saints and appointed feast days unto his name, on the fifth day of the month of April. May God recompense him [Ferrer] according to his deeds.[4]

*   *   *

As the *juderías* of Spain erupted in flames, two things were true. First, conversion to Christianity could, and did, save lives—provided the priest got to the scene before the murderous mob. In 1391 religion was a matter of faith, not race, and since doctrine held that baptism altered the soul, the "stain" of Judaism was instantly blotted out. From that moment the baptized Jew was perceived as an instant (if unwilling) member of the Christian majority in an officially Christian land.

Second, Spain was, without doubt, an officially Christian land, but at the heart of this reality lived another, less orthodox truth. Far from being minority outsiders, the Jews of fourteenth-century Spain had lived integrated lives in a longstanding multicultural world. Far from being marginal, the degree of their involvement in the economic and cultural life of their country had been nothing short of astonishing.

Two questions emerge as we observe this turning point in the history of Spain. How did this plural society come into being in the first place? And why did it begin to disintegrate in flames?

Notes

1. Philippe Wolff, "The 1391 Pogrom in Spain: Social Crisis or Not?" *Past and Present* 50 (1971).

2. M. Francisco Dánvila, "El Robo de la Judería de Valencia en 1391," *BAH* 7, fasc. 5 (1886); analyzed by Isidore Loeb, "Le Sac des Juiveries de Valence et de Madrid en 1391," *REJ* 19 (1888): 239ff.; José Amador de los Rios, *Historia de los Judíos en España y Portugal* (1875–1876), 3 vols., 2: 463ff.

3. Henry Lea, "Ferrand Martínez and the Massacre of 1391," *AHR* 1 (1896): 217ff.

4. Rabbi Joseph ben Joshua ben Meir, *Chronicles,* Bialloblotsky translation, 1: 265–67, cited in Lea, "Ferrand Martínez," 218, note 2.

2

Setting the Scene: Two Nations in One: Christ and Muhammad

It is a remote time, the fifth century C.E., and for the past five hundred years Hispania has been a far-flung, western outpost of the vast Roman Empire.[1] A succession of consuls and generals subdued the indigenous Celtiberians who had lived here since time immemorial. Brilliant engineers built roads, bridges, and aqueducts across this scorched terrain of deserts and mountain ranges. They introduced Roman law, openly extended Roman citizenship to everyone living in the territory, promoted education and Latin literature, and ruled with a relatively even hand.

There are many Jews living here in the Iberian Peninsula. Later on Jewish mythologists will claim the community first settled here in the sixth century B.C.E, after the destruction of the first temple in Jerusalem, or, even more prestigiously, that they arrived with Phoenician traders in the tenth century B.C.E at the time of King Solomon. Two thousand years later, in the tenth century C.E., during the so-called Golden Age of their long history in Spain, proud Jews proclaimed their lineage back to King David himself.[2] Lineage was a Spanish obsession, and the Jews were no exception to the rule. They called their country Sefarad—a place cited in the prophesy of Obadiah where the Jews, exiled from Jerusalem, lived.

The factual record is somewhat less glamorous: indeed, there is no reliable evidence with which to date the arrival of the Jews in the Iberian Peninsula, although it is generally agreed that one wave probably accompanied the Roman legions as merchants, and another came as refugees after the fall of the Second Temple in 70 C.E. The first documentary proof of a Jewish presence comes from the third century C.E.: a gravestone from Adra marking the burial place of a girl with the unmistakably Jewish name of Salomonula.

Like their native, Celtiberian compatriots, the Jews of fifth-century

Hispania live largely undisturbed lives. They cultivate the soil, alone or with slaves, and enjoy equal rights. But a fatal hurricane is blowing in from two directions, one spiritual, one political. Rome has adopted Christianity, the new faith, sewing the seeds of future conflict with Judaism, the parent religion that will eventually be pushed outside the boundaries of official acceptance. On the political front, barbarians from the north are pouring out of Germany and overrunning the once invincible empire. The sweep of the Visigoths across Hispania in the early fifth century is overwhelmingly brutal. "They murdered men and women, uprooted the crops, killed domestic animals, and attacked entire cities," one horrified Roman observed. "Famine and plague followed, and there were so many bodies strewn about that the country looked like a huge morgue."[3]

The Visigoths (who are Arian Christians, not Catholics) have unfamiliar names like Athanagild, Leovgild, Gundemar, Wamba, and Witiza, and their three-hundred-year-long reign in the Iberian Peninsula is marked by war and internecine royal assassination. Eventually, Hispania has no army, no industry, no trade, and no literature. Roman authors such as Virgil, Tacitus, and Livy are condemned as pagan atheists. Science and the arts are forbidden. (The most prominent archeological remnant of this impoverished culture seems to be belt buckles and a handful of crowns.)

But the Visigoths do seem to have a special talent: the persecution of minorities, in particular the Jews whom they forbid from holding public office, following their dietary laws, celebrating Passover, and marrying Christians (established interreligious marriages are declared void).

Religious minorities had coexisted under the Romans, even after Rome officially adopted Catholicism, and for a hundred years the conquering Visigoths expended their considerable energies on trying to promote conversion to their Arian brand of Christianity. But in the late sixth century a singular event occurred that politicized the exclusion of the Jewish minority. King Reccared of the Visigoths converted to Catholicism, then declared his new faith to be the official religion of the state. This was a dangerous combination, a crucial shift that gave birth to a politically powerful clergy.

In 633 the Fourth (Church) Council of Toledo tests its strength by ordering Jewish children to be removed from their parents and educated in convents, or at the very least by Christians. A religious command is now the law of the land. In 638 the Sixth Council goes further still. In an ominous foreshadowing of later events, the Visigoth clerics now declare that "only Catholics can live in Spain."

Short of having the power to place a priest on the throne, the clergy fiddle behind the scenes to ensure that the policies of the Church prevail. In 680, believing that King Wamba has been less than appropriately enthusiastic in his oppression of the Jews, the bishops arrange to slip a herbal potion into his royal cup. When Wamba falls into a coma and rumors of his imminent demise sweep the palace, the bishops rush to his side, piously shave his head, and dress the king in monk's robes to help ease his passage into the next world. But the uncooperative Wamba refuses to die. Instead, he wakes up to find himself a frocked, tonsured monk who is, by law, unable to sit on the throne. Does he fight back? By now the Church is much too powerful. The pathetic king accepts his fate and retires to a monastery, leaving the throne to a new monarch who has been hand-picked by the bishops.

The scheming machinations of seventh-century bishops jockeying for primacy may be the stuff of tragicomedy, as Polonius might have concluded, but something serious and entirely rational is being acted out. The Catholicism adopted by King Reccared has openly pitted two opposing visions of history against one another: one Jewish, one Christian. By denying that the Messiah has already lived on earth in the person of Jesus Christ, Judaism contradicts the essential premise of Christianity. At the same time, Christianity contradicts the essential premise of Judaism: that the Messiah has *not* yet come to save the world, but will do so one day. While religious coexistence was the rule, as under the laissez-faire Romans, this inherent conflict did not rise to the surface; but once Catholicism and the political state merged into one indivisible entity after the conversion of King Reccared, the mere presence of unconverted Jews in the land became politically intolerable. When church and state were one, the Jewish "challenge" to Christianity was, at the same time, a challenge to government.

Seen in this light, the anti-Jewish laws of the Visigoth rulers and their priests were not in the least arbitrary, and it is hardly surprising that the Jews were routinely accused of *political* subversiveness. They were charged with scheming to take over the kingdom, plotting to destroy the Church, and seeking to murder Catholics. As punishment for these "evil deeds," the Visigoths announced plans to confiscate the Jews' property and sell entire families into slavery.

These were harsh and dangerous times, but the inept Visigoths proved more skilled at pronouncing new laws than at carrying them out, and little came from their threats but lives of fearful expectation. In any case, by the early eighth century a new invader was eyeing the Iberian Peninsula, this time from the south. They were Muslims, believers in the new religion of Muhammad, and they swept from North Africa into Spain just decades after the death of the prophet.

When the Moors (as the Muslims of North Africa and Spain were called) rode their sleek Arabian horses through the stone-arch gates of

Toledo, the royal city of the Visigoth kings, a brutal era came to an end—except for the ideals that had informed the centuries of their rule. The stark war of the messiahs that underscored the repressive, antiminority policies of the Visigoths did not die, but remained alive in the minds of Christian survivors and their descendants as a model for future days.

*   *   *

On a night in April in the year 711 C.E., an army of seven thousand men sets sail from the coast of what is now Morocco. Stealthily, they traverse the water, their sights fixed on the rock now known as Gibraltar. They anchor in a natural harbor along a stretch of sandy beach and disembark, clinging to the mules they have brought with them; then they hide in caves along the seashore.

Later on, people will whisper that Tariq ibn Ziyad, the captain of the flotilla, was invited to invade by a disgruntled member of the royal house of the Visigoths who had been edged off the throne by the current king, Rodrigo. Others will insist that the Moors were summoned by one Count Julian, whose daughter, Florinda, was raped by King Rodrigo as she bathed in the River Tagus at Toledo.

The truth of these legends has long been lost, but Tariq the Moor intends to stay, regardless. As soon as his men disembark he burns every one of their ships.

King Rodrigo and Tariq meet in battle at Rio Guadalete in the crushing heat of July 711. Tariq's small army of seven thousand has been bolstered by five thousand reinforcements from North Africa. The Visigoth king arrives in an ivory chariot, dressed in a suit of gold cloth. Beside him paces his splendid white horse, Orelia. Rodrigo's forces number sixty thousand, but they are an undisciplined band of slaves and disloyal nobles who desert when the fighting gets rough. During the course of battle King Rodrigo disappears. One day later Orelia, Rodrigo's royal sandals, and his "upper garment and buskins, covered with pearls and precious stones"[4] are found on the bank of the River Guadalete, but the king is never seen again.

Who can understand a king who simply vanishes from the face of the earth? Certainly not his eighth-century subjects. They believe a magical power has destroyed him, and instantly transform the story of Rodrigo into legend. (A thousand years later, ballads about the king's strange disappearance were still being sung.)

Tariq the Moor presses over the Iberian Peninsula with ease as the awed inhabitants of city after city surrender without a struggle, and in 712 he reaches the capital of Toledo, the royal heart of the country. Here, as well, the story of his supernatural victory over Rodrigo has preceded him. The terrified bishops and nobility of the Visigoth court are in no mood to test the Devil's magic. They flee before the prodigious infidel whose magic scimitar has left no trace of their king.

But rumors of something new and utterly astonishing are on everyone's lips. Tariq the Moor has sent advance couriers to announce that his new regime is offering unheard-of terms: anyone who wants to leave Toledo can do so, but Christians and Jews of the city who choose to stay will be free to own property and practice their religion, including governing themselves according to their own civil and religious laws. In return they will have to pay a head tax, refrain from public processions, and agree not to punish any coreligionist who has chosen freely to convert to Islam.

The acceptance of other religions was set out in a verse in the Quran itself:

> Say, O believers! I shall not worship what you worship. You do not worship what I worship. I am not a worshipper of what you have worshipped, and you are not worshippers of what I have worshipped. To you, your religion. To me, my religion.[5]

After centuries of oppression, it is hard to imagine that the persecuted Jews and oppressed serfs of Visigoth Spain would not have welcomed a change of regime; in fact, the Jews were instantly accused of throwing open the gates of Toledo to the invaders, and the charge may have been well founded. True or not, the story of the Jews, the Moors, and the gates of Toledo was quickly mythologized as a seminal element in a new body of anti-Jewish, anti-Muslim propaganda that would grow and endure for centuries.

Given the liberal choice they were being offered, hundreds of thousands of Jews and Christians did decide to stay in the occupied territory and live under the Moors; and over the years a high degree of acculturation took place. Mozarabs—the name eventually ascribed to the Arabized Christian population—were unique to Spain. The Jews also were Arabized in natural ways.

But the diehard Christian Visigoths who refused to live with the Moors were also creating the nucleus of something new—a starkly different ethos that would eventually come to define the other "nation" in the Iberian Peninsula. From their strongholds in the mountains of northwest Cantabria, this surviving remnant of the Visigoths organized the beginnings of military resistance to the Moors: the Holy Christian Reconquest. What was to become "Spain" was forged in the cauldron of this struggle between two nations, one multireligious and liberal, the other exclusive and profoundly conservative. This conflict endured, on and off, for seven hundred years until the defeat of the last Arab kingdom in Granada in 1492.

The Astonishing World of the Moors

The ambience that marked the early centuries of Arab rule in Spain could not have been further removed from the brutal Visigoths, or from Christian Europe in general. While Europe embraced ignorance and superstition, the Moors promoted scholarship. While Christianity denigrated the senses, the feel of Arab Spain was nothing short of sensual. The Moors loved silks, linens, and fine wool, and their new science of agriculture made the expert production of these materials possible. They planted rice, olive trees, vineyards, corn, sugar cane, and cotton; they mined iron, copper, silver, gold, and other precious stones, and fished the seas for coral and pearls. All these products were traded with the friendly Muslim states to the east.

By the ninth century, the Andalusian capital of Cordoba was dotted with gardens dubbed "The Meadow of Murmuring Waters" and "The Golden Meadow." Gardening was an obsession. Following the example of a caliph with an interest in botany, courtiers, priests, army generals, and local governors feverishly planted and pruned. Oaks and beeches were uprooted from the sides of surrounding mountains and figs, almonds, and pomegranates were planted in their place, filling the air with perfume.

The caliphs channeled water from mountain rivers in lead pipes so that fountains, basins, and baths might grace their cities. Baths in the ninth century? An astonished contemporary remarked that "the Arabs of Andalusia are the cleanest people on earth. . . . Indeed they carry cleanliness to such an extreme that it is not an uncommon thing for a man of the lower classes to spend his last dirham on soap instead of buying food . . . and thus go without dinner rather than appear in public with dirty clothes."[6] On the other hand, commented another chronicler, the Christians in the north "live like animals, enter each other's houses without asking permission, and wash neither their bodies nor their clothes which they only remove when they fall into pieces."[7]

One hundred years later, Cordoba rivaled fabulous Byzantium in reputation. Local bazaars displayed crystal, gold, silver, carved ivory, rubies, sapphires, and pearls from the Orient, and every herbal drug known to medicine. There was nothing one could not buy in the magic city, and travelers from all over the world rushed home carrying exquisite treasures with which to amaze their compatriots.

The architecture born of this striking aesthetic genius was crowned by two early monuments: the Mezquita, or Mosque of Cordoba (constructed in 786 on the foundations of a Christian basilica), and the palace of Az-Zahra, which also was begun in the eighth century.[8] In the Mezquita 1,200 multicolored marble columns gathered from various parts of the ancient Roman Empire separated eleven distinct aisles. The walls glittered with porphyry and jasper, and the air was perfumed with incense. The roof of the Az-Zahra was supported by four thousand columns of marble and the halls of the palace were paved with marble of differing colors. Streams ran through lovingly tended gardens. Travelers, merchants, ambassadors, poets, and pilgrims swore that no one had ever seen the like. A transported contemporary gasped,

> Soldiers, pages, and slaves of all nations and religions move to and fro attired in silk and brocade . . . and a crowd of judges, theologians and poets walks through the halls. . . . The number of male servants in the palace has been estimated at 13,750, for whom the daily allowance of meat is 13,000 pounds. The number of women . . . comprising the harem of the Caliph is said to be 6,314. . . . The daily allowance of bread for the fish in the ponds is 12,000 loaves. . . . No imagination however fertile could have formed an idea of it. Praise be to God Most High for allowing His humble creatures to design and build such enchanting palaces as this.[9]

Public literacy was a government priority. Successive caliphs built libraries that were open to all; in fact, one tenth century ruler, Hakam II, was so obsessed with books that he sent emissaries to Baghdad with orders to buy every manuscript that had ever been produced. Hakam's personal library was reputed to hold four hundred thousand hand-written volumes, many of which were annotated by himself, and the catalogue of his titles alone occupied forty-four volumes. (An equivalent twentieth-century library would comprise millions of books.)

Although Spain of the Moors—*Al-Andalus*—was a thoroughly male world, women also were educated during the reign of Hakam II, and free schooling was provided in the city mosques. The caliph invited foreign scholars to his court in Cordoba to teach and absorb each other's research. Sailors drew nautical maps. New works on geography were compiled. The compass was invented so faithful Muslims could knowingly face Mecca for their daily prayers. Paper was manufactured for the first time (until then all writing was done on hard-to-obtain Egyptian papyrus), and surprised travelers fought for pieces of the new substance to carry home for the showing. Arabic numbers replaced the more cumbersome Roman ones and became the foundation for everyday arithmetic. The bases of algebra and trigonometry were established. Astronomy and astrology were deemed equally important, and a planetarium was built to depict the stars, clouds, and lightning. Even sophisticated Cordobans were thoroughly amazed: Ziryab, a court musician, ordered his tailor to make him a suit of feathers with wings, then on an astrologically auspicious day he dressed, excitedly flapped his "wings," and tried to fly to the stars.

The overt sensuality of this world has been preserved in its poetry where male sexual longing prevails. A drinking party takes place on the river in the darkness of night. Slim, round-hipped girls pour wine and dance to the music of the lute. A slave girl slips out of her dress "like a bud unfolding from a cluster of blossoms." Poetry was the medium of history, thought, satire, desire, love, courtly patronage, and communication in general.

The Jewish poets of Andalusia were profoundly influenced by their Muslim compatriots, and from the tenth to the twelfth century, during the justly named Golden Age of the Spanish Jews, they, too, wrote remarkably beautiful verse. "In the days of Hasdai the Nasi they began to chirp, and in the days of Samuel the Nagid they sang aloud," noted one observer with an eye for metaphor.[10] Although Arabic was their language, the Jews wrote astonishingly beautiful religious *and* secular poetry in Hebrew, much of the latter associated with the "wine party," a cultural happening they copied from the Arabs.

The wine party carries us into the sensuous heart of this civilization. Wine is served after the evening meal in gardens or on the banks of a river. The participants sit on cushions; beside each is a small table and a goblet. Musicians play lutes and other instruments while a serving boy pours from a wine-skin.

Talk touches on the issues of the day, but dwells on poetry: Poetic riddles, recitations, and improvisations; descriptions of the beauty of the environment and the wine itself; evocations of the poet's inner life. The party lasts all night while the drinkers drift in and out of sleep. The object is to induce a separate reality, a heady experience of night, intoxication, and pleasure.

> How exquisite the fawn that woke at night
> To the sound of viol's thrum and tabor's clink,
> Who saw the goblet in my hand, and said
> "The grape's blood flows for you between my lips,
> Come drink."
> Behind him stood the moon, a letter C,
> Inscribed on morning's veil in golden ink.[11]

It is believed that the great twelfth-century poet Judah Halevi was "discovered" at one such party in Granada. As integrated as he and his compatriots were in Arab society, Halevi's verse reveals that Jerusalem was not forgotten.

> O Zion, will you not inquire of your captives?
> The exiles, the remnant of your flock, who so desire
> your well-being?
> Receive greetings from those near and far—and the
> blessings of this captive of desire
> Who sheds his tears, like the dew of Hermon,
> and longs to have them fall upon your hills.
> I am a jackal that weeps for your affliction,
> But when I dream of the exiles' return,
> Then I am a lute for your songs.

*   *   *

Politically, the caliphs of the first, Umayyad dynasty* largely followed Tariq's tolerant lead. Conversion to Islam was encouraged, but without coercion, and churches and synagogues in every city came under royal protection. These policies bore fruit: During the first one hundred years of the Muslim occupation of Spain not one religious revolt occurred.[12]

The Umayyad caliphs knew they needed the mediating skills of Jews and Christians who had long-established links throughout the peninsula. More importantly, they seem to have been unburdened by a church-is-state religious ideology that might have led them to share their power with the Muslim clergy.

The caliphs honored and protected the Jews who, in turn, helped create an exceptionally dynamic civilization; there was even a minorities-protection office of government run by a functionary known as the *Kátib* of protection. Before long, Arab Spain was a refuge for persecuted Jews elsewhere in Europe, and for enlightened Christians who wanted to live in a unique pluralistic society. One ninth-century German deacon scandalized his entire nation by moving to Saragossa, marrying a Jewish woman and converting to Judaism.

The cross-over assimilation produced by this open society was perceived as a distinct threat in Christian Europe, where the Moors of Spain were written off as loathsome, godless infidels. As early as 782, and again in 785, Pope Hadrian I complained, with a certain justification, that some

---

*The Umayyad dynasty (756–1031 C.E.) represented the high point of Arab civilization in Spain.

Christian Mozarabs were converting to Islam, or to Judaism, and that others were confused about Easter and predestination. He was especially upset that easy contact among people of different religions was promoting mixed marriages and divorce.

If this sounds strangely modern, consider the words of Pablo Alvaro, a ninth-century Mozarab layman who railed against the influence of Islam on Christians in generation-gap, the-world-is-going-to-the-dogs language that is as contemporary as our own decade, with only minor adaptations for content: "Who, I ask, is there today among our faithful laymen who studies the sacred [Latin] scriptures?" he berated his coreligionists.

> Rather our Christian young men . . . [are] distinguished by their pagan learning and proud of their Arabic eloquence. They know not the beauty of the Church and they despise the streams that water the paradise of the Church. Alas . . . the Latins do not study their own language, so that in the whole assembly of Christ one would scarcely find one among a thousand who is capable of addressing a letter of salutation to his brother in correct form.[13]

Pablo Alvaro's excessive religious enthusiasm encouraged some Mozarabs to publicly revile the Prophet Muhammad, an offense theoretically punishable by death; but it is typical of the delicate ethos of the day that the caliph tried to absolve the "criminals" by quietly suggesting their insults had been "involuntary."[14]

One of Pablo Alvaro's concerns was the prickly question of priestly celibacy, since the open sensuality of the Moors came into direct conflict with Christian doctrine. However, the Mozarab Christian clergy of Arab Spain were considerably less outraged; indeed, by the eleventh century the clerics of Seville were so contemptuous of celibacy rules that a *Muslim* chronicler saw fit to attack them. "[They are] debauched fornicators and sodomites," the writer fulminated. "Christian women should be forbidden to enter the church except on days of liturgical services and religious feasts since they customarily go there to eat, drink and fornicate with the clergy. . . . There is not one of the latter who does not have two or more mistresses."[15]

Sexual mores were perplexing for non-Muslims in Arab Spain since no one could avoid noticing that the ruling caliphs sometimes had thousands of women in their harems, or that even ordinary Muslims were allowed up to four wives. The Jewish solution to contemporary sexual ambiguities was perhaps easier: Judaism does not demand sexual abstinence from its clergy, and the Jews were not subject to critical scrutiny from an outside religious center equivalent to Rome.[16] Rabbinical interpretations of religious law were not rigidly codified, which meant that the ethos of Arab society could eventually be reflected in religious ordinance. Jewish law traditionally forbade multiple marriage, but over the years bigamy came to be accepted in Spain under certain conditions.

Jewish life harmonized with the Muslim world in other ways. Since Judaism prescribed study, the Spanish rabbis encouraged a secular application of that study, a decision that met the needs of the caliphs and allowed the Jews to pursue secular as well as religious interests. Before long Cordoba was the most important center of Jewish learning in the world. Culture flourished, the law that governs Jewish religious life was codified, and theology was systematized. Scholars established the bases of Hebrew philology and grammar, and poets wrote brilliant Hebrew verse, reflecting the dominant Islamic culture that prized literature. Islamic scholars learned to read the Scriptures in Hebrew, just as Jews read the Quran. In addition, Jewish merchants traveled widely. They learned new languages (many already knew both Arabic and Hebrew as well as the local vernacular of their regions), and served as ambassadors, diplomats, and emissaries of the caliphs.

In the tenth century a talented scholar named Abu Yusuf Hasdai ibn Shaprut (or simply Hasdai) rose to become chief advisor to Caliph Abdur Rahman III (912–961), the first of a breed of Jewish courtiers who would sit beside the kings of Spain. Hasdai was born in 915, and his remarkable schooling helps to explain the sophistication of the tenth-century community he led.

Hasdai learned Arabic, Latin, Hebrew, and the Bible, and was host to a large community of artists, scholars and poets from inside and outside the country who gathered at his home. He studied medicine and became famous for purportedly rediscovering a long-lost miracle drug that was thought to be effective against snakebite, poisons, stomachaches, asthma, jaundice, myopia, impotence, plague, and anything else worth worrying about.[17] (As a result of this discovery Hasdai was named chief court physician, and in 956 he was asked to treat Sancho the Fat, king of the northern Christian kingdom of León, who was suffering from dropsy [water retention]. That the bloated and ridiculed Christian king could seek medical treatment at the court of his enemy is another indication of the caliph's openness.)

Hasdai was known for his delicacy and frankness, and Caliph Abdur Rahman III frequently asked him to receive official visits in the magnificent hall of the Az-Zahra palace. In 944, diplomats from Emperor Constantine of Constantinople arrived in Cordoba. The ambassadors entered the Royal Garden pavilion of the palace and were awestruck by the richness of the rugs on the floor and by the walls shimmering in green and.

gold silk. Before them sat the caliph himself on a raised throne made of solid gold. Beside the caliph sat Hasdai, surrounded by the entire court. (The sight must have been overwhelming for we are told that the head of the delegation fell to the floor in a faint.)[18]

The Constantinople delegation had come to deliver a precious book to the caliph, a copy of a Greek medical work by the first-century physician Pedanius Dioscorides.[19] Pedanius Dioscorides had traveled with the armies of the Roman Emperor Nero, studying the medicinal properties of hundreds of plants including cannabis, hemlock, and peppermint, and in his book he gave directions for the chemical preparation of sleeping potions and surgical anesthetics as well as other drugs. The caliph wanted this book for medical use and research, but the beautiful, illuminated manuscript was in Greek, a language no one in Spain understood. Emperor Constantine had sent along a monk who knew Greek and Latin and could translate from the former to the latter, but someone—a physician who could understand the meaning of the text—would have to translate the Latin into Arabic.

Hasdai was the only physician in all of Arab Spain who knew enough Latin to translate this text. He worked with the monk from Constantinople for several years until the famous manuscript was translated from Greek into Latin, and then into Arabic—and his renown grew. Among the Jews he was called *Nasi*, or prince, and he was the first to achieve a public position that was powerful enough to protect the community should ever a threat of danger arise.[20]

The rich synthesis of learning and culture nurtured in Muslim Spain produced a remarkable era of science, philosophy, philology, biblical commentary, and literature; and the intellectual activity that characterized this civilization would have a profound effect on the rest of Europe. The writings of the ancient Greeks, eclipsed for hundreds of years, were reborn; the scientific and philosophical treatises of Aristotle, the geometry of Euclid, and the original writings of Plato (as opposed to the transformation of his work into the mystically inclined neo-Platonism so beloved by early Christianity) were translated into Arabic and Hebrew, then again into Latin and the vernacular languages of Europe. Medicine also was transformed. The writings of the Greek physician Galen had been prominent in the Hellenistic world since the third century, though unknown in Europe. By the late ninth century all 129 of his works were translated into Arabic and Aramaic, and in the eleventh century a Latin translation revolutionized European practice. (Galen's theories of the four humors—all organs are created from blood, phlegm, yellow bile, and black bile, which must be in balance for health—remained the basis of Western medicine until well past the Renaissance.)

The startling achievements of Arab Spain were born from a literate society of more than a millennia ago, and were unique in Europe; in fact a parallel class of educated laypersons did not emerge elsewhere until the thirteenth century. Something unique distinguished Moorish Spain from northern Europe: Accomplishment grew from a foundation of cultural pluralism, which welcomed new people, new languages, and new ideas, while the exclusive ideology of Christianity set roadblocks in the way. The intellectual, artistic, and cultural brilliance of Arab Spain was the harvest of an open cross-fertilization unimpeded by religious rejection.

The multicultural, multireligious society fostered by the Moors was morally repugnant to the Spanish Visigoth-Christian clergy in the north of Spain, for in their orthodox worldview the very idea of pluralism was perceived as a threat. God spoke in one voice only, for if other sounds were heard, the certainty of the single, universal, and true religion would be open to question. If other sounds were heard, some might come to the conclusion that faith was a matter of choice.

From an orthodox point of view, there was legitimate reason for concern. As we have seen, Mozarab Christians were adapting liturgy, while the Jews were changing religious law to conform with Muslim social practices. Muslims, Jews, and Christians may have identified themselves according to religion, but many people were devoting their lives to secular and literary pursuits. The multicultural world of Andalusia undoubtedly promoted social assimilation (this was the key to its cultural, intellectual, and worldly success), and it is not incongruous that people engaged in the exploration of science, or in thinking about and translating ancient Greek writings on philosophical rationalism, would begin to question the fundamental certainties of revelation.

Eventually, a rationalism born of secular study came to threaten the religious authority of all three religions in Spain, and beyond. The issue began with the rediscovery of Aristotle in the ninth century.

Ibn Rushd (known in the non-Muslim word as Averroës), a twelfth-century Cordoban jurist, philosopher, and physician, was the first to propose a synthesis of reason and revelation. He argued boldly that both reasoned philosophy *and* revealed religion are true, and since all truth is in harmony, there is no inherent contradiction between reason and revelation. Scripture should be interpreted allegorically, not literally; only logic will penetrate the secrets of the world and beyond.

Averroës's troubles started at home, in his own city of Cordoba. The Muslim clergy were willing to tolerate the ancient Greeks when it came to mathematics and medicine, as long as their own domain was left intact, but a *religious* challenge from philosophy was too much. They rose in anger. There was a public burning of Averroës's books.

When the translated works of Averroës reached Christian Europe, the clergy there was hardly more tolerant. Averroës was reviled for hundreds of years after his death, the hatred against him reaching a climax some time in the fourteenth century when an enraged churchman invented a slanderous speech in which he has Averroës (the heretic) proclaim, "Moses, Christ and Mohammed are the three great imposters who have deluded the human race."

Curiously, Averroës's greatest impact was probably felt among the Jews, through the work of his contemporary and good friend, the physician and philosopher Moses ben Maimon of Cordoba, known to us as Maimonides.

Just as the education of Hasdai reflected the high cultural standards of the Jews of Andalusia in the tenth century, so the early education of Moses Maimonides, two hundred years later, helps us understand how Hebrew society evolved in the interim, and how a rational, religious thinker such as Maimonides might have emerged. Maimonides studied the usual religious subjects, the Bible and the Talmud, but he also learned languages, literature, mathematics, astronomy, science, and medicine. And he studied Aristotle, the bane of the clerics.

In the spirit of pluralist Cordoba, Maimonides was influenced by both Christian and Arab thinkers.[21] And like his good friend Averroës, he wanted to prove that religion is not in contradiction with philosophy since both emerge from the spirit of God. Truth, according to both Averroës and Maimonides, may be understood by ordinary people through revelation, riddles and parables; but the intellectually superior individual—the philosopher—will comprehend truth on a higher level.

Just as Averroës enraged the Muslims and the Christians, Maimonides' attempt to reconcile Judaism with rational philosophy instigated a bitter schism among the Jews. Traditional keepers of the faith—artisans and others among the less educated who neither appreciated nor understood philosophy—fought back. Maimonides' works also were publicly burned. Rationalists were clearly a threat in all three religions.

In spite of book burnings, schisms, and internecine hatreds, a rationalism based on Aristotle gave birth to a recognizably "modern" intelligentsia that believed reason might coexist with faith, or even supersede it. Science, philosophy, and other nonreligious learning was elevated to a plane where once only God's word had lived. A small class of intellectual revolutionaries, some of them budding "secularists," came into being in an age when no one dared think of living an openly nonreligious life.

A tragedy would unfold from this. A society of different peoples with common interests naturally engendered new thought forms, but rational "secularism" had not yet reached its historical hour and the clergy, especially the Christian clergy, lay in perpetual wait. During the pogroms of

1391, almost seven hundred years after the arrival of the Moors in Spain, power would shift irreversibly toward the Catholic Church and its religious-orthodox agenda. When this happened, the spiritual "children of Aristotle," especially those of the Jewish persuasion, were lost.

*　　*　　*

The rulers of Arab Spain presided over a creative, even brilliant society, but they were less successful as politicians, and the entire period was marked by internecine rivalries. In the eleventh century the Almoravids, a tribe of Islamic crusaders, arrived from North Africa. The caliphate of Cordoba was destroyed, but openness and culture were not, for the small Arab kingdoms that emerged in its place rivaled one another in magnificence and continued to sponsor philosophy, poetry, and science. Then, at the end of the twelfth century, the fanatical Almohads invaded, once again from North Africa. This time Jews and Mozarabs were forced to convert or emigrate north to the Christian territories.

The arrival of the Almohads marked the end of an era. The bright light of Cordoba flickered and went out like a dying star, never to shine again.

Christian Spain

Twelfth-century Christian Spain is a rough society of illiterate knights and rude peasants, a universe removed from the lushness of Andalusia. To enter this world is a shock for both Mozarab and Jew.

But just as they enriched Arab Spain with their diversity centuries before, so will they now transform the Christian north. Mozarabs and Jews bring with them a passion for learning, born from a civilization that loved knowledge, and a sophisticated, esthetic culture. They bring with them the Arabic language and an experience of innovative agricultural techniques. Once again they adapt to new social conditions, so much so that Moses Ibn Ezra, the illustrious Hebrew poet from Granada, is appalled at the transformation of his people when he too moves north.

> Fortune has hurled me to a land
> where the lights of my understanding dimmed,
> and the stars of my reason were clouded
> by faltering knowledge and stammering speech.
>
> I have come to the iniquitous domain of
> a people scorned by God and accursed by man,

amongst savages who love corruption
and ambush the righteous and the innocent.
They have adopted their neighbours' ways,
anxious to enter their midst,
They share their deeds and are counted among them.
Those nurtured in their youth
in the gardens of truth,
hew in old age the wood
of forests of folly.[22]

In another poem he wrote scathingly:

I am with them a gentleman amongst savages
And a lion amidst a flock of apes and parrots.[23]

What Moses Ibn Ezra missed most was the elite society of Granadan Jewry where he had been at the center of a group of brilliant poets. Self-conscious pride was central to this world. Ibn Ezra had once declared that the Hebrew literature of Spain was superior because Spanish Jews were descended from Jerusalemites who excelled over other Israelites "in the purity of language and the tradition of legal science."[24] Other notables held equally exalted views of their origins. In the eleventh century Samuel ha-Nagid, a poet and courtier, asked himself in literary form, "Are you capable of properly praising God?" and answered, "I am the David of my generation."[25]

In fact the structure of Jewish life has changed little in the flight north from Andalusia. Since the Christian nobility wages war and nothing else (work is anathema and learning an ideal they do not aspire to), the rulers of Christian Spain are happy to appropriate the administrative talents of the immigrants from the south, and before long, educated Jews are co-opted as royal advisors, ambassadors, and physicians—just as they had been under the Moors. Like the caliphs, the Christian kings of Castile and Aragon become protectors of "their Jews."

But beneath the seemingly smooth surface of this transition is change of a different sort as the seeds of religious intolerance planted centuries ago by the Visigoths quietly take root. The multiculturalism of the Moors is adopted in Christian Spain for practical reasons, but the memory of Cordoba, where such habits of acceptance were born, is increasingly reviled. The ungodly infidel ruled there: the rhetoric of twelfth-century Christianity is unambiguously exclusive.

In the centuries to come, few will remember the practical wisdom of the first Abdur Rahman when instructing his son Hisham in the year 787 C.E. Before his death the caliph called in the governors of the six provinces into which Andalusia had been divided to witness the royal succession. Then he addressed the prince:

> Remember, my son, that these are God's kingdoms, God who gives and takes away at his leisure. . . . Be just to all men, equally to the poor and the rich, for injustice is the road to ruin; at the same time be gentle and merciful with those who are dependent on you, for they are all creatures of God. Trust the government of the provinces to wise, experienced men and punish without pity those ministers who oppress the people. Treat soldiers with gentle firmness so that they remain the defenders of the state and not its destroyers. Encourage and protect the cultivators, for it is they who provide us with our sustenance. . . . Never cease to merit the affection of your people; in their good will is the security of the state, in their anger there is danger, and in their hatred certain ruin. And rule so that the people bless you, so that they live happily in the shadow of your protection; for in that is the glory and joy of a king.[26]

Notes

1. The Romans first landed in 218 B.C.E. They completed their conquest in 19 B.C.E.

2. The Golden Age of Spanish Jewry is generally thought to be the tenth to the twelfth centuries. By contrast, the Golden Age of Spain itself is the sixteenth century.

3. Paulus Orosius, cited in U. R. Burke, *A History of Spain*, 1: 42.

4. Ibid.

5. Sura 109.

6. U. R. Burke, *A History of Spain*, 1: 156, note 2.

7. J. Conde, *Histoire de la domination des arabes en Espagne* (1821), cited in Viardot, *Essais*, 191.

8. Part of the foundations of this palace have been excavated. Beyond this, nothing remains.

9. Arabian account cited in Stanley Lane-Poole, *The Moors of Spain*, 141–42.

10. Abraham Ibn Daud, *The Book of Tradition*, cited in Raymond P. Scheindlin, *Wine, Women and Death*, 3. Schleindlin is excellent on this subject.

11. Samuel ha-Nagid, eleventh century, quoted in Scheindlin, *Wine*, 69.

12. In the following century, laws enacted against Christian Mozarabs regarding their use of Latin as opposed to Arabic, among other things, resulted in an uprising.

13. Joseph F. O'Callaghan, *History of Medieval Spain*.

14. They insisted and he was forced to execute them.

15. Ibn Abdun, *Seville Musulmane*, cited in O'Callaghan, *History*, 309.

16. The Babylonian Academy was effectively replaced by Cordoba.

17. Eliyahu Ashtor, *The Jews of Moslem Spain*, 1: 160ff.

18. Stories of the Az-Zahra were collected from contemporary chronicles by Conde and cited in Lane-Poole, *The Moors of Spain*, 143, and Viardot, *Essais*, 98, note 1.

19. Called *De Materia Medica* in Latin.

20. *De Materia Medica* was translated into at least seven languages and remained the most important text on pharmacology until the end of the fifteenth century.

21. This thesis is developed by Norman Roth in *Maimonides*.

22. O'Callaghan, *History of Medieval Spain*, 328, and Y. F. Baer, *A History of the Jews in Christian Spain*, 1: 63–64.

23. Norman A. Stillman, "Aspects of Jewish Life In Islamic Spain," in *Aspects of Jewish Culture in the Middle Ages,* edited by Paul E. Szaarmach, 70.

24. Norman Stillman, *The Jews of Arab Lands,* 58.

25. Samuel ha-Nagid, in Scheindlin, *Wine,* 57.

26. Fragment from a chronicle of the reign of Abdur Rahman I, translated and cited in Viardot, *Essais,* 60, note 1. English translation by Erna Paris.

3

Setting the Scene:
The Face of Early Christian Spain

On our side, Christ, God and man. On the Moors', the faithless and
dammed apostate, Muhammad.
  What more is there to say?

—Chronique latine des rois de Castille

The most open society Europe had seen flowered during the centuries of
Arab occupation, but at the same time, in the far north of Spain, another
"nation" with distinctly different values was emerging. This was a society
profoundly opposed to the laissez-faire policies of the Muslims, a mili-
tantly Christian society that was committed to the exclusion of minorities,
just like its Visigoth ancestors.

The Visigoth nation-in-exile is born as the army of Tariq the Moor
pushes inexorably toward the capital city of Toledo in the year 712. "The
Devil is coming," Toledans whisper to each other with a shudder. Is Tariq
not the same terrifying heathen who magically spirited away the body of
their King Rodrigo from the battlefield? He must have swallowed him
whole, or sucked his blood, or recited an incantation that made the king
vanish into thin air. Foreigners and infidels can do that because they are
not baptized Christians.

Ordinary folk nervously await the arrival of the king-swallowing infidel, but the Visigoth nobility run for their lives. They speed north, away
from the approaching Moors; north to the remote mountains of
Cantabria where Basques and other indigenous peoples have lived for so
long, and in such isolation, that they barely noticed the invasion of the
Romans or the Visigoths, let alone the Moors. The Visigoth escapees
think of themselves as survivors, and they have one overriding goal: to
reconquer their lost land and regain their lost power.

All nations are built from mythologies that unite the tribe in a web of shared belief, and in the mountains of northern Hispania the unifying thread of these "survivors" is Christianity. Before long their sporadic attempts to expel the invader and retake their lost territory have acquired the status of a Holy Reconquest, a heroic struggle between Christianity and the infidel, God and the Devil. The idea of a greater good will inspire them to give their lives for the "nation."

Since the Holy Reconquest needs an inspiring leader, a suitable candidate is quickly uncovered. In 718, during a skirmish, a man named Pelayo prevents a small army of Moors from overtaking a mountain stronghold. This small, but sufficient claim to fame is seized upon to trumpet the first notes of the new, national mythology. Pelayo's little victory is instantly transformed into source material for the myth-makers of Christian-Visigothic Spain. It will become the foundation stone upon which an entire national edifice is painstakingly constructed.

One hundred years later Christian chroniclers are describing Pelayo as a grand-nephew of King Rodrigo and claiming that he was elected king by members of the royal family who accompanied him into exile. By the sixteenth century two miracles now characterize his modest victory. In one of these miracles a "shower of stones and darts" the Moors shot at the Visigoths suddenly changed direction and "flew back at the Moors." In another, a God-inspired landslide fell into a river killing the Moors as they retreated, and "for many years after, bones and pieces of armour were dug out of that place."[1]

In spite of Pelayo's symbolic value to the Christian armies, the Moors managed to hold on to occupied territory; and after a century of largely unsuccessful, sporadic battles the Visigoths began to believe that something important must be missing from the inspirational equation. Although he was heroic, Pelayo had lived as an ordinary mortal. He was human; as such he lacked the transcendental qualities needed to inspire future generations of Christian knights to risk their lives for the Reconquest. The Moors could look to Muhammad, the central figure of Islam. Might that be the reason they were so strong? The Christians needed someone, too, a holy figure whose sacred name they could shout to summon courage as they faced the armies of the infidel with their formidable, low-slung Arabian horses, their wildly colored turbans, and the terrifying scimitars they waved so dangerously above their heads.

Having acknowledged this need, the knights of the Reconquest were forthwith granted another miracle, one even more impressive than those ascribed to Pelayo. Early in the ninth century word leaked out that an extraordinary tomb had been discovered. A hermit saw a bright light illuminate a certain spot and heard angels singing. Naturally he informed his local bishop who rushed to the scene and found, *mirabile dictu*, the site of the tomb of Christ's apostle Saint James the Elder.

The historical James, son of Zebedee, had been beheaded by the Roman king Herod Agrippa I of Judaea, around 44 C.E., but now it was learned that his body had been miraculously transported to Spain and buried there. The church of Santiago de Compostella was constructed on the site to memorialize this marvelous event, and before long thousands of pilgrims began to arrive from all over Europe, by foot, by mule, and by wagon (fortuitously opening commerce and increasing settlement along the way). Christian Spain now had a religious and national patron to hold up to Muhammad, and for the next six hundred years the knights of the Holy Reconquest carried the cross aloft and shouted *Santiago!* (Saint James) as they galloped into battle against the Moors.

By the eleventh century, earth-bound Pelayo seemed in need of renewal, and a second, worldly hero was created to help with symbolic endeavors. El Cid (from the Arabic title *sidi,* or lord) was an illustrious warrior knight, but nothing he actually did approximated the fame he would garner a century later when he was enshrined in popular literature. The epic *Poema de Mio Cid* (Song of My Cid) is one of the earliest examples of the heroic epic, and in recounting and romanticizing El Cid's deeds, the poem added a third glorious leader to the rostrum of the Holy Reconquest. Santiago could intercede with God on behalf of the Christian armies, while Pelayo and his update, El Cid, inspired warrior knights to imitate their heroic feats.[2]

Even the humiliating defeat of King Rodrigo underwent an ideological transformation. No one could possibly deny the king's military failure in the battle against Tariq in 712, but it was always possible to infer a moral victory. By the sixteenth century a Christian chronicler was safely able to write, "The kingdom and nation of the Goths were subverted, in my opinion, by a peculiar providence, that out of their ashes might rise a new and holy Spain, greater in strength and dominions, to be the defense and bulwark of the Catholic religion."[3]

Here was the Christian-Visigoth tribe arising from the ashes of defeat.

*   *   *

A single political goal informed the religious-national rhetoric of the Holy Reconquest: the recovery of land and power; but by the eleventh century, a wide chasm stretched between the symbolic language of the Reconquest and the prosaic realities of daily life. Sloganeering to the contrary, the everyday world of Christian Spain readily adopted the tolerant policies of the Moors as territory was retaken, in battle after battle, and Muslims, Mozarabs, and Jews came under the jurisdiction of Christian kings. Pacification was in everyone's interest. Why destroy good agricultural land when Christians would now be the beneficiaries? Why destroy a city that would otherwise pay an ongoing tribute in gold? The monarchs of Christian Spain had other things on their minds than abstract notions of religious orthodoxy; they had to settle border territories that had been battlegrounds for centuries and promote the local economy. For this they depended on the skills of their newly incorporated citizens, which meant accepting minority cultures and religions, just as the Moors had done.

Real life in the Christian territories from about the middle of the eleventh century was ludicrously remote from Reconquest propaganda, and this reality continued to set multicultural Spain apart from the rest of Europe. Ironically, the true record of El Cid, the knight who came to symbolize the Holy Reconquest, best exemplifies the gap. El Cid's exploits were exaggerated in the epic *Poema,* but the events described there are thought to be largely accurate, and his story tells us much about the cultural and social ambiguities of the times. El Cid was born to the landed nobility in 1043 as Rodrigo Diaz de Vivar and died in 1099 as the virtual ruler of reconquered Valencia; but far from personifying the religious ideals of the Reconquest, as he was later held to do, he was (like the majority of contemporary knights) a mercenary, who hired himself out "to earn his bread," as he put it. El Cid served two Christian kings of Castile, which is understandable, but he also served the Muslim ruler of Saragossa (who purportedly paid him handsomely). In eleventh-century Spain it was often hard to know who was fighting for, or against, whom—Christian or Moor.

El Cid was held to be the ideal knight because he reconquered Valencia in 1094 and pushed the Reconquest borders further south; and in this he personified the archetypal masculine figure of medieval Spain. Such a man belonged to the warrior class whose job was chivalry. Ideally, it was the duty of a knight to serve the king's military interests with tenacity and courage, to think carefully before he spoke, and to be loyal to his word. The true knight lived by the sword, defending justice and virtue; and he believed firmly in God, whose interests (such as the Reconquest) happily coincided with those of the king.

The chivalric ideal mixed religion and politics, and mirrored the ideals of Christian nationhood underpinning the Reconquest. It set formulas containing principled goals to strive for. Once anointed, a knight was expected to be ever in the public eye. When called upon to serve, he was obliged to ride off to renew the war against the infidel; at other times he jousted at the king's tournaments or dueled in the name of honor. Chivalry was a moral system that governed and (it was hoped) elevated the behavior of the nobility. Through example, the chivalric code was meant to improve the conduct of society at large.

However, as in the case of the individual hero El Cid, reality was somewhat messier. The Reconquest armies were notably inefficient, and there was no workable hierarchy of command. More importantly, as we have seen, a Spanish king had to count himself lucky if his men were not fighting for the Moors on the other side. As if that weren't problem enough, a knight, or an entire contingent, might decide to desert if the prospective booty from a battle did not look profitable enough. Away from the battlefield, knights fought among themselves and demanded ever more in the way of money, property, and privileges from the king as payment for their services. And everyone in eleventh century Spain shared in an unbridled greed for gold, in spite of unending remonstrances from the Church against materialism. When the Cid sent criers into Navarre, Castile, and Aragon calling for knights to help him "win the battle of Valencia for Christendom," he was joined, the *Poema* tells us, by men who were "thirsting after wealth," of which they found plenty. ("The gold and the silver, who can count it?" rhapsodized one chronicler.) The Moors were believed to have stashed away quantities of gold and precious stones in remote mountain caves and every warrior knight dreamed of finding this buried treasure. (Sometimes they did discover a glittering cache: When El Cid captured the Arab city of Denia he reputedly found a hiding place in the mountainside stuffed with gold, silver, and jewels.)

Because they lived in a truly mixed society, Reconquest crusaders of the eleventh century felt little real hostility toward the Moors they met on the battlefield, and their apparent willingness to switch from one side to the other did not escape the notice of Christians elsewhere in Europe. In 1063, Pope Alexander II summoned the knights of Christendom to speed up the defeat of the Muslim infidel in Spain, and a large army of French crusaders crossed the border to join a contingent from Aragon for an attack on the Moorish city of Barbastro, a market town in a fertile plain situated at the foot of the Pyrenees.

With this call the pope injected a new element into the Spanish Reconquest which had, until then, proceeded according to its own rules; in fact, the presence of French crusaders in Spain would open the way to a transformation of the Iberian Peninsula.

*   *   *

With plenty of provisions at hand, the Moors of Barbastro ought to be able to sustain a defense of their city. But a large stone falls and blocks an underground water aqueduct, cutting off the city's water supply. After forty days of siege, they are forced to surrender.

As usual, the Spanish army is prepared to spare lives in return for loot, land, and payment of a regular tribute to the king, but something new happens. The French, who are part of the victorious contingent, despise the tolerant Spaniards, and as prisoners are marched out of the city they slaughter six thousand of them on the spot. Seven thousand more are captured as slaves, including fifteen hundred women who are delivered like cattle to the French commander and papal standard-bearer Guillaume de Montreuil, along with five hundred loads of jewels, clothing, and other goods.[4]

When the battle of Barbastro is over, there are other temptations. The French knights have never seen anything quite so luscious as the lifestyle of the Moors, and when they have finished raping, burning, and looting, they abandon themselves to the pleasures of a slave harem. A messenger sent to ransom the daughter of a wealthy Moor who is being held by a French count-crusader finds the count reclining on a couch, in flowing robes, and surrounded by baskets of gold and young women playing lutes. The happy crusader adamantly refuses to release the Moor's daughter.[5]

What has happened to religious rectitude? The pope had been counting on the French to bring a little more rigor to the battle against the infidel than the decadent Spanish knights were traditionally willing to muster. Back home the French clergy are asking the same question. They are enraged at these soldiers of the Holy Cross who are being "consumed by the hell fires of love," as one of them puts it. But no one seems to be listening, least of all the French crusaders.

The papacy and the French clergy have taken an active interest in Spain and have found attitudes toward Muslims and Jews there seriously wanting. The French abbé Pierre of Cluny is perfectly clear regarding the Jews: "What is the good of going to the end of the world, at great loss of men and money, to fight the Saracens, when we permit among us other infidels a thousand times more guilty toward Christ?" he asks in language that is a clear harbinger of days to come.[6]

Toward the end of the eleventh century, another monk from the Cluny Order undertook the long, arduous voyage over the Pyrenees to preach Christianity to Muslims living in reconquered territory, but according to his biographer the mission failed:

> To prove the certitude of the Christian faith and to uproot the hardness of Saracen [Moorish] cruelty he offered to undergo the ordeal by fire. But the Saracens would not agree to his conditions, namely that if he emerged unscathed they would hasten to baptism. When through blindness or hardness of heart they refused to be moved in any way, he shook the dust from his feet and returned to his monastery.[7]

The failure, however, was only a temporary one. The Church's war on religious pluralism in Spain had only just begun.

French Fanaticism

On May 25, 1085, the troops of King Alfonso VI of Castile mass excitedly outside the arch of the old Bisagra Gate that opens into the fortress wall of Toledo. Perched on a hill that dominates the surrounding plain and encircled by the blue waters of the Tagus River, the stone monuments of the great city gleam under a cloudless sky.

With the help of Christian knights from France, Germany and Italy, the most important battle to date in the long Reconquest wars has been won: Toledo, capital of the ancient Visigoths and symbol of lost Christian Spain, has been recaptured from the Moors. The uncertain tide of the Reconquest has turned.

Rodrigo Diaz de Vivar led the battle for this prize of a city. Having been lost by a Rodrigo, it would be won back by a Rodrigo, he once predicted. Today El Cid assumes the place of honor beside the king of Castile as horses and banners line up for a victory procession through the Bisagra Gate.

The king in his glittering battle attire personifies the peculiar religious mix and ethnic flux that characterizes Spain. Although Toledo had been "lost" to the Christians since the eighth century, this monarch spent several years at the Muslim court of the capital as part of his education. Later on in his life, the royal daughter of the Muslim ruler of Seville will bear him a son.[8] Nothing exposes the truth about this pluralist nation better than the eleventh-century monarch's own life.

The king and El Cid spur their horses and move forward under the arch of the Bisagra Gate, followed by their army. The narrow street climbs steeply, horseshoes click loudly on cobblestones. The Moors, Jews, and Christian Mozarabs of Toledo line the streets in wary expectation as the royal train moves forward. Then suddenly a miracle occurs. Bystanders swear that El Cid's horse actually kneels before the main mosque of Toledo, which was constructed hundreds of years before on the ruins of an old Visigoth church. The Christian soldiers dismount and rush inside. There they find a Visigoth lamp illuminating a hidden crucifix.

Joy at the taking of Toledo and its accompanying symbolic miracle erupts throughout Christian Spain, and to demonstrate the importance of his victory, Alfonso VI begins to call himself emperor. Soon he is calling himself Emperor of the Three Religions in an expression of the openness that characterizes Spanish life. Mirroring the liberal offer Tariq the Moor made to the defeated Visigoths of Toledo 373 years earlier, Emperor Alfonso promises royal protection and freedom of worship to the Moors and Jews of the city in return for a head tax. Those who choose to stay in Toledo will be guaranteed the continued use of mosques and synagogues and will be allowed to keep their own laws and judges. Those who prefer to leave may take their goods and property with them.

But Alfonso VI is married to Constance of France, and the queen is deeply offended by her husband's attitude to religious minorities. Were the infidel Moors not properly defeated in battle? What might the king wish to accomplish by offering such liberal terms to Moors and Jews who were now being incorporated into Christian Spain?

Queen Constance personally negotiates the appointment of a French abbot as the new archbishop of Toledo, and Bernard de Sauvetot is as shocked as she is by Spanish pluralism. One day, in the absence of the king, the new archbishop orders soldiers to seize the chief mosque of Toledo which he immediately reconsecrates as a church. He renames it *Cristo de la Luz* (Christ of the light) in honor of the miraculous Visigoth lamp that El Cid purportedly found burning there.

The Muslims riot. King Alfonso rushes home to be faced with a critical choice: he can act decisively on behalf of the offended Moors, or he can choose to appease his queen and the archbishop of Toledo. Alfonso decides to forgive the queen and the archbishop; perhaps he believes forgiveness a small price to pay to protect the prestige of his queen and the most important cleric of the city. Peace returns to Toledo, but the decision of the "emperor of the three religions" not to punish the violent act of the French archbishop marks an important moment in the breakdown of Spanish pluralism.

For now, most of the old habits persist. During the twelfth century, the Reconquest continues to wrest land from the Moors. New territories need settling, arable land needs farming, and new merchant links need to be established. Nobles are created from the merchant classes who regularly fight in battle and raise the necessary capital, a group which includes many Jews. In the thirteenth century, King James the Conqueror of Aragon rewards his knights with prosperous Muslim farms as an incentive to continue the Reconquest, and ever more privileges are granted to entice both commoners and nobles to settle the conquered territories. Peaceful coexistence is the rule.

The Jewish World of Thirteenth-Century Saragossa

Across Europe the thirteenth century was a prosperous time. Town life grew and strong trade links developed. In Saragossa, a former Roman city built on the rich plains alongside the banks of the River Ebro in Aragon, the ethnic mix that typified Spain was especially vibrant.[9] Relations among members of the three religious groups were amiable and easy. Jewish and Christian shoemakers had a common guild; and silversmiths, needle makers, sword temperers, leather toolers, and other trades cooperated freely.[10] Even Church authorities were relatively friendly to religious minorities, in spite of their frequent conversion campaigns, and when the Franciscan priests of Saragossa built a new convent, they invited the Jews to hold meetings inside. In the same spirit the municipality of Saragossa did not dispute royal pardons for individual Jews and Muslims of the city, except in cases of homosexuality and sexual intercourse with Christians, both of which were strictly forbidden by the Church, but happened anyway. Everyone spoke a common vernacular reflecting a high degree of mutual acculturation. Worshipers were called parishioners regardless of their religion, and rabbis frequently dated their documents using the Christian, not the Jewish, calendar. Exclusionary papal ordinances that arrived through the ecclesiastical pipeline from Rome ordering Jews and Muslims to wear distinctive dress and forbidding Jews to work as royal envoys or have authority over Christians were largely ignored.

About three thousand Jews, representing 3 to 5 percent of the total population, lived in the maze of narrow, unhygienic streets of the Saragossa *judería*. Rich or poor, Jew, Christian or Moor, everyone lived in unhealthy squalor in the thirteenth-century city. Stinking garbage was piled high at every turn in every road. Latrines were nonexistent, except among the rich whose palaces sometimes bordered rivers, in which case elementary piping systems dumped waste directly into the water. Street rats were comfortably at home everywhere.

In the thirteenth century, some of Aragon's most influential families lived in the *judería* of Saragossa, in elegant living quarters and tree-shaded patios hidden behind thick, outer walls. Evidence of their communal life is still visible in the city in spite of the passage of seven hundred years. The old ritual baths, for example, are perfectly preserved far below the present street-level inside what is presently an ordinary-looking apartment building. Down the stairs and behind a small door lies an intact room that originated about one thousand years ago as a cistern sunk deep into the earth. There one sees an astonishingly beautiful display of thirteenth-century gothic arches and columns resembling the crypt of a church *and* a mosque—strong evidence of the synthesis of art and culture that marked the period.[11]

Thirteenth-century Saragossa was the richest city in Aragon, and largely because of Jewish commerce. Jewish artisans produced elegant filigree silver, and their best customer was the Catholic Church, which placed regular orders for chalices and other religious objects. On El Medio Street, where their shops lined both sides of the narrow passage, the Jews crafted leather shoes that were renowned all over Spain.[12] They were famed artists, renowned manuscript illuminators who produced stunning Haggada miniatures of biblical stories from Genesis and Exodus.[13] They were tailors, boiler makers, and kosher butchers (Christians and Jews alike prized kosher meat), and every Thursday they brought their wares to an open market that was frequented by people from all over the city. A second Jewish market, called the Alcaiceria, was a flamboyant bazaar specializing in silks reputed to be the best in Aragon. A third market specialized in grain. The only green space in the Jewish quarter was the cemetery.

Alongside the artisans and small-scale merchants was a small group of skilled administrators whose business was finance. These men were the Bank of Saragossa, so to speak, and they looked after the savings of everyone in the city. The Saragossa bankers made loans to kings, nobles, clerics, and peasants alike for their collective and individual ventures. They sold investment bonds, and when these came due velvet-clad knights and monks in hooded capes lined up in front of the bankers' houses in the *judería* claiming payment of their principal plus interest.

A few privileged court Jews in both Aragon and Castile competed with Christian knights for the king's favor. They collected taxes, supplied the king's armies, traveled, negotiated with Muslim rulers to the east with the aid of international letters of exchange representing different monies (this innovation meant that coinage did not have to be transported), and administered the royal treasury. These court Jews "protected" the humbler folk of their communities by giving voice to their concerns, the way Hasdai had done hundreds of years earlier at the court of Cordoba, and like Christians of their class they enjoyed wealth and noble privilege.

Lending and borrowing were indispensable and the basis of what appears to have been an early, protocapitalist economy, but the disproportionate involvement of educated Jews in the business of money was disturbing. A guilt-producing contradiction lay at the heart of economic life in thirteenth-century Spain, in a society whose value system was religious regardless of whether or not Church teachings were respected. Lending at interest was legal and everyone was engaged in it to a greater or lesser degree. On the other hand, Christianity taught that the *principle* of lending was sinful. According to the Church, economic life ought to be based on a "just price" calculated as the cost of materials plus labor without the addition of profit. To operate outside this ideal, which everyone did (including the clergy), was to pique troubling problems of conscience.

Since the Church prohibited Christians from lending money to each other with interest (and the Talmud did the same with regard to the Jews) a convenient double standard evolved. Both religions allowed their members to lend to the *other* group. (The problem for Christians was further diminished by employing Jews whose spiritual well-being was of no interest anyway.) But the negative view of the Church clung to the business of money, and eventually all lending at interest came to be labeled usury. Usury implied cheating, and where money is concerned cheating is a perennial temptation, but like all broad accusations the usury label effectively denigrated everyone and was profoundly harmful to the Jews who were the main handlers of money. Shielded by Church approbation, the blanket charge of usury—whether true or false, depending on the case—became an easy justification for persecution.[14]

Collecting taxes on behalf of the king did not increase the popularity of Jewish notables. Everyone was taxed mercilessly: There were taxes on income, taxes on buying and selling, and taxes on consumption, all of which were collected every Sunday. When the king needed more money, which he always did, he invented new taxes. In 1266 James the Conqueror appropriated revenue from the Jewish baths in Saragossa for a two-year period so he could build a bridge over the Ebro River. One hundred years later his descendant, Pedro IV, needed to repair the same bridge and dreamed up taxes on wine and meat, the basic staple foods of the country. Pilfering was punished harshly and any theft of food from the taverns of Saragossa before the taxes were tabulated was punished by religious excommunication.

The Jews paid extra duties: taxes to keep up their quarter and taxes to recompense the deemed kindness of the king, the Church, and the municipality. (In Saragossa the community paid the Christian Council of the city four thousand sueldos* annually.) Medieval Spanish royalty was constantly on the move in order to take care of government business throughout the country, and in return for the protection the Jews received, they were expected to provide for the royal retinue whenever the monarchs resided in their city. This included beds, cooking and eating utensils, and meat to feed the caged lions that traveled with the king. Keeping lions was a royal commonplace.

Every Jew over the age of eighteen paid between six and eighteen sueldos a year (excepting the blind, the handicapped, and the poor) based on an evaluation of family property carried out by a commission of six Jewish notables and levied at two sueldos for every 100 of assessed value. Any man or woman who thought he or she was being assessed unfairly

---

*As the Spanish currency was then called.

could appeal personally to the king who might intervene directly on his or her behalf. Government was always a hands-on affair, and attempts by post-Reconquest Christian kings to protect "their Jews," as they called them, were real and not illusory, even if they sometimes failed in times of crisis. A published collection of royal ordinances in Aragon between 1213 and 1327 details a record of taxes, help in settling disputes, and hundreds of "privileges" extended to Jews during this period.[15]

Saragossa was also home to the greatest scholars and poets of Aragon, and by the thirteenth century Jewish males were being educated to a degree that was nothing short of encyclopedic. Boys were taught the entire spectrum of knowledge: the Bible, Hebrew, poetry, the Talmud, Euclidean geometry, the mathematics of Nicomachus and Archimedes, optics, astronomy, music, mechanics, medicine, natural science in all its branches, metaphysics, ethics, Aristotle's logic (as interpreted by Averroës), and the relationship between philosophy and revelation. The rationalism of Aristotle as retailed by Averroës and Maimonides had an important impact.[16]

Saragossa was the most important center of Aragon, but Toledo, at the heart of neighboring Castile, had emerged as the new center of learning after the "death" of Cordoba in the twelfth century. Toledo was famed throughout Spain as a center of Jewish life, a worthy successor to Cordoba and Granada.

A contemporary Jewish traveler described it this way:

> I came to the great city of Toledo, capital of the realm—which is adorned with the sciences, showing its beauty to people and princes alike. For the tribes have migrated here, the tribes of the Lord.
>
> There are so many palaces in this city that make one want to rush to light the altar lamps—such is their magnificence and splendour. There are so many synagogues of incomparable beauty. Here every soul praises the Lord. In its midst is a congregation adorned with justice, as numerous as the plants of the field.[17]

By the thirteenth century, the Toledan school of translation—continuing the tradition of intellectual discovery that so brilliantly marked the Moorish kingdoms—was famed all over Europe. The Arab, Mozarab, Jewish, and Christian translators of the city knew a variety of languages and cultures. They worked from Arabic and Hebrew into Latin, then into the vernacular languages of Europe, translating ancient Greek works of mathematics, astronomy, astrology, and even the occult. Occasionally they worked in groups. For example, a team of four scholars translated the Quran into Latin: one Muslim, two Christian Latinists, and a Mozarab who straddled the two traditions. A Latin translation of the work of the eleventh-century Arab physician Ibn Sina (Avicenna) was carried out in two phases: a Jewish scholar put the Arabic into Castilian, and a Christian put the Castilian into Latin.

The translators of Toledo owed their success to the king of Castile. Alfonso X, "The Wise," was interested in everything from chess to astronomy, and under his patronage Toledo attracted scholars from all over Christian Europe—from Bath, Tivoli, Bruges, Paris, and Chartres as well as from other centers of Spain—just as Cordoba had done centuries earlier. Europeans were increasingly excited by the new window opening on Arabic and ancient Greek learning. Some may have sensed that in this rich font of human knowledge, which had been lost to the West for centuries, lay the true hidden treasure of legend, far more potent in its future uses than the gold they lusted after.

Alfonso the Wise surrounded himself with learned people, many of whom were Jews. His official treasurer was a renowned student of the Talmud.[18] His personal physician was a Jew, although this was hardly unusual since the practice of medicine had been "Jewish" since the early days of *Al-Andalus*. But one man—the prayer reader in the synagogue of Toledo—was the king's favorite: Zag (Isaac) Ibn Said, the most prominent astronomer (and astrologer) of his day. Alfonso X commissioned Ibn Said to draw up astronomical tables to measure time, and the still-famous "Tables of Alfonso" made the lasting reputation of the king.[19]

In this rough-hewn world where war and only war had occupied the noble classes for centuries, Alfonso the Wise founded university courses in Latin *and* Arabic (the speech of the supposedly hated infidel), and fostered the codification of vernacular Castilian as a formal language. He established university chairs in medicine, surgery, music, and plain song at the University of Salamanca, and put together a famous code of laws called the *Siete Partes* (Seven parts) in which he (unsuccessfully) tried to set standards for the conduct of military campaigns. He set up a school at Murcia with a teaching faculty that represented the three religions of Spain, and under his patronage Jewish and Muslim scholars wrote treatises on chemistry and other sciences. This remarkable king also penned a great deal of forgettable poetry himself.

During Alfonso's thirteenth-century reign, twelve thousand Jews lived in Toledo. They built their synagogues of columns, arches, and mosaics in the architectural style of the culture that had been theirs for centuries, Moorish Spain. Young men of high birth trained to fight in continuing Reconquest battles with the few remaining unconquered Arab kingdoms to the south, while their fathers raised capital for the enterprise. In this integrated, multi-ethnic society, the Christian mystic Ramon Llul composed an Arabic dialogue in which the three principal characters were a Christian, a Jew, and a Moor, and the king of Aragon established a school at Mallorca to disseminate the work throughout the Islamic world.

The prosperous thirteenth century closed on the hybrid civilization of Christians, Jews, and Muslims characterized by Llul. It closed on a burgeoning merchant class that had opened new trade routes and enriched the Spanish kingdoms—a class consisting almost exclusively of Jews whose linguistic and educational backgrounds had prepared them to fill these ambassadorial roles just as they had done under the caliphs. Wherever the Reconquest retook territory, the familiar symbiosis of Moorish, Christian, and Jewish cultures was perpetuated until there was little real difference between "Christian" Toledo and "Islamic" Cordoba. At the end of the thirteenth century, Spanish society, though officially Christian, was as mixed and multifaceted as any the world had seen, or would see again, for centuries to come.

*   *   *

Within the Jewish communities, however, an uneasy tension had taken hold: a serious split, a class division, now separated the prominent, well-educated believers in Aristotle's rational approach to the world from the masses of the faithful—the traditionalists, the hard-laboring poor, the simple, the mystics, and the messianists for whom the long season of diaspora life was but an interlude before the Jewish version of the end of days, when the Messiah would arrive to lead them back to Jerusalem. This internal friction led to the emergence of numerous self-appointed prophets, some of whom were privileged with visitations. For example, the "prophet of Ávila" entertained an angel who dictated a long manuscript called *The Book of Wondrous Wisdom*. This prophet (along with a cohort, the prophet of Ayllon) foretold that on a certain July day in 1295 the Messiah would blow his horn to summon the Jews.[20]

Rumors of prophecy spread, and in all the communities of Spain faithful Jews fasted, did good works, and prayed. They packed their belongings in chests. On market days they spoke of nothing else. Even the sophisticated, upper class aristocrats were intrigued.

On the appointed day, thousands of men, women, and children dressed in white, as on Yom Kippur, the Day of Atonement, and congregated in their synagogues. Breathless and expectant, their chests at home, packed, and ready for the voyage, they awaited the moment of prophecy they and their ancestors had prayed for, the hour of redemption when the true Messiah would appear before them to confirm the ancient religion of Moses.

And something exceptional did happen, of course—how could it not?—but sadly it was not what the Jews were waiting for. Carried away by excitement, fear, anxiety, and in an emotionally suggestible state, they experienced a mass, collective vision as they waited for a sign from above. They "saw" crosses appear on their clothing. A horror! Screaming, tearing at their clothes, the Jews fled to their homes, but the crosses were there, too, on the linens packed in the chests that were ready for the voyage.

Some cried that this was a sign from Jesus telling them that he alone was the true Messiah, and they demanded to be baptized on the spot. Others thought the vision was the work of the Devil who was up to his usual tricks. (The rabbis later adopted this explanation.) Still others admitted to being simply baffled. One thing was certain: Following this terrifying event, large numbers of Jews converted to Christianity.[21]

Shared anxieties lay exposed, but where had they come from? Spanish Jews were not noticeably uncomfortable in the late thirteenth century. With few exceptions, royalty in Castile and Aragon ignored papal pronouncements against minorities and continued to promote the multicultural policies they had inherited from the Moors. Pluralism was a national habit. Perhaps it was the very openness of a society that was seen to encourage "secularism" and assimilation among the educated, Jewish upper classes that had provoked a backlash from the faithful; perhaps they were frightened to observe the most talented members of their community repudiate tradition. These salt-of-the-earth believers openly feared for the survival of the tribe, and of Judaism, itself. Whatever the cause, the "vision" of the crosses laid bare their inner apprehensions. They lived in a world whose powerful spiritual root was Christianity and now, at the perceived end of days, as they awaited a Messiah who would rival and replace Jesus in the world, even the strong quavered. In this moment of truth, the ultimate question arose. What if they were proved wrong?

The Jews still rode the double track they had inherited from Averroës and Maimonides: a rationalist intelligentsia was well assimilated into the highest echelons of society, but was increasingly condemned by the masses for abandoning religious orthodoxy. This split would devastate the community as pressure on the Jews increased.

Notes

1. U. R. Burke, *A History of Spain*, 1: 103.

2. El Cid's fame endured. In the seventeenth century the great French dramatist Pierre Corneille recreated part of the myth (the unsubstantiated part) in a work that dramatized the supposed conflict of love, honor, and duty El Cid and his wife, Jimena, were forced to confront.

3. Juan de Mariana, *The General History of Spain*, 6: 102.

4. Contemporary chronicler Ibn Hayyan, cited in R. Menéndez Pidal, ed., *Historia de España,* 83–84.

5. Ibid.

6. Cited in Léon Poliakov, *The History of Anti-Semitism: From the Time of Christ to the Court Jews,* 48.

7. Cited in Joseph F. O'Callaghan, *History of Medieval Spain,* 312.

8. The sources are in conflict as to whether Alfonso actually married Princess Zaida after the death of Queen Constance of France.

9. Details on life in medieval Saragossa can be found in M. Kayserling, "Notes sur l'histoire des juifs d'Espagne," *REJ* 28, and Angel Canellas-Lopez, "La Judería Zaragozana," conference on the Jewish Quarter of Saragossa, 1974.

10. Silver work, leather tooling (especially shoes), bookbinding, and sword tempering were considered Jewish arts.

11. These baths were first documented in the early thirteenth century.

12. El Medio is now called Rufus Street. It is still a street of shoe makers and repairers who work out of tiny shops.

13. The Haggada contains the ritual service that is recited during the Passover seder.

14. For an interesting discussion of ethics and usury in the Middle Ages see Jacob Katz, *Exclusiveness and Tolerance: Studies in Jewish-Gentile Relations in Medieval and Modern Times,* ch. 5 and 102ff.

15. Jean Régné, *A History of the Jews in Aragon, Regesta and Documents, 1213–1327,* throughout.

16. I. Abrahams, *Jewish Life in the Middle Ages,* 355ff.

17. Cited in *A Guide to Jewish Toledo,* 1990.

18. His name was Meir de Malea.

19. In general, astronomy, astrolabes, the drawing of maps, etc., were considered Jewish arts.

20. There had been an earlier prophecy by the great thirteenth-century authority of France, Rabbi Moses of Coucy, proclaiming the coming of the Messiah in 1240. Rabbi Moses preached throughout Spain from 1236 to 1240.

21. This remarkable story is recounted in Y. F. Baer, *A History of the Jews in Christian Spain,* 1: 280.

4

That Liar the Devil:
The Fourteenth Century

With the growing success of the Holy Reconquest, all of Spain had become a multireligious society. A king of Castile had even called himself emperor of the three religions. Yet at the end of the fourteenth century a nationwide, grisly pogrom erupted against the Jews. What could possibly have happened to destroy centuries of established tolerant behavior?

The question looms large, for the tensions Spain experienced during the fourteenth century have been felt many times since, and with similar, brutal results. What happened in Spain was rooted in the social, religious, and economic soil of the era, and the deadly fruit of hatred took infinitely longer to ripen. But seen through a historical mirror, the breakdown of tolerance six hundred years ago assumes a pattern that is now strikingly familiar.

The misery began with the century itself. In the first decade a strange cold strangled the whole of Europe and the Baltic Sea froze twice. It was, in fact, the beginning of what has been called the Little Ice Age.[1] The population of Spain had increased over the boom years of the thirteenth century, but with the cold the growing season shrank. In some regions agriculture failed entirely, and the difficult mountain topography made transportation of foodstuffs from one part of the country to the next almost impossible. The result was localized starvation.

In the second decade of the fourteenth century it rained so hard and for so long that crops were wiped out in some places and famine spread. Preachers recalled the parable of Noah and his ark. Surely God was punishing people for their sins.

But the most frightening blow of all was not to the physical body, for in the fourteenth century the prospect of disaster was ever present. It was, rather, to the spirit. The unifying center of life and society—the Catholic Church—was in grave trouble.

69

By the fourteenth century the priesthood was the favored career of men in search of a pleasure-filled and often powerful life. (Even earlier the son of King James, the Conqueror of Aragon, had reportedly entered a monastery so he could lead a sensual life with impunity and was rumored to have died from debauchery.) Pious Christians had long railed at the ignorant, venal friars who were supposed to guide them through a maze of earthly temptations, but were at least as sinful as their flock.

A tongue-in-cheek satire on the clergy, written by a contemporary priest so clever that both he and his lengthy poem are still the subject of debate, has survived intact. The *Libro de Buen Amor* (The book of good love) was, in fact, a graphic description of how to get a woman into bed, but the author, Archpriest Juan Ruiz, was far too subtle to get caught in a trap of his own making. In his introduction he announces that *buen amor* means love of God and his commandments while, on the other hand, *amor loco d'este mundo* is the silly love of this world. His *true* intention, he warns, is to reveal the foolishness of the latter so godly people can rightly choose the former.[2] This is already a joke, of course, and what follows is a raunchy, blasphemous, and probably autobiographical account of sex and gluttony in fourteenth-century Spain, all told in the name of religious salvation. It is also a rare window into contemporary society.

"To save their souls, some join an order, some become warriors, while others dedicate themselves to the serving of their lords,"[3] the archpriest informs his readers. As everyone knows, the success or failure of these monks, knights, and vassals is predetermined at birth by the conjunction of the stars and planets. But since he, the author, was lucky enough to be born under the sign of Venus, the reader will appreciate that his amorous inclinations fall into the category of "the natural course of things."[4]

Ruiz begins with a careful disquisition on how to choose a "beautiful, graceful and lively lady, [who is] neither too thin nor a dwarf." The goal is to convince—or trick—this lady into her lover's bed, and since the fourteenth century predates the sexual inhibitions of later eras, the author assumes that women are as lusty as men. The protagonist relays very specific advice: "Inquire about [the lady's] entire figure. If your hag [a go-between] tells you that the lady's armpits are sweaty and her legs short, her loins long, her hips wide, and her feet tiny and well-arched, know that such a woman is not to be found in every marketplace. She will be wild in bed, but prudent at home. Keep her in mind."[5]

The key to the "hag's" loyalty is money, the sly priest's second subject. Money runs the world, according to the protagonist of the poem.

It makes the lame run and the dumb man speak. Even a man without hands reaches out and grabs for money. A man may be an idiot, but money will make him a noble or a sage. If you have money you can have luxury, pleasure, and joy, and benefices from the pope; you can buy Paradise and earn salvation. Piles of money bring piles of blessings.

In Rome, the seat of holiness, I myself observed them all curtsying and scraping before Money, and doing him solemn homage. They humbled themselves as they do before the Crucifix. There money created many priors, bishops, and abbots, archbishops, doctors, patriarchs and men of power. Money consecrated many clerics and priests, certifying that they had sufficient knowledge, while the poor were informed they lacked learning. . . . I have often heard monks in their sermons condemn money and its temptations—and immediately grant pardons, waive penances and offer prayers—for money. These monks may scorn money in the public square, but back in the cloister they hoard it in vases and chalices. Money has more hiding places than do thrushes or magpies.[6]

The poem concludes with a more playful attack. The archbishop sends a letter to the town of Talavera informing the local priests that the pope will excommunicate anyone who keeps a mistress. The clerics are outraged, and the next day they decide to appeal to the king of Castile because "the king understands that we are all made of flesh."

"Am I to discard Orabuena whom I took up last year?" asks one. "By my tonsure, she had a bath only last night. I would renounce all my benefices, my high office, and my stipends rather than let my Orabuena be insulted like this!"

"What does the Archbishop have against us?" asks another. "He wants us to denounce what God has forgiven. I appeal, for if I now keep, or ever kept a maidservant in the house she is neither my kin, nor my relative. She was an orphan, and I brought her up! And I am not telling a lie. To support an orphan or a widow is a work of mercy—that's the absolute truth. If the Archbishop looks on this as evil, then let us give up good works and turn to evil ones."[7]

Juan Ruiz's mordant joking hints at the depth of general corruption within the Spanish Church and at the hypocrisy surrounding sex and money, both perennial subjects for satire. And the poem's easy eroticism is just one more sign of the pervasiveness of Arab culture that characterized Christian Spain.

Contempt for the Church was widespread throughout Europe, but at the beginning of the fourteenth century no one was quite prepared for the degree of cynicism displayed by King Philip the Fair of France. Philip accused the pope himself of heresy, murder, sodomy, blasphemy, sorcery, simony (the selling of offices), and every other sin he could think of. Then he dispatched an envoy to Italy to kidnap the pontiff and return with him to France where he would be tried and deposed. Pope Boniface VIII was, indeed, kidnapped, and so outraged that he died of shock a few weeks later.

Philip of France kept his royal hand in the papal cookie jar by ensuring the subsequent election of a *French* pope, Clement V, who avoided Rome entirely and moved the papal See to Avignon in 1309, where Philip could keep an eye on things. Clement V's papacy, and those that followed, were characterized by cynicism, sensuality, and a wild materialism which was financed by the frenetic selling of dispensations for everything imaginable—in particular to legitimize the children of priests.[8] The fourteenth-century popes became so wealthy that one of them, John XXII, bought gold cloth from Damascus for his gowns and an ermine-trimmed pillow—possibly to complement the tresses of his mistress.[9]

For the faithful, the painful question was this: If the Church could not rise above base venality, how could it perform its central function, which was to save souls from eternal damnation? A deep anxiety burrowed into every heart. Hell was a palpable reality: under the best of conditions only a select few would enter paradise.

A depiction of the Last Judgment was painted above the altar of the cathedral of Salamanca so the faithful could absorb its meaning during mass. In the painting the souls of the dead rise from their graves. Those destined for heaven are dressed in white gowns; their hands join in prayer and their eyes look upward toward the resurrected Christ. On the other side of the tableau sinners writhe in graphic horror, naked in their shame and about to enter hell. They recoil in fear as they are propelled toward the mouth of an enormous, many-toothed monster. Horned devils reach out from inside the creature's maw, pulling them in haphazardly. To the good citizens of Salamanca this was the reality of Everyman, the moment of destiny no mortal would escape.

No artist portrayed this terror more eloquently than the fourteenth-century poet Dante Alighieri. In his *Divine Comedy* Dante and Virgil descend together into the circles of hell where the theme is sex and simony—the top-rated sins of the day—and where the most visible sinners are the clergy.

> And everywhere along that hideous track
> I saw horned demons with enormous lashes
> move through those souls, scourging them on the back.
> . . . One of those lashes fell and a demon cried,
> "Move on, you pimp, there are no women here to sell."

A tonsured priest cries out in his suffering to Dante and Virgil:

> . . . the flatteries I sold the living
> have sunk me here among the dead. . . .[10]

It was enough to terrify all but the most sanguine.

If the Church had lost its moral authority to save men and women from the specter of hell or to provide answers to the enigma of life, it could no longer offer protection from a frightening, random universe. As general anxiety grew, new "return-to-the-source" religious movements sprang up, especially in France where spiritualist Franciscans were preaching poverty and the conversion of the Jews. (The debased papacy in Avignon did not object to the conversion of the Jews, but it did object to the perverse idea that Christianity might be connected to poverty. The spiritualists were promptly condemned as heretics, and in 1318 four were burned at the stake in Marseilles.)

Anxious attempts to purify Christianity were intensified by attacks on Judaism, since the universal religion could be "true" only if the others were "false." In 1320 the French inquisitor, Bernard Gui, put the Talmud on trial and found it "guilty" of heresy and blasphemy.[11] In the same decade a movement called the Shepherd's Crusade (led by the so-called *Pastorelli*) vowed to wipe out the remaining Muslims in Granada. While they waited to leave on their holy mission they occupied themselves by murdering Jews and lepers, both of whom were accused of poisoning wells. The *Pastorelli* circulated a ridiculous but significant story to back up the well-poisoning charges: the Arab king of Granada offered the Jews money to get rid of his Christian enemies. Knowing they were already suspect in Christian eyes, the Jews hired the lepers to execute the deed on their behalf.

The psychological underpinning of this fantasy is interesting. It revives the historical collaboration between Jews and Moors in Spain and, by implication, the legend that the Jews had opened the gates of Toledo to Tariq the Moor after he defeated King Rodrigo on the battlefield and thus helped destroy Visigoth, Christian Spain. The story also confirms that the relationship between Moors and Jews in Arab Spain before the Reconquest was common knowledge elsewhere in Europe—and a source of discomfort.

The *Pastorelli* struck first in Toulouse, then crossed over the border into Aragon and Navarre where they wiped out entire Jewish communities before being thrown out of Spain. However, the fanaticism that marked the French revivalist movements inevitably affected attitudes in Spain, too, because the conditions of Church corruption and economic suffering that had precipitated their rise in France were as true on one side of the Pyrenees as on the other. The French influence in Spain was not new, as we have seen. Spain had already experienced the effects of religious interference as far back as the "crusade" to Barbastro in the eleventh century, after which the French Archbishop of Toledo took it upon himself to convert the central mosque of the city into a church.

Money was another problem. As usual, the poor resented the rich, and as the decades of the fourteenth century brought famine, flood, and disease, the enemy became the tax collector. Peasants and the lower urban classes paid heavy taxes, regardless of their circumstances, and they increasingly resented the Jews who came to collect in the name of the king. Soon the tax collector *and* his entire community were in constant danger. He might be accosted, beaten, robbed, or murdered on the road in the course of performing his duty of collecting and delivering the revenues to the king. No matter. A starving peasantry was growing desperate, and it was easier to scapegoat the king's messenger than to confront the king.

Desperately unhappy men and women could not influence the weather to make crops grow, nor could they negotiate with the king to defer or lower their taxes, but they could express their suffering in other ways. One release was to attack the tax collector physically.

* * *

Deeply felt religious desire had produced the Christian spiritualist movements, and now a similar rift tore through the Jewish communities of Spain. In the 1320s, growing rationalism combined with the worldly pleasures of consorting with lord and king continued to seduce educated Jews away from traditional religion. Some of them bragged openly about the clout they wielded: "In times of trouble I go to the house of the emperor and who but I can gladden his heart? Can a moneyless man obtain the annulment of a decree?" asked one haughty individual.[12]

The class conflict of the preceding century grew more serious. Uneducated artisans and the poor remained faithful to the old orthodoxy while their leaders attacked the new rationalism in defense of the faith. As antirational mysticism grew (in tandem with Christian mysticism), traditionalists denounced the wealthy intelligentsia who served lords and kings and seemed to have forgotten the God of Israel. An anonymous prophet from the city of Saragossa begged the Jewish aristocrats to think about what had happened in their own lifetime:

Behold fourteen years after the banishment of 5066 [the Jews were temporarily banished from France in 1306], in the year of wrath and anger, the

Shepherds came and slew about eight thousand men of Israel, as was shown to me by my teacher of blessed memory three years before the event, in uninterrupted visions, two years after he had departed this life. And concerning this matter I preached to the multitudes on the verse "for the hand of the Lord hath not waxed short for salvation"—meaning salvation from the Shepherds—"nor is His ear dulled from hearing"—meaning from hearing the accusations made against us of having poisoned the waters, on account of which they slew the most holy ones in France. . . .

And what was the cause but your sins that separated us from God; and what are they but that your hands are foul with blood, that is to say, with plunder; for he who deprives his fellow of a penny is as one who has taken a life.

The thirteenth-century *Zohar,* or *The Book of Splendor*—the most authoritative book of the Jewish mystical movement known as Cabalism— fiercely attacked the rationalism of the upper classes, whom the mystics reviled as spiritual descendants of Maimonides.

Fools who know not and discern not wisdom say that the universe operates though mere chance without divine guidance. . . . They are fools. They lack faith. Woe unto them, woe unto their souls! 'Twere better had they never come into the world.[13]

The reformers were especially outraged by the easy sexual mores of the Jewish notables. Since the days of the Cordoba caliphs, Christians and Jews had openly (or covertly) imitated Muslim polygamy, sometimes through double marriage if a wife was barren, but more often through concubinage. By the twelfth century the Church in Spain also seemed noticeably ambivalent on the subject. Concubines were routinely recognized as "semiwives," and in one notorious case an enthusiastic abbot who had been convicted of keeping seventy concubines, then removed from his clerical position, was nonetheless supported by the Church for the rest of his life. Enforcing celibacy in a sensual society was a doomed cause. By 1322 the Church Council of Valladolid in northern Castile was complaining that local parishioners were insisting that the priests take concubines as the only way to protect the community's wives and daughters.

Spanish rabbis also pondered tricky sexual issues and some were known to change their minds frequently. In a document dated 1267, King James, the Conqueror of Aragon, states that Jewish law permits bigamy, and there can be no doubt that he got his information from the Jewish authorities of the day.[14] Maimonides approved of polygamy, in theory.[15] One thirteenth-century rabbi wrote that multiple marriage was perfectly acceptable, then changed his mind and said it was perfectly perverse.[16] Still another railed against concubinage: "Degrade not thy daughter by making a harlot of her, lest the land fall into harlotry, and the land become full of lewdness," he quoted from Leviticus.[17]

No religious institution has ever successfully suppressed the liveliest instinct, but in the confusion of the fourteenth century, codes governing morality were strained.

Advocating reform and a return to basics, the Jewish mystics studded their writings and oratory with messianic prophecies and apocalyptic visions. "Prophets," both Jewish and Christian, wandered the roads praising poverty, preaching repentance, and conversing with whomever would listen under the cool shade of a leafy tree, or in caves where they took refuge from the highwaymen who stalked the roads at night. Both Cabalists and Franciscans despised the "arrogance" of science. Both promoted the faith of the "little man."[18] And both were opposed by their respective "aristocracies": by the skeptical Jewish notables, advocates of Aristotelian rationalism by way of Averroës and Maimonides; and by the Dominican Order, whose members also were enthusiastic followers of Aristotle as well as being the favored religious order of the Christian establishment.[19] Class divisions did not wait to be discovered by Karl Marx.

As prosperity and the comfort of predictability dissolved year by year, apocalyptic fervor grew. Unlettered Christian peasants were visited with prophecies of the future, sometimes presented in perfect Latin which the recipient could not understand. Among the Jews there had already been mass messianic movements, as in the devastating Messiah-and-the-crosses affair of 1295. Physical life was becoming increasingly difficult and traditional religious life less secure. In the wake of this transformation, shifts in public and private behavior emerged.

Abner: The First of a Kind

Among those who were deeply troubled by the vision of the crosses affair in 1295 was a young Jewish physician named Abner of Burgos. Abner treated children who had developed emotional problems as a result of the vision (perhaps as a response to their parents' overt fears) and he became profoundly disturbed by the religious implications of the experience. That the Messiah had not appeared according to the prophecy was a blow to Abner's convictions, and the fact that this disappointment coincided with rifts and splits within the Jewish community over questions of fundamental dogma contributed to his depression.

Abner was a prototype for the intellectual apostate who later came to typify the upper classes of Spanish Jewry. He was well-read in Muslim and

Jewish philosophy as well as the theological works of Augustine, and among his peers Maimonides was considered the great teacher. Religious and intellectual issues were the lifeblood of civilized discourse among this educated class, and there was nothing in the least frivolous about young Abner. For twenty-five years after the vision of the crosses he pondered the truth of Judaism versus the truth of Christianity:

> I saw the poverty of the Jews, my people, from whom I am descended, who have been oppressed and broken and heavily burdened by taxes during their long captivity—this people that has lost its former honor and glory; and there is none to help or sustain them. One day I went to the synagogue weeping sorely and sad at heart. And I prayed to the Lord, saying, "I beseech Thee, O Lord God, for compassion. Why art Thou so angry with Thy people these many days. Why should the Gentiles say, 'Where is their God?' "[20]

One night in a dream, a "tall man" appeared to Abner. The Jews had only themselves to blame for their problems because they stubbornly refused to give up Judaism and accept Jesus as their Messiah, said the phantom. Then he leaned over the sleeping Abner and whispered in his ear:

> I say unto thee that the Jews have remained so long in captivity for their folly and wickedness and because they have no teacher of righteousness through whom they may recognize the truth.[21]

Late in the year 1319, Abner of Burgos converted to Christianity. He changed his name (as did all converted Jews), emerging from the baptismal font as Alfonso de Valladolid, a believer in Christ (but still a Jew by culture), and a Christian polemicist who was to dedicate himself to a passionate struggle against Judaism *and* the Jews.

For the remainder of his life Alfonso de Valladolid defended himself against his Jewish detractors: Tradition and respect are no substitute for independent thinking and coming to personal conclusions about received truths, he said, shrewdly referring them all to Abraham who held back from declaring *his* faith until he was over fifty. Then he took up the cudgel declaring that Christian morality was better than Talmudic ethics; Christian family law was better than Jewish family law; the Talmud was hostile to Christians; and, most importantly, the Messiah had already come in the person of Jesus Christ.

Before long Alfonso's rage took a more ominous turn. He argued that Jews and Christians should not eat together or socialize in any way, and he warned Christians against using the services of Jewish doctors. This last call was already a commonplace; in the fourteenth century sick people often died of whatever was ailing them, and Jewish doctors were frequently charged with murder on religious grounds. On the other hand, when the warning came from someone who had once been a Jewish doctor, it carried new weight.

Eventually Alfonso moved into uncommon territory. He initiated a call for active persecution:

> A blow of the rod is a means of directing a boy toward study and good behavior. [Similarly] when Jewish communities are massacred, and the particular generation of Jews is thereby reduced in numbers, some Jews immediately convert to the dominant Christian faith out of fear. In this way a handful are saved. This experience [the massacre] brings salvation to subsequent generations, that is, to the descendants of the suffering generation who turned to the right path.[22]

From a twentieth-century, post-Freudian vantage point, Alfonso's bitterness toward Judaism and his former coreligionists takes on a complex hue. What his hatred *and* the mass hysteria of the crosses suggest, at least in part, is that the pendulum was moving away from the easy tolerance of earlier days. With worsening economic times, the breakdown of comforting religious certainty among both Jews and Christians, overtaxation, and the envy of the lower classes, the Jewish minority was no longer as comfortable as it once had been. Some of its members, feeling targeted and ill-at-ease, yearned to "belong." This took the form of conversion to the dominant religion and a rejection of their former selves.

Abner-Alfonso was the first significant figure to seek comfort, safety, and salvation in baptism and anti-Jewish polemic. Unfortunately for the Jews of Spain, he was not the last.

Behold a Pale Horse

There was famine, flooding, and the painful erosion of deeply held conviction, but the fourteenth century had not finished delivering up misfortune. In mid-century all of Europe was devastated by unprecedented calamity, and in its wake came terror for the non-Christian minority.

"In A.D 1348, the people of France and of almost the whole world were struck by a blow other than war," wrote Jean de Venette, the prior of a Carmelite monastery in Paris.[23]

Looking back at that terrible year the goodly prior suspected he had been permitted to see a celestial portent of the plague:

In the month of August 1348, after Vespers, when the sun was beginning to set, a big and very bright star appeared above Paris, toward the west. It did not seem, as stars usually do, to be very high above our hemisphere but rather very near. At length, when night had come, this big star, to the amazement of all of us who were watching, broke into many different rays. Whether it was a comet or not, whether it was composed of airy exhalations and was finally resolved into vapor, I leave to the decisions of astronomers. It is, however, possible that it was a presage of the amazing pestilence to come.[24]

Since 1346, strange rumors had been circulating through Europe telling of a terrible disease that was spreading through Asia and killing entire populations. But Asia was far away and the idea of contagion was unknown. In any case, disease somewhere else only meant that God was punishing other people for their sins.

In 1348 one of the trading ships that plied the seas between the Far East and Italy delivered a terrifying cargo into the harbor of Genoa. The blackened bodies of dead sailors lay across their oars while a few dying companions managed to row the ship into shore. The sick men had large, black swellings in their groins and armpits that oozed pus and blood. They were dizzy, shaking with fever, and suffering terrible pain. A few seemed to be delirious; others did not have the swellings, but coughed incessantly and spat blood on the deck. All of them seemed to be bleeding from deep within, for everything coming from their bodies—sputum, vomit, urine, excrement—was bloody and tainted by a foul odor. Those with the cough were dead in a day. Almost all the rest were dead within five days.

It was bubonic plague, and there were, in effect, two strains. One was characterized by swelling of lymph nodes, called buboes, and was transmitted to human beings by fleas that had bitten infected rats; the other was pneumonic, a contagious infection that fills the lungs with water. The death rate for the first strain was about 60 to 80 percent; for the second, 100 percent.

The bubonic plague reached the Catalonian port of Barcelona in the spring of 1348, and within six months it had decimated the whole of Aragon, Navarre, Castile, and Portugal. The disease spread under exceptionally favorable conditions. Spain had almost doubled its population over the relatively peaceful years of the thirteenth century, industry and international commerce had surged ahead, and thousands of rural peasants had moved to the walled cities where garbage rotted in the streets and the black rat, the deadly carrier of bubonic plague, soon replaced the common rat of the back alleyways. Worse still, floods and famines had physically weakened the population and made them vulnerable to disease.

Lawlessness and debauchery increased, looters raided shops, and the poor boldly squatted on the abandoned lands of dead nobility. Agricultural production ground to a halt. In Barcelona, workers demanded salaries four or five times higher than before the plague.[25] In Gerona, in northeastern Catalonia, the town notables appealed to the king to exempt them from taxes because the city was almost entirely depopulated.

By the end of 1348, the plague had spread along the Mediterranean coast to Corsica, Sardinia, Spain, and France "where it attacked several cardinals [in Avignon] and took them from their whole household. Then it spread little by little, from town to town, from village to village, and finally from person to person."[26] By 1349 Austria, Hungary, Germany, Flanders and parts of England were devastated. In 1350 the plague had reached northern England, Scandinavia, and the Baltic countries, stretching to Iceland and Greenland. "All this year and the next, the mortality of men and women, and the young even more than the old was so great that it was impossible to bury the dead. People lay ill little more than two or three days and died suddenly, as it were in full health. He that was well one day was dead the next and carried to his grave."[27]

A contemporary described the ravages of the plague in the central Italian city of Orvieto:

> In May 1348, a great death came to Orvieto. Things grew worse daily, until June or July, when one day five hundred people died, young and old, men and women. Death and the horror people felt was so extreme that they died suddenly; one morning they were in good health and the next morning they were dead. All the shops were closed, many families were decimated, and many houses remained uninhabited; it is said that nine-tenths of the population died. The survivors remained sick and horrified, and in terror they abandoned their houses and their dead.[28]

In Spain, a traveler stopped at an inn in the town of Salvatierra, near St. James of Compostella. He ate, talked with the innkeeper and his wife, and went to bed for the night. When he awoke the next morning the house was strangely quiet. The entire family was dead.[29]

For most people there was only one explanation: God had sent the plague as an expression of his anger at human sin. There was no use wondering which sin. Every individual had his or her own personal storehouse of guilt. The Church railed against human frailty—adultery, avarice, blasphemy, greed, pride—but without success. Guilt hollowed out deep crevices in the souls of believers and doubters alike.

Doctors and scholars seized on a more "logical" explanation for the catastrophe: In his anger God had ordered a pernicious conjunction of the stars and planets, they explained. The proof was that on March 20, 1345, certain astrologers had observed a dangerous juxtaposition of Jupiter, Saturn, and Mars under the sign of Pisces: an early portent of calamity.[30]

The fourteenth century believed that diseases were carried through air or water.[31] This was partly true, of course, but since medicine lacked a crucial concept of contagion, or infection, physicians could go no further. They thought the air was "corrupted" by astral influences, or by winds that carried pestilence, or by various miasmic stinks, including the odor of decomposing bodies. And since there was no known cure for plague, physicians concentrated on prevention. Aromatic plants such as cypress, roses, and thyme were placed in the main plazas of Spanish cities to perfume the "corrupted" air, and frightened people duly sprinkled their houses with vinegar morning and night. Doctors prescribed amulets which were to be worn near the heart. (Those made with sapphires and emeralds were said to be the most effective.) The physicians recommended chicken, partridge and eggs, but warned against beef, duck, lamb, goat, rabbit, and pork. (Pork and duck were the most dangerous because they created humors which threw the body out of balance.) Bread had to be eaten within three days; apples or pears were to accompany the first meal of the day; and only dry white wine was safe. All fish was bad, except lobster. And everyone killed their cats and dogs since their hair was thought to carry the disease.

One cheerful author concluded his narrative of prevention by advising his stricken contemporaries to "live happily and with decent diversion, such as music."[32] Needless to say, his advice applied only to the wealthy. The poor scrounged what they could, where they could, and left thoughts of happiness to others. "Nothing helped, neither physicians, nor medicament," despaired the chronicler Marchione di Coppo Stefani in his *Cronica Fiorentina*. "Either this disease is new and hitherto unknown, or the doctors have never studied it. There seems to be no remedy."[33]

In the face of terror, human beings did the usual thing: they beseeched God for mercy and looked for scapegoats. But turning to God was now a risky proposition, for who could fathom the depth of divine rage if this awful disease was its most visible sign? In Andalusia processions of the faithful transported relics of holy martyrs to local churches, where they prayed to the dead saint to intercede on their behalf. Cathedrals were hastily repaired or newly constructed. People contributed to charities and did good works, hoping to gain points with the Almighty. (The rich of Castile donated so much land and wealth to the Church that the prelates grew magnificently rich and the entire economic structure of the country fell into disarray.)

If sin had brought about this strike from above, might one still be saved? Church corruption made the faithful despair, but more and more priests trafficked in the sale of indulgences.

Not surprisingly, a new back-to-basics religious movement spread across Europe in tandem with the plague. Barefoot and dressed in dark, hooded robes with a large red cross embroidered on front and back, men and women calling themselves Brothers of the Cross traveled from town to town, punishing themselves twice a day with a three-pronged whip tipped with iron. (The men whipped themselves in public, the women in seclusion.) Through self-inflicted pain the Flagellants, as they were known, hoped to recover the purity of their original baptism—a state without sin—and therefore protect themselves from the plague. To direct anger at God was impossible: to inflict suffering on themselves in God's name was permissible. (Others rebelled against the established Church order by turning for help to witchcraft, magic, and satanism.)

The Flagellants needed an outlet for their rage, and as soon as they arrived in a new town they headed straight for the Jewish quarter, with the excited mob of townsfolk storming behind. Their charge against the Jews was a simple one: Jews were poisoning the wells in order to rid the world of their enemies, the Christians. Once this motive was firmly established, the Flagellants mustered indisputable proof that the Jews had the capacity to carry out this conspiracy. They were doctors, apothecaries, and grocers, were they not? Therefore they had access to the spectrum of poisons.

In 1348 in the southern French city of Toulouse, forty Jews were tortured and eventually "confessed" to poisoning the wells. They were massacred by a mob. (Many were thrown into the wells, which *did* poison the water.) Jean de Venette chronicled the attacks:

> As a result of this theory of infected water as the source of the plague, the Jews were suddenly and violently charged with infecting wells and water and corrupting the air. The whole world rose against them cruelly on this account and many thousands were burned everywhere, indiscriminately. The unshaken, if fatuous, constancy of the men and their wives was remarkable. For mothers hurled their children first into the fire that they might not be baptized and then leaped in after them to burn with their husbands and children.

The friar was nonetheless skeptical about their supposed guilt:

> In truth, such poisonings, granted they actually were perpetrated, could not have caused so great a plague nor have infected so many people. There were other causes; for example, the will of God and the corrupt humors and evil inherent in air and earth.

But a fellow chronicler named Jean le Bel (a knight before becoming a priest) had fewer doubts. The Jews poisoned the wells, he alleged:

in order to poison all Christendom and to have lordship over the world, wherefore both great and small were so enraged against them that they were all burned and put to death by lords and judges of the places along the route of the Flagellants. And they all went to their death dancing and singing joyously as though they were going to a wedding, and they would not be converted, nor would fathers nor mothers permit their children to be baptised . . . saying that they had found in the books of the prophets that as soon as the sect of the Flagellants had overrun the world, that all Jewry would be destroyed by fire, and that the souls of those who remained firm in their faith would go to paradise. Wherefore as soon as they saw the fire, men and women leaped into it, always singing and carrying their little infants with them for fear that they might become Christians.[34]

The higher Catholic clergy was appalled and disturbed by the Flagellants' success, and in July and September of 1348 Pope Clement VI published two bulls declaring that the poison-well accusation was preposterous. Anyone with eyes could see that the Jews were losing as many people to the plague as Christians, he pointed out; in Saragossa, for example, 80 percent of the Jews had died of plague.[35] The pope went on to explain that Christians who blamed the Jews were being "seduced by that liar, the Devil,"[36] but a combination of public hysteria and disdain for the Church mitigated the impact of his intervention.

In defiance of the pope, King Philip VI of France accused the Jews of receiving poisons from their "grand master" in Toledo and commanded them to stand trial for well poisoning. The poisons were said to have been extracted from venomous scorpions, spiders, and toads, which were powdered then carried to France in "stitched leather satchels." Jews were massacred all over Europe—in France, Switzerland, Germany, Poland, and Lithuania. In the city of Strasbourg, on February 13, 1349, nine hundred individuals were hurled into bonfires.[37]

It is of interest that not one of the chroniclers relaying these fevered accusations even pretended to verify the existence of a toxic substance capable of poisoning water with plague: rumor sufficed in the fourteenth century, as it occasionally does today. It is also worth noting that although the great scientific collaborations of Christians, Jews, and Muslims in the translation centers of Toledo had excited the intellectual classes of Europe, they had apparently frightened ordinary people who made up the bulk of the population everywhere. In the popular mind Toledo was a "Jewish city" where mysterious, anti-Christian science was explored, such as grinding up scorpions to make poisons. The impulse was a familiar one: those who are not one of us must necessarily be against us.

Although accusations of well poisoning brought about the worst antiminority attacks of the entire Middle Ages, Spanish Jews were largely

spared. There were a few anti-Jewish uprisings in 1348, sometimes instigated by debtors who could not, or would not, repay their loans; but only
in Barcelona and Lérida did violent pogroms causing death occur, and
both of those Catalonian cities were geographically close to France and
subject to French influence.

By 1351 the plague had largely passed (although there were to be frequent recurrences throughout the rest of the fourteenth century and the
fifteenth as well).[38] Between 25 and 30 percent of the population of
Europe was dead—about twenty-five million people in all: in fact, in one
small French parish the records indicate more deaths for the period of
August 1 to November 19, 1348, than for the previous twenty years.[39] In
Spain the preplague population had been 7,470,000. When the ravages of
the disease subsided 4,000,000 remained.[40]

The plague was followed by a widespread psychological aftershock, as
stunned and brutalized survivors struggled to resume their lives. The survivors had witnessed the agonizing death of loved ones. They had watched
doctors and clergy abandon the dying, and they felt overwhelmed by the
magnitude of sin they believed they and their families must have committed to have been punished so severely. Eventually they could no longer
care about the heaps of uncollected bodies rotting in the streets, and,
finally, they could think only of their own personal survival. Deepening
their anguish was the belief that thousands had died without the benefit
of last rites before the pope eventually issued a general dispensation. To
die without confession was to risk burning in the fires of hell in perpetual
torment.

The shock of massive death invaded all of Europe and was mirrored
through the dark lens of art. Death personified—a grinning skeleton
brandishing scythe and hourglass—interrupts the joyous celebrations of
young and old. He bides his time in gleeful expectation or actively carries
away his victims under the helpless, horrified watch of their companions
who are, of course, next in line to go. No army can defeat him. He is the
Fourth Horseman of the Apocalypse from the *Très Riches Heures* of the
Duc de Berry, painted by Jean Colombe in 1470: "And Behold a pale
horse, and he that sat upon him his name was Death."[41]

A desperate dissoluteness now marked Europe. In Valencia houses
were looted in broad daylight and murders were committed in the streets.
Gambling tables operated in public squares and the richest families reck-
lessly threw away their fortunes, borrowing heavily at uncontrolled interest rates to maintain the spending frenzy. Courtiers paraded about in rich
gowns of red, blue, and green velvet or silk, their sleeves and bodices
draped in lavish folds. Wealthy widows were quickly remarried to new
husbands with an eye for opportunity. A careless disregard for the future

pervaded society; only the present mattered. Jean de Venette offered the following lament:

> Woe is me! the world was not changed for the better but for the worse. For men were more avaricious and grasping than before. They were more covetous and disturbed each other more frequently with suits, brawls, disputes and pleas. Greater evils than before abounded everywhere in the world. And this fact was very remarkable. Although there was an abundance of all goods, yet everything was twice as dear, whether it were utensils, victuals, or merchandise, hired helpers, or peasants or serfs. Charity began to cool, and iniquity with ignorance and sin to abound, and few could be found in the good towns and castles who knew how or were willing to instruct children in the rudiments of grammar.

Disruption in Spain

There was little relief. Pestilence recurred (though not on the same scale), but now there were consequences to the long-standing, widespread propaganda that had blamed the Jews for the plague. For the first time since the days of the Visigoths, anti-Semitism seeped into secular politics. In Castile, in 1366, Enrique of Trastámara rebelled against his brother, King Pedro I, initiating a civil war that drove out the king and installed the usurper Enrique in his place in 1369. Pedro's enemies mockingly called him "king of the Jews" because of the traditional presence of Jewish advisors in his entourage. For the first time a king's purportedly evil doings were attributed to the Jews.

Increased anti-Semitism encouraged more escapes-by-conversion, which in turn demoralized the already divided Jewish communities of Spain. The mystics continued to rail in vain against the *conversos,* as the converts were called, against the upper-class intelligentsia and the men of the court, against the rabbis, and against the community notables: "Woe unto those who joyfully and pridefully flaunt their colorful garments, forgetting that they are exiles among nations, far away from their homeland. They should wear black, and groan, and weep," admonished one mystic.[42]

Many Jews and Christians yearned for an end to recent horrors, for a return to the religious source, to the spring of life as they had known it, to the world as it had been before misery overtook the fourteenth century.

So it was that in the 1380s, when a certain fanatic archdeacon named Ferrán Martínez began to preach against the Jews of Seville, he had before him a dismayed and despairing audience that had long forgotten the halcyon days of Alfonso VI of Castile, "Emperor of the Three Religions," and the unique history of their own complex and tolerant land. The massacres that began in the narrow streets next to the cathedral of Seville and then spread to Valencia and over the entire surface of Spain had been a century and more in the making. The face of old Visigoth Spain was reemerging. Behind it was the body of the Catholic Church.

Notes

1. I am indebted to Barbara Tuchman's *A Distant Mirror*, chapter 2, for a general overview of the fourteenth century.

2. Juan Ruiz, *The Book of Good Love*, c. 1343, trans. Rigo Mignani and Mario A. Dicesare.

3. Ibid., 3.

4. Ibid., 62.

5. Ibid.

6. Ibid., 121.

7. Ibid., 330ff.

8. Barbara Tuchman, *A Distant Mirror*, notes that out of 614 grants of legitimacy in the year 1342–43, 484 went to members of the clergy.

9. Tuchman, *A Distant Mirror*, 28.

10. Dante Alighieri, *Divina Commedia*, Italian manuscript, Codex 74, fol. IV, reproduced in *The Horizon Book of the Middle Ages* (1968), 286.

11. This was the second time this occurred. The first took place a hundred years earlier.

12. Baer, *A History of the Jews in Christian Spain*, 2: 19

13. Ibid., 1: 263.

14. Jean Régné, no. 359, cited in Baer, *A History of the Jews in Christian Spain*, 1: 256.

15. Abraham E. Neuman, *The Jews in Spain*, 2: 51–52.

16. Solomon ben Abraham ibn Adret, 1233–1310, rabbi of Barcelona and financial and legal counselor to the kings of Aragon.

17. Solomon ibn Adret, cited in Baer, *A History of the Jews in Christian Spain*, 1: 256.

18. This movement was not restricted to Spain, nor did it end with the Middle Ages. In twentieth-century France, for example, unquestioning belief of this type is called "the coal man's faith."

19. In the thirteenth century, after a formidable struggle within the Church, Thomas Aquinas successfully incorporated Aristotle into Catholic doctrine. Maimonides' work was less successful in convincing the majority of ordinary Jews that reason and faith could be united in some measure. A full discussion of this issue is important in the history of both religions, but beyond the scope of this work.

20. Baer, *A History of the Jews in Christian Spain*, 1: 328–29.

21. Ibid.

22. Cited in Baer, *A History of the Jews in Christian Spain*, 1: 353–54.

23. *The Chronicle of Jean de Venette, 1340–1368*, trans. by Jean Birdsell (1953), 48. Jean de Venette was a peasant turned friar who, in spite of his lowly station, acquired a Masters of Theology degree at the University of Paris. He was prior of a Carmelite monastery from 1339 until 1342.

24. Ibid. The plague had actually been present in France since May 1348.

25. Charles Verlinden, "La grande peste de 1348 en Espagne," *Revue Belge de Philologie et d'Histoire* 17 (1938): 103ff.

26. *Jean de Villette*, 49.

27. Ibid., 48ff.

28. "Discorso historico con molti accidenti occorsi in Orvieto et in altre parti principiando,

1342–1368," cited in Elisabeth Carpentier, *Une ville devant la peste noire de 1348,* 112. Medieval chroniclers were less than fastidious about numbers. According to Carpentier, it is highly unlikely that five hundred people died in one day, given the population of Orvieto, or that nine-tenths of the population died.

29. Cited in Jean Noel Biraben, *Les hommes et la peste en France et dans les pays européens et méditerranés,* 1.

30. Tuchman, *A Distant Mirror,* 103.

31. Panchon Carreras, *La peste y los Médicos en la España del Renacimiento.*

32. Alonso de Burgos, "Tratado de peste, su essencia, prevención y curación" (Cordoba, 1651), cited in Juan Ballesteros Rodriguez, *La Peste en Córdoba, estudios Cordobeses.*

33. Jean-Noel Biraben, *Les hommes et la peste en France,* 55.

34. Cited in *Jean de Venette,* 189, note 22.

35. Baer, *A History of the Jews,* 2: 25.

36. Cited in Tuchman, *A Distant Mirror,* 113.

37. Jean-Noel Biraben, *Les hommes et la peste en France,* 61.

38. The bubonic plague did not entirely disappear from Europe until the eighteenth century.

39. The parish registry of Givry, cited in *Jean de Venette,* 186, note 50.

40. Juan Ballesteros Rodriguez, *La peste en Córdoba, estudios Cordobeses.*

41. Revelation, 6:8

42. Baer, *A History of the Jews,* 1: 371.

5

After the Pogroms

Alas the synagogues
Are all in ruins,
Kites and vultures made their nests there
When the sons of Israel departed,
And through devastated portals
Strangers entered.

—Yaacob Albeneh[1]

The Toledan poet Yaacob Albeneh reflected the desolation of those who lived. Every survivor had seen his or her parents, children or friends murdered or baptized. Localities could no longer pay their taxes and had to receive special dispensation from the king. "In Aragon by divine compassion, remnants survive of all our communities. Nothing remains to us but our bodies," wrote the political and spiritual leader of the Jews of Barcelona, Rabbi Hasdai Crescas, in a letter to the Jews of Avignon.[2]

More than anything else the pogroms were a failure on the part of the monarchy which was unable to protect "their Jews." Enrique III of Castile was a sickly eleven-year-old child (known not-so-fondly as "The Invalid"). A regency governed in his name and it was this gap in direct authority that gave Archdeacon Ferrán Martínez the opening he needed to prepare the mob in Seville for an attack. In Aragon, King Juan I was as tolerant toward minorities as his predecessors had been, and he certainly wished to protect "his Jews" from a popular insurrection that was a direct threat to royal authority. But King Juan's forte was pleasure, not politics (he was called "The Indolent" behind his back) and he always chose hawking, hunting, music, and poetry over the affairs of state. Poor Juan I had none of the macho qualities so admired by his contemporaries. This perception of weakness helped encourage the brush-fire of violence that swept his kingdom.

(Contemporary social attitudes also played a role in the failure of government protection. Faced with a popular riot, the medieval lawmaker put his faith in God, and God, as everyone knew, always made his wishes known by the outcome. Just as trial by ordeal established guilt or innocence, so it went with a pogrom. If a besieged community survived, divine providence had spoken in its favor; if the community went under, divine providence had spoken against.)

After the riots, King Juan I of Aragon promised to punish the instigators of the Valencia pogrom. He wrote, "Neither civil nor canon law allow that a person should be made a Christian by force; this can only happen in complete freedom."[3] But the nobility of the city had compromised themselves by participating in the riot and vigorously deflected the king's efforts. In fact, just thirteen months later they obtained a royal pardon for most of the participants. The king did authorize the city council to hang five or six ordinary people no one cared about, but he waited an entire year before visiting Valencia, that is, until the riot had been forgotten, when it was duly recorded that "he was received by the populace with much joy."

The happiest post-pogrom constituency was the Christian clergy, and from their point of view it seemed wrong to let the momentum die now that the miracle of the baptism of the Jews was established. Riots were reprehensible, no question; but peaceful conversion was in the best interests of non-Christians and society at large—and would hasten the Second Coming of Christ on earth. For the first time since the Visigoths were defeated seven hundred years before, the religious-nationalist ideals of *Christian* Spain seemed poised to become reality.

The conversion of the Jews emerged as the most important social phenomenon of the early fifteenth century in both Castile and Aragon, and before long religious pluralism itself was being described as the cause of social unrest. If everyone conformed to a uniform identity, there would be nothing left to fight about. The opening decades of the century following the pogroms were a time of changing consensus. The Visigoth ideal of religious exclusion had spread from the clergy to the population at large and was gaining important ground.

*　*　*

At the heart of this shift was an individual we have already met: the honey-tongued Dominican priest from Valencia whose preaching had incited his compatriots against the Jews in 1391.[4] Friar Vicente Ferrer was intense, persuasive, known to be incorruptible, and subtler by far than his coarse colleague in Seville, the archdeacon Ferrán Martínez. The authoritarian Martínez had issued confrontational anti-Jewish edicts and openly incited violence. Vicente Ferrer was a far more intelligent deliverer of propaganda, and his massive and relentless campaign had a smooth tone that captured the imagination of Spanish Christians (and terrified everyone else). None of this went unrecognized. Ferrán Martínez was censured by the monarchy and the Church. Vicente Ferrer was named a saint.[5]

Sometime after El Cid reconquered the Moorish city of Valencia in 1094, the main mosque on the central plaza was destroyed and a great Gothic cathedral built in its place. (Christianity thus demonstrated its superiority just as the Moors had once built over Roman temples to proclaim the preeminence of Islam.) Every week Friar Vicente preached a sermon in this cathedral urging the conversion of the Jews. *Maestre Vicens,* as he was called, had a scholar's knowledge of scripture and a gift for rhetoric that amazed his illiterate audience. He knew how to reach into the despairing souls of his parishioners and raise their hopes for a purer Church; he was an antidote to the corruption they feared, and an instrument of the healing they longed for. If the presence of religious minorities had caused the terrible riots of 1391 (as everyone believed by the early fifteenth century) then the Moors and the Jews had to be baptized into Christianity.

Unlike other priests who paraded about grandly and were followed by retinues of retainers, Vicente Ferrer was an ascetic, a reformer and a purifier. He was born in 1350, during the plague, so his very survival was something of a miracle; and he had grown to maturity during a period of unprecedented economic and social disorder. Vicente Ferrer was convinced that sin had brought about the calamities of his lifetime, and he decided to dedicate himself to eradicating the sickness.

Like the wandering friars he had observed during his youth, Friar Vicente removed his shoes, wore coarse robes, ate frugally, and lived in a monastic cell. His fame grew with each renunciation, and by 1390 he had attracted his own, but very different, retinue: a throng of about three hundred penitents who followed him wherever he went, flagellating their bodies until they drew blood.

Friar Vicente's sermons, which are preserved in the library of the Valencia cathedral, open a revealing window on the early fifteenth century. He preached endless tirades against women, whom he compared as a group to Salome who corrupted her stepfather, Herodias, and attempted the same with John the Baptist; he fulminated against the temptations of Eve and attacked the freedom allowed young people of both sexes (that female sexuality was universally acknowledged had been amply demonstrated in the *Libro de Buen Amor*); he devoted serious attention to a contemporary debate over whether priests should be allowed to visit prostitutes. And throughout his sermons he repeated a stirring, rhetorical phrase that was guaranteed to drive his theme home. *Per quae peccat quis, per haec torquetur*, he warned ominously: "We are tortured (punished) for our sins."

But Friar Vicente's central and abiding interest was the conversion of the Jews, and by 1405 he had developed his main lines of argument: Conversion should be voluntary, not forced; and all friendships and business relationships among Christians, Jews, and Moors should cease entirely, even if this prevented people from obtaining the necessities of life. "Jews and Muslims should be walled off from Christians, for we do not have greater enemies," he sermonized. "Infidel physicians should not be allowed, nor should anyone purchase food stuffs from them. Christian women should not be wet nurses to Muslims or Jews; nor should Christians eat with them. For the Holy Scriptures say that even a small sin will corrupt the whole person."[6]

Ferrer ordered all Jews and Jewesses over the age of fourteen to attend his sermons and to stand together as a group behind the altar. If any individual neglected to turn up, he or she would be fined 1,000 florins. Jews and Moors alike were commanded to wear a distinguishing sign. Finally, any *Christian* who disobeyed these new restrictions would face excommunication. In January 1412 all of Vicente Ferrer's recommendations were officially legislated in Castile. What the friar had in mind was a ghetto with a single locked door.

A sixteenth-century historian recounted the list of Ferrer's famous laws, including an interesting origin for the badge of shame.

> In Castile, the conversion of the Jews was carried on, and to humble those obstinate people it was ordered that they should not put out money to use, and that to be known they should wear a round or red cloth on their right shoulder three fingers broad. Three years after [1408] it was ordained that the Moors should wear a larger round of blue cloth in the shape of a half moon. Twenty-five years before this King John [Juan I of Aragon] . . . [had] enacted that the mistresses of priests should be distinguished from honest women by wearing a piece of cloth three fingers broad on their head cloths.[7]

Vicente Ferrer's ability to convince the monarchy of Castile to adopt his draconian legislation represented a major triumph for the Catholic Church, which had been struggling against religious pluralism for centuries, and marked a break in the tradition of Spanish kings and queens who historically ignored the antiminority edicts of the Church, including papal Bulls emanating from Rome. Friar Vicente Ferrer was the first to successfully introduce the Church's anti-Jewish agenda into secular law.

* * *

One of the most powerful men in early fifteenth-century Castile was Pablo de Santa María, the scholarly and renowned Bishop of Burgos. Before becoming a bishop—before becoming Pablo de Santa María—his name had been Solomon Halevi. Then he was the chief *rabbi* of Burgos and a leading scholar and intellectual in the Castilian Jewish world.

Some said Halevi had been baptized in 1390 after listening to the sermons of Vicente Ferrer; others insisted that he converted during the chaos of 1391. In either case it seems that his entire family was baptized at the same time he was, with the notable exception of his wife who refused to convert and remained a Jew. (Pablo divorced her. Had they remained married he could not have become bishop of Burgos.)

Having joined the Christian mainstream, the brilliant Pablo rose like a comet in the ecclesiastical hierarchy until he was bishop of the great see of Burgos, by then the capital of Castile, itself. Like Abner of Burgos, his counterpart of a century before, Pablo de Santa María transformed himself into a formidable enemy of his former people. Not only did he participate in the royal decision of 1412 legalizing Vicente Ferrer's demands, he insisted on adding further humiliations—subtle indignities that foreshadowed the psychological finesse of German Nazis many centuries later. No Jew had the right to be addressed with the respectful designation of Don or Doña, he ordered; and no Jew or Jewess was allowed to dress in fine clothing. Both sexes were to wear long, shapeless cloaks made of sacking upon which was sewn the round, red badge of shame. Men were forced to let their hair and beards grow untrimmed on pain of one hundred lashes. A contemporary Jew described the results of the edict:

> Inmates of palaces were driven into wretched nooks, and dark and lowly huts. Instead of rustling apparel we were obliged to wear miserable clothes, which drew contempt upon us. Prevented from shaving the beard, we had to appear like mourners. The rich tax-farmers sank into want, for they knew no trade by which they could gain a livelihood, and the handicraftsmen found no custom. Starvation stared everyone in the face. Children died on their mothers' knees from hunger and exposure.[8]

At the same time—history rarely moves in straight lines—ordinary people continued the familiar tolerant practices of old. Jews, Christians, and Moors who had lived together and were friends were not likely to pay attention unless they were forced to, and in truth, once the anti-Jewish rhetoric of discrimination had been established, royalty itself had little reason to enforce laws that would deprive them of their most capable constituency. As a result, many of Vicente Ferrer's harsh reforms were modified or abandoned within just a few months of their legislation. The Catholic Church was determined to win the long battle for power and control, but at street level, multireligious Spain was not dead yet.

In April 1412 Ferrer and his *compañia* of flagellants arrive in the city of Teruel in the southern part of the kingdom of Aragon. Most of the local Jews have already fled since by now everyone knows what is going to happen.

The *Maestre* likes to preach after hours so peasants who work in the fields can attend, and a platform has been built for him in the main plaza (Ferrer was physically small and wherever he went a dais was provided).[9] As usual the scene is dramatic and haunting. Flickering torchlight illuminates the dark sky. Long shadows leap across the paving stones of the plaza. Bright pools of yellow fire light the stage where the *Maestre* will stand.

There is a huge, noisy crowd here this night. Ferrer's appearance in Teruel is an event no one wants to miss. Everyone falls quiet as Aragon's most famous priest mounts the podium. *Maestre Vicens* begins to speak in the well-rounded, incendiary phrases for which he is renowned. His audience listens intently and crowds in close.

Behind and off to one side of the platform are the Jews. They huddle together searching the faces before them for signs of incipient danger. These events are always unpredictable. Vicente Ferrer is overtly opposed to violence; this is a stance which sets him apart from cruder men and actually endears him to some Jews, but his preaching incites others—an obvious reality the good friar can scarcely ignore. The psychological barriers that formerly held hatred in check were breached in 1391, and Ferrer, a universally admired man, has made anti-Semitism respectable. By now ordinary people who were sincerely revolted by blood in the streets in 1391 can, and do approve of his iron fist in a velvet glove; by now all of Christian Spain shares the *Maestre*'s fervent conviction that non-Christians must, and will, be baptized.

Friar Vicente's authoritative, convincing voice is enhanced by the dark and the torchlight as he recounts familiar parables from the Bible and tells tales of Jews who have seen the light of Truth. In one of his favorite stories a Jew who is unable to find a hostel in Rome takes refuge in a church where he is confronted by an idol surrounded by devils. The Jew refuses to be seduced or intimidated by the frightening demons, and when God sees this he sends fire to destroy them. But before the devils disappear, they speak: "God's intervention is a sign you must be baptized," they say.[10] A murmur of agreement washes through the crowd in the Teruel plaza.

Ferrer continues: "You must embrace, honor and love them [the

Jews] for Jesus Christ was a Jew. It is a sin to mock them." In other words, the Jews are to be treated well, though their faults be grievous. Ferrer speaks with the same undertone of double meaning later conveyed so brilliantly by Shakespeare in Mark Anthony's funeral oration.

> The noble Brutus hath told you Caesar was ambitious,
> If it were so, it was a grievous fault . . .
> For Brutus is an honorable man;
> So are they all, all honorable men.[11]

When he has finished speaking, Vicente Ferrer steps down from the podium. Holding a large cross aloft, he leads a procession of his *compañia* straight to the Jewish quarter where he reconsecrates the synagogue as a church to the cheering of the Christians and the despair of the Jews.[12]

Ferrer had done this before, in Toledo, in 1405. He was preaching in a church called Santiago del Arrabal (St. James on the Outskirts) from a beautiful Mudejar pulpit ornately carved in pink and white stone under delicate rose windows that filtered in the daylight. The forcibly assembled Jews stood in an alcove to the right of the high altar. Close by was another alcove containing a gorgeously sculpted baptismal basin.[13] It was Ferrer's intention to baptize the Jews there when the sermon ended.

But Toledo was the center of Spanish Jewry in 1405, or what remained of it after the 1391 pogroms, and the Jews standing beside the altar that day happened to include some of the most famous rabbis in the country. When these men refused to be swayed, Vicente Ferrer grew angry. Holding his crucifix high in his left hand, he marched out through the great wooden doors of the church, down the stone steps and into the narrow street. People hung over their wrought iron balconies to watch the *Maestre* pass; he was close enough to touch.

With his disciples in lockstep behind him and the curious in tow, Friar Vicente followed the street, hiking up and down the hills of the city until he reached the Jewish quarter near the cathedral. There he entered the main synagogue and stood with his followers under the Moorish arches. Among the white columns, capitals, and geometric interlacings carved gloriously into stone, he reconsecrated the synagogue to the Virgin Mary as Santa María la Blanca.[14]

Vicente Ferrer did not brook contradiction. When two Jews of Perpignan suggested he had misunderstood certain biblical commentaries, Ferrer had them arrested "for having pronounced words that were injurious to God and to Friar Vicente." (The men were held in prison until the king ordered them released.)[15]

Threatened with assault, even death, thousands of Jews sought refuge in baptism whenever Vicente Ferrer preached in their towns. A contemporary chronicler estimated the number of converts at 100,000,[16] although a sixteenth-century writer later praised the *Maestre* for having converted "8,000 Moors and 35,000 Jews besides the Christians he reclaimed from their wicked lives."[17] Later still a nineteenth century historian estimated that Vicente Ferrer was personally responsible for the conversion of 20,500 Jews.[18]

Medieval numbers are impossible to pin down with precision and we may never have an exact tally. What counts is the knowledge that the vulnerable succumbed to the pressure to convert, especially the educated upper classes who were leaning toward secular rationalism anyway. Only the most devout held fast. Unfortunately, they were the simplest, and entire communities were left "headless," so to speak. Within two decades the impact of 1391 on the Jews of Spain was compounded by the shock of being abandoned by the most talented men and women in their midst.

Although the practical details of the anti-Jewish legislation he sponsored were quietly ignored in many places, Vicente Ferrer was the first to formally distance government (the monarchy) from the tolerant practices that had characterized Spain since the first days of the Moors. He continued the "work" of the pogroms without the violence. He furthered social transformation by altering public consensus regarding the established "right" of the Other to live in peace. Ferrer changed Spain irreparably. After his death in 1419 other strongmen of the Church found it easier to follow in his wake.

Notes

1. Cited in *A Guide To Jewish Toledo,* 1990. Translation from Spanish by Erna Paris and T. M. Robinson.

2. Cited in Baer, *A History of the Jews in Christian Spain,* 2: 115.

3. Cited in Wolff, "The 1391 Pogrom in Spain: Social Crisis or Not?" *Past and Present* 50: 18.

4. Sources on Vicente Ferrer include: R. Chabás, "Estudio sobre los sermones Valencianos de San Vicente Ferrer," *RABM* 7 (1903); Bernardino Llorca, S.J., "San Vicente Ferrer y el problema de las conversiónes de los Judíos," IV Congreso de la Historia de la Corona de Aragón, 1 (Mallorca, 1955); Francisca Vendrell, "La actividad proselitista de San Vicente Ferrer Durante el Reinado de Fernando I de Aragon," *Sefarad* 13 (1953); Bernardino Llorca, S.J. "San Vicente Ferrer y su labor en la conversion de los Judíos," *Razón y Fe* 152 (1955).

5. Vicente Ferrer was canonized by a fellow Spaniard, Pope Calixtus III, in 1455.

6. R. Chábas, "Estudio sobre los sermones," 111ff.

7. Juan de Mariana, *The General History of Spain,* 323. It is interesting to note that the stigma of the cloth, be it a circle or a star, was first used to identify priests' mistresses, and that it was the woman, and not the priest, who was stigmatized.

8. Cited in H. Graetz, *History of the Jews,* 4: 220

9. Ibid., 89, note 7.

10. R. Chabás, "Estudio sobre los sermones."

11. *Julius Caesar,* act III, sc.II (c.1590).

12. This scene occurred all over Castile and Aragon between 1412 and 1414. In Aragon alone synagogues in five cities including Saragossa were reconsecrated.

13. This beautiful Mudejar church has been restored and the original pulpit and the baptismal font are still in place.

14. José Amador de Los Rios, *Historia de los Judiós en España y Portugal* 4: 426. This structure has been magnificently restored and can once again be visited.

15. Francisca Vendrell, "La actividad," 87ff.

16. Gil Gonzalez Davilá, *Historia de Enrique III* (1405).

17. Mariana, *The General History of Spain* 19: 322.

18. Graetz, *History of the Jews* 4: 223.

6

A Pope from Aragon
Tightens the Noose on the Jews

He was Benedict XIII, antipope of Avignon, and one of the most outrageous individuals of his age, or any age for that matter. Wily old *Papa Luna,* as he was affectionately called in his native Spain (his birth name was Pedro de Luna) personified the intrigues of the era. In many ways his lengthy career foreshadowed the later pope-princes of the Renaissance who with their scheming, plotting, and high living brought about the Protestant Reformation from sheer popular desperation.

Pope Benedict and Vicente Ferrer were friends (Ferrer was the pope's confessor) and they shared a singular passion: a determination to convert the Jews of Spain. Pedro de Luna was known for his erudition, and long before he became pope he had sought out debates with Jewish scholars over the universal truth of Christianity. At his death his personal library was found to contain 1,090 handwritten manuscripts (making it one of the biggest, contemporary collections in all of Europe), among which were a number of current and historical anti-Jewish polemics.[1] But Pedro de Luna had his own reasons for desiring the conversion of the Jews of Spain, and they had nothing whatsoever to do with holy fervor.

Pedro de Luna was born in 1328 into one of the most noble families of Aragon. He entered the priesthood, became a professor of canon law at the University of Montpellier, then a cardinal to the papal court in Avignon in 1378. (The papacy had moved to Avignon in 1309 after King Philip of France had arranged the brazen kidnapping of Pope Boniface VIII in Rome.) The year 1378 was also the beginning of the Great Western Schism in the Catholic Church, a demoralized and demoralizing period in Church history (the "Babylonian Exile"), which was to provide the canny Papa Luna with the best dramatic role of his lifetime.

The disturbing double papacy had been brought about in 1378 when a disputed papal election finished with not one, but two claimants to the papal office—one in Avignon, the other in Rome. Avignon was on the border of the French kingdom and the papacy there had been under the influence of the French for more than half a century. When Urban, the Roman candidate, won the papal election, the French refused outright to accept the results and declared Cardinal Robert of Geneva as pope in Avignon. (This strategy was so palpably political that when Robert became Pope Clement VII, the French king exclaimed, "Now I am pope.")[2]

The presence of two popes, one in Rome, the other in Avignon, was a declaration of war among Christians since each pope claimed to represent all of Christendom and had his own curia, and each was propped up by rival nations antagonistic to one another. It was proposed that an independent Church council resolve the impasse, but the suggestion alone enraged both popes. Clement VII took this perceived assault on his authority particularly hard. Within three days of hearing about the ghastly idea, he dropped dead of apoplexy.

When the shock of Clement's demise had subsided, everyone agreed it was time to reunite the Church. But the cardinals of Avignon (led by none other than Pedro de Luna) were deeply committed to their privileged positions. The pernicious side to all this talk of Church unity had not escaped their careful attention. Without a pope in Avignon, there would be no cardinals.

Pedro de Luna proposed a cunning solution that would allow the pope and the cardinals in Avignon to preserve their power while continuing to approve of eventual Church union. He suggested that whoever was elected pope automatically abdicate if asked to do so by a majority of the cardinals.

Eighteen of the twenty-one cardinals agreed, and signed an oath saying so. One of their number was proposed as pope. He hesitated, then refused. "I am feeble and perhaps would not abdicate," he bluntly confessed. "I prefer not be exposed to the temptation."[3]

"I on the other hand would abdicate as easily as I take off my hat," interjected Pedro de Luna just a little quickly.[4]

Cardinal Pedro de Luna was duly elected Pope Benedict XIII on September 28, 1394, and so began a byzantine career that would rock the Christian world and hasten the Reformation. The machinations of this crafty and brilliant pope-politician would also accelerate the transformation of Spanish society.

As a shrewd manipulator of power Benedict XIII set out to strengthen the public perception of his legitimacy through the major propaganda device of the age: popular ballads sung by troubadors who recited flattering tales of his papacy. (This activity so annoyed King Charles VI of

France that in September 1395 he forbade Benedict to create "songs" about the Great Schism.)[5] But it soon was apparent that nothing had changed. There was no effort on the part of Avignon to reunite the papacy. A movement against Benedict coalesced led by the influential clerics of the University of Paris. The rector, Nicolas de Clamanges, spoke passionately begging Benedict to resign. By doing so he would gain "eternal honor, imperishable renown, a chorus of universal praise and immortal glory," the rector argued. Once Benedict had abdicated, his rival in Rome would certainly do the same, cajoled Clamanges, and a single, legal papacy would be reestablished.

Infused with a sense of transcendental personal destiny, Benedict conveniently forgot about the hat that was supposed to fly off his head when the inevitable request arrived. After all, he retorted, how could he be sure that his rival in Rome would also resign? He, Benedict XIII, might be pressured into abdicating only to find the triumphant Roman pope in sole possession of the papal tierra. He, Benedict XIII, had been duly elected by the cardinals of Avignon. By God, he would never yield.

For the next three years Benedict held fast in Avignon while his opponents drummed up support for his deposition. Finally King Charles VI of France met with Wenceslas IV, the son of the Holy Roman Emperor and King of Bohemia. Since Wenceslas officially supported the Roman pope, Boniface IX, and Charles officially supported Benedict, it was hoped that the two monarchs could reach an agreement whereby both popes would be forced to abdicate.

The meeting was held on March 23, 1398, and it must have been an astonishing affair. Wenceslas was a drunkard who could only do business early in the morning, before the alcoholic fog grew so dense that he would agree to anything; and he was known to be so erratic that he had once had his cook roasted for having prepared a stew he didn't like. Charles who was also known as "The Mad," was entering a new bout of illness as he arrived. On such occasions the king's seizures caused him to tear his clothes, smash furniture, and fail to recognize those closest to him, including his wife. While in this condition (episodes lasted six to nine months) he also believed he was made of glass and would break if he moved. As the meetings proceeded indisputable signs of a new attack appeared, and the conference with King Wenceslas was abruptly adjourned.

Benedict remained adamant. "I desire the unity of the Church," he announced, "but since God has granted me the papacy by divine grace I shall remain pope as long as I live, and never will I renounce my title in submission to king, duke, count, or to any treaty, or trial whatsoever."[6]

Diplomacy had clearly failed. King Charles withdrew his support from Benedict and imposed a military siege of the papal palace in September

1398; but the wily Benedict had prepared by storing up a three-year supply of wine, grain, lard, oil and other necessities.[7] Other nations withdrew
their loyalty, the supply of heating wood ran out in the papal palace, and
several of Benedict's remaining cardinals tried to escape, but still Benedict
would not be moved.

For four years during which his beard grew long (he swore never to
shave while a prisoner), Benedict put together a secret army of four hundred loyalists. One night he escaped in disguise taking with him only a pyx
with which to say mass, and took refuge in a safe house in Avignon where
he was welcomed by a company of rebel French nobility who opposed the
king. He was eighty years old.

The French were furious, and Benedict XIII was reviled in remarkably
sordid terms. One doctor in theology said of him, "He [Benedict] would
rather kiss the ass of a filthy whore than the mouth of [Saint] Peter."[8] It
is small wonder that ordinary Christians abhored the clergy and despaired
of salvation.

Benedict escaped once again, this time home to Aragon.

In March 1409, ten thousand ecclesiastics and royal ambassadors
attended the General Council of Pisa and excommunicated both Benedict
and his papal counterpart in Rome. Then they elected a new pope,
Alexander V. Both of the schismatic popes were officially disgraced, but
both refused to resign. Now the Christian world had three popes instead
of two.

A contemporary German monk expressed the general desperation:

> The pope, once the wonder of the world, has fallen, and with him the heav-
> enly temples. The Papal Court nourishes every kind of scandal, and turns
> God's houses into a market. The sacraments are basely sold; the rich is hon-
> ored, the poor is despised, he who gives most is best received. Gold was the
> first age of the papal Court; then came the baser age of silver; next the iron
> age. Then came the age of clay. Could aught be worse? Aye, dung; and in
> dung sits the papal Court. All things are degenerate, the papal Court is rot-
> ten; the pope, himself, head of all wickedness, plots every kind of disgrace-
> ful scheme.

Pope Benedict's sense of personal entitlement was nothing short of
awesome. Now he needed something dramatic to offer to the Christian
world in his defense: a cause, a crusade, anything that might encourage
kings and notables to rally around his claim to the papacy. He cast about
for a concrete symbol of his piety as proof that he placed the interests of
Christianity above his own stubborn conceit. The showier the symbol, the
better.

At home, in Spain, the obvious solution stared him in the face: the conversion of the Jews of Aragon. If the Jews disappeared from the face of Spain, not by pogrom, murder, or expulsion, but by becoming Christians, why then only good would have been served. This process was already well underway, thanks to the pogroms of twenty years before and the tireless efforts of Benedict's friend and confessor, Friar Vicente Ferrer; and the baptisms in Spain were causing much pleasure elsewhere in Europe where people feared and despised the strange multicultural world across the Pyrenees.

Now the time was right. A new push to baptize the Jews was the perfect tool with which to battle Benedict's enemies, the initiative that might keep him on the papal throne.

The Disputation of Tortosa[9]

It was 1412, just months after Friar Vicente's ferocious edicts against the Jews were translated into law by the regency of Castile. In November Pope Benedict issued a summons ordering every Jewish community in Aragon to send its best scholars to his new papal court in the coastal city of Tortosa for instruction in the Christian religion. A disputation between their scholars and his would open early in 1413, he announced.

The premise of the debate had been decided, said the pope. It was: The Messiah has already appeared on earth and His presence was foretold in the Talmud.

The Jews of Aragon sensed trouble. They knew of Benedict's lifelong obsession with their conversion *and* of his on-the-job problems, so to speak. The connection between their harassment and the pope's rehabilitation was not difficult to see. Furthermore, they were being ordered to Tortosa at a time when they needed to help their decimated communities at home, and religious disputations had been known to last for months, even years. Such debates between Christian and Jewish theologians were not uncommon, and everyone knew Pope Benedict was an acknowledged master of the genre.[10]

The Jews tried to extricate themselves in the usual ways—through bribery and by sending delegations of notables to plead their cause. But Benedict was adamant for obvious reasons, and the Jews had no choice but to obey. By January 1413 the most respected among them had made their way to Tortosa from across the kingdom, by foot, by wagon, and by mule.

The day before the opening session Benedict attempted to reassure them in customary, if somewhat ambivalent, terms: "You notables of the Jewish people, a people chosen by the ancient Chooser and rejected for your own sins. Have no fear of the disputation. You will meet with no guile or wrong whatsoever."

No one quite believed him.

The Disputation of Tortosa was held in a room attached to the cathedral behind a small, wooden door that opened then (and now) with a huge key. It was a large room by medieval standards, surpassed only by the Chapter House in Barcelona. Hundred of years later the well-preserved gothic arches still stretch across a ceiling of ornately sculpted wood, and the visitor can still observe the outlines of an arched doorway that led into a smaller room from which the overflow crowd watched nervously or triumphantly, depending on their allegiance.

The Disputation was solemnly inaugurated on February 7, 1413, by Pope Benedict, who presided. The pontiff sat on a raised throne at one end of the room surrounded by a dozen cardinals and bishops dressed in gorgeous robes. Visiting dignitaries perched on benches along the walls, and the audience stood in the center of the room.[11]

In the place of supreme honour directly beside the pope sat Jerónimo de Santa Fe, a prominent convert from Judaism. Jerónimo had once been a physician, scientist, and scholar of the Talmud named Joshua Halorki, a member of the learned Jewish aristocracy of the city of Alcaniz. He had also been the personal physician of a certain high-ranking priest—one Pedro de Luna, now Pope Benedict XIII.

Halorki/Santa Fe had walked a long road, from Jewish physician to right-hand advocate of the pope. In the 1390s, although thousands of educated Jews like himself were defecting to Christianity after the pogroms, he had been astonished to learn that the chief rabbi of Burgos, Solomon Halevi, was among the converts. There were few as learned as Solomon Halevi, or as concerned, or (it had seemed) as steadfast.

All those years ago, Joshua Halorki had written a letter to Solomon Halevi (now Pablo de Santa María) expressing his surprise and chagrin, but at the same time admitting that he, too, had certain spiritual misgivings, and the painful questions he put to Santa María offer a poignant glimpse into the inner suffering of Spanish Jews after 1391. Did Santa María "lust after riches and honors?" Halorki wondered in his letter. Did philosophy "cause you to regard the proofs of faith as vanity and delusion?" In other words, had the Aristotelian rationalism of upper-class Jews brought him to disdain the revelations of faith? Had philosophy made Santa María believe "that our fathers had inherited falsehood?" Or had the terrible afflictions that fell on the Jews during and after the plague years made Santa María believe God had abandoned his people and "that the name of Israel would be remembered no more?"[12]

I knew you delved into the hidden treasure of Christian books, commentaries, and principles, having a mastery of their language [Latin], and there found many things not discerned by any of the Jewish scholars of our time. Would that I could fly and dwell under the shadow of your roof tree, that you might teach and tell me what has been revealed to you of these foreign matters, one by one. Perchance you might still the tumult in my heart and resolve for me a multitude of doubts concerning these interpretations.[13]

Like Abner of Burgos more than a century before, Joshua Halorki wrestled with his conscience for more than twenty years. Until 1412, when Friar Vicente Ferrer visited Alcaniz. Halorki had been "waiting" for Friar Vicente like an autumn leaf on a branch waiting for a breeze. His conversion was swift and total. As Jerónimo de Santa Fe, he became one of the *Maestre*'s most illustrious disciples.[14]

In his letter to Pablo de Santa María, Halorki had opposed Christianity and argued in favor of Judaism; in particular he had refused to accept the central Christian belief that the messiah has already lived on earth. But when he metamorphosed into Jerónimo de Santa Fe, all this changed. He prepared a manuscript in both Hebrew and Latin in which he marshaled arguments for Christianity and against Judaism; and it was common knowledge that he was spoiling for a fight with his former coreligionists. Soon Jerónimo was a confidant of Pope Benedict XIII himself; and now, within two years of his conversion, he was here in Tortosa, at the pope's side, ready to debate on behalf of Benedict and the Catholic Church against the most renowned Jews of Aragon—all of whom he knew personally.

* * *

Thirteen Jewish notables entered the Chapter House in Tortosa. They stood upright, facing the pope and Jerónimo. Benedict XIII addressed them. The disputation was not a debate over the respective merits of Christianity and Judaism, he insisted. Judaism was once the true religion, but it had been surpassed by Christianity: this fact was not in doubt and not debatable. What they had been summoned to acknowledge, on behalf of the Jews, was that the Messiah had already come to earth as Jesus Christ, and that their own book, the Talmud, had prophesied this coming.[15]

Then Jerónimo de Santa Fe took the floor. He was well prepared for this battle. In addition to his formidable knowledge of the Talmud he had made himself an expert on Christian theology and a master of scholastic argumentation.

Jerónimo looked confidently at his former friends, whom he could now observe from a place of undisputed power. Then he opened his remarks with an ambiguous quotation from Isaiah 1: "Come now, let us reason together. But if you refuse and rebel, you shall be devoured by the sword."

This choice of openings did not reassure the assembled rabbis.

Jerónimo intended to prove that Jesus of Nazareth was the Messiah, he said, and he would do so by means of a logical syllogism that went like this:

> He who fulfils the prophesies is the Messiah,
> The prophesies were fulfilled by Jesus,
> Therefore, Jesus is the Messiah.

Only the middle premise needed to be proved, Jerónimo explained, since the other statements were simply and indisputably true. Jerónimo claimed he would demonstrate with reference to the Talmud that the Messiah was prophesied to come toward the end of the period of the Second Temple and that he would be born in the town of Bethlehem. Furthermore, he, Jerónimo, would prove it was prophesied that the Messiah would be born of a virgin mother, and that he was the son of God, and that kings from the Orient would arrive offering gifts of gold, incense, and myrrh; and that on his arrival the souls of the just would be saved from hell, and that after his mortal death he would return to earth, then ascend to heaven to take up his seat next to God the Father. Finally, Jerónimo promised to demonstrate that the Talmud was filled with abominations, heresies, and falsities, and that the Jews were being punished by God for their sin of rejecting Jesus.

The debate would be conducted according to the scholastic method which included deduction, inference, and the making of distinctions and subdistinctions within closely reasoned arguments. The tool was logic, as understood and practiced all over Christian Europe. The object was to win the minds of reasonable people.

This approach created problems for the Jews. First, they could hardly expect an open investigation of the subject since it was already decided in advance that the conclusion was "indisputably true." Second, the Talmud was not a book of literal religious dogma, as Jerónimo well knew. The Talmud was anecdotal, literary and allegorical, a loose compendium of topics as diverse as geography, history, Jewish law, astrology, astronomy, ethics, fables, metaphysics, theology, magic, natural sciences, and mathematics, all presented in a unique dialectic style that combined centuries of oral tradition and complex debate. To dispute the minutiae of the Talmud according to the rules of syllogistic logic was an inherent distortion, like forcing square blocks into round holes.

Finally, although most of the rabbis knew Latin by the early fifteenth century, they were largely untrained in scholastic debate and would be at a distinct disadvantage.

During the early sessions the rabbis held their own in the formulation and counterformulation of arcane arguments. But as time passed they began to lose heart. Only days into the proceedings, one Moses Abenhabec cried out, "We have listened enough to the reasons of *maestre* Jerónimo! We do not need to reply further!"[16] His colleague, Astruc Halevi, jumped in: "Since the Christians impute many strange things which are difficult to believe to their Messiah, why should they wonder that the Jews believe that the Messiah may live a thousand years or more until the time comes for him to reveal himself?" he shouted.[17] Pope Benedict was intensely angered by these impromptu remarks and ruled that all future comments were to be submitted to him in advance.

Jerónimo de Santa Fe cited passages from the Talmud the rabbis claimed did not exist and refused to produce the text he was quoting. If the rabbis thought he was wrong the onus was on them to prove it, he said. Finally, he delivered his coup de grâce.

> You Jews must admit that the terrible sins for which you are being punished in your exile are much more grave than those committed by your ancestors. For your ancestors' sins, the Jews were exiled to Babylon, but only for seventy years. Your current exile has already lasted more than 1,400 years; therefore you must be continually offending God with forms of idolatry, murder and execrable adulteries. If this is so, the earth ought to swallow you, and Christians ought not to allow you to live among them. What else could produce such an exile? What sin have you committed to be so cruelly punished? Are you audacious enough to presume yourselves innocent? Do you commit the even graver sin of believing God to be unjust?[18]

Their most vicious sin, he concluded, was that they refused to accept Jesus as Messiah.

Here was the heart of the matter: the ancient belief that the exile of the Jews was God's punishment for the sin of rejecting Jesus. And with the phrase "Christians ought not to allow you to live among them" came a glimpse of future expulsion and an echo from the past. In 638 the clergy of Visigoth Spain had ordered that "only Christians can live in Spain." The spirit of old Visigoth Christianity was present here in the Chapter House of the Tortosa cathedral, its powerful message of exclusion and religious intolerance ironically enjoined by a former Jew.

When Jerónimo had concluded his powerful address, ten Jews from the audience asked to be baptized. Their request was granted immediately and the *procès-verbal* of the Disputation of Tortosa relates that "they were purified of the Jewish leprosy at the baptismal font."[19]

The Chapter House was crowded with Jews from all over Aragon who had come to hear their rabbis defend the ancient faith, but when they saw the great scholars of their communities falter they despaired. Small groups of men and a few women anxiously paced back and forth along the path of the cathedral cloister, their agitation in sad contrast to the tranquil beauty surrounding them. The Tortosa cathedral cloister is today as it was then. With an imaginative leap the visitor can discern the faint echo of their steps.

The number of people converting to Christianity grew daily. Church records have preserved a written description of what took place:

> During this time, numerous Jews came each week and each day to a knowledge of the truth, and they publicly professed the Catholic faith. They arrived in twos and threes, and sometimes in larger numbers, asking to be baptized in the presence of the entire curia of our lord the pope, without counting those who were converted in various parts of the realm as in Saragossa, Calatayud and Alcaniz. In effect, those who were present heard Jerónimo put forth proofs against the Jews that were so strong, so remarkable and so transcendent, and argued so scientifically that in that summer [1413], more than 250 Jews were converted.[20]

*   *   *

While the Disputation proceeded in the Chapter House, Friar Vicente stepped up his itinerant preaching accompanied (as always) by his coterie of self-flagellating disciples; only now when the Jews heard he was coming, some of them climbed over the walls of their towns and fled, and the Moors hid their children. Eventually Ferrer turned up at Tortosa, where he was welcomed by Pope Benedict and Jerónimo—and gaped at by an awestruck audience. Ferrer was the holy man who had seized upon the chaos of 1391 to do God's work, and even now his persuasive voice spread the word of the gospels among the unbelievers. The brilliant Jerónimo was his acknowledged disciple.

The conversions were wreaking havoc in Aragon. Families and friends of the new converts were enraged. In Calatayud, the former friends of a convert physician named Berenguer Cabra robbed and tore down his house. Now the king of Aragon was forced to become involved, for it was his royal duty to protect the Jews. Berenguer Cabra complained to King Ferdinand I that his own family was withholding the rest of his property. Another new convert complained to the king because his family refused to pass on his maternal inheritance. One Yucé Abencabra (he was now Martín de la Cabra) had founded the Calatayud synagogue; now he wanted to reconsecrate it as a church. The Jewish community was infuriated, but Cabra had already received permission from the pope and he wanted additional confirmation from the king. (He received it.) Two more converts petitioned the king because their families had hidden their children from them.

King Ferdinand I took quick action whenever he heard reports of violence. On one occasion he wrote an angry letter to his son ordering him to intervene in the city of Daroca because Christians were harassing the Jews. "Violence is counterproductive. You must watch closely and punish those who take part in violence," he warned, demonstrating a genuinely principled nature as well as the historical tradition of protecting minorities. Ferdinand also wrote to the governor of Aragon ordering him to secure the safety of the Jews and punish anyone who "tries to commit unjust, vexatious acts."[21]

Nonetheless, the king encouraged the ongoing baptisms, paying special attention to the conversion of important Jewish notables he wished to keep in the service of the state. Restrictive laws were still in force, and many Jews were being driven out of administrative posts; but the king wanted and needed them there. Bribery was the usual, preferred means of persuasion. Ferdinand offered brocades, furs, tax exemptions, and even noble status to important Jews who might subsequently convince their entire families to convert. What mattered was the future, the next generation; a baptized man had to persuade his wife and children to become Christians, or the conversion would begin and end with one individual.

The family King Ferdinand wanted most was the respected, learned, and wealthy Caballería clan of Saragossa whose noble scions had been in royal service for more than a century. The Caballerías financed royal battles, and Ferdinand was in the middle of an important and expensive siege. If they refused to convert, anti-Jewish legislation might eventually limit their public life and their ability to serve the king in the accustomed way.

Many upper-class Jews had been persuaded by Vicente Ferrer and had already converted to Christianity. The Caballerías had not.

King Ferdinand had his eye on a member of this family who was beloved in Aragon among both Jews and Christians: Vidal Josef de la Caballería—a Hebrew poet, a scholar, and a man of profound sensitivity.

Vidal Josef de la Caballería was born in the early 1370s and he had been taught by the most celebrated Hebrew poet of his generation, Solomon de Piera. As a young man Vidal was a star in the literary circles of Saragossa, a new "Renaissance man" who was learned in science, classical literature, and philosophy. Vidal was one of a small group of avant-garde intellectuals who were trying to introduce the Italian Renaissance into Spain.[22] Their focus was to make literature more widely accessible by translating Latin into the vernacular. Vidal had personally translated Cicero into Castilian.

Vidal's youth had spanned a period of extreme disruption in the Jewish communities, when conversion to Christianity was already in the minds of the skeptical upper classes, and he undoubtedly thought about, read about, and talked about Christian and Jewish theology over many years, vacillating perhaps, like others, in his commitment to Judaism.

When the Jewish delegation convened at Tortosa in early 1413, Vidal de la Caballería, now forty, was in their midst, and his admiring peers might well have described him as the individual who best straddled the Christian and Jewish worlds of his day. Vidal was well acquainted with Jerónimo de Santa Fe: Jerónimo had been a friend of the Caballería family before his conversion, and Vidal had even translated a medical treatise Jerónimo had written while he was still a Jewish physician.

Ferdinand was anxious to convert Vidal as well as his grandfather, Bonofos de la Caballería, an octogenarian who had accumulated power, wealth, and prestige over his lifetime as royal treasurer to the king.[23] Ferdinand believed, with reason, that the entire Jewish community of Saragossa might lose heart and follow in the footsteps of these two men should they convert to Christianity, and in September 1413, he wrote Pope Benedict suggesting that since both Vidal and Bonofos were in Tortosa, they might be amenable to a little friendly persuasion. The disputation might just loosen the ripe fruit from the tree. Ferdinand was firm about the persuasion part of his request. He respected the Caballería family and there was to be no pressure exerted on them, he said.

Whether or not Pope Benedict pressured Vidal and Bonofos is not known, but something in the mood of the proceedings, or in the arguments of their old family friend Jerónimo apparently touched a nerve in both men. Vidal de la Caballería and his grandfather, Bonofos, converted to Christianity, in Tortosa, on February 2, 1414, at the cathedral of the city. They were joined by fifteen members of their family, including servants.

Vidal took the Christianized name Gonzalo de la Caballería, and soon turned up holding one of the top financial posts in the kingdom. Bonofos became Fernando de la Caballería, and before long he was being referred to as counselor and "tesorero del senyor Rey" (treasurer to the king), a position that was officially no longer accessible to Jews.

The Caballería conversions were a great coup for the king, the pope, Friar Vicente, and Jerónimo de Santa Fe—and a terrible blow to the Jews of Spain. The loss of their beloved Vidal was one of the saddest moments in their history.

Vidal and his old tutor, the poet Solomon de Piera, broke off relations.[24] Another poet wrote of his pain at Vidal's defection, comparing the man who had embodied the hope of the Jews to the sun:

> The goodly sun in our West has set. Why then
> Upon its circling path does it not rise again?
> How long—oh say—shall no day
> Make its way after our night?
> Can we await a better fate
> When Time breeds woes without relief?
> The eyes, the heart, they cannot bear
> To look upon this crushing grief.[25]

He sent a second pained lament to a relative:

> When I see how hearts and faces are transformed,
> and how the learned speak those things which
> the Torah condoneth not,
> Scholars who were precious beyond words,
> who girded themselves with valor.
> Their names are engraved on my forehead. How,
> now that they are gone, shall I erase those beloved
> names from my doorpost?
> I cry for desolation and dispersion. I weep like the sea
> For my redemption which exile postpones
> Yea, I cry, and they laugh.[26]

Anger and confusion erupted among the Caballería clan, but with the exception of one entire branch of the family, most of Vidal's and Bonofos's relatives converted in the days and weeks following the baptisms. This did not prevent an angry cousin from writing bitter polemics against Vidal, or the emergence of a poignant struggle within Vidal's immediate family. Vidal's father, Benvenist, had died in 1411, but his mother, Tolosana, remained a devout Jew as she watched her father, Bonofos, her brother, Leonardo, and five of her seven children convert to Christianity. Two of Tolosana's daughters, Puria and Reyna, remained faithful to Judaism, and they and their mother tried to prevent a third daughter, Oria, from seeking baptism with the others. In fact, they refused to let her leave the house.

But Oria wanted to convert. Vidal and his brother Juan pleaded with their mother, without success. Finally they appealed to King Ferdinand who issued a royal order preventing Tolosana and her daughters from leaving Saragossa (it was rumored they were planning to escape with the hapless Oria) and ordering Tolosana to allow her daughter to convert of her own free will. With the official authorization of the king, Vidal took his sister from their mother's house and witnessed her baptism.

The Caballería family would never be the same again, and neither would the decimated Jewish community of Saragossa; but in 1443 Tolosana's last will and testament, which has survived, gave evidence of her undiminished commitment to Judaism and her equally undiminished love for all her children, in spite of the choice they had made three decades earlier. She bequeathed money to the synagogue of Saragossa with the rider that if its status was changed for any reason—that is, if it were turned into a church—the money was to be transferred to the largest Jewish community of Aragon. She left money to the Talmud Torah for the education of the young, to the local Jewish burial society, and to several other charities. Finally she stipulated that her bequest was to be administered in perpetuity by the closest relative by the name of Caballería, and if there was no one of that name in Saragossa who was still a Jew, that the closest Jewish relative be called upon, whatever his or her name.

In her will Tolosana de la Caballería alluded only fleetingly to what must have been one of the greatest sorrows of her life. In detailing the equal sums she was leaving to each of her seven children she dictated the following sentence using their new, Christian names: "I leave to Gonzalo and Juan de la Caballería, my sons, and to Beatriz, Juana, and Brianda de la Caballería, my daughters, and to Puria and Reyna de la Caballería, Jewesses, my daughters. . . ."[27] The additional word, Jewesses, was her only mention of the critical break in one of Spanish Jewry's most illustrious families. The Caballería family went on to play a prominent role in the second turbulent half of the fifteenth century, but as converts, and never again as Jews.

*   *   *

The Disputation of Tortosa ended on November 13, 1414, after twenty-one months during which the rabbis were forbidden to visit their homes. It was generally agreed that Jerónimo de Santa Fe had won, although the contest had never been equal. The pope and Jerónimo had made that clear at the outset. To the disruptions of the past two decades—the pogroms of 1391, the destruction of Jewish communities throughout Aragon and Castile, the forced conversions, the fiery preachings of Vicente Ferrer, the conversions in the Jewish upper classes, the oppressive laws of 1412 restricting Jewish life and livelihood, and the growing anti-Semitism of the larger population—was now added the ignominy of supposed theological defeat and the demonstrated "proof" that Jesus Christ was, indeed, the Messiah.

Although he had "won" at Tortosa (it was said that more than three thousand Jews were baptized during the course of the disputation),[28] Pope Benedict XIII emerged angry that the rabbis still refused to concede officially to Jerónimo's syllogistic proofs of the coming of the Messiah. In May 1415, the pope promulgated a papal bull designed to compel the recalcitrant scholars and other holdouts to convert after all. To the edict of 1412 and the persuasions of Tortosa, Benedict added what was, he hoped, the final squeeze.

The new bull had thirteen clauses including the following ten draconian interdictions:[29]

1. All Jews were forbidden to listen to, read, or teach the Talmud, and within the space of one month all copies of the Talmud and commentaries on the Talmud were to be relinquished to local bishops. Official searches would be carried out twice a year to ensure that no one was hiding a copy of the "depraved doctrine."

2. All Hebrew books that contradicted the dogmas and rites of Christianity were banned.

3. No Jew was permitted to pronounce the names of Jesus, or Mary, or the saints. Neither could they bind Christian books, or manufacture crosses, chalices, or other religious objects. (This ordinance affected the livelihood of many people, for Jews were bookbinders and reputed artisans in gold and silver. Benedict, himself, owned many religious objects produced by Jews including a gold-plated silver ciborium (designed to hold the sacred wafers for the Eucharist), which was made for him in Provence while he was pope in Avignon. Even more intriguing, Pope Benedict ordered a silver cross from one Bernardo Astruch, the head of a famous dynasty of Morella silversmiths, in 1415, the same year as his bull was promulgated. The object was not delivered until 1419.)[30]

4. No Jew could be a judge for either criminal or civil cases. No new synagogues could be built, or old ones refurbished.

5. No Jew or Jewess could practice the professions of physician, surgeon, pharmacist, midwife, business agent, trader, matchmaker, or moneylender. Nor could he, or she, collect or administer rents or property, employ Christian servants, or socialize with Christians in the local baths or elsewhere. No Christian could aid Jewish neighbors by lighting lights for them on the sabbath. Jews were forbidden to make or sell unleavened bread for the Passover.

6. All Christian kings and princes were warned to lock the Jewish quarters of their towns and cities when they bordered on Christian neighborhoods.

7. All contracts concerning Jews were null and void.

8. All wills disinheriting converts were null and void and all converts would henceforth legally inherit from their "infidel relatives."

9. Every Jew and Jewess over the age of twelve was ordered to attend three sermons a year in which the priest would sermonize about the coming of Christ the Messiah, the blindness of the Jews in stubbornly embracing the errors of the Talmud, and the truth of the prophesies that foretold the exile of the Israelites. At the end of each sermon, the ordinances of this Bull would be read aloud.

10. Every Jew and Jewess was obliged to wear a distinctive red or yellow badge.

Much of Benedict's bull reproduced the earlier ordinance of 1412 since parts of the latter had already been repealed by royalty. But the legal oppression of the Jews reached new heights with this latest document that was designed to complete the work of Tortosa.

Pope Benedict need not have worried about the influence of those remaining leaders who refused to convert, for the Jews of Aragon were totally demoralized. A poet asked:

> Have we not found a refuge in Aragon's remnant of scholars?
> Or is it only a respite, like a grain overlooked by the reaper,
> Or like a booth hanging in the air without pillars?[31]

Benedict XIII could not have predicted the social problems his Bull would create; for example, the monarchs of Spain had long depended on the Jewish communities as a source of tax revenue, but as Jews converted and left the community, the tax base diminished, along with the content of the royal coffers. The king was forced into a dilemma. He was bound to defend the Jewish minority, but this ancestral duty was increasingly difficult since Benedict's papal Bull legitimized anti-Semitism and tacitly condoned violence as well.

The new muscle of the Spanish Church was beginning to interfere with secular traditions, and it is historically important that Ferdinand I declined to challenge the usurping power of the Church, choosing damage control instead. Benedict's bull came just three years after the Vicente Ferrer's anti-Jewish legislation was agreed to by the court of Castile in

1412, setting a precedent, and King Ferdinand's acquiescence continued the undermining of state control by the Church. The king's failure to protect secular traditions also recalls an earlier trigger point in the transformation of Spanish pluralism: the refusal of King Alfonso VI of Castile to condemn the French-born Archbishop of Toledo who had turned the chief mosque of the city into a church in the king's absence. Alfonso VI called himself "Emperor of the Three Religions," but his cowardice in allowing an injustice against one of the "three religions" to be perpetrated with impunity marked a turning point in the pattern of social relations.

Benedict's papal bull indirectly legitimized violence and anti-Semitism, and the king found himself caught in a struggle to keep newly liberated hatreds under control. In early 1416, the Jews of Aragon appealed for protection, saying that zealous Christians were preventing them from exercising their livelihoods, and that they were literally dying of hunger. Ferdinand quickly reprimanded the offending communities. Then the Jews of Jaca complained that wearing the red and yellow badges put them in danger when they traveled the remote mountain roads of their region. Ferdinand exempted them from wearing the badge while on voyage. Also in Jaca the Christian population unilaterally decided to cancel all their outstanding debts to the Jews, which meant that moneylenders could not recover their loans. The king commanded the citizens to repay what they owed.[32]

Violence, led by none other than Jerónimo de Santa Fe, erupted in Saragossa, where many converts continued to live in their old houses in the Jewish quarter. Jerónimo had been assigned to the city to implement Pope Benedict's new laws, and had ruled in his zeal that converts could stay in their old homes, but the Jews had to move to another neighborhood. A riot broke out during which Jerónimo's young son stabbed a Jew. Ferdinand concluded that Jerónimo and his son had provoked the riot and warned Jerónimo not to overstep his jurisdiction. The king would tolerate no harassment of the Jews of Saragossa, he said. Then Ferdinand ordered that since they were fewer in number the converts, and not the Jews, should move out of the Jewish quarter.

The most ominous development of all was the news that converts were also being treated badly in some places, even worse than their Jewish relatives. They were being penalized in their business dealings by Old Christians (as distinguished from converts who were sometimes called New Christians) who said they were wolves in sheep's clothing, the same people in new dress. They were being verbally insulted.

What could this mean? A baptized man or woman was a Christian, pure and simple. And Christians did not insult other Christians on grounds that they were still Jews. Ferdinand was "angry and indignant" and ordered local officials throughout his kingdom to protect the new converts. But this turn of events was profoundly disturbing.

Neither King Ferdinand I, Pope Benedict, Friar Vicente Ferrer, nor Jerónimo de Santa Fe could possibly have imagined the fruit that was poised to grow from the seeds of religious conversion, for whatever their motives (including Benedict's) they believed that the baptism of the Jews was God's work, and that when all Jews were Christians the conflicts of the day would be resolved. Thousands of new converts also thought that their difficult lives would change for the better once they were baptized. They were all tragically wrong.

Throughout, no one doubted that God watched and judged. Almost two hundred years later a Jewish chronicler writing from exile in Fez, North Africa, recalled that a violent storm suddenly tore across Spain during the Disputation of Tortosa while hundreds of Jews were converting to Christianity. "In this same year [1412–1413], God raised up a terrible wind that tore boulders from mountains, uprooted trees, and sunk the surprised ships in the sea. God sent these calamities upon his people as punishment for the sins of Israel," he wrote.[33] In a God-centered world every natural event brought further proof of weakness, sin, and guilt. With such clear signs of divine anger, the remaining Jews of Spain had nowhere to turn for comfort.

The Curtain Falls on Benedict XIII

Although he had mounted the most dramatic theological disputation Europe had ever seen, definitively "proved" that Christ had fulfilled the prophesies of the Talmud itself, and converted untold numbers of Jews to Christianity, the spectacle at Tortosa did not resolve the career problems of Benedict XIII. International pressure mounted anew to get rid of this tenacious, undeniably brilliant octogenarian who could talk circles around his opponents.

Benedict was finally and definitively deposed in 1417 by the Council of Constance, representing the collective notables of European Christendom. The world had never seen as great a sinner, they declared. He was a perjurer, and a heretic, he had encouraged disunion, and schism, and he was an enemy of all Christians. On July 26 of that year they excommunicated him. After thirty-nine years the Great Western Schism was effectively over. For twenty-four of those years Benedict XIII had been pope in Avignon.

Isolated, excommunicated, and a virtual prisoner in his fortress castle of Peñiscola overlooking the blue of the Mediterranean, old Pedro de

Luna never gave up maintaining that he was Benedict XIII, the rightful pope. In fact, as late as November 1422 he brazenly created four new cardinals. Only death brought his personal crusade to an end. It was 1423 and he was ninety-five years old. Even then, it was hard to believe that such a man could die of natural causes, and it was rumored that he was poisoned "in some wafers he used to eat after Meat."[34]

The Great Western Schism had confirmed the worst fears of the faithful—that the worldly clergy was no longer competent to help them find salvation; and in his use and abuse of power no one exposed this ethos more brazenly than *Papa Luna*. When his last public-relations spectacle, the mass conversion of thousands of Jews at Tortosa, did not win him the approbation he needed to secure the papacy, his cause was lost. The Disputation at Tortosa was a Pyrric victory for the pope, a purported success that ultimately failed in its objective. But the central drama of the event, the baptisms that followed in its wake, joined by Benedict's formidable, anti-Jewish legislation, had unforseen repercussions.

Benedict and Friar Vicente Ferrer died within four years of each other. They had added irreversible power to an increasingly political Spanish Church.

Notes

1. In the mid-fourteenth century, the library of the University of Paris contained 1,300 volumes. In the late twentieth century, many research libraries contain upwards of eight million volumes.

2. Cited in Philip Hughes, *A History of the Church,* 3: 241.

3. Cited in M. Creighton, *History of the Papacy,* 1: 147.

4. Ibid.

5. Jean Froissart, *Chroniques 1392–1396,* 16 (ed.1871).

6. Ibid., 124.

7. Ibid., 130.

8. Hughes, *A History of the Papacy,* 268.

9. Sources for this chapter include: Francisca Vendrell, "La política proselitista del rey D. Fernando I," *Sefarad* 10 (1950); ibid., "En torno a la confirmación real, en Aragón, de la pragmática de Benedicto XIII," *Sefarad* 20 (1960); ibid., "Aportaciónes documentales para el estudio de la familia Caballería," *Sefarad* 3 (1943); José Amador de los Rios, *Historia de los Judíos de España y Portugal,* 2; Heinrich Graetz, *History of the Jews,* 4; Y. Baer, *A History of the Jews in Christian Spain,* 2; A. D. Posnanski, "Le Colloque de Tortose," *REJ* 74, 75 (1922, 23); A. Pacios López, *La Disputa de Tortosa,* including the complete *Actas* of the proceedings (Latin text).

10. Another famous debate on the same subject took place in Barcelona in 1263 under the patronage of King James I of Aragon.

11. The number of people who were present at the Disputation has been distorted in the usual way in the contemporary accounts. There were hundreds, but not thousands, as recorded, and there were probably a dozen or so cardinals, not seventy-five. It is also interesting to note that Spaniards stood in their churches until the mid-twentieth century.

12. Known as the Halorki Letter. Cited as of the late fifteenth century, Baer, *History of the Jews,* 2: 143.

13. Ibid, 145. Pablo de Santa María's reply has been lost. Baer speculates it was destroyed by Jewish copyists who did not want to transmit his views.

14. Many of the Jewish converts took names that corresponded to Christianity and the Christian faith. *Santa Fe* means Holy Faith; *Santa María* means Holy Mary, and so on. There may have been something about changing one's name as well as one's religion that contributed to dissociating some converts from their former selves, adding to the fanaticism of their conversion.

15. See A. D. Posnanski, "Le Colloque de Tortose et de San Mateo," *REJ* 74, 75 for the *procès-verbal* of a number of sessions.

16. A. D. Posnanski, "Le Colloque de Tortose et de San Mateo," *REJ* 74 (1922): 189.

17. Baer, *History of the Jews,* 2: 180.

18. Posnanski, *REJ* 74: 191.

19. Ibid.

20. Ibid., 194. For the consequences of the Tortosa conversions and the role played by King Ferdinand, see Vendrell, "La política," 350ff.

21. Ibid.

22. They were well ahead of their time. The Renaissance did not fully reach Spain until the middle of the fifteenth century when Naples became a dependency of Aragon (1443), and printing was introduced (1474).

23. Vendrell, "Aportaciónes documentales," p.134.

24. There is mixed evidence suggesting that de Piera converted later on at the age of seventy.

25. Solomon Bonafed, cited in Baer, *History of the Jews,* 2: 213.

26. Ibid., 216.

27. Manuel Serrano y Sanz, *Orígenes de la dominación Española en América,* 1: 186.

28. J. Amador de los Rios, *Historia de los Judíos,* 2: 505.

29. Archivo de la Santa Iglesia de Toledo, reproduced in ibid., 627.

30. Both these items are currently on display in Benedict's family fortress castle at Peñiscola. The ciborium is signed in Hebrew. The artist may have been a convert, but converts changed their distinctly Jewish names.

31. Solomon Bonafed, cited in Baer, *History of the Jews,* 2: 218.

32. F. Vendrell, "En torno a la confirmación real."

33. R. Abraham ben Solomon de Torrutiel, *El Libro de la Tradición,* late sixteenth or early seventeenth century, cited in M. Gaspar Remiro, *Los Cronistas Hispano-Judíos* (1920), 27ff.

34. There are those who still hold that Pedro de Luna was the true pope and a victim of libel, slander and outright crime. On one of the walls of the old castle of Peñiscola hangs a plaque placed there by members of the University of Saragossa as recently as 1923. On it is written a message to posterity: "Aragon asks you to pray to God for Benedict XIII, a great Aragonian of pure, austere and generous life, a life that was sacrificed for an idea of duty. The final judgment will reveal mysteries of his life that are hidden in history. . . ."

7

The Fate of the Conversos

Although there had been early problems—King Ferdinand I of Aragon having to protect converts as well as Jews, for example—the assimilation of conversos looked like an outstanding success a generation after Tortosa. Conversos continued on without missing a beat in exactly the same occupations they had held as Jews. This was no surprise: they were, after all, the same multifaceted, educated elite the day after their baptism as the day before. Royalty in both Castile and Aragon protected and sponsored them for the same reasons they had always protected and sponsored the Jews: conversos and their descendants were better trained administrators than any other class of Spaniards.

As former Talmudic scholars, many conversos applied their well-trained minds to the new theology and rose quickly through the hierarchy of the Catholic Church. Freed from the on-again, off-again legal constraints imposed on Jews, many conversos merchants grew wealthy enough to marry their sons and daughters into old Christian nobility. Such marriages provided new Christians with noble status and old Christians with new infusions of money—a profoundly satisfying trade-off. In fifteenth-century Spain there was nothing more important than noble status—except, perhaps, an infusion of money.

As relative newcomers to nobility, conversos were even prouder of their station—their *hidalguía*—than the legions of old Christian dukes, counts, and lords whose families they had joined. Some intermarried to the very highest level of the land—right into royalty. Just one generation after the massive conversions instigated by Vicente Ferrer and Pope Benedict, the very queen of Aragon was of converso origin. Queen Juana was mother to Spain's most famous monarch, Ferdinand II of Aragon, husband to the equally famous Isabella of Castile (a fact which lends considerable psychological interest to the king's later sponsorship of the Inquisition).[1]

Since the Church had proclaimed that baptism was the only line that divided "us" from "them," there seemed to be no obvious way for ordinary people, who resented elites in general, to protest the rise of the conversos. Their envy was rooted in common class anger, but the source of full social acceptance was Catholicism and the Catholic church accepted the conversos. There seemed to be no formal way to exclude the conversos who were holding so many of the top jobs. Legislation had been passed against the Jews—over and over again—but these conversos were Christians and therefore exempt. Except that they didn't seem like Christians. They hadn't adopted the attitudes along with the baptismal water, and neither had their children. The aristocracy among them did not disdain learning the way the old Christian nobility did; and the poorer classes of conversos didn't metamorphose into peasants. They remained what they had been: merchants, small-scale artisans, administrators, and physicians, among other things—that is, the country's "middle class."

The conversos themselves were having a certain degree of difficulty with the transformation, for there were deep emotional repercussions to changing one's religious identity in a civilization where religion was everything. Many people tried to reinvent themselves with the quasi-universal practice of changing a Jewish name to something overtly Christian, such as "Holy Mary" in the case of Pablo de Santa María, or "Holy Faith" as in Jerónimo de Santa Fe. In a world that had yet to discover the unconscious, such blunt efforts were deemed sufficient.

Many, perhaps most, new Christians did not integrate well, and they grew into a hybrid social class at the very heart of society. In reality, they were neither Christian nor Jewish, and the satirical name they were given, *alboraycos,* underscored their ambiguous status. According to legend, the *Alborak* was a magic steed brought to Muhammad by the angel Gabriel for the prophet's ascent to heaven. It was neither horse nor mule, neither male nor female.

There were, of course, exceptions—people who had converted out of conviction; but the majority of conversos did not wake up as pious Christians. The majority Christian culture had promised acceptance and "belonging" if one converted, and to join this culture meant adopting, or pretending to adopt, the outward forms of faith. If one knew what they were. Jews who were forcibly converted in 1391 had been given no instruction in Christian dogma, and the same was true for those thousands more who were persuaded to convert by Friar Vicente, or who converted in the aftermath of Tortosa. As for the skeptics who had changed religion out of opportunism or convenience, they knew nothing of Christianity, nor did they care. Many were "modern," essentially secular people who were forced to adopt a label of one sort or another in order to survive.

The labeling was simple enough: you were or were not a Christian, depending on whether or not you had been baptized. The problem lay elsewhere for many people. Religion is an inner experience, an infinitely complex commitment that touches the deepest recesses of emotion. Although as Jews they had been *outwardly* indistinguishable from their Christian counterparts in language, dress, and general social attitudes, old customs and dozens of cultural touchstones tied the conversos to their lives in the Jewish quarter. But they were expected to give it all up—their homes, their families, and their friends, as well as the seasons and feast days that make up the rhythms of Jewish life. They were forced to abandon their innermost selves.

It is not surprising that many conversos did whatever they could to maintain the continuity of their emotional lives. They continued to practice Judaism, if only for reasons of comfort, familiarity, and companionship, and they led painfully schizophrenic inner lives. Officially they were Christians, but in reality they were anything but. Officially they were outside the Jewish ambit, but many of them lived double lives. Women passed on the rites and practices of Judaism, although the meaning of what they were doing grew hazier as the decades passed. Christianity may have defined their official identity, but conversion from force, fear, opportunism, or even faith could not erase the inner person, nor alter the complex weave of attitudes, values, and habits that make up the texture of a life.

Although they lived apart, the conversos frequently visited the old Jewish quarters of their towns—sadly, confusedly and in an atmosphere of tension, for their Jewish relatives actively tried to woo them back into the fold. They shared meals with family members and former neighbors, for what is more comforting than to break bread with loved ones and what is sadder than to be deprived of this intimacy? Given the importance of sharing food, it is not surprising that adopting "Christian" dietary habits was a major problem for the first generations. They could not get used to eating pork, the forbidden food; they claimed it made them physically sick—which was probably true given the powerful biblical prohibition they were breaking. (Later, when converso life became infinitely more dangerous, many tried to avoid the suspicion that they were not true Christians by forcing themselves to devour huge quantities of pork in the most public way possible.) Some conversos complained loudly that they had bad stomachs and could not eat bread, thus providing themselves with an excuse to eat *matzo,* or unleavened bread, all year long so they could be in tune with Jewish religious requirements when Passover came along.[2]

In the beginning most conversos were open about their doubts, or skepticism, concerning Christianity, and open about their Jewish practices. In any case keeping secrets in the village atmosphere of a medieval town was hardly possible. Streets were narrow and there was little noise to muffle the sounds of speech. Busybodies easily overheard private conversations taking place in courtyards or inside open windows.

Innocently, converts and their descendants continued to use familiar Jewish oaths in their dealings. "I swear by the Ten Commandments of the holy law of Moses," was a favorite.[3] So too was, "I swear by the day of Yom Kippur." Yet many became exceptionally proud of their lineage. A simple fishmonger was convinced that being a new Christian meant one could not die poor. "God promised this to Moses," she proclaimed confidently to a friend. Another believed that a new Christian who married an old Christian would be poor, but an old Christian who married a new Christian would be rich. (There was more than a little truth to this.) There was also no shortage of small-minded pettiness as well as the occasional, refreshing injection of pure honesty. One man admitted he had converted to Christianity out of revenge because he had been refused a seat in the synagogue, while a cheerful cynic acknowledged to a friend that he had converted "for the goods and prosperity of this world."

Some conversos lived in fear that they had offended the God of their ancestors. A young girl was killed falling down a flight of stairs and her mother's friend knew exactly why: "Because we have accepted the religion of the gentiles," she explained. Others were convinced that Judaism was the true religion and thought they would be dammed if they did not practice Jewish rites. (Wiser souls reasoned that Jews might perhaps be saved through their religion and Christians through theirs but, as usual, they were the minority.)

Some conversos were sure it made excellent sense to keep all their options open since one never knew what might happen on the day of the Last Judgment, or when the Messiah of the Jews finally decided to make an appearance. They hoped a judicious mishmash of religions might do the trick.

"What religion do you belong to?" a Jew from Daroca asked a converso named Juan de Sayas. "I see you do not observe your law [Christianity] and you speak ill of the Jewish law and of the Moorish law. By God, what are you going to do in the next world?"

"You are crazy," retorted Juan de Sayas. "Don't you know that there is nothing in this world but to be born and to die, and that the soul of a dog enters the body of a man, and that of a man enters the body of a dog? All in all, I intend to commend my soul to all three religions, and whichever turns out to be the right one, I'll be prepared."[4]

What characterized the converso class was its rejection of the essence of Christianity: the belief in the divinity of Jesus. This was their rebellion. Privately, many people ridiculed Christ, whom they took to have been a mortal man; others hid Jewish texts inside their breviaries to read during Sunday mass. But there were times when pretense and the accompanying inner struggle must have been overwhelmingly painful. The record tells of a Saragossa convert named Maria who dared to speak about what she had lost to a single, trusted friend. Maria admitted she had converted "not from devotion, but from fear," and that she continued to try to live as a Jew. She always cooked "the hot dish" on Fridays so it would last through the sabbath on Saturday, but her husband was so angry at this that he had destroyed her oven. When she was a Jewess she had been in love with a Jewish man, she said, but "they" had married her off to her present husband who was a Christian. Even now, she admitted, she and this Jewish man were lovers. Maria's brother was still a Jew, and from him she had learned much about "the religion of Moses."

"Look at yourself, Agueda," Maria confided to her friend. "If you became a Jewess how could you possibly give up following Christian ways? This is what you must understand. In these things one must do what comes naturally."[5]

This conversation took place as late as the early 1480s, after the inauguration of the Inquisition; in other words, it was an exceptionally dangerous admission on Maria's part. Why did she take such a chance? One must think that the strain of leading a double life simply became too heavy, and that she had to unburden herself to a trusted friend.

The Marginalization of the New Christians

There was an ambiguity to converso identity. They were Christians, albeit new Christians—dutifully baptized in the usual way—but "different," and increasingly disliked by the peasantry for the same economic and class reasons that the latter disliked the Jews. Yet there were no obvious grounds for excluding the new Christians. On Christian unity, the Church was absolutely clear.

Three generations had passed since the 1391 pogroms and the start of massive Jewish conversions when the monarchy suddenly collapsed in Castile. The ensuing political instability intensified the anger many old Christians (especially peasants and the lower, urban classes) held toward the successful conversos in their midst. Something similar had happened a century before when the plague ravaged Europe and upset the social order. Then the scapegoat was the Jewish "other." Now, the target was the converso.

How this actually happened is worth noting since economic and political instability historically nurture racism.

In 1419, just as Friar Vicente and Pope Benedict were winding down their careers, a fourteen-year-old king came to the throne of Castile. Poor Juan II was the wrong ruler at the wrong time. He sang and danced beautifully; he was a lover of literature and sensitive to the strains of Renaissance humanism radiating from the intellectual centers of Italy; he encouraged writing and the translation of classical works into Castilian; and his court was home to the best poets of the age, many of whom were conversos. He even wrote a great deal of terrible poetry himself. But the boy-king was unable to control the proud, enormously wealthy nobles who held their own courts and waged war against each other with private retinues of knights. The nobility of Castile wore its ancient family crests with overweening pride. Some of them even fabricated genealogies linking them to a heroic past up to and including the Visigoths and that symbolic icon of the Christian Reconquest, Pelayo. Their opulence rivaled the king's, which only increased their boldness by reducing the distance between ruler and ruled. If the king threw extravagant banquets, so did they. In honor of several visiting knights from Aragon and Valencia one Juan de Velasco hosted a feast consisting of four thousand pairs of hens, two thousand sheep and four hundred oxen. Food for this one meal was delivered to his kitchens in two hundred wagons.

A weak king was vulnerable, and a vulnerable king meant volatility and danger. The pogroms against the Jews in 1391 had amply proved the point just a generation earlier. But someone had to run the country if the young king refused to do so. Juan II made a decision: He left all matters of state to his closest friend and concentrated on jousting, hunting, tournaments, and versifying.

The king's friend, Alvaro de Luna, was still a child when he was introduced by his uncle, Pope Benedict XIII, to the court of Castile. Alvaro impressed all who met him with his grace, intelligence, and ease of conversation. As a young man he danced and sang to perfection, dressed beautifully, and was considered exceptionally handsome (which is of interest, since he was purportedly short and bald with bad teeth and tiny eyes). He was certainly intelligent, energetic, and socially astute. But one fact became indisputable. Alvaro de Luna was the most cunning man in the country. And he single-handedly ruled Castile for forty years from behind the throne: forty crucial years during which the status of Jews, Moors, and now conversos, would undergo permanent change.

Alvaro de Luna became Constable of Castile, which meant he was the most powerful man in the kingdom, the sole and final arbiter of every civilian, military, and ecclesiastical post in the land. He was, in other words, a hurdle along the road of every man's ambition. Alvaro was Grand Master of the Order of Santiago, Duke of Trujillo, Count of Ledesma, Count of Santisteban de Gormaz, and lord of at least sixty towns and magnificent castle fortresses. (The walls, turrets, and towers of his holdings can still be seen perched on mountain tops all over Castile.) No title was too small to covet, no rent too insignificant to appropriate. Alvaro even misinterpreted scripture in order to justify his rapaciousness. He once wrote to a friend, "*Qui venerit ad me non ejician fuera,*" echoing the words of Christ, "He who comes to me, I shall not cast away." Either Alvaro's understanding of Latin was abominable, or he was counting on the fact that his friend was poorly educated; in either event he conveniently mistranslated "he who" as "what," and interpreted the quotation as "*What* comes to me, I shall not cast away."[6]

Extravagant to the last degree, the nobles hated Alvaro for his even greater ostentation: Alvaro had a private army of three thousand lances, an annual income of one hundred thousand gold *doblas,* and twenty thousand personal vassals.[7] To say he was envied for his wealth and power would be to understate the flood of anger that seethed and swelled around him.

The magnates of Castile despised King Juan II for being easily dominated, and for loving Alvaro "like a mistress," as a nineteenth-century Spanish historian put it.[8] It was whispered that the two men were lovers and that Alvaro also made bold love to the queen. Some said that the Constable had woven a magic spell over the king, but even without the help of the supernatural Alvaro's power over Juan II was extraordinary. The nobleman Fernán Pérez de Guzmán put it this way: "The most amazing of all that was said or heard was that even [the king's] natural acts were controlled by the Constable. Although the king was an attractive young man, and he was fond of the queen, his wife, who was a beautiful young woman, he would not go to her bed without the Constable's permission."[9]

As discord between Alvaro and the nobles of Castile grew more intense, both God and nature seemed to rage. Plague broke out in neighboring Portugal seeding terror all over the Peninsula. The winter of 1435 was "dangerous in Castile by reason of the great rains," wrote the historian Juan de Mariana.

> The roads were so deep there was scarce any traveling. Many buildings were carried away by the floods. In forty days no corn was ground so that the people fed upon the grain boiled for want of bread. At Seville, the river Guadalquivir swelled within a [meter] of the top of the walls, [and] some of the inhabitants lived aboard ships for fear of being drowned. The rains began on the 28th of October and continued without ceasing until the 25th day of March.[10]

Some of the most powerful players at the court of Alvaro and Juan II were conversos, as were thousands of crown officials, regional governors, town mayors, poets, scientists, physicians, lawyers, scholars, tax collectors, and professionals of every stripe. Soon all were identified with the hated regime. Trapped by circumstance, the underclasses sank further into misery. In every way and in every sector the time was ripe for rebellion.

*   *   *

If, in the 1430s, ordinary people could not even think of attacking those in the stations above them, and if conversos in high positions remained safe because of their official Christian status, there was, it seemed, an acceptable way to identify and exclude the Other: true Christians versus false Christians. Heresy within the Christian faith.

Famous conversos had already raised verbal swords against unconverted Jews; now others tried to head off an impending attack against their class. In 1434 Bishop Alonso de Cartagena (Pablo de Santa María's son and successor) obtained a papal decree authorizing bishops to punish any new Christian caught practicing Jewish rites. (This decree was an early harbinger of the Spanish Inquisition-to-be, still a half century away.) Alonso de Cartagena was sincere, devout, and profoundly aware of the need to distance himself from openly irreligious conversos, but his decree came to nothing since the Constable of Castile, Alvaro de Luna, did not approve of persecuting useful people; in fact it backfired. Public distrust of *all* conversos was seen as having been legitimized by one of the most illustrious of new Christians. Before long "converso" was synonymous with "heretic" in the popular mind.

*   *   *

On January 26, 1449, Alvaro de Luna is in Toledo to raise money for the king. He demands a loan of twenty thousand doublas from the inhabitants of the city and instructs Alonso Cota, a high-standing converso, to collect the tax.[11]

Something spontaneous happens. Two low-ranking priests ring the great bell of the church (formerly the synagogue) of Santa María la Blanca. A mob runs to the city square, led by a local wineskin maker. Suddenly a full-blown attack against the conversos is underway.

The crowd storms the converso quarter of St. Mary Magdalen looking for the tax collector Alonso Cota. When they cannot find him they burn his house to the ground. The mob takes control of the city gates and the defense towers positioned along the fortified walls.

King Juan II arrives, but the rebels lock the gates of the city against him. They lob rocks and cabbages from behind the walls, and shout insults at their monarch. The king's own son, Prince Enrique, takes the side of the rebels against his father.

"The conversos are enemies!" cries Pero Sarmiento, the governor of the royal palace of Toledo. "They support Alvaro de Luna and the king! They told Alvaro to destroy our city with taxation." Sarmiento then formally articulates the new, linking mythology. "The conversos are like their Jewish ancestors," he shouts, "the traitors who opened the gates of our Toledo to Tariq the Moor seven hundred years ago!"

The crowd gathered in the square of the city in front of the cathedral roars their agreement. Encouraged, Pero Sarmiento shifts from the political to the religious. "The conversos are false Christians," he cries. "They are the enemies of the Holy Mother Church. They continue to practice Judaism. They call Jesus 'that hanged Jew whom the Christians think is God.' At Easter they slaughter lambs and offer sacrifices."[12]

Months pass and still the rebels are in control of Toledo. On June 6, 1449, Pero Sarmiento calls a public meeting and reads aloud a new law called the *Sentencia Estatuto,* a statute of exclusion. According to this law, no person descended from Jews can henceforth hold a public post. This is, of course, the point of the exercise. Thousands of Toledan Jews were baptized during the conversion years, and in the half-century from then until now many have moved into important positions in municipal government and other public posts, displacing others.

The *Sentencia* takes effect immediately. Some thirteen city councilors, judges, and notaries are instantly ousted from their posts for reason of "impure blood."

There were anti-Jewish riots in 1391 and thousands of conversions to Christianity over the next several decades. The laws of 1412 passed by the acting regency of Castile, at the urging of Vicente Ferrer, were directed against the Jews and had promoted still more conversions. Tortosa had its effect, as had the hard-line papal bull proclaimed soon afterward by Benedict XIII.

But now, for the first time in Spanish history, blood and race were the issue, not faith, as had previously been the case. A half-century had passed since 1391 and the start of the mass conversions that were supposed to resolve the social problems that had purportedly produced the pogroms in the first place. But the problems of the late fourteenth century were complex, as we have seen, and pogroms were almost certainly a consequence of plague fatigue, envy, and economic despair, not religion. The former were the real conditions of life; and little had changed.

Once conversos had been effectively reidentified as Jews by the statute of exclusion, all the ancient anti-Jewish accusations could be revived with impunity. Guilds, colleges, and military orders quickly passed their own *estatutos*. "Purity of blood," or *limpieza* (cleanliness) exploded into a national obsession.[13]

Again, however, like the abstraction of the ideal knight and the religious-patriotic-militaristic ideology of the Holy Reconquest, the anti-Jewish imagery rekindled so vehemently in Toledo by Pero Sarmiento mixed uneasily with custom and tradition. Pluralism was under attack and a general level of tension was on the rise, but in the daily life of towns and villages, ordinary Jews, Moors, Christians, and new Christians maintained relatively cordial relations. Because they had never been baptized and were therefore immune from the charge of Christian heresy, Jews were, ironically, better accepted than their Christian convert relatives. Most specifically anti-Jewish laws had been repealed, and synagogues and copies of the Talmud restored. A few learned Jews (who had resisted conversion) had resumed traditional roles as physicians and financial advisors (although they were never again powerful enough to restore the strength of their communities, composed now of artisans, shopkeepers, and other "little people," for the most part). Blood-purity propaganda targeted conversos, not the Jews. Most importantly, blood purity cracked open the fundamental medieval notion that baptism alone determined who "belonged" to the majority culture and who did not.

Soon a credo equating food and religion emerged as a way of isolating conversos and their descendants, and no one articulated this better than Andrés Bernáldez, a contemporary chronicler-priest. "They [the conversos] never abandoned their habits of Jewish eating, their stews, their onions and garlic fried in oil, and their meat cooked in oil instead of pork fat," he complained sourly.

> These things cooked in oil had a bad odor, and their houses smelled bad, and so did they. The Jews smelled [bad] because of the dishes they cooked, and because they were not baptized.
> Those who were baptized brought the Holy Faith into disrepute by practicing Jewish rites. They would not eat pork unless they were forced to do so; they ate meat during Lent; they patronized the kosher butchers; and they ate unleavened bread.[14]

The cooking practices described by Bernáldez were common to the entire Mediterranean basin, then as now, with the notable exception of Spain where more pork was consumed. It is tempting to speculate that the habit of eating large amounts of pork (a habit that has persisted) came from a direct attempt to force thousands of conversos into "Christian" practices, or to isolate them as false Christians if they did not comply. (Since the central industry of medieval Spain was wool, it might have made more sense to favor lamb.)

Castilians, or "Spaniards," as they were increasingly called, consumed pork, bread, and wine—a diet they claimed proved they were true Christians; while Jews and conversos ate *adefina,* a slow-cooking stew that was traditionally put on the fire before the sabbath began. (The Moors were equally despised for their diet which largely eschewed meat altogether in favor of grains and fruit. In general the converted Moors, or Moriscos, escaped the venom of the blood-purity cult because, unlike the converted Jews, they were not socially or economically influential.)[15]

In this climate of mounting attack, the powerful conversos fought back. The earlier strategy of protecting themselves by attacking the less-than-pious in their midst had failed. Alonso de Cartagena had tried that back in 1434 with his failed papal decree; it had backfired by highlighting old Christian accusations against conversos in general. Now the high-standing converso clergy struggled to counter the charge that all new Christians were false Christians. They did so by invoking Christian unity. Juan de Torquemada, Cardinal of Saint Sixtus, (a grandson of converts and the uncle of the future Chief Inquisitor, Tomás de Torquemada) wrote a famous defense of the new Christians.[16] So, ironically, did Alonso de Cartagena.[17] The potential dangers of *limpieza* (cleansing) could scarcely go unnoticed in a mixed population that also included Christians whose Jewish ancestors had converted centuries ago when the oppressive Visigoths were around. King Juan II rallied to the conversos' side and urged Pope Nicolas V to expedite a papal bull condemning the statute of exclusion pronounced in Toledo in 1449.

A rumor spread that new Christians were about to be massacred in the northern Castilian city of Burgos. The attack did not take place, but the status of conversos had deteriorated so quickly and become so precarious that another prominent member of the Santa María clan made plans to leave Castile.[18] That danger might threaten the great family of Pablo de Santa María signaled just how unpredictable the world had become for converts and their descendants. By the time converso churchmen acknowledged the shifting social consensus, switched gears, and began a rear-guard battle on behalf of the unity of all true Christians, it was, in a sense, too late. They argued that the issue was faith, not race. Some conversos were certainly heretics; others (themselves, for example) emphatically were not. But the blood purity obsession sweeping Spain put the lie to their claims. All conversos were tarred with the brush of "Jewishness."

Alonso de Cartagena was a tragic case in point. The bishop was a man of refined intelligence and broad education who was spearheading a move to adopt the artistic and intellectual reforms of the Renaissance. His cathedral in Burgos displayed brilliant stone and marble sculptures commissioned from the Flemish artist Gil de Siloé. He had translated Seneca from Latin into the Castilian vernacular and the *Nicomachean Ethics* of Aristotle, as well as other works of moral philosophy and theology. Bishop Alonso was known to speak graciously and was "very clean about his person, in the clothes he wore, and in the service of his table, and everything he touched was treated with great cleanliness. He detested men who were not clean because exterior cleanliness is a sign of inner purity, but he also did not approve of cleanliness of body and clothing if this did not correspond to sincerity of thought and purity of deed."[19]

As Bishop of Burgos, Alonso de Cartagena continued to preach mass before the high altar of his cathedral under the brilliant stained glass windows that scattered paths of coloured light around him. Facing him were the faithful of his city, but they now included men who threatened the entire class of Christians descended from converts, including himself.

What thoughts might have passed through the mind of this converso bishop as he looked over the heads of the worshipers standing before him, and as he listened to his voice echo from the stone walls and spires of his church? As a bishop, as a citizen of Renaissance Castile, Alonso de Cartagena was exalted to the highest degree. At the same time he was in personal danger.

Alonso's father, Pablo de Santa María, had viciously attacked his former people, the Jews, in the name of Christianity. Ironically, Alonso was subject to a similar attack directed against the conversos, as though they were Jews.

Other conversos tried to defend themselves by flagrantly denying they were of new Christian origin—a dubious enterprise since the truth still resided in living memory. Pedro de la Caballería—a renowned expert on jurisprudence and a member of the famous Saragossa family—boldly prepared a family genealogy "proving" that the Caballerías were descended from old Christian stock, even though there were plenty of people in Saragossa and elsewhere who had known them as illustrious Jews.

Some conversos sought to protect themselves by zealously accusing their fellows of false Christian practice, just as Alfonso de Valladolid (Abner of Burgos), Pablo de Santa María (Salomon Halevi), and Jerónimo de Santa Fe (Joshua Halorki) had tried to shore up their new Christian status by attacking the Jews.[20] Pedro de la Caballería—he who brazenly traced his lineage back to old Christians—hurriedly sat down to write a powerful polemic against "Jews, Saracens, and Infidels."[21]

Even the greatly admired, now elderly, Pablo de Santa María came under scrutiny. He, however, was vigorously defended by Fernán Peréz de Guzmán. Peréz de Guzmán was a knight of liberal inclination and certain courage. "Even the apostles fell back on certain familiar Jewish customs after they were converted by Our Lord, until little by little they affirmed themselves in the faith. I do not wonder at people [who do this] such as women and others who are not instructed," he wrote compassionately of the conversos.[22]

But Peréz de Guzmán was the exception: Writer-poets of all persuasions—new Christians, old Christians, and Jews—satirized the generic converso mercilessly in verse, the communications medium of the day. One of the first of these attacks was written soon after the Toledo riot of 1449 where conversos were first identified as Jews. It described a fictitious privilege bestowed by King Juan II upon an old Christian nobleman who had asked to enjoy the special benefits of being a *marrano*. (This was yet another pejorative word for converso; it meant pig, and may have originally been used by the Jews to heap scorn on renegades who broke the prohibition against eating pork.)[23]

According to the author of this attack the "benefits" of being a *marrano* included: the right to practice trickery on old Christians with impunity; the right to play with the fortunes of others; the right to deny Catholic articles of faith and "to venerate the image of the Torah," or to believe in nothing at all except the reality of birth and death; the right to observe the Jewish sabbath behind closed doors and eat *adefina*; the right to control all public revenues and to set old Christians at each other's throats; the right to be a priest and use the confessions of old Christians against them; the right to be a doctor or pharmacist and kill old Christians under the cover of medical treatment in order to make off with their wives; the right to be circumcised in spite of being baptized; the right to have a secret Jewish name; the right to maintain Jewish funeral customs; the right to hide a tax-farming register inside one's breviary during Mass; among other things.[24]

The sharpest of many such satiric poems describes a new Christian who hedges his bets for the afterlife, requesting that when he dies the Cross be laid at his feet, the Quran at his breast, and the Torah, "his life and light" at his head.[25] This literary fool was set up for laughs, of course; all the same the authenticated reply of Juan de Sayas, whom we have met (the converso who intended to commend his soul to all three religions just for safety's sake), conveyed precisely the same message.

Although these parodies of converso life within society were exaggerated to incite contempt, they were and remain a remarkable illustration of the central paradox: new Christians were socially marginalized, yet they were at the very center of social, political, and economic life. The object of these literary attacks was a well-known type: the skeptic whose conversion to Christianity had had little to do with religion. Several decades later an interesting story came to light concerning the jurist Pedro de la Caballería, polemicist and self-genealogized old Christian. A Jewish weaver told the Inquisition that Pedro had often shared the sabbath meal with his family. One day the weaver asked Pedro why he had converted to Christianity when he was so learned in the Torah. Pedro purportedly replied: "Silence, fool! Could I as a Jew have risen higher than a rabbinical post? Now I am one of the chief councilors of the city. For the sake of the little man who was hanged [Jesus] I am accorded every honor, and I issue orders to the whole city of Saragossa. Now I do as I please."[26]

But there was something peculiar about the anticonverso satires regardless of whether they were authored by old Christians, Jews, or other conversos. They were liberally sprinkled with Hebrew words. In other words, the mixing of religions and cultures persisted as a subtext to society in spite of the Church, in spite of politics, and in spite of the shifting public consensus regarding conversos. The integration of former Jews had enriched the blood line of the nobility by broadening the intellectual base of a stagnant old elite and introducing new ways of thinking and new forms of language.[27] The Church's push toward massive religious conversions over the first half of the fifteenth century had been designed to eliminate difference and therefore unify society; it had, on the contrary, extended the historical hybridization of Spanish culture, a process that had been continuous since the eighth century when both Jews and Christians had adapted themselves, culturally, to the rich civilization of the Cordoban caliphs. At a political and social level significant change was taking place, but at its core the ethnic stew pot that was Spain simmered on, assimilating the flavors of a unique history.

The year 1449 marked another step in the slow transformation of society and the emergence of intolerance. The riots in Toledo liberated long-smoldering resentments, and before long the old accusations, with their familiar anti-Semitic content, were being brought against some of the most powerful people in the kingdom, baptized men and women who were linked by blood to the great ancient families of the land.

Blood purity became a powerful weapon in the hands of the overtaxed peasantry and town proletariat that customarily had no voice at all, for suddenly the entire noble class, whom they hated, was "revealed" to be "tainted" while they were "pure" because their members did not intermarry with conversos. No matter what their social status, conversos now scrambled to protect themselves from a growing scrutiny of their tainted origins. Like Pedro de la Caballería, many decided that the best defense was an outright lie: a fabricated genealogy.

Purportedly "Jewish" traits were reviled. As the decades passed, ignorance became a badge of pride and any Christian who could read and write was likely to be identified as a converso—soon a most dangerous label. While the fires of the Spanish Inquisition burned, the sixteenth-century author of *Don Quixote,* Miguel de Cervantes (who was of converso origin), has one of his fictional characters ask a peasant if he knows how to read.

"Certainly not," replies the indignant individual. "No one in my lineage has so little judgment as to learn that nonsense which brings men to the stake."[28]

The transformation of Spain was completed during the century that lay between the 1449 statutes of exclusion and the wary response of Cervantes's shrewd peasant. What remained of Tariq the Moor's legacy of tolerance would shrivel in the flames of holy fire.

Notes

1. Ferdinand II's mother was Joana Henríquez of the powerful Henríquez clan of Castile. She was the second wife of Juan II of Aragon who was a son of Ferdinand I.

2. R. Solomon ibn Verga, *Shebet Yehuda* (Scepter of Judah), 1550, trans. from Hebrew to Spanish by Francisco Cantero Burgos (1927), note 64. French scholar, Isidore Loeb, called *Shebet Yehuda* "the most original and lively of all the Hebrew chronicles relating to the history of the Jews in the Middle Ages." The author's memories were written as fiction but are considered largely authentic.

3. Details cited of converso life are drawn from Inquisition records. See E. Marin Padilla, "Relación judeoconversa durante la segunda mitad del siglo XV en Aragón," *Sefarad* 24 (1986): 29-30.

4. Ibid.

5. Ibid.

6. Ferán Pérez de Guzmán (1376–1470), *Generaciónes y Semblanzas,* ed. by J. Dominguez Bordona (1954), 135.

7. M. Lafuente, *Historia General de España,* 6: 205, note 2.

8. Ibid., 201.

9. Pérez de Guzmán, *Generaciónes,* 121–22.

10. Mariana, *The General History of Spain,* 360.

11. Sources for this event are *Crónica del Halconero de Juan II,* ed. by Juan de Mata Carriazo (1946); *Crónica de Alvaro de Luna,* ed. by Juan de Mata Carriazo (1940); Mariana, *The General History of Spain,* ch. 9; Fernán Pérez de Guzmán, *Crónica del Señor Rey Don Juan* (1779).

12. Most probably a reference to the Passover seder which falls at the same time as Easter.

13. See A. A. Sicroff, *Les Controverses des Statuts de Pureté de Sang en Espagne du XVe au XVIIe siècle* (1960), and John Edwards, "Race and Religion in 15th and 16th century Spain: The 'purity of blood' laws revisited," *International World Congress of Jewish Studies* 2 (1990).

14. Andrés Bernáldez, *Memorias del reinado de los Reyes Católicos,* ed. by Juan de Mata Carriazo (1962): 94ff.

15. The late twentieth-century visitor to Spain will notice that local restaurant cuisine still emphasizes pork, wine, and bread with very few vegetables. When the Reconquest was completed and the Jews expelled, "Christian" cuisine was entrenched.

16. Juan de Torquemada, *Tractatus contra Madianitas et Ismaelitas,* ed. by N. López Martínez and V. Proaño Gil (1957).

17. *Defensorium unitatis christianae* (1450).

18. Alvar Garcia de Santa María, chronicler of King Juan II.

19. F. Pulgar, *Claros Varones de Castilla,* ed. by J. de Mata Carriazo (1943), 137

20. *Scrutinium Scripturarum* (1432).

21. *Zelus Christi contra Judaeos, Saracenos et Infideles* (1450).

22. *Generaciónes,* 91.

23. *El Privilegio.* See H. Pelaum, "Une ancienne satire espagnole contre les Marranes," *REJ* 83–86 (1927): 131ff.

24. Ibid.

25. Ibid., Alfonso Alvarea de Villasandino on Alfonso Ferrandes Semuel.

26. Baer, *A History of the Jews in Christian Spain,* 2: 227. The weaver's testimony may have been fabricated, but as Baer suggests, the degree of detail indicates the story was probably authentic.

27. See Seymour Resnick, "The Jew as Portrayed in Early Spanish Literature," *Hispania* 34 (1951); and Joseph M. Sola-Solé and Stanley E. Rose, "Judíos y conversos en la poesía cortesana del siglo XV: el estilo polígloto de Fray Diego de Valencia," *Hispanic Review* 44 (1976).

28. *The Mayors of Daganzo,* cited in Sanford Shepard, "Crypto-Jews in Spanish Literature," *Judaism* 19 (1970).

8

Anarchy and Renewal

Castile had suffered political anarchy for almost half a century ensuring the marginalization and eventual persecution of minorities. Juan II of Castile was a failure. In 1449 his subjects in Toledo pelted him with cabbages, and things did not get better. When the king lay dying in 1454 he confided pathetically to his physician, "I would rather have been born a simple craftsman than the king of Castile."[1]

But at least Juan II had encouraged the Renaissance arts. His son and successor, Enrique IV, could claim no redeeming qualities whatsoever. Chaos marked his reign, unpunished crimes were committed with nose-thumbing bravado; and with this breakdown in the social structure came overt attacks on conversos who were identified with the hated regime.

King Enrique preferred hunting to governing, so he held court in Segovia and Ávila, where the hunt was best; then he enhanced his reputation for cheating by covertly stocking a mountain enclosure with three thousand deer, wild boar, and other animals. He minted coin to pay for his pleasures until inflation multiplied prices by six and people could not afford the basics of life. Like his father, he abdicated the affairs of state to powerful favorites to whom he granted full authority to "punish, exile, or execute" without trial, and he summarily wiped out all previous rights of appeal and asylum.[2]

The king shocked his contemporaries with his cynicism in religious matters; he particularly enjoyed calling ecclesiastical documents "sheep skins covered with absurdities,"[3] purposely named unworthy people to ecclesiastical posts, and ordered a ceremony ridiculing the Church to take place in Seville. When a hurricane devastated Seville, he ordered a priest to sermonize that this was a natural phenomenon and not divine intervention; then to amuse himself he ordered a group of "experts" to come together to report on what terrible punishments heaven was announcing. (In his quasiscientific skepticism Enrique IV was thoroughly modern and apparently not without a sense of humor.)

Most of all, Enrique hated the powerful archbishop of Toledo and Primate of all Castile, Alfonso de Carrillo: a battle-seasoned, noble warrior-priest who could lead an army and wield a lance like few others and was known to have fathered at least one son.[4] Enrique cut off funds to the archbishop and other vicars of the Church, and removed an abbess whom the archbishop had appointed because "there was debauchery among the nuns," he explained disingenuously. (He then appointed one of his own mistresses in her place.)

Every level of crime went unpunished in the Castile of Enrique IV. A royal page brazenly abducted the daughter of a prominent family while the king was visiting Seville, and when the girl's horrified parents protested, Enrique accused *them* of failing to supervise their child. Nobles ambushed one another on the highways, and killed and robbed with impunity. The powerful knight known as the Master of Calatrava actually tried to rape Queen Isabella, the widow of Juan II and King Enrique's stepmother. Either the king did not care about this attack on a member of his own family, or he was too weak to intervene. The crime was simply ignored. (Corruption did have limits for the masses of ordinary people, however. When the archbishop of Santiago raped a young woman at whose marriage he had just officiated, the indignant population literally threw him out of town.)

Courtiers and subjects took their cue from the degenerate ruler and a chronicler describes the queen's attendants as "wearing [dresses] *décolleté* to the stomach [and] painting themselves up to the thigh so that when [their legs showed] all was a uniform white colour. They passed the year [1455] eating sweets, flirting with the young men, and sleeping."[5] The prior of San Juan, wearing a mask of a female courtesan and accompanied by two clerics disguised as ruffians and drunkards, rode a mule through the streets. The Count of Haro pretended to be a monk and rode about on a donkey, and the king publicly compared him to a blacksmith's dog.

Hoping to keep the peasants from rising against him, Enrique doled out titles and privileges for the asking, but he only succeeded in whetting an appetite for more and, as one chronicler put it, "converting [the peasants] into lions."[6]

But scandal—a sexual scandal—eclipsed all the rest and effectively changed the course of Spanish history, including the future of Jews and conversos.

Poor Enrique IV was known throughout Spain and Europe as Enrique the Impotent. A childless thirteen-year marriage with Blanche of

Navarre was declared void by both the bishop of Segovia and the archbishop of Toledo "for *impotencia respectiva* owing to some malign [astral] influence," and confirmed by the pope.[7] Then in 1455 the king married again. His new bride was Juana, a vivacious, fun-loving child of twelve, and the sister of the king of Portugal. All of Castile celebrated. Might their king yet produce an heir to the throne?

On February 28 1462, after seven years of childless marriage, Queen Juana gave birth to a daughter, also named Juana. But whose child was she? Certainly not Enrique's, "for the impotence of the king was known, and the great nobles believed that the queen had conceived by another man and not the king; and they affirmed that it was one of his favorites who was named Don Beltran de la Cueva, Duke of Albuquerque, whom the king loved very much."[8]

Enrique stubbornly insisted that the infant Joana was his daughter and obliged the nobility to recognize her as heir to the throne of Castile and León. But the rumors persisted. Some said that during the thirteen years of his marriage to Blanche of Navarre, the king had never lain with her "as a husband ought to with a wife."[9] Nor had he lain with any of the many women of all ages and social classes with whom he met, although they were constantly in the palace and were often alone with him. The chronicler Fernando de Pulgar wrote:

> Many times he had slept with them in his bed, but they admitted that he had never had carnal relations with them. This testimony was given not only by the Princess Blanche, his wife, and by all the other women with whom he was in intimate rapport, but also by the doctors, women, and other people who looked after him when he was a child.

Some people whispered that the king had commanded his wife to sleep with Beltran de la Cueva so he could claim any child who was born as his legitimate heir. But most people blamed the young queen. That Juana was beautiful and vivacious also was held against her.

"Fragile woman, ancient and principal instrument of the destruction of humanity," fulminated a contemporary;[10] an emotionally charged theme that was the subject of a million sermons. The charming young queen was suddenly transformed into Eve, Lilith, and the whore of Babylon, the dangerous, sexual woman of myth.

Eventually the king relented and the queen was imprisoned in the castle fortress of Seville where her guard claimed that he, too, had relations with her: he lowered her from the tower in a basket, he said, and they made love in a field. These slanders were satisfying to righteous folk, at once salacious and stimulating. Most importantly, they disgraced a powerful woman and put her in her place. Unsubstantiated stories circulated claiming that the queen became pregnant during her captivity and wore loose clothes to cover her condition (a rumor that purportedly prompted a new dress fashion among similarly afflicted maidens.)

As for the putative father, Beltran de la Cueva disparaged the disgraced queen in terms that he might have reserved for a prostitute. When his friends made fun of her "imprudence" he replied that he had not the slightest sexual interest in the queen and that "he had never liked her thin legs."[11] He also suffered no personal or career disadvantage—quite the contrary: during the baptismal ceremony of the royal infant, King Enrique publicly honored Beltran with a brand new lordship.

The child was known contemptuously as *la Beltraneja,* in honor of her putative father. The mighty queen of Castile had been brought down.[12]

While scandal and anarchy tore through the kingdom, the heavens foretold terrible calamity. A great flame appeared, seeming to divide the sky in two, and in Burgos and Granada "there fell a shower of great stones" which killed many cattle. The king's lions fought at Segovia and the smallest lion killed and ate the biggest: a frightening portent. In the town of Penalver, a three-year-old child predicted that the chaos in the land would continue unless people did penance for their sins. Terrified peasants, townsfolk, and nobles alike walked in processions entreating God's help. "But they mended not their lives," reported the sixteenth-century historian Juan de Mariana, confirming timeless humanity.[13]

* * *

With a monarch thought to be mentally debilitated on the throne and a scandal that brought the legitimate succession into question, the powerful nobles decided to go all the way. They enacted a symbolic ceremony of dethronement which must rank among the strangest events of European history.

It is June 5, 1465, and a wooden stage has been erected on one of the dust-brown hills that surround the walled city of Avila. A throne has been placed on this platform, and on the throne is a life-size statue of King Enrique IV carrying all the trappings of royalty: sword, scepter, and crown. The assembled rebel nobility of Castile mills about in expectation.

Ordinary townspeople run through the gates in the city walls towards this scene, shouting and asking each other what is going on. Others watch, stupefied, from the eleventh century ramparts that encircle the city.

The crowd falls quiet as the Bishop of Calahorra approaches the statue of the king. He is carrying a manifesto which he opens and reads:

"It is well-known, *Señores,* that the kingdom is the body and the king is the head and that justice dictates that the kingdom must not be deprived of a just succession."[14] This vision of the medieval community as a living organism with the king as the "head" and his subjects as the body was first elaborated by Thomas Aquinas in the thirteenth century and remains unquestioned two hundred years later.

The bishop formulates four accusations against Enrique:

"The king has corrupted the dignity of the crown," he announces. At this the archbishop of Toledo rushes forward and knocks the crown off the head of the statue.

"The king has perverted the administration of justice." The Count of Plasencia grabs the royal sword and throws it to the ground.

"The king has impeded proper government of the realm." The Count of Benavente tears away the scepter from the right hand of the statue.

"The king has debased the throne." Diego López de Stuñiga lifts the statue of Enrique from the throne and violently hurls it to the ground.

People sob to witness the "death" of their king. A king rules by the grace of God. "The Kinge, . . . yea, though he be an infidele, representeth as it were the image of God upon earthe," wrote the English bishop of Winchester a full century later. It is the same here on the hills of Avila. This terrible scene is tantamount to deicide.

Now eleven-year-old Prince Alfonso, half-brother to Enrique IV, is led to the throne. A crown is placed on the child's head, and suddenly— yes—suddenly the people are no longer sobbing. They are cheering. Trumpets sound and the traditional cry rises from a thousand throats in thrilling unison: "Castile, Castile, for King Don Alfonso!"

When he is informed of this treason, King Enrique falls into a deep depression and quotes fulsomely from the Book of Job: "Naked I came from my mother's womb, and naked must I go down to the earth."[15]

Supporters of the two royal factions introduce civil war into Castile until, toward the end of the decade, Prince Alfonso dies suddenly and mysteriously. He is traveling on the road near Avila with his sister, Princess Isabella. They stop for lunch in an inn where Alfonso is presented with his favorite dish, breaded trout. Instantly he falls to the floor, unable to speak. Most people are convinced he has been poisoned through the auspices of his half-brother, Enrique IV.

On hearing of Alfonso's death, the archbishop of Toledo and the rebel grandees of Castile rush to the side of the prince's sister, seventeen-year-old Princess Isabella. They tell her that she and she alone is the legitimate successor to the crown of Castile.

A Curse on the Conversos

The lower classes blamed the conversos for the civil war over the succession to the throne of Castile. Conversos acted on behalf of both "rulers" in the schism and were perceived as influential; they were easily attackable stand-ins for royalty. In 1462 an assault on the converso community broke out in the city of Carmona. Ominously, the municipal authorities did not protect the victims as they had always done in the past. The governor of the city "handed [the conversos] over to hostile evildoers who were thirsty for their riches. In the name of religion, they sacked, murdered, and committed other violence, and perpetrated all sorts of infamies such as had been done before in Toledo," wrote the chronicler Alfonso de Palencia.[16]

Nor did King Enrique intervene to help the conversos, as was the habit of royalty, refusing even to discipline the governor who had betrayed the new Christians "to hostile evildoers." Once again Castilians were confronted with the issue of legal impunity and the breakdown of traditional protections. The result was that vigilante bands grew more brazen in their attacks and the unprotected conversos grew more desperate and vulnerable.

In 1467, conversos in Toledo mounted an oddly miscalculated offensive. They covertly stockpiled crossbows, muskets, caltrops (iron balls with spikes), and ten thousand knotted ropes with which they apparently planned to tie up their prisoners. On July 21, they attacked the cathedral of the city.

They never had a chance to get to their stocks of crossbows and caltrops, or their knotted ropes. Masses of peasants rushed in from the countryside and massacred the conversos indiscriminately. More than a thousand houses were burned to the ground. Those who escaped from the city wandered about without assistance until they died.

The significance of these events cannot be overstated, for familiar patterns were changing. Conversos were identified with the upper nobility and the court, but in this time of chaos and civil war "the court" had split in two, with rival kings, and the conversos were an easy substitute target for the enemies of both sides. Significantly, neither "king" seemed prepared to extend the protection Spanish minorities had taken for granted for hundreds of years. Castilians of all stripes—Moors, Jews, Christians, conversos—yearned for a return to law and order; a return to the old days of strong government and peace.

The Princess of Their Dreams

She was seventeen years old, blue-eyed, and fair-skinned (a legacy from her English grandmother, Catherine of Lancaster, daughter of John of Gaunt). She was pious and smart (notably pious, they said, and amazingly smart); why, she was just a wisp of a girl, and so clever.

The rebel nobles who backed her after the death of young brother Alfonso were the same who had "dethroned" her half-brother, Enrique IV, and simultaneously (they hoped) blocked the succession of his illegitimate daughter, *La Beltraneja*.

King Enrique needed to get rid of Isabella, but he didn't dare poison her in the usual way. Instead, he opted for the next best strategy: a marriage that would strangle her chances of wearing his crown. Enrique had the perfect husband in mind: Alfonso of Portugal, a widower with children. And yes, Alfonso just happened to be the uncle of *La Beltraneja*, so he was naturally sympathetic to the child's cause.

The canny archbishop of Toledo warns Isabella that Alfonso's commitment to his older children will prevail over any offspring he and Isabella may have together, and all the gossips agree. Nervy troubadors sing satirical ballads in public squares all over Castile: "If the princess accepts the hand of old Alfonso she will become step-mother to people older than herself!" "Castile and León will come under the yoke of enemies!" (As blocking Isabella was precisely what King Enrique had in mind, he threw the troubadors in jail.)[17]

Since marriage was essential, and the *right* marriage the key to the throne, Isabella began her own search. Sixteen-year-old Richard, Duke of Gloucester and brother of Edward IV of England, was an early suitor. (Had he been successful both English and Spanish history would have taken a different turn. Richard grew up to become the presumed [though debated] monster-murderer of his two nephews in the Tower of London in August 1483, after which he had himself crowned as Richard III.)

Next came the Duke of Guienne, heir to the throne of France. Isabella sent her chaplain to the French court to observe this would-be husband, but when he reported back that the duke was "a feeble and effeminate prince with limbs so emaciated as to be deformed, and with eyes so weak and watery as to incapacitate him for the ordinary exercises of chivalry" she rejected him out of hand.[18]

Isabella's choice was neither old, feeble, widowed, nor foreign. Her chaplain visited the court of Aragon and told her that eighteen-year-old Prince Ferdinand was a man "of comely, symmetrical figure, a graceful manner, and a spirit that was up to anything"[19]—an attractive prospect for an equally spirited young woman. Ferdinand spoke her language and understood her customs; in fact he was a distant cousin. Topping the list of his qualities, Ferdinand would inherit the kingdom of Aragon, just as she would inherit Castile. Isabella was clever enough to see a unique opportunity to unite the neighboring states of Spain, especially since Castile was by far the most powerful of the two.

Who was Ferdinand of Aragon, this man who would become the husband and equal partner of a legendary queen? He was a man descended from Jews who would inaugurate an inquisition against those who were, like himself, of converso origin, then expel the Jews and Muslims who were unwilling to convert from Spain. He was a man of wily character who was so admired by none other than Nicolò Machiavelli that he is thought to have been the model for Machiavelli's famous book, *The Prince*. Ferdinand would eventually defeat the last Moors in Granada under the flag of the Holy Reconquest, then dispatch one Christopher Columbus to places unknown across the sea.

Ferdinand was a product of the Renaissance: cool, calculating, with an unsentimental cast of mind, like his royal father, who was called "Juan without faith" behind his back.[20]

Ferdinand had a sharp eye for politics and exceptional administrative skills: he had received an excellent Renaissance-style education at his parents' court, had been provided with the finest teachers, instructed in state affairs and the chivalric arts, and encouraged to observe the practical workings of government. But there was something harder to pin down about Ferdinand of Aragon, a repressed passion, perhaps, that sharpened intention and resolve, a cagey opportunism, a studied ruthlessness. More obvious was his willingness to tell lies in the service of his massive ambition—a quality that was observed in fine detail by Machiavelli, his cunning Italian neighbor. Ferdinand divorced politics from ethics and married government to national interests, making him the first of a modern breed. These, one will recall, were the Machiavellian ideals.

Isabella was flaunting the wishes of her brother King Enrique in choosing Ferdinand as her husband-to-be, and she would remain in danger until her marriage was a reality. Accompanied by two trusted ambassadors of the princess, Ferdinand walked to her, secretly and in disguise, from Saragossa to Valladolid, a distance of hundreds of miles. When they reached a small village inhabited by a few peasants, the prince pretended to be the servant who looks after the mules. Danger was all about: the entire countryside was patrolled by Enrique's armed knights.

(Today, the path the young Ferdinand took to Valladolid is still no more than ten feet wide in places, and it still weaves through vast tracts of olive groves. Shepherds and their flocks stand guard along the banks of the Duero River, and the ruins of the tenth century castles that fortified the front line of the Reconquest continue to dominate the mountains. Dusty villages still sleep in the afternoon sun; troglodytes build homes into the rockside. In rural Spain little has changed.)

Ferdinand slipped into Valladolid the night of October 11, 1469, and was conducted to the apartments of the princess. One of the ambassadors who had led him into Castile had gone ahead and was waiting there with Isabella. He pointed out Ferdinand excitedly. "*Ese es! Ese es!*" "That's him! That's him!" (To commemorate this auspicious moment the envoy was allowed to place the letters SS, which in Spanish sound like the exclamation, *ese es,* on his family escutcheon.)[21]

Ferdinand kissed the hand of the princess and they began to talk, but the omnipresent archbishop of Toledo, who had appointed himself chaperon, was intent on curbing any unseemly enthusiasm on the part of the young couple, "for their hearts were filled with the joyous contemplation that soon they would be joined by the licit bonds of matrimony."[22]

On October 18, 1469, Ferdinand returned to Valladolid to be married. The archbishop of Toledo and the grandees and knights of Isabella's entourage officially welcomed him, and the people of the city lined the streets cheering, playing instruments, and waving banners. Armored knights pranced about on horseback among the elegant arcades of the central plaza of the city.

Enrique IV was not there, of course, but his spies were. There were those who were overtly opposed to this marriage for the damage it would do to the cause of the king and his daughter, *La Beltraneja,* men who had tied their fortunes to the king in return for the influence they might wield over him. Intrigue rumbled beneath the surface of events. Plots hatched within plots, interests within interests. Noble families attached to the Enrique or Isabelline factions and locked in bitter feud were all in Valladolid that October day, watching one another with suspicion.

Ferdinand was escorted into Isabella's apartments and the terms of the marriage were read aloud: Isabella would retain control over the affairs of Castile, contrary to the usual duty of wives to defer to their husbands. Ferdinand's authority in Castile would ultimately derive only through her, but their names would appear jointly, and it was conceded that his would come first. The couple joined hands, were pronounced upon by the archbishop of Toledo, and the people of Valladolid danced and celebrated in the streets.

Enrique was outraged. The factional civil war over the succession of his "daughter," on the one hand, and Isabella, on the other, persisted, and now it also included an escalating conflict between Old Christians and New Christian conversos. As the social fabric of cities and towns disintegrated, the conversos were blamed and targeted as enemies—as *Jewish* enemies. Hatred exploded in the streets. In Cordoba in 1473 a young converso girl was accused of emptying a bed pan on a religious procession that was passing beneath her window. A riot ensued. "Horrible cruelties were committed against the conversos," reported the chronicler, Alonso de Palencia. Many conversos fled to Seville where they put together yet another secret militia of three hundred horses, five thousand armed infantrymen and a storehouse of crossbows. Others took refuge in Palma de Mallorca, or escaped to Italy or Flanders.

Another pogrom erupted the following year in Seville. Once again Alonso de Palencia captured the heart of it:

> Feigning religious fervor, some evildoers in Seville who were eager for booty and blood, accused [the conversos] of not sanctifying Sunday as the sabbath, but Saturday, instead. Some old Christians went from house to house to contain this rabble, but at the end the latter found their pretext in the quarrels of children and began the looting and the horrors.[23]

Palencia's description of the riot in Seville foreshadowed an underlying element of the approaching Inquisition, which was less than a decade away: the accusation of religious hypocrisy was often a pretext for robbery and ethnic violence.

The nation was in chaos. "The cities and towns of Spain suffered greatly from robbery, murder, sacrilege, adultery, and all kinds of delinquency," observed an eyewitness.

> People were unable to defend their homes from attackers who feared neither God, nor king, nor could they protect their wives or daughters, for there were so many evil men. Some of these usurped all means of justice. They raped married women, virgins, and nuns and committed other carnal excesses. Others cruelly robbed and murdered traveling merchants. Some occupied the fortress castles belonging to the Crown, and from them they sallied forth to attack the entire region. These same men kidnapped many people and held them to ransom for the same sum of money as if they had captured Moors or other barbarians who are enemies of our holy faith.[24]

A converso courtier, Fernando del Pulgar, corroborated the state of anarchy. "In these divisive times, no one was able to execute justice in the cities, or towns or anywhere in the kingdom. No one paid their debts unless they wanted to, nor did they obey any authority. Citizens and laborers and peaceful people had no recourse against robbery and violence."[25] Pulgar also wrote candidly to the archbishop of Coria about the feuding nobility of Andalusia. The Guzman and the Ponce clans had retinues of armored knights who "robbed, destroyed and murdered throughout all of Andalusia," he said. "I assure you, Señor, that no letter, messenger, magistrate, or questor has traveled from the kingdom of Murcia to the Kingdom of Navarre for more than five years."

On the economic front, the currency of Castile was so debased that ordinary people were refusing to accept coinage and had reverted to barter. Government revenues had fallen by approximately 87 percent over the century.[26]

King Enrique IV died on December 11, 1474, at the age of fifty, of a long-standing sickness "of the liver and stones" which had caused him pain and weakness for several years. Fool to the end, he had not prepared a will in spite of his illness because, commented a chronicler, "he did not expect to die so soon."[27]

Pedro Gonsález de Mendoza, the archbishop of Seville and cardinal of Spain, prepared an official notice of death:

> The most illustrious Enrique the Fourth, King of Castile and León, most merciful prince and pious lord. His death and absence, [his] humanity, mercy and magnificence will be mourned.

Never was the flattering language of royal homage less true. There were few who mourned the malfeasant king, with the possible exception of his pathetic *Beltraneja*.

* * *

Isabella was in Segovia when she learned of Enrique's death and she demanded to be crowned immediately, even though Ferdinand was absent in Aragon. On Tuesday December 13, 1474, she was welcomed by the nobility and clergy at the palace and conducted along the narrow street (one can walk it still), under a brocade canopy, to the central plaza of the city where a platform had been hastily erected. Royal banners flew in the winter wind, Moorish jugglers performed, and musicians played their instruments.

Isabella rode on a small white horse. Before her walked an officer of the court carrying the royal sword, symbol of strength and justice, the sword that would symbolically defend the kingdom. The archbishop of Toledo was waiting. Slowly the princess mounted the platform and seated herself on a throne that had been placed there. "Castile, Castile for the king Don Ferdinand and Doña Isabella, sole queen of these kingdoms," cried the assembled mass of courtiers and commoners.

They raised the standards of Castile and León and rang the church bells as Isabella swore the customary oath to maintain the liberties of the kingdom. Then she stepped down from the platform and walked in slow procession to a church just steps away. A choir sang the *Te Deum* and the music swelled and soared carrying the hope of thousands of weary Castilians. The pious young queen stepped forward alone to pray. Isabella was twenty-three years old. She was assuming a disputed crown in a country torn by civil war.

Her rival, *La Beltraneja,* entered a convent in Portugal. Juana never acknowledged defeat. Until her last day this woman of tragic birth defiantly signed herself, "I, the queen."

* * *

The fourteenth century had ravaged body and spirit, and in the fifteenth century a weak king and his dissolute son had undermined what was left of the economy and further undercut the values people lived by. A terrible sexual scandal had destroyed a queen and disturbed the legitimate succession to the throne. Since the monarchy ruled by divine right, did this chaos signify that God had forsaken the world?

End the civil war! Heal the wounds! Isabella had been crowned queen of Castile by historical accident, and the demand that she do something to save her people was universal. To end the violence against the conversos was a priority: The queen needed these educated administrators to run her government.

To add to her difficulties, Isabella had assumed the throne of a spectacularly ultramasculine world of fiestas, tournaments, jousts, and galas where a display of courtly love (one fought to honor one's lady) and simulated war were one and the same. Bull-lancing from horseback was the most popular sport of the Castilian nobility and such events were dangerous to both participant and spectator. On special occasions bulls ran through the streets (this sport has a vestigial descendant in modern-day Pamplona). Sometimes armored knights pitted themselves against wild animals captured for the occasion, or herded them into artificial forests for a stimulating, bloody hunt, then dragged the carcasses unceremoniously to the feet of cheering spectators.

To be a powerful woman was a dangerous occupation in fifteenth-century Castile, and Isabella had much to be wary of. Her world was now imbued with the teachings of Aristotle, who had argued that women were not fully human because they were less rational than men. The young queen would prove herself to be the most rational monarch Castile had seen in the entire fifteenth century, but given the contempt in which women were held, the palace "press" was exceptionally careful to emphasize Isabella's wifely relationship to her husband. The narrow tight-rope every woman walked had become sharply visible with the public disgrace of Queen Juana, whose putative lover had been free to disparage her with impunity. Isabella's sexual and wifely reputation was protected by constant recourse to soothing homilies: she had to be seen as the most "moral" of living mortals.

"Although she was the most powerful monarch in Europe, she never lost an opportunity to demonstrate her joy in having tied her fate to that of Ferdinand," wrote a nineteenth-century historian of the Isabelline period echoing the carefully cultivated line that was nurtured and established during her reign.

> Their initials were engraved together, [their symbols] the yoke and the arrows were united on the coinage, on books, [and] on public buildings. She was an example of licit love to all wives. She was zealous, it is true, but her zeal was decent, and nothing dishonoured her or her husband. She was passionate, but indulgent, loving but respectful, and she never spoke, or wrote of her husband without there following an expression of her love and reverence.[28]

There was about the young queen a severity, a rectitude, and an inflexibility that enabled her to push through reform without vacillating. Isabella was abstemious and frugal (it was said that she and her family ate for less than forty ducados a day; later on her grandson, Carlos V, spent four hundred),[29] and she was so modest that when she received the last sacrament before her death she refused to allow her feet to be uncovered. Isabella was incorruptible, a lover of pure justice applied without consideration for class or differential punishment. This single-minded rigor underscored the respect with which she was held. Isabella of Spain was a puritan in a decadent age.

Her first priority was to end the looting and murder on the roads. That was relatively easy. She revived an old institution called the *Santa Hermandad,* or Holy Brotherhood, a sort of vigilante police force, and assigned it jurisdiction for crimes of rape, robbery, and resisting justice, and for violence on the highways and in the cities. The operating system was simple: Every one hundred households maintained a horseman whose duty it was to arrest wrongdoers: a vigilante neighborhood watch, in other words. When a crime occurred the town bells rang and the "brother" galloped off in hot pursuit. Where one horseman left off another took up the relay.

Few criminals escaped and the penalties were severe. Simple robbery was punished with whipping, the loss of a hand (the latter derived surely from Muslim practice), or death. (The condemned received the last sacrament, then were quickly dispatched to the hereafter before their relatives could protest too loudly.) Before long a half-century of lawlessness had been brought under control.[30]

The queen's next target was Andalusia where rival noble clans were terrorizing the entire region. In July 1477, Isabella entered Seville and set herself up in the magnificent Alcazar of the city to hear cases of public abuse. Every Friday she sat on a chair covered with gold cloth, surrounded by her counselors, and listened to petitions from the aggrieved.

In just three years the queen's reputation for enforcing the law was such that when the criers announced she was coming to Seville, four thousand worried individuals fled the city. They were not misguided. The words "off with his head" rang out so frequently in the Alcazar that the old archbishop of the city had to remind the young queen that justice also included mercy.

Having established her strength, Isabella considered leniency. She announced a general amnesty, and all four thousand wrongdoers crept back to town.

Next, she addressed herself to the depleted royal treasury. Since the time of Juan II the nobility had refused to pay their annual rents to the crown, and some families were many times richer than the royal house. Although they represented just 1.65 percent of the population, the grandees of Castile controlled more than 97 percent of the land.[31] A skilled laborer was paid one ducat for eight days work, but the Marquis de Villena, for example, had an income of 100,000 ducats a year.[32]

Isabella summoned the great nobles of Castile to Toledo. She had already demonstrated her authority and they had little choice but to come; and little choice but to contribute to the national treasury when she demanded it. Families who received royal pensions on a yearly basis without contributing any services whatsoever were ordered to return the money in its entirety. Anyone owing money to the state was allowed to keep only that part which corresponded to services performed.

The queen explained herself in language politicians of all times would appreciate. "No monarch should consent to alienate his estate since the loss of revenue deprives him of the best means for rewarding the loyalty of friends and making himself feared by his enemies," she announced.[33]

She was incorruptible and intractable. One Alvar Yanez de Lugo, of the northern province of Galicia, had forced his scribe to forge a signature so he could appropriate someone else's inheritance; then he killed the scribe to prevent him from talking and buried him under the floor of the house. There were no witnesses, but the scribe's wife was suspicious and appealed to the queen. Alvar Yanez confessed, then in a desperate bid to

save his life he offered Ferdinand and Isabella forty thousand gold doublas to be used for the war against the remaining Moors in Granada. This
was an enormous sum, the equivalent of an entire year's income for the
royal house.

Some royal advisors argued heatedly that the holiness of the cause was
reason to accept the gift. But Isabella was adamant. She ordered Alvar
Yanez's head cut off and his money used to reimburse the people he had
robbed. Furthermore, she refused to touch any part of his property so that
"people will not think that greed was our motive for executing justice."[34]

Isabella and Ferdinand also forbade the proud lords, dukes, and
counts of Castile to build new fortress castles, or to use royal escutcheons
on their family crests. Most obeyed, but the monarchs eventually tore
down fifty castles belonging to recalcitrants. This was absolute power
with a new slant. Ferdinand's and Isabella's reforms in the name of
national salvation demanded the suppression of the self-interested,
volatile, feudal aristocracy of Spain.

No group was spared, including the ignorant, wealthy clergy whose
debauchery was so commonly accepted that the child of a priest could
inherit legally if the father died intestate. "Enough!" ordered the pious
Isabella. Not all priests found the new prohibitions to their liking. Rather
than give up the delights of the flesh four hundred friars in Andalusia converted to Islam and moved to North Africa.

Merit became the principal route to power. Ferdinand and Isabella
were "modern" rulers born into a generation that was increasingly influenced by the Italian Renaissance. They admired learning—a trait that
countered the anti-intellectual attitudes of Spanish nobility. They were
intent on modernizing the structures of government, which meant calling exclusively on educated men to act as accountants, secretaries, managers of estates and administrators—in other words, promoting Jews and
conversos from all classes.

There had always been Jews, then later conversos, in top positions at
court; but now the lineage-proud old Christians whose family names had
guaranteed court careers found themselves and their children squeezed
out. A new slogan was making the rounds: *Dios hizo hombres, no linajes*
(God made men, not family lineages),[35] and nothing, but nothing, upset
the old Christian nobility more. *Hidalguía* (nobility) with its attendant
privileges was at the heart of Castilian life.

Rising resentment in the Old Christian nobility dovetailed with the
bitterness of the poorer classes, and the tax collector and the men who
administered public life from the court right down to the municipality
were the object of deep-rooted rage. Ferdinand and Isabella were smart
enough to know that such teeth-grinding envy was not subject to the

bureaucratic reforms they had initiated which were working so well else-where. All the same they were intent on having the most talented people in their administration.

Pragmatic as she and Ferdinand were, Isabella's decisions depended ultimately on religious considerations. The issue for the queen was not that her favorites might be Jews or conversos. She was not an anti-Semite. The problem, if problem there was, concerned heresy: the possibility that eminent conversos might be false Christians who were secretly practicing Judaism.

Since the success of Jews and conversos had long been a source of envy and anger, it was easy for anti-Semites to whip up popular fury using the argument of religious hypocrisy. The queen was not stupid, nor was she a cynic; however, if it could be shown that false Christianity, or heresy, was a fact, and a source of public unrest, her desire to surround herself with the best administrators in the kingdom would take second place. "Heretic" was the most resonant word in the vocabulary of the pious queen. Heresy was the one crime she had refused to include in her general amnesty at Seville in 1477, and the issue that troubled her most.

The Spanish Church had been waiting a very long time for political power, since the long-ago days of the Visigoth kings; but for hundreds of years the secular habits of royalty and traditions of religious pluralism had stood in the way. Now, in the fertile soil of Isabella's piety and Ferdinand's ambition, dormant seeds would bloom.

Notes

1. M. Lafuente, *Historia General de España,* 6: 205.
2. A. Paz y Mélia, *El Cronista Alfonso de Palencia,* 383.
3. Ibid., 382.
4. Alfonso de Palencia, *Notas Biograficas,* ed. by Juan de Mata Carriazo, 370.
5. Ibid.
6. Ibid.
7. Ibid., 67, note 5.
8. Pulgar, *Crónica de los Reyes Católicos,* 2.
9. Ibid., 8.
10. Alfonso de Palencia, *Crónica de Enrique IV,* ed. by Paz y Mélia, 1: 354.
11. Palencia, *Notas Biograficas,* ed. by Juan de Mata Carriazo, 376.
12. The Middle Ages provides hundreds of examples of male sin-related sexual anxiety and fear of women such as the *Speculum* by the thirteenth-century encyclopedist Vincent de Beauvais. De Beauvais describes universal Woman as "the confusion of man, an insatiable beast, a continuous anxiety, an incessant warfare, a daily ruin, a house of tempest, and a hindrance to devotion." Following a line whose roots can be discovered in early Greek thought, medieval "woman" is depicted as the lowly body of humanity while "man" is the superior intellect capable of ruling, thinking, and reaching toward God. This hierarchy was analogous to the medieval theory of government in which the kingdom is perceived as the body while the monarch is the head.

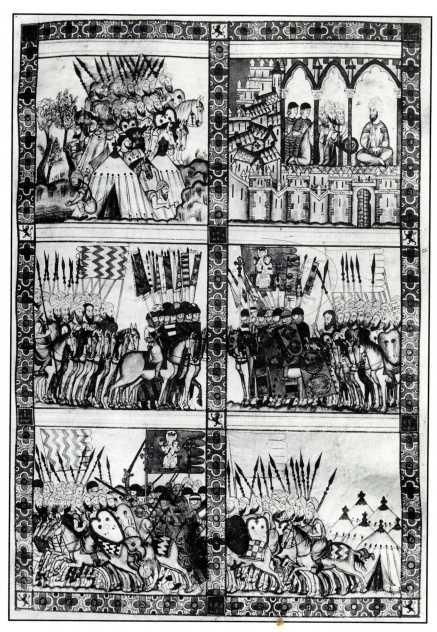

Fig. 1. Thirteenth-century battle scenes of the Reconquest from the famous *Cantigas de Santa María* of King Alfonso X of Castile. The Moors are bearded and in turbans. The Christian knights carry the standard of the Virgin and Child (El Escorial, Madrid).

Fig. 2. Alfonso X, also called "the Wise," encouraged learning in many different ways. He founded a school of translation, initiated university courses in Latin *and* Arabic, and patronized a teaching faculty representing the three religions of Spain. This fragment from *The Book of Chess*, which he commissioned, reveals the social harmony that existed among Christians, Jews, and Muslims (El Escorial, Madrid).

Fig. 3. Friar Tomás de Torquemada offering the communion wafer to
Queen Isabella. Torquemada was confessor to Isabella from her earliest
childhood and had great influence over her. At his urging, Isabella and her
husband Ferdinand inaugurated the Spanish Inquisition in 1481 (they named
Torquemada the first Inquisitor-General), and expelled the Jews from
Spain in 1492 (fifteenth-century painting by Pedro Berruguete, Valbuena
de Pisuerga, Palencia).

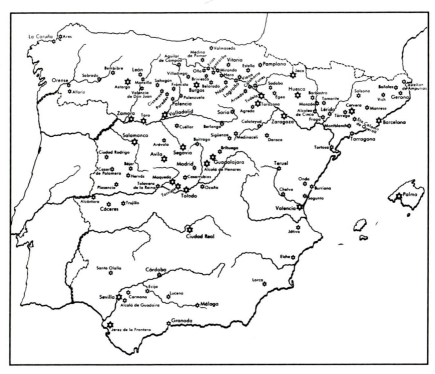

Fig. 4. Map of the Jewish communities of Spain in the late fifteenth century, on the eve of the expulsion. Large stars represent important centers with more than one synagogue (Instituto Amatller de Arte Hispanico).

9

The Holy Office of the Inquisition

O duro Oficio, quien te llama Santo?*

By the beginning of the 1480s, Isabella and Ferdinand had fairly whipped Castile back into shape. The economy had improved, and the richest families were once again paying taxes to the crown. Law and order. Although Spanish nobles were the most independent of all Europe, this girl of a queen had ruthlessly curbed their power. Even the libidinous priests had been scolded and brought into line.

The Holy Office of the Inquisition was the final reform in the arsenal of the Catholic monarchs, as they were called—the ultimate "cleansing" of religious impurity from the land. Ironically, unconverted Jews were safe, at least at first; only "false" Christians, *heretical* Christians, were the objects of inquisitorial scrutiny.[1]

The idea of an inquisition against depraved heresy appealed to Isabella on grounds of piety, but it also looked like an appealing way to appease millions of peasants—the "little people" who seethed with anger at the middle and upper classes and congregated in mobs at the smallest pretext, and who believed they were morally superior to conversos since they had 100 per cent "pure blood." An inquisition might also serve as a sop to old Christians who were losing their historical claim on influential careers at court and elsewhere in the kingdom.

A centralized inquisition could be shaped to consolidate the power of the royal couple throughout both Castile and Aragon. An inquisition under the banner of Christ would serve to promote national unity among the motley, feud-loving, power-monging peoples of the peninsula as noth-

---

*O cruel Office, who calls you Holy?

153

ing had done since the days of the Reconquest. Here was a chance to reinvent the religious-national ideals of Pelayo and his symbolic offspring, the Cid. Here was the Holy Reconquest against the Infidel redirected and reemployed.

Ferdinand and Isabella also understood that an inquisition to purify the faith would send out a powerful message to pious Christians that the Church reform they yearned for and dreamed about might actually come to be. With heretics properly exorcized from the community through death or repentance, believers might begin to trust in the salvation of the nation as well as the salvation of their souls. The king and the queen would facilitate this salvation; the queen because she truly believed, and the king because, as Nicolò Machiavelli observed, he was surpassingly shrewd.

And yes, they needed the conversos who were about to be targeted, but medieval custom had always found ways to exempt important people from legislation. Besides, there was the question of the royal coffers, a subject of consummate interest to Ferdinand. These were not quite as empty as they had been during the profligate reigns of Juan II and his imbecile son, Enrique, but they weren't exactly full either. An inquisition would confiscate property right off the top.

Ferdinand of Aragon was ambitious in other ways, and if there was one victory he wanted more than anything it was to complete the Holy Reconquest against the last remaining Arabs in Spain—the kingdom of Granada. He knew that to win that final war after almost eight centuries might catapult him into the same league as, say, Alexander the Great and that his name would be sung for centuries. And the present king of Granada just happened to be particularly weak. But wars cost money—lots of money; and that is what an inquisition would provide.

Psychologically, one cannot ignore the reality of the king's own converso origins on his mother's side. What, for example, did Ferdinand of Aragon think about his own "tainted blood"? Could it be that like so many other descendants of former Jews, he felt the need to attack in order to demonstrate his Christian orthodoxy? Did his own converso background play a role in his enthusiasm to establish the Inquisition? The king did not leave a record on this subject and we will never know, but the question is worth pondering.

*   *   *

There had been a "papal" inquisition in Europe since the thirteenth century when Pope Gregory IX first asserted the right of the Church to put heretics on trial following a bloody crusade against the Albigensian sect of southwestern France. The Albigensians believed there were only two principles in the world, one good, one evil, and that all material life was evil. They denied ecclesiastical authority and the sacraments.

Although their beliefs about the evils of the body implied they might have problems producing future generations of little Albigensians, and although crusading barons from northern France had already left rivers of blood flowing through the narrow streets of Toulouse, the decision of Pope Gregory IX to establish an inquisition against heresy suggests that the Albigensian dissent from orthodox religious doctrine warranted continued ecclesiastical vigilance. The "papal" inquisition was inaugurated in 1213, and its chief personnel, or inquisitors, were priests—mostly of the Dominican order. These carefully chosen men of high dignity soon created a bureaucracy of notaries, police, commissioners, and spies. Big Brother was born, and he had a thousand eyes and ears.

The papal inquisition spread into the kingdom of Aragon (never into Castile), but the rulers of that pragmatic and comparatively tolerant society ignored it altogether until it existed in name only. By the early decades of the fifteenth century, most Aragonians barely knew the Inquisition existed.

Before any single idea can successfully dominate an era, one or more "inspired" individuals must make that issue the center of their lives and use the currents of their time to make it appear desirable, then inevitable, to their contemporaries. This has certainly been true for the successful upheavals of the twentieth century—of the political Left and the Right— and, intriguingly, late-fifteenth-century Spain was a prototype. In retrospect, one man can be seen to have seeded the terrain that Alfonso de Valladolid, Vicente Ferrer, Jerónimo de Santa Fe, Benedict XIII, and Pablo de Santa María had plowed such that a new inquisition grew inevitably from its soil. He was Alonso de Espina, a Franciscan priest of old Christian lineage.[2]

Espina was respected as a learned and holy man, and he yearned for a strong inquisition to cleanse the Church of heresy. In the 1450s, with King Juan II and his powerful Constable Alvaro de Luna both dead, Espina was recorded as complaining angrily: "Some are heretics and Christian perverts, others are Jews, others Saracens [Moors], others devils. There is no one to investigate the errors of the heretics. The ravening wolves, O Lord, have entered thy flock, for the shepherds are few."[3]

Espina asked the Franciscans for help in instigating an inquisition, and a royal hearing was arranged with the new king, Enrique IV. Espina hoped Enrique would be more attentive to the dangerous threat of heresy than his predecessors, although one can hardly imagine he was unaware that this was the monarch who called ecclesiastical documents "sheepskins covered with absurdities."

The Franciscans entered the royal chamber and approached the throne. The king waited. "Sire," said one of the priests solemnly, "are you aware that conversos are circumcising their sons?" As evidence, the friar claimed to have a large number of foreskins in his possession.

This was precisely the sort of allegation Enrique IV loved to mock, and he ordered the priest to produce his collection of baby foreskins. When he could not, the king (who had other things on his mind, such as the hunt) lost interest in Espina's inquisition.[4]

Not a man to accept defeat, Friar Alonso de Espina set about developing a body of propaganda to underscore his cause. Espina had a fine grasp of the essentials of mythmaking, and his formula for disseminating believable "information" was fail-safe. Start with false, or better still, half-true premises that will ring bells of recognition in the intended listener, then follow through with carefully constructed conclusions.

Hatred of Jews and conversos was Alonso's obsession, and his message was threefold. First, he said, the Jews are the Devil incarnate. The idea of Jews as devils had become commonplace in northern Europe, although not in Spain; but as a learned man Espina could scan the Latin literature of Europe for "evidence." He probably found this part of his message in the Gospel of John. In chapter 8:43-44,47, John quotes Jesus saying to the Jews, "Why do you not understand what I say? You are of your father, the Devil, and your will is to do your father's desire. You are not of God." The charge that Jews were devils had also been propounded with more than a little bombast by the fourth-century archbishop of Constantine, St. John Chrysostom. "The synagogue," said Chrysostom, "is . . . the repair of wild beasts . . . the temple of demons devoted to idolatrous cults . . . the cavern of devils . . . a place of meetings for the assassins of Christ . . . the refuge of devils."[5]

Furthermore, argued Espina, all conversos are false Christians. Therefore they are heretics. Finally, Jews and conversos are one and the same people—a race. The implication was unmistakable: If Jews were a race, there could be no such thing as a Jew who "becomes" a Christian.

The boundary between converso and Jew was already crumbling in the public mind, but Alonso de Espina put forth a spectacular effort to erase it entirely in a book titled *Fortalitium Fidei* (Fortress of the Faith),[6] published around 1461. In this work Friar Alonso boldly accused Pablo de Santa María, the most revered converso ecclesiastic in Castile, with reciting prayers against Christians. Santa María denied the charge, but it was written, and the written word prevailed. Espina had struck at the highest and strongest point of the converso edifice in order to bring the entire structure crashing down.

The *Fortalitium Fidei* introduced into Spanish literature a compendium of all the poisoned well and ritual murder stories that had circulated in northern Europe for centuries, and from which Spain had been insulated. The hatred that underscores this work is startling. Jews are diabolical, semimagical creatures whose goal is the destruction of Christians and Christianity. They worship the Antichrist, who is their long-awaited Messiah. Jews are "inhuman." In an enchanted realm somewhere they have multiplied until there are enough of them to populate twenty-four kingdoms.

But conversos are worse. They continue to practice Judaism openly, and there is no one around to put them to death for their crimes. Here the friar reached the heart of his crusade.

Alonso de Espina had produced a medieval alchemy of the true (many conversos did practice Judaism), the false, and the fantastic, all carefully mounted to sway the minds of people who hardly needed to be convinced that Jews and conversos were devils; and his *Fortalitium Fidei* marked a milestone along the road leading to the isolation and demonization of both groups—a psychologically necessary milestone if the general populace was to be properly prepared for the sort of inquisition Espina had in mind. Anticonverso satires abounded, as we have seen, and the peasant classes were trumpeting the purity of their Christian blood, but conversos still lived at the heart of the middle and noble classes. Their degradation would have to be thorough before an institution as violent as the Inquisition would be accepted and approved.

With Espina, the centuries-long campaign of the medieval Catholic Church to destroy religious pluralism in Spain had come full circle. Under the Visigoths, when Church and state were one powerful unity, Jews were similarly accused of scheming to take over the kingdom as well as plotting to destroy the Church and murder Catholics. But during the hundreds of years that separated that far-away time from the present there was strong resistance to this ancient message. A different ethos had held sway. If the riots of 1391 had changed the world for the Jews, the riots in Toledo in 1449 had changed the world for the conversos. By borrowing the one thousand-year-old language of a fourth century archbishop of the early Church, Alonso de Espina successfully introduced a framework for true oppression.

The Inquisition Is Born in Seville

In 1477, Queen Isabella moved her court to Seville, where she presided over matters of law and justice in the magnificent Alcazar of the city (and gave birth, as it happens, to her beloved son, Prince Juan.) But the queen had no sooner left Seville for nearby Cordoba when a Dominican prior named Alonso de Hojeda galloped after her to tell of dark rumors that were circulating in the city. He said that on the night of Good Friday, 1478, a group of Sevillian Jews and conversos had met secretly to perform Jewish rites and ceremonies. No, he couldn't prove it. But everyone knew it was true.

Alonso de Hojeda whispered another terrifying tale. A certain young knight from the illustrious Guzmán family had fallen in love with a Jewish girl. This knight had observed his lover's family and their baptized converso friends insult an image of Christ and—most horrible—"crucify a Christian child."

"Your magnificent Highness, the poison of heresy has infected the whole of Andalusia," warned the priest. "Your Highness *herself* is surrounded by impious conversos."[7]

Alonso de Hojeda called for an inquisition, and he was supported in his demand by two very important men: Pedro González de Mendoza, the cardinal of Spain and archbishop of Seville, and Tomás de Torquemada, a Dominican priest: Torquemada (who was of converso origin) was the prior of the Santa Cruz monastery in Segovia and nephew of the respected cardinal, Juan de Torquemada. This family connection had served Tomás well. He had been confessor to Queen Isabella since her childhood, and was rumored to have extracted a promise from her that if she ever came to the throne she would "devote herself to the extirpation of heresy for the glory of God."[8]

Torquemada was well aware of the influence he carried with the young queen. She trusted, respected and admired the preceptor of her youth.

Unlike Torquemada, Cardinal Mendoza was neither zealot nor fanatic; in fact, he had recently tried to solve the so-called heresy problem with something less punitive. Mendoza thought education might be the answer and had

> ordered all the sacraments of holy doctrine [that] a true Christian must follow all the days of his or her life to be posted in all the churches of [Seville], and ordered the clergy to instruct their parishioners so that everyone could keep them and teach them to their children so they would know that the eternal damnation of their souls and the destruction of their bodies and property would follow if they practiced Judaism.[9]

How well the local clergy followed these orders is hard to gauge. What we do know is that according to Friar Alonso de Hojeda (whose report was certainly not disinterested), Cardinal Mendoza's education initiative "failed."

The king and the queen listened carefully to the three ecclesiastics, but they would make their own choices. There were six hundred thousand to one million conversos in Spain at the time, representing about 7 percent of the total population, and if even a small percentage of these were found to be heretic judaizers, an inquisition would have far-reaching consequences.[10]

Ferdinand was quickly in favor. The king desired the unity of Castile and Aragon (this, after all, had motivated his marriage to Isabella) and he wanted absolute control over every aspect of social, economic and political life in his realm. The centralized authority of an inquisition would speed up the process of consolidating power. Ferdinand of Aragon understood that better than anyone.

The king applied to Pope Sixtus IV in Rome for permission to establish an inquisition, and on November 1, 1478, the pope issued the requisite bull allowing Ferdinand and Isabella to choose priests "of irreproachable virtue" as inquisitors, provided they were over forty years of age. Pope Sixtus IV was not about to stand in the way of Ferdinand's request since an inquisition in Castile would also enhance the power of the papacy. On the other hand, Ferdinand and Isabella were not about to allow Rome to control *their* inquisition, or siphon off the wealth it would appropriate from convicted heretics. The pope did not approve of giving up control of a religious institution, but he could see the benefits of a compromise: the Catholic Church gained advantage merely by agreeing to create an inquisition in Castile.

Permission was in place. But in 1480 Queen Isabella had still not agreed to go ahead. The queen admired and needed her converso advisors, and she had yet to be convinced that an inquisition was necessary. The conversos were lobbying her directly not to bring an inquisition to Castile.

That year the queen held a meeting of the *Cortes* of Castile, in Toledo. The parliament renewed its old rules: Jews were to wear a distinctive badge, live in separate quarters, not practice medicine, trade with Christians, or work as barbers, and so on down the list. In other words, the usual restrictions that were often ignored. Not a word was spoken about conversos or the possibility of an inquisition. Isabella had not made up her mind.

But Ferdinand had made his up years ago, and in September 1480, he succeeded in convincing the queen on the only grounds that would have appealed to her. There were heretics among the converso class and they were sullying the faith.

When the first tribunal of the new Spanish Inquisition opened in Seville in 1481, thousands of conversos fled their homes, jamming the roads of Andalusia, and there were immediate economic repercussions: almost all the merchants and managers of the city were conversos. This was, of course, the outcome Isabella had feared, but she did not back down. Fernando del Pulgar recorded her official response:

> Since the absence of these people depopulated a large part of the country, the Queen was told that commerce was declining; but setting little importance in the decline in her revenues and prizing highly the *limpieza* (purity) of her lands, she said that the important thing was to purify the country of the sin of heresy, for she knew it to be in God's service and her own. . . . And the representations that were made to her on this subject did not change her decision.[11]

Isabella was a true believer, and if false Christians were "corrupting" the Church they had to be weeded out. Regardless of the cost to the country.

From the queen's point of view, heresy was true reason for the Inquisition. All the same, there would be uses for the large amounts of money the Holy Office was certain to expropriate from its prisoners. Pious uses. It can scarcely be thought coincidental that as the first fires burned in Seville, the Christian armies of the king and queen were massing in preparation for the final assault of the Holy Reconquest against the infidel in Granada.

*   *   *

The first inquisitors of the Spanish Inquisition were two simple Dominican monks, Miguel Morillo and Juan de San Martín, each of whom was assigned two associate priests to act as prosecutor and assessor. Their duties began in Seville, home to the wealthiest new Christians in Castile.

At the arrival of the inquisitors, thousands escaped to the estates of the Duke of Medina-Sidonia, the Ponce de León family, and other old Christian nobles with whom they were connected. But the old ways of seeking safety were passé. On January 2, 1481, the inquisitors Morillo and San Martín issued an edict ordering the dukes, marquis, counts, knights, and other grandees of Castile to give up their protected friends within fifteen days under pain of excommunication and the loss of their own rights and privileges. Here was a first sign of exceptional and unusual power. The inquisitors' edict was backed up immediately by Queen Isabella.

Morillo and San Martín ordered the old Christian nobles to bring every converso they were protecting to Seville, and also to seize and inventory the conversos' property. Already the nobility was being transformed into an arm of inquisitorial oppression. How ironic. How ambiguous. For who could tell who was who in the year 1481, almost a century after the forced conversions of 1391 and seventy years after the Disputation of Tortosa? By this time the entire noble class had intermarried with descendants of converted Jews.

The nobility of Andalusia complied, regardless; indeed, the most famous families bowed before the Inquisition in a collective act of obeisance that signaled the true end of their former, rampant power. They walked, or rode to the city with their prisoners, many of whom were their relatives, and as they approached Seville, there must have been much nervous tallying of the degree of "Jewish blood" they carried in their veins.

Soon there were so many captive conversos in Seville that the Inquisition was forced to move to the Triana castle where there was more dungeon space.[12] Inquisitors Morillo and San Martín had the following cryptic message carved on the castle gates: "Arise O Lord and judge thy cause. The fox endangers us."[13]

Having so rapidly established their authority, the inquisitors issued an Edict of Grace: heretics who came forward voluntarily to confess within a period of thirty days would be allowed to repent and be treated mercifully. But if they did not come forward and were denounced by others they would be pursued with the full force of the law. The promised "mercy" did not mean that a man's or a woman's status would be decided privately, however. Public humiliation was an essential tool of inquisitorial control. (In 1483 the rule forbidding a private resolution in cases of voluntary confession was formally spelled out, along with the confirmation that confiscated property was never to be returned.)

After the Edict of Grace was announced, seventeen thousand conversos voluntarily denounced themselves, and only then did they learn what was to be exacted from them in return. The promised absolution was conditional: no one would be released from custody until he or she had informed on every new Christian who had ever prayed over a candle on the Sabbath, entered a synagogue, or practiced any other Jewish rite, or was rumored to have done so.

Hoping to save themselves, frightened individuals "remembered" as many names as they could. Betrayal was made easy; informants were promised total secrecy. Victims of the Inquisition were never told who had denounced them, or for what.

The inquisitors published helpful lists detailing how to identify a heretic.[14] According to their guidelines a heretic was:

- a baptized Christian who is awaiting the Messiah, or says he has not yet come, or that he will come to save his people and deliver them from captivity to the promised land.

- a Christian who says that the religion of Moses is just as likely to save souls as Christianity.

- a Christian who keeps the Jewish sabbath, and wears clean clothes on that day, or puts a white tablecloth on the table, or does not light a fire in the house.

- a Christian who cuts the fat off meat, or bleeds the animal after slaughter while washing it under water, and does not eat certain parts of the animal.

- a Christian who keeps the Jewish fast known as the fast of the pardon, or expiations, or *kippur* which takes place during the Hebrew month of Tisri. One knows this if the person goes barefoot during the fast, as do the true Jews, or if he or she is in the company of Jews at this time, or asks them for forgiveness during that night, or if a father places his hand on the heads of his children without making the sign of the Cross, and if he says, "Be blessed by the Lord and by me."

- a Christian who fasts during the feast of Esther which the Jews observe in memory of their captivity under the reign of Ahasuerus.

- a Christian male who recites certain prayers of the Jews while raising and lowering his head with his face turned toward the wall.

- a Christian who celebrates the feast of unleavened bread, or the feast of the Tabernacles. One can recognize this if the person builds a shelter of green branches in front of the house and exchanges gifts of food with others.

- a Christian who blesses the food at the table in the way of the Jews.

- a Christian woman who has failed to attend church for forty days after giving birth, or has a child who is circumcised.

- a Christian who washes the part of the baby's head that has received the holy baptismal water.

The list was long. An informant had only to remember, and be saved.

The arrests begin. A knock on the door at the still hour of midnight. Scuffling noises, denials, cries for help. The victim is led away. His or her property is scrupulously inventoried. Children are abandoned to the street unless they are taken in by others. No one will see the victim again until the day of his or her sentencing at the auto de fe.

Family members shrink from one another, including from small children who might innocently reveal what has gone on in their homes. Every night when darkness falls parents clasp their children to them and creep from the city, crouched shadowy figures furtively hugging the sides of roads. More than four thousand of them manage to escape to the north of the country or to Portugal, France, and North Africa. Many of the escapees are tried in their absence; some are burned symbolically in effigy. The bones of people who died before the advent of the Inquisition are removed from their graves, put on trial, and similarly burned.

It is all happening so suddenly. The converso community in Seville trembles in shock, and so do their old Christian, Jewish and Moorish neighbors. Something new and terrible has taken place; the world seems to have changed overnight.

The Jews of Spain watched what was happening to their converso relatives in Seville with mounting fear, and in the mystical, allegorical style of the day there were those who claimed that all had been seen and foreseen from the beginning. One hundred years later, the author of the narrative *Shebet Yehuda* claimed that the fate of the conversos was predicted.[15] It is written, he says, that during the first days of the Inquisition Rabbi Judah ibn Verga, a famed astronomer of Seville, placed three pairs of doves in his window. One pair was alive and unplucked. On their necks was a label: "These will be the first to escape." The second pair of doves was plucked, but still alive. Their label said: "These are the middle ones." The last pair of doves was slaughtered and plucked. Their label read: "These are the *anusim* (forced converts) who will be the last to escape."[16]

The Seville inquisitors displayed the full force of their power as early as they could, for effective terror depended on public spectacle. On February 6, 1481, a group of conversos who had governed the city just weeks earlier were led out of the Triana castle dungeons and paraded through the streets. They were unkempt, barefoot, and carried unlighted candles. The penitents wore yellow *sanbenitos,* the Inquisition's cloak of shame: a tunic painted front and back with a large, red cross indicating that these prisoners were absolved and "reconciled" to the Church. ("Reconciled" was not as gentle as it sounds. It could mean prison in perpetuity, public flogging, or being chained to the oars of war galleys for the rest of one's life. Punishment depended entirely on the temper of the inquisitor. Property was confiscated forever, and the "reconciled" and their descendants were forbidden to hold public office and sometimes to practice their trade. Frequently they were commanded to wear the sanbenito for the rest of their lives whenever they left their houses.)

Those who were condemned to death wore black sanbenitos painted on both sides with flames and grotesque devils. They were "released to the secular arm," meaning they were handed over to the secular authorities of the city for their final dispatch. This euphemistic device allowed the Inquisition to suggest it had no direct involvement in the reality of corporal execution. The Holy Office of the Inquisition was a religious institution. Its official purpose was to save souls, not to destroy bodies.

On that February day in 1481, Inquisitors Morillo and San Martín strode proudly at the head of their motley procession carrying high the cross of the Inquisition and looking imposing in the white habit and black cloak of the Dominican order. The prisoners stumbled behind, winding their way through a crowd of silent, intimidated onlookers who lined the narrow streets next to the cathedral where Alonso de Hojeda was preparing to preach the sermon over the condemned. The friar's lifelong dream had finally been realized, as had the dream of his spiritual predecessor, Alonso de Espina. (Ironically, Hojeda would live only a few more days. Plague broke out and he was among the first to die.)

Human beings react to danger in different ways. Some conversos instantly understood the scope of the threat and escaped. Others tried to hide—not an easy task in a medieval town. On the other hand, some powerful individuals simply refused to believe their status had changed so quickly. One of these was Diego Susán, a respected notable of the city and a man so wealthy he was reputed to be worth "ten million maravedis."[17]

As the danger grew, Diego Susán convened a secret meeting of magistrates, clergy, and other prominent conversos, and five hundred years later one can still sense their collective surprise and profoundly wounded egos. An anonymous account of their assembly in the church of San Salvador in Seville has survived: "[There were] many rich and powerful men from the towns of Utrera and Carmona. These said to one another, 'What do you think of them acting thus against us? Are we not the most propertied members of the city, and well loved by the people?' "[18] They decided to collect weapons. If any one of them was arrested the others would murder one of the inquisitors.

The converso majordomo of the cathedral was arrested in one of the first roundups of the new Christian community, and weapons to arm one hundred men were found in his house. The Inquisition did not know their origin, but the plot to murder one of the inquisitors was betrayed—by Diego Susán's own daughter, who was engaged to an old Christian knight of the city. She told her fiancé, and he told the Inquisition. The conspirators were seized, hastily tried, and burned to death on March 26, 1481, at the very next auto de fe.

The psychological fallout from patricide, matricide, or infanticide—a consequence of denouncing one's parent or child—would have been devastating, and the suffering of Diego Susán's daughter suggests the degree of pain that thousands of other family informers likely experienced over the years. The girl entered a convent, but left without taking vows. According to legend she became a street prostitute (although more than a hint of moral rectitude clings to this part of the story and may have been adduced by later chroniclers). When she died she asked that her skull be placed over the door of her house as a warning to others.[19]

Because all the peoples of the Iberian Peninsula felt themselves to be profoundly Castilian, or Aragonese, or "Spanish" (although that collective identity was not yet entrenched), the new reality of official persecution was hard to understand. Diego Susán and his friends were unable to accept that their status had evaporated, even though anticonverso hatred had been growing steadily for thirty years and the Inquisition had already burned its first victims. They felt outrage and disbelief, followed by a profound sense of injustice. The "rules" according to which they had lived and thrived were changing. A groundswell movement to scapegoat them for the ills of the nation had ballooned out of control in the decades since Pero Sarmiento proclaimed his Statutes of Exclusion in Toledo, but in an all too human way they hadn't "noticed," because what was happening didn't correspond with their view of themselves.

They lacked the perspective to see the obvious. A converso was now heretical, gouging, dirty, and traitorous—by definition; after all, the word *marrano* meant pig. A converso was—a Jew.

*   *   *

On November 4, 1481, Sevillians were shocked by a spectacle whose magnitude they could not have imagined. On that one day 298 conversos were paraded through the city and condemned as heretics.

Soon there were so many executions that the municipality was forced to build a massive burning site on a field outside the city: a permanent platform made out of stone and marked at each of its four corners by large plaster statues of Old Testament prophets. The name of the site was simple enough: *Quemadero,* or The Burning Place. It remained there until 1810 when it was torn down to make room for a battery against the army of Napoleon.

The statues were paid for by a new Christian named Señor Mesa who was rewarded for his pious act by being made an official "familiar," or spy, of the Inquisition and receiver of confiscated property. But such desperate, contrived acts were of little help. Before long the unfortunate Señor Mesa was convicted of "judaizing" and burned on the very stage he helped create.[20]

The chronicler Fernando del Pulgar (himself a converso) was appalled by the brutal happenings in Seville, and he did something brave and dangerous: he wrote a carefully worded letter to the archbishop of Seville "about the execution of the conversos."

> I believe, my lord, that there are at least 10,000 young women of from ten to twenty years old in Andalusia, who from their birth have never been absent from their homes, or heard of, or known any other religion than that which they have seen and heard practised under the parental roof. To burn all these would be a most cruel act. . . . [The inquisitors] . . . are very good men; but I know that they with their flames will never make such good Christians as will the Bishops Don Paulo [Pablo] and Don Alonso [of Burgos] with their [baptismal] water.[21]

An anonymous troublemaker did not hesitate to remind people of Pulgar's converso origins and to accuse him of heresy, but Pulgar defended himself successfully and survived to become the official chronicler of the monarchy.

Sevillians whispered to one another that the heretics chosen by the Inquisition were the richest men and women in the city. The receiver must be raking in gold, silver, and jewels, they murmured in carefully lowered voices. And all those magnificent houses! Even the great Fernando del Pulgar had dared suggest the Holy Office might be more interested in wealth than religious purity.

In fact, the confiscations were the unspoken heart of the enterprise, and a look at the uses to which the money was put lends a new dimension to our understanding of the Inquisition. Ferdinand and Isabella divided all appropriated goods into three parts. The first went to the Inquisition. The king and queen ruled that the Holy Office would pay for itself, including capital costs and salaries; not one single *maravedi* would come from the royal purse. A second part of the booty went to the starved royal treasury for the Reconquest wars against the Moors in Granada. A third part was reserved for general religious purposes, and before long, dozens of new churches and monasteries were founded.[22]

By December 1482, two thousand women and men had been burned in Seville, two thousand more had been burned in effigy, and seventeen thousand had been "reconciled" with varying degrees of punishment—and all of their property had been divided into the requisite three parts.[23] Conversos were objects of a nationwide hunt, the focus of an exploding racist consciousness masquerading under the cloak of religion. The metaphor of the doves on the window had come true: most of those who did not escape were still alive, but already plucked.

Fernando del Pulgar had sounded a note of opposition—a courageous and rare occurrence both then and later—but Andrés Bernáldez, the curate of Los Palacios, a town near Seville, undoubtedly spoke for many more people when he described conversos with nose-crinkling distaste.

> I do not wish to write more about this for it is impossible to describe the sickness of this depraved heresy. Except to say that [now that] the fire has been lighted, it will burn to the last stick . . . burn until every judaizer is dead, and [there remains] none over the age of twenty who is touched by that leprosy.[24]

Religion and racism had fused into one. Where once religion, and only religion, had informed the ideals of the Holy Reconquest against the Infidel and the conversion drives of the century, a new element had now been added. Officially, and on the surface of things, the Inquisition was still uniquely concerned with religious matters; however, at a pragmatic level, the Holy Office was supported and underscored by ordinary people who had discovered that blood purity was a potent weapon for use against the middle and upper classes who had intermarried with conversos over the decades. Their hatred of conversos was a convenient prop, a matter of designating a necessary enemy upon whom one could project the woe, despair, and suffering of the age. Hatred of the Other was a way of avoiding a dangerous confrontation with God, who allowed such pain into the world.

By establishing a Holy Inquisition against Depraved Heresy, Ferdinand and Isabella could claim to have initiated a final crusade: the Church's symbolic defeat of the enemy within. Extirpate the worm from the apple and the integrity of the fruit will be restored. The queen was fulfilling her childhood promise to her confessor, Friar Tomás de Torquemada.

With the Inquisition in place under the secular jurisdiction of the monarchy, the Church had finally achieved what it had strived for since the halcyon days of the Visigoths: a religious institution wielding absolute power buttressed by the rulers of the political state.

For their part, the king and queen had created an institution that would carry them further toward their goal of absolute, centralized authority in every realm of life. Law and order had replaced social anarchy, economic disintegration, and moral dissoluteness. Long-suffering Castilians cheered this—and who could blame them? What they were cheering, however, was the advent of Europe's first fascist state, where unity was secured by a strong-armed central authority that was, in turn, tied to *limpieza,* or the "cleansing" of the body politic.

Notes

1. I have found the following general histories particularly useful in the writing of this chapter: H. C. Lea, *A History of the Inquisition of Spain*, 1–4, and *Chapters from the Religious History of Spain*; H. Kamen, *The Spanish Inquisition*, and *Inquisition and Society in Spain*; Juan Antonio Llorente, *Histoire Critique de l'Inquisition d'Espagne*.

2. Until the twentieth century it was widely believed that Espina was a converso, but it is now agreed that his knowledge of Judaism did not come from Jewish, or converso sources.

3. *Fortalitium Fidei*, Prologue, 1461.

4. H. C. Lea, *A History of the Inquisition of Spain*, 1: 152–53.

5. Cited in Dennis Prager and Joseph Telushkin, *Why The Jews?* 94.

6. An English translation of the *Fortalitium Fidei* was provided by T. M. Robinson.

7. H. Kamen, *The Spanish Inquisition*, 43ff.

8. J. Zurita y Castro, *Anales de la Corona de Aragón*, 4, fol. 323.

9. Fernando de Pulgar, *Crónica de los Reyes Católicos*, 136.

10. The 1482 census counted just over nine million people. B. Netanyahu, *The Marranos of Spain from the Late Fourteenth to the Early Sixteenth Century*.

11. Pulgar, *Crónica*, 2, ch.77.

12. The Triana castle remained the seat of the Inquisition in Seville until 1626.

13. Zuñiga, *Anales de Sevilla*, 389.

14. Kamen, *The Spanish Inquisition*, 165.

15. Solomon ibn Verga, *Shebet*.

16. Baer, *A History of the Jews in Christian Spain*, 2: 325.

17. A. Bernáldez, *Memorias del reinado de los Reyes Católicos*, ch. 44.

18. *Relación Histórica de la Judería de Sevilla* (1849), 24–26, cited in Kamen, *The Spanish Inquisition*, 37.

19. J. Amador de los Rios, *Historia de los Judíos en España y Portugal*, 3: 247–48, cited in Lea, *A History of the Inquisition in Spain*, 163, note 1.

20. Lea, *A History*, 1 and 4: 164, note 1.

21. Pulgar, *Crónica* cited in W. Walsh, *Isabella of Spain*, prologue, and A. Castro y Rossi, *History of Religious Intolerance in Spain*, 17ff. Pulgar is referring here to Pablo de Santa María and his son Alonso, Pablo's successor as Bishop of Burgos. It is likely that he chose the example of young women since, being homebound, their innocence is easily demonstrated.

22. Kamen, *The Spanish Inquisition*, 151.

23. J. de Mariana, cited in Juan Antonio Llorente, *Histoire Critique de l'Inquisition d'Espagne*, 239.

24. Bernáldez, *Memorias*, ch. 44.

10

The Grand Inquisitor

The two inquisitors laboring in Seville were accumulating so much incriminating information about conversos all over Castile that it seemed a pity to limit the scope of their work. Ferdinand and Isabella applied again to Rome, and in February 1483, Pope Sixtus IV appointed seven new inquisitors for the cities of Cordoba, Cuidad Real, and Jaen. All were respected men, but the most prominent among them was Queen Isabella's childhood confessor, Tomás de Torquemada. With Espina and Hojeda both dead, the prior of Santa Cruz was the most zealous heretic hunter in Castile.[1]

There have always been people who "express" their names, but Tomás de Torquemada may be the strangest example of this in history. The word *Torquemada* can be loosely translated as twist and burn, which is precisely what Father Tomás did to people. The newly appointed inquisitor was a type of individual known to all times and places, a man of single-minded, obsessive will. When Torquemada took the requisite vows of poverty he did not allow himself a little quiet comfort on the side, as did most of his more indolent contemporaries, but never again ate meat, wore linen next to his body, or slept on anything softer than a board.

The Inquisition had many enemies and Torquemada took no chances. When he traveled from city to city he surrounded himself with a retinue of fifty mounted guards and two hundred foot soldiers; in fact, he was so worried about an attempt on his life that he reputedly kept a "unicorn's horn" on his table which he used to detect the presence of poison in his food.

One can infer something of Torquemada's narrow emotional horizons from his cruel treatment of his only sister, who was entirely dependent on him. Because he chose a rigid, ascetic life she, too, was penniless.

Unable to marry without a dowry, she was forced to enter a nunnery in order to eat and be clothed.

Although he was himself of converso origin, Torquemada was the first to introduce blood-purity laws into a Dominican monastery, his own convent of Santa Cruz. How he managed to exempt his own "tainted blood" has not been recorded, but as in the case of King Ferdinand, one is led to ponder the complex psychology that would push a member of an endangered class to head an inquisition against his own group. The desire to disassociate oneself from a pariah class is a universal, if less than admirable impulse, but another reason looks equally likely: given the atmosphere of suspicion and accusation that swirled around the conversos, including the most influential, there was probably no better way to avoid being investigated than to call for and supervise the investigation.

Torquemada seems to have been independently cruel, and this aspect of his character set the tone for the Inquisition and was uniquely emphasized for centuries—largely by Protestant writers who created the so-called Black Legend of the Spanish Inquisition.[2] But it is also worth noting that later on, in his role as Inquisitor-General, Torquemada emerged as a consummate bureaucrat, an administrator, and a cog (albeit an important one) in the wheel of a public institution: the Holy Office of the Inquisition. In a pre-echo of contemporary dictatorships, Torquemada structured a faceless, abstract bureaucracy where the reality of death at the stake was easily forgotten in the myriad details of efficient organization. The Inquisitor-General had a policing job to do and he did it dutifully. In spite of his enormous personal power, he was a man who had superiors to report to—a man who could claim to be merely a part of the larger whole.

Little is known about Torquemada's background except that he was born in Valladolid into a converso family that gained renown during the first half of the fourteenth century, almost certainly as Jews, and that he was the son of Pero Fernandez de Torquemada, the brother of Cardinal Juan de Torquemada. Like his learned uncle, young Tomás became a Dominican priest, and a brilliant one by all accounts. He was elected prior of the Santa Cruz monastery in Segovia in 1455 and his reputation for learning and sanctity coupled with his family connections led to his appointment as confessor to the young Princess Isabella.

In attempting to understand Torquemada at a distance of five hundred years it is worth remembering the circumstances of his early life. Torquemada was born in 1420 just as Juan II acceded to the throne of Castile, and he was fifty-four years old when Isabella was crowned queen; in other words, the anarchy that characterized those decades encompassed his entire experience until well into midlife.

Like his contemporaries, he was subject to potent symbols of prophecy, and as a high-ranking member of the clergy he would have led the procession of frightened penitents that threaded through the streets of Segovia after a tiny child predicted there would be no end to anarchy until Christians did penance. Torquemada knew that only sin could have caused the apparent dissolution of his country—the sum of public and private sin; and when Isabella, the woman whose spiritual values he had helped to shape, was crowned queen, he would have rejoiced in the hope that a return to the ways of God might save Castile. But Torquemada also recognized a matchless opportunity; he had already extended the scope of his influence by becoming spiritual confessor to Ferdinand as well as the queen. From the beginning Torquemada had positioned himself to head the Inquisition that prominent members of the Church had so long desired, and his presence in Cordoba on that day in 1478 when Friar Alonso de Hojeda galloped in breathlessly to inform the queen about the contamination of heretics in the land was certainly no coincidence. As a political strategist, Torquemada rivaled the canny king, Ferdinand.

* * *

The Holy Office of the Inquisition spread muscular tentacles over the vastness of Castile, spewing terror, gathering victims, isolating families and friends from one another, crushing dissent, and instituting the willingness to betray as a condition of survival. But Ferdinand and Isabella weren't entirely happy. They needed to contain this growing power, for it would be absurd to have reformed the clergy and wrested control of the Inquisition from the pope himself if the Dominicans running the Holy Office became more powerful than the crown.

In 1483, the Catholic monarchs created a special body called the Council of the Suprema and General Inquisition with responsibility for all matters connected with heresy. The *Suprema,* as it was called, established a formal hierarchy of command with a special position at its apex—the Inquisitor-General who was appointed by the monarchs and was responsible to them—and six other members, including representatives of the Dominican Order and the Council of Castile. It was a tight unity of Church and State and there was no appeal beyond its jurisdiction—not even to the pope in Rome.

No surprise, Tomás de Torquemada was their preferred candidate for Inquisitor-General. He was their close confidant, and even more importantly, no one was ever likely to uncover a hint of human weakness to discredit him or bring the position into disrepute.

The first modern historian of the Inquisition, Henry Charles Lea, tells a revealing tale. During the 1480s the inquisitors at Medina were considering acquitting several of their prisoners, but knowing the character of the Inquisitor-General they thought they'd be advised to check with him first. Torquemada demanded that they retry the accused, which they did. But when they decided on acquittal once again, the Inquisitor-General flew into a rage. "Burn them all!" he shouted. The victims were rearrested and tried in another district by different inquisitors. Their fate is unknown, but not hard to predict.[3]

Torquemada drew up a list of twenty-eight instructions for the Holy Office, most of which were based on the procedures of the moribund papal Inquisition. Each tribunal was assigned two or three inquisitors, depending on its size, plus an assessor of confiscated property, a prosecutor, and an *alguacil,* or bailiff who was the arresting officer. When a man or woman was apprehended, the alguacil and the assessor were both required to be present, the alguacil to serve notice of arrest and physically remove the individual, the assessor to notarize every item of property down to the last cooking pot. These jobs were well remunerated, indicating their importance. By 1498 both posts commanded the same salary as inquisitors.[4]

The "notary of the secret" took verbatim notes during interrogations. He recorded the exact time a prisoner left his or her cell and returned, and kept track of the cost of the food he or she consumed. (In the early years wealthy people paid for their food from their own, confiscated money while the poor were fed "at the wish of the Inquisition and when it was possible."[5] This unequal practice provoked predictable anger in the jails, and it was eventually decided that everyone would eat the same amount to a limit of twenty-six maravedis a day.)

Inquisitors were assisted by lay servants of the Inquisition called *familiars*—one for every two hundred citizens. Familiars were dreaded, and for good reason. They spied on friends and families, informed, and denounced. Castilians were appalled when they realized "they were deprived of the liberty to hear and talk freely, since in all the cities, towns and villages there were persons placed to give information of what went on."[6] Familiars were the concierge network of an earlier era, an information web of strategically placed men and women with solid roots in the community. Through them the Holy Office reached into the very heart of the community and controlled society from the bottom up.

Familiars were allowed to carry arms, a privilege which gave them instant power over everyone else. They were entitled to so many perks that to serve the Inquisition soon became an honor and Old Christians vied with each other for the distinction.

From the beginning the expropriation of property assumed the highest priority, and the amount of money confiscated was astronomical by any standard. Within no time at all, Ferdinand and Isabella had amassed ten million ducats for Grenada wars; (at the end of the century one ducat could buy a full 185 litres of wine, or 220 kilos of bread).[7] The Inquisition funded itself handsomely. Torquemada took to living in castles—for reasons of security, he explained—and the Spanish Church built lasting monuments. In Avila, Torquemada founded the Dominican monastery of Santo Tomás where the royal emblem of Ferdinand and Isabella—the yoke and the bundled arrows—still adorns every decorative motif. The Catholic monarchs used the Santo Tomás monastery as a summer residence, and in their private cloister gilded pomegranates—*granadas* in Spanish—still hang from the ceiling symbolizing their determination to win the final Reconquest war, in Granada. As a further measure of Torquemada's high standing Prince Juan, who died in 1497 at the age of nineteen, was buried in the monastery church.

The monastery of Santo Tomás was also the seat of the Inquisition for the city of Avila. As Inquisitor-General, Torquemada had been careful to attach prison cells and a torture chamber, to his building plans.

*　*　*

Pre-nineteenth century tyrants did not need Freud to discover the power of conditioning minds; attitude-shaping has always been a top priority of those who wield absolute power. The Inquisition was no exception, and from its earliest days, Castilians were taught to recognize a heretic.

Reading the records of the Holy Office, one is continuously struck by the crushing banality of the designated "criminal" behavior. A man or a woman might be denounced for wearing clean clothes at the end of a week, since this was a certain sign he or she was preparing for the sabbath. One woman was reported to the Inquisition for seeming to smile when she heard the name of the Virgin Mary.[8]

Hundreds of pairs of eyes peered through windows, trained ears listened behind doors. Soon the reality of what constituted "guilt" was blurred and amorphous. Was one guilty for committing an act, for thinking a thought, for a word heard (or misheard) in the street? Conversos were seized with terror and some of them openly blamed the queen.

"All the evils that have befallen us are the fault of women, and that cheap whore, the Queen, is the cause of our going about as exiles in the world," wrote one Franciscus Gerrett with typical fifteenth-century misogyny coupled with hatred for Isabella.[9] Others shot frightened, backward looks at long-gone parents, grandparents, and great-grandparents whose Christianity now appeared tainted on inspection—as tainted as their own "Jewish" blood. The overwhelming imperative was survival.

Escape was no longer possible. Better to make oneself useful to the oppressor, to prove one's loyal commitment to religious orthodoxy by pointing a finger at others, heart pounding, palms sweating, voice strangled with fear: no, don't take me, take her, take *her.* Better to accuse oneself before being denounced by another. Yes, accuse oneself, assume the guilt, shed the burden, hope for mercy.

Pious Christians denounced themselves. In the old days when their Jewish neighbors were well tolerated they had bought kosher meat and joined them at weddings and funerals. Now they worried about being accused of heresy for activities that took place twenty-five and thirty years prior, and preempted the investigation.

A collective hysteria shook Castile and no one was exempt. Old Christians were threatened with excommunication if they refused to inform on their converso neighbors. Unfortunately, this intimidation was often unnecessary. Many people were happy to discover an unlooked-for opportunity to settle old scores.

Torquemada deliberately intensified the atmosphere of suspicion and hatred that was poisoning Castile, for without general approval for the oppression of conversos, the Inquisition might fail to gain the necessary level of support. In addition to the volume of anticonverso literature that was already in wide circulation, he personally authorized the writing of two specific tracts, both of which attacked the Christian identity of conversos and turned them into "Jews."

The first of these was an attack on presumed heresies in the Talmud and the preface, written by Friar Fernando de Santo Domingo, was dedicated to Torquemada in the words of Jeremiah 1.10: "See, I have this day set thee over the nations and over the kingdoms, to root out and to pull down, to destroy and to overthrow, to build and to plant." The friar's homage left little doubt about the goals of Torquemada's Inquisition.

Friar Fernando hoped the booklet would convince liberal-minded doubters of the Inquisition that men and women who clung to the old Jewish practices were not simply mistaken, or perhaps atavistic in their habits, but heretics through and through. And since all the laws of the Talmud contain heresies from the Christian point of view, conversos who observe the laws of the Talmud must die.

The second tract Torquemada commissioned was a no-holds-barred satire that became an instant hit.[10] An earlier variation on the theme, written soon after the 1449 riots in Toledo, had described the "privilege" of being a converso, or marrano. In this latest attack, conversos are likened to the Alborak, the legendary steed that reputedly carried Muhammad to heaven. (That Muhammad's steed was the preferred metaphor of a Catholic priest in an attack on converted Jews is further proof of a truly pluralist society in which cultural references had lost their particularity. The presence of Hebrew words in contemporary anticonverso literature spelled out the same message.)

The author's arguments are superficially comical from a modern perspective, but beneath the skin of their fifteenth-century-specific content, the anti-Semitism is disturbingly familiar. The legendary *alborayco* turns out to be part horse, part mule—like the hypocrite conversos who are neither Jew nor Christian. High-bred horses are known for their ability to spill blood in battle; so converso *alboraycos* are killers of prophets, apostles and martyrs, for *they* spilled the blood of Christ. Conversos are unfit for real work and hang around the royal court cheating Gentiles. They are bad priests because they are heretics, bad soldiers because they are dishonest, and bad laborers because they are lazy. They spread heresy the way snakes spread venom. Although the true Messiah already came to earth, they pretend he will come to Seville or Lisbon in the person of a rich knight riding in a golden chariot.[11] They help the infidel Turk destroy Christians (the Turks had taken Constantinople in 1453, and were an ongoing threat to Christian Europe). Conversos return to the religion of Judaism: to circumcision, to the sabbath, to eating *adefina*—like a dog returning to eat its excrement. They are like cranes; if one is touched all the others cry "gru, gru!" They are as vain as peacocks, but however rich they may be, they have only to look at their feet (to see their humble origin). Among Christians they say, "We are Christians." Among Jews they say, "We are Jews." They invented sodomy. Like Muhammad's horse, they trample Christians underfoot and enslave them.

Though anonymous, this polemic is known to have been written by someone connected to Torquemada's monastery of Santa Cruz. Its transparent and only purpose was to eliminate public sympathy and heat the fires of the Inquisition.

Implicating the Jews

In 1485, the inquisitors in Toledo called a meeting of all district rabbis. On pain of death they forced the rabbis to report all conversos of their acquaintance who were practicing Jewish rites, and to excommunicate and pronounce a ban—a rabbinical curse—on any Jew in their congregation who did not do the same. Inquisitors all over the country subsequently held similar meetings, tightening the vise on both converso and Jew. Conversos had confided their doubts about Christianity to Jewish friends and relatives. The Jewish community had been their refuge.

Unconverted Jews had been relatively safe, since a "heretic" could only be a faithless, baptized Christian; but now the Inquisition was extending its tentacles into the Jewish world as well. Some Jews defied the ban at their peril, but others hated the wealthy conversos whom they considered traitors to Judaism and were happy to inform on them. The Inquisition was well aware of long-standing conflicts between the worldly and the orthodox in the Jewish communities of Spain, and of tensions between Jews and conversos. The decision to put pressure on the Jews by exploiting these divisions was a careful strategy.

The Jews were of interest to the Inquisition for yet another reason; Torquemada was convinced that their presence in Spain was inimical to Christian purity. The Jews, he said, were slyly seducing conversos from established Christian families back into the fold. The prospect of expelling the troublemaking Jews in order to check the spread of heresy among conversos was already much in the air. In 1483 (the year Torquemada became Inquisitor-General) the Inquisition had succeeded in chasing the Jews out of the southern region of Andalusia. Many had fled next door to the last Arab kingdom of Granada, where they were allowed to practice freely.

As the pressure on their communities increased, a powerful revival of messianism seized the Jews. In Jewish eschatology the Messiah will arrive at the end of days, after a period of anguish known as "the birth pangs of the messianic age." Given the trials they were forced to endure, could anyone doubt that the Messiah would make his presence felt momentarily? An anonymous being in the Muslim east was rumored to be the Messiah. He was called, simply, "the Turk," and the Jews believed he would soon come riding into Seville in a golden chariot. In their vigil they were joined by thousands of hunted conversos, for if new Christians had once been relatively indifferent to Judaism, their suffering now propelled them to seek comfort in the faith of their ancestors. The very terror of the Inquisition was creating "heretics."

It is not surprising that the beleaguered Jews and conversos of Castile looked to the Muslim world for refuge, for the Moors of Spain had created a society in which they had thrived. On the other hand the Ottoman Turks were building an empire, and Christian crusader armies had failed to check their fast expansion. The Turks had conquered fabled Constantinople in 1453. By 1468 they had extended their territory to the Euphrates River, and appeared unstoppable. The Jews' naive faith in a *Turkish* savior only served to alienate them even further from Christian Spanish society.[12]

Torquemada's Fanaticism

Nothing angered the Inquisitor-General more than the presence of converso priests within the Spanish Church, but the powerful bishops, whom he hated most, were out of his grasp. They could only be tried by the ecclesiastical court in Rome. However, converso clergy at the lower levels of the Church hierarchy were easy targets.

The trials of several priests from the Order of San Jerónimo expose the typical range of charges that were levelled against converso clergy.[13] One monk was charged with having chosen to become confessor to converso parishioners in order to learn about Judaism from them, of donating some of the monastery's oil to a local synagogue, and of having received a Hebrew book as a gift. Even more seriously he was accused of declaring that whatever he knew about God he knew through reason, not faith; and that Christianity was "a belief in idols and holy pictures [presided over by] Mary, who was a Jewess, and Christ who was circumcised."

Another monk from the same order was indicted for avoiding making the sign of the cross, refusing to eat pork, and for eating eggs and meat during Lent. Furthermore, his congregants claimed that during Mass he always raised the Host upside down. The priest did not deny this apparent aberration. "God is on every side," he explained disingenuously. (During the trial he reported that his eyesight was bad and he hadn't noticed that the Host was upside down.)

In another trial a certain Pedro Fernández de Alcaudete, chief treasurer of the Cordoba cathedral, was accused of succumbing to the devil and stuffing a consecrated host in his shoe so he could "continually step on Jesus Christ, for he was His secret enemy."[14] One day as Pedro went to the cathedral his foot began to bleed, recounted the prosecution for the Inquisition. His colleagues noticed this and accompanied him to his home, thinking he had a wound, and when the blood increased they forcibly pulled off his shoe. There they discovered a bleeding host. The awful truth now lay naked and exposed.

Under torture, Pedro confessed that he had deliberately desecrated the consecrated host. The outcome of his trial was not in doubt: "The treasurer was burned alive in the Field of Truth," recorded the trial scribe dutifully.

Whenever possible, the Inquisition memorialized its successes. In this case the cathedral of Cordoba engraved the entire story on a stone, "and displayed the shoe of the said Jew."[15]

The trial of poor Padre Pedro indicates that the earlier, seminal work of Alonso de Espina was bearing fruit. The *Fortalitium Fidei* had introduced northern European myths about demon Jews intent on destroying Christianity into Spain. In the trial of Padre Pedro, the theory of the devil Jew-Converso was "proved" true.

* * *

The date is February 12, 1486—five years after the first converso-heretics were lashed to the stake and burned in Seville. The place is Toledo, the ancient heart of the nation: Toledo, the center of Jewish culture for centuries, and later the center of converso life. The first rebellion against the converts and their descendants took place here in 1449, marking the beginning of the blood purity fetish that is currently obsessing the entire country. The inquisitors have been receiving thousands of denunciations and arresting thousands of people. It is time for a show of force.

An eyewitness left an account of seven hundred and fifty "judaizing heretics" who were processed by the Inquisition on this day, one after the other, in a spectacular display. The writer's matter-of-fact description highlights the disgrace and shame of men and women who had been among Toledo's most prominent citizens.

> They went in procession from the church of St. Peter Martyr in the following way. The men were all together in a group, bareheaded and unshod, and since it was extremely cold they were told to wear soles under their feet which were otherwise bare; in their hands were unlit candles. The women were together in a group, their heads uncovered and their faces bare, unshod like the men and with candles. Among all these were many prominent men in high office. Along with the bitter cold and the dishonor and disgrace, they suffered from the great number of spectators (since a great many people had come from outlying districts to see them), [and] they went along howling loudly and weeping and tearing out their hair, no doubt more for the dishonor they were suffering than for any offense they had committed against God. Thus they went in tribulation through the streets along which the Corpus Christi procession goes until they came to the cathedral. At the door of the church were two priests who made the sign of the cross on each one's forehead, saying, "Receive the sign of the cross which you denied and lost through being deceived." Then . . . they arrived at a scaffolding erected by the New Gate, and on it were the father inquisitors. Nearby was another scaffolding on which stood an altar at which they said mass and delivered a sermon. After this a notary stood up and began to call each one by name, saying "Is x here?" The penitent raised his candle and said, "Yes." There in public they read all the things in which he had judaized. The same was done for the women. When this was over they were publicly allotted penance and ordered to go in procession for six Fridays, disciplining their body with scourges of hempcord, barebacked, unshod, and bareheaded; and they were to fast for those six Fridays. It was also ordered that all the days of their life

they were to hold no public office such as alcade, alguacil, regidor or jurado, or be public scribes or messengers, and that those who held these offices were to lose them. And that they were not to become moneychangers, shopkeepers, or grocers or hold any official post whatsoever. And they were not to wear silk or scarlet or colored cloths or gold or silver or pearls or coral or any jewels. Nor could they stand as witnesses. And they were ordered that if they relapsed, that is if they fell into the same error again, and resorted to any of the forementioned things, they would be condemned to the fire.[16]

The scaffolding at New Gate was just steps away from the church where Friar Vicente Ferrer had preached for the baptism of the Jews of Toledo eighty-one years before. This auto de fe, supreme and final, was the ironic fruit of his crusade.

Notes

1. Sources on Torquemada and his family include U. R. Burke, *A History of Spain*; Juan Antonio Llorente, *Histoire Critique de l'Inquisition d'Espagne*; *Historia de la Iglesia en España*, 1980; Fernando de Pulgar, *Claros Varones de Castilla*, ed. by J. Domínguez Bordona (1954).

2. Historical writing about the Inquisition was, for centuries, exclusively polemical. Juan Antonio de Llorente, the eighteenth-century inquisitor, was the first person to write a negative account of the Holy Office—from the safety of France. In a lecture delivered in Madrid in 1811, Father Llorente said, "You will hardly find a book printed in Spain from the time of Charles the Fifth to our days in which the Inquisition is not cited with praise."

3. H. C. Lea, *A History of the Inquisition of Spain*, 1: 175.

4. José Martinez Millan, *La Hacienda de la Inquisición, 1478–1700*, ch. 2.

5. Ibid., 283.

6. Juan de Mariana, *The General History of Spain*.

7. H. Kamen, *The Spanish Inquisition*, 147.

8. Ibid., 164.

9. Quoted in M. de Bofarull, *Colección de documentos inéditos del archivo general de la Corona de Aragon*, 28, cited in Baer, *A History of the Jews in Christian Spain*, 2: 500, note 66.

10. For a summary of this tract see Isidore Loeb, "Polémicistes chrétiens et juifs en France et en Espagne," *REJ* 18 (1889): 1–34. See also Baer, *A History of the Jews*, 2: 394ff.

11. This corresponded to the current messianic vision of "The Turk."

12. By the mid-sixteenth century the Turks had conquered almost all of the Balkans, which accounts for the contemporary presence of Muslims in that part of the world.

13. H. Beinart, "The Judaizing Movement in the Order of San Jerónimo in Castile," *Studies in History, Scripta Hierosolymitana 7* (1961).

14. Cited in Rafael Gracia Boix, *Autos de Fe y Causas de la Inquisición de Cordoba*, 2.

15. Ibid.

16. Fidel Fita, *La Inquisición Toledana* (1887), cited in Kamen, *The Spanish Inquisition*, 188–89, and Lea, *A History of the Inquisition*, 169–70.
Over the years the auto de fe was transformed from a vehicle for inspiring terror into an exciting public spectacle reminiscent of a Roman circus. The stated purpose of the auto continued to be the extirpation of heresy, but eventually autos de fe were mounted to celebrate official occasions of a general nature and cost millions of maravedis each. In 1665, an auto de fe held in Cordoba cost 2,038,610 maravedis. The breakdown of expenses is revealing: 479,000 mar-

avedis for imported wood to construct the platforms and dais, 273,326 maravedis to build comfortable chairs and couches for dignitaries, 103,258 maravedis for a sumptuous banquet for inquisitors and other functionaries. As for the prisoners, the cost of their food on that most auspicious day of their lives also made the notary's list: 49,989 maravedis. So did the cost of the *leña* (kindling) with which they were burned to death as part of the spectacle: 1,020 maravedis. Martinez Millan, *La Hacienda de la Inquisición*, 288–89, 306.

11

Murder in the Cathedral

It was May 1484, and a white-hot sun scorched the desert plains of Aragon. From the walls of the city of Teruel, guards watched a retinue of men approach slowly on horseback. Two of them were dressed in long clerical robes; the rest seemed to be retainers.[1]

The guards alerted the city councilmen who had been waiting for this moment. The priests on horseback were known to them; they were inquisitors appointed to Teruel by Tomás de Torquemada, Inquisitor-General of the Holy Office, and it was common knowledge that they had been ordered to stay in Teruel until every abominable heretic was arrested and brought to trial.

The city fathers—both old Christians and new—had prepared themselves to resist this flagrant assault on their independence. Torquemada was a foreigner, from Castile, and they did not like foreigners, especially those who were apparently licensed to impose frightening new laws that were not of their making. A Castilian daring to exercise power in Aragon? Daring to appoint deputies? Even the king himself was obliged to be resident in Aragon before he could appoint government officials to represent him. The confiscation of wealth was just as new and just as shocking. Was not property ownership the basic right of the kingdom?

For hundreds of years the proud feudal lords of Aragon had only nominally accepted the authority of their king, and when they deigned to pledge allegiance they did so with the following oath: "We who are as just as worthy as you make you our King and Lord on condition that you preserve our laws and freedoms; and if you do not, we do not!"[2]

The notables of Teruel lined up behind the gates of their city, and when the inquisitors, Juan Colivera and Martín Navarro, arrived in a cloud of road dust, they bluntly refused them entry. Enraged, the priests retreated to the nearby village of Cella where they plotted what to do next. Inquisitors were not to be humiliated.

They retaliated. Each and every Teruel notable was excommunicated, and each and every citizen of the city was prohibited from receiving church sacraments. Second, the inquisitors promised the local peasantry that upon payment of a small sum to the coffers of the Holy Office, anyone who owed money to a soon-to-be-designated Teruel heretic would instantly be freed from his debt. The peasants of Aragon owed large sums in tax arrears. They were, of course, delighted.

The wealthier citizens of Teruel went straight to the papal appeal court, where they greased the appropriate palms and obtained a reversal of the inquisitors' edicts. But in this war of nerves the inquisitors held the heavy ammunition. They had the support of King Ferdinand. His royal backing had permitted the new Inquisition of Castile to enter Aragon in the first place.

Still issuing edicts from their perch in Cella, the inquisitors announced on October 2, 1484 that all positions and appointments in Teruel had reverted to the Crown, and that the people who held these offices were fired. Ferdinand backed them in their decree and ordered the nobles of Aragon to assault the rebellious city, arrest the inhabitants, seize their property, and hand the criminals over to the inquisitors for punishment. Anyone who refused this order would be fined twenty thousand gold florins and dismissed from whatever office he held.

Some refused, citing this unheard-of breach of their historic and constitutional rights, but Ferdinand's army attacked in April 1485, under the leadership of Juan Garcez de Marcilla. It was an unequal battle. Before the month was over the inquisitors had entered Teruel in triumph.

A cold fear crept into the heart of the city. Juan Garcez de Marcilla was appointed governor with absolute dictatorial powers and he arrested or banished everyone the inquisitors pointed at. The governor's fanaticism knew no bounds. Before 1485 had drawn to a close his converso wife, Brianda de Santángel, her brother, and her sister were arrested, tried, and convicted of heresy from his own evidence.

Some two hundred miles away over mountain range and dusty plain the nobles of Saragossa watched what was happening in Teruel with growing unease. Saragossa was the capital of Aragon; individuals from its famous converso families—the Caballerías, Sánchezes, and the Santángels, among others—held the five most important administrative posts in the kingdom, while other new Christian notables occupied at least half of the remaining senior positions. The Caballería family alone could boast Alfonso de la Caballería, vice-chancellor of the kingdom of Aragon and political counselor to Ferdinand and Isabella; an admiral; a top administrator at the University of Saragossa; several clergy in high positions, and a treasurer of the kingdom of Navarre.[3] Gabriel Sánchez was treasurer-general to Ferdinand and Isabella, the most powerful financial post in Spain. Luis de Santángel was chief comptroller in the king's court, and Jaime de Montesa was chief accounting officer of Aragon.

The converso nobility of Saragossa did not have long to wait before the Inquisition also reached their city. Torquemada appointed two inquisitors for the city: Gaspar Juglar and Pedro de Arbués alias Pedro de Epila, a canon of the Seo cathedral. Within days of their arrival, a full inquisitorial court was in place.

Terror insinuated itself into the sumptuous, private palaces that lined the streets of Saragossa. Men and women eyed one another, their servants and their neighbors with trepidation, for it was rumored that Inquisitor Pedro de Arbués was paying for information and hiring dozens of local *familiars* to spy. There was also the Edict of Grace to worry about, that brief time span during which one might reveal all one knew about secret Jewish practices (one's own or other people's) and have one's own punishment mitigated. The time for decision was short, and few could be trusted.

Arbués and Juglar wasted no time arresting and convicting their first prisoners; just six days after their appointment in May 1494, they held their first auto de fe in the Seo cathedral. Four people—a married couple and two women—were led into the street barefoot, wearing the penitent's yellow robe of shame. One was convicted of eating meat on Fridays and during Lent; another was condemned for fasting on the Jewish holy day of Yom Kippur. All four were "reconciled" to the church. Their property was confiscated, they and their descendants were forbidden to hold public office, and they were ordered to wear the robe whenever they appeared out of doors.

On June 3, 1484, a second auto de fe was held in the patio of the archbishop's house next door to the cathedral. *Maestre* Pedro de Arbués officiated, but this time the citizens of Saragossa were exposed to the full terror of the death sentence. Two men and one woman were condemned to the fire, the woman for giving clothes to "twelve poor Jews in honor of the twelve tribes of Israel." The inquisitors were obliged to produce a symbolic effigy for burning, for the condemned woman was already dead and had been found guilty in her absence. Unfortunately for them, the men were alive. They were convicted of "Jewish practices," but one repented at the last moment and benefited from merciful treatment: he was strangled before being tied to the stake.

The powerful conversos of Saragossa quickly understood that they and their families had become the object of a deadly hunt. If they could not stop the Inquisition legally with the support of the old Christian nobility, they knew they were lost. Old Christians were bound to help, for in this new era of acute racial awareness they, too, were under a threat. What the peasants had claimed was true: the status of old Christians was ambiguous since, as in Castile, almost every noble house in Aragon had intermarried with conversos and now had "tainted blood." Beyond these racial concerns, the Inquisition menaced their traditional constitutional rights. They were going to fight.

Shaken by the arbitrary arrests of dozens of people, the Saragossa notables held meetings during November and December of 1484, hoping to find a way to prevent the Inquisition from entrenching itself in their city. The Aragonese chronicler Zurita observed:

> Those recently converted from Judaism, and many other leaders and gentry, claimed that [the Inquisition] was against the freedoms of the kingdom, because for this offence [heresy] their property was confiscated, and they were not told the names of witnesses who testified against them. As a consequence the conversos had all the kingdom on their side, including persons of the highest estate, both old Christians and gentry.[4]

The noble clans converged on Saragossa from all over Aragon to plan their offensive. Barons came on horseback having rounded up all the military strength they could muster, and so did the widows of powerful knights who had been killed in battle. Their first tactic was well-worn and traditional: bribery and coopting influence. In the latter category the famed converso jurist Jaime de Montesa and a wealthy merchant Juan de Pero Sánchez, brother of the king's treasurer, Gabriel, both tried to arrange quick marriages between their daughters and the sons of Martín de la Raga, an official of the Inquisition whose job it was to assess confiscated property. When this did not work the converso nobility set about to raise funds for an appeal to the king, or to Rome if necessary.

A delegation from Saragossa visited Ferdinand and Isabella in Cordoba. They pleaded, implored, argued legalities, and bribed. There was plenty of reason to think the monarchs would want to see the royal war chest replenished; the war in Granada was well underway. But Ferdinand was unmoved, and wrote a letter making his position perfectly clear.

> [We have] no intention of infringing on the *fueros* [laws], but rather of enforcing their observance. It is not to be imagined that vassals so Catholic as those of Aragon would have demanded, or that monarchs so Catholic would have granted, *fueros* and liberties adverse to faith and favorable to heresy. . . . If there are so few heretics as is now asserted, there should not be such dread of the Inquisition. It [the Inquisition] is not to be impeded

in sequestrating and confiscating and other necessary acts, for be assured that no cause or interest, however great, shall be allowed to interfere with its proceeding in future as it is now.[5]

The notables of Saragossa replied to these fateful words with a dignified, clear, respectful justification of their ancient constitutional rights; and their deeply felt sense of thwarted justice reverberates across the centuries. This letter would be their last communal stand.

> Very high and very powerful Prince, King and Sir:
>
> . . . In response to Your Highness, our intention never has been, nor ever will be other than to aid the Inquisition and its ministers, as much on account of the reverence it displays for God our Father as that which concerns Your Highness. Nevertheless, we believe Your Majesty is not unaware of our responsibilities, and with what great trials and punishments we are bound and obliged to guard and defend the freedoms of this kingdom. We cannot bring about the violation of this freedom either directly or indirectly. . . . Therefore, we humbly beseech Your Majesty to see fit to look upon these kingdoms with merciful eyes and to wish to conserve them in their freedoms, which are their very souls and which have been earned and won from the kings of glorious memory, predecessors of Your Majesty, with such great and notable services and shedding of blood. They (the kingdoms) expect no less from your Highness. Thus, as long as it does not impinge upon our defense of liberty, be assured, Your Highness, that we will aid the inquisitors, provided that the Inquisition follows the laws and liberties of this kingdom canonically and justly. And let God the Father bring you prosperity and long life, Your Royal Majesty, as is desirable; and let us, your humble servants and vassals, know your wishes.
>
> Saragossa, the fifth of January 1485.[6]

To everyone's dismay, all entreaties failed.

Ferdinand was not likely to be moved by the delegations from Aragon and their arguments for justice, legality, or loyalty; and even less by their pleading. He was certainly not interested in preserving the historical rights of the Aragonese nobility. On the contrary, in order to centralize authority and unite the kingdoms of Castile and Aragon as he and Isabella desired, he needed to *reduce* their power, and the Inquisition was a means to this end. The struggle against the entry of the Holy Office into Aragon was lost before it began. The Aragonese nobility knew their importance; they were infused with the history of their families and their influence. Their eyes dimmed by feudal tradition, the nobility were unable to calculate the extent of change. A new era had opened without their noticing.

*   *   *

A private meeting was held in the palatial home of Jaime de Montesa with its tiled, inner courtyards, overhanging balconies, fountains, flowers, and high-ceilinged rooms. Montesa, a renowned jurist, was close to seventy. During the 1460s he had been the representative of the chief justice of Aragon (the municipal records of Saragossa indicate that in 1466 he conducted an arbitration for which he was paid "two pairs of partridges"),[7] and in 1485 he was the chief justice for the city council of Saragossa, among his other public duties.

Montesa was privately distressed. Rumor had reached him that the inquisitors had commissioned private testimony about his secret Jewish practices from a young man who had had a liaison with one of the servants in his household. Friends had begged this man to retract his accusation, but he had refused. Montesa was smart enough to know that unless something drastic happened he was finished.

About thirteen richly dressed men gathered at Jaime de Montesa's home, including some of the most famous names in the kingdom. Sancho de Paternoy was the chief financial officer for all of Aragon, and the son of an illustrious converso family. Juan de Pedro Sánchez, Alonso Sánchez and Guillén Sánchez were all brothers of Gabriel Sánchez, treasurer to Ferdinand and Isabella. Luis de Santángel had been knighted twenty years earlier by Ferdinand's father, King Juan II of Aragon, for his wartime services, and he was known to be as good a jurist as he was a soldier. Santángel had strong court connections as well: his daughter was married to Gabriel Sánchez, and his illustrious cousin, also named Luis de Santángel, was chief comptroller for the king and queen.

Martín de Santángel was another member of the famous family. Beside him stood Francisco de Santa Fe, legal advisor to the governor of Aragon. Francisco was the grandson of Jerónimo de Santa Fe, the brilliant convert who had debated against the Jews on behalf of Pope Benedict XIII at the famous Disputation of Tortosa in 1414.

This meeting of desperate men was the outcome of the conversion of the Jews so passionately fought for by Jerónimo, Benedict, and Vicente Ferrer a half-century earlier. They and their contemporaries assumed, among other things, that a simple change of religion would relieve the social problems that had resulted in nationwide pogroms in 1391. But those problems had had nothing to do with religion as such; they were born of envy, disorder in government, and the sort of group cohesiveness that encourages majorities to scapegoat minorities living in their midst. A few drops of baptismal water had changed none of these underlying conditions.

The men gathered in Jaime de Montesa's study that evening were all openly frightened. Every legal avenue had failed. Sancho de Paternoy whispered he had heard that the notary for the Inquisition, Juan de Anchias, had asked a Jewish tailor whether he, Paternoy, had a seat in the synagogue. If a man with the stature of Paternoy was being secretly investigated none of them was safe.

They exchanged stories. A well-to-do tanner named Salvador Esperandeu had been arrested and was languishing in an Inquisition cell. There had been no public charges, of course; his family was not allowed to visit, and no one knew how long he would be in prison, or if he would ever be released. Esperandeu's house, his business, and everything he owned had been seized. Leonardo Eli also had been arrested, and Eli was known to be a sincere and faithful Christian. They were all quietly worried about their mothers, wives, and daughters. More women than men were involved in secret Judaism, and servants had intimate knowledge of their activities.

We must fight harder, raise more money, they said. Each man made a contribution to cover expenses for more petitions to the king. Montesa, Gaspar de Santa Cruz, and Juan de Pedro Sánchez agreed to solicit funds from converso communities in other places.

They met again several weeks later, this time at the home of Luis de Santángel. The Inquisition was taking root so quickly and the bribes, letters, petitions, and delegations were turning out be useless. Several among them had actually tried to threaten the jailer of Leonardo Eli, but Ferdinand had learned of this and condemned "certain evil persons" who were attempting to interfere with the activities of the Inquisition.[8] Many more people were being arrested in surprise night strikes. What had happened to Salvador Esperandeu and Leonardo Eli could happen to any one of them—at any moment.

They were overwhelmed by the precariousness of their situation, and who could blame them? For almost a century their illustrious families had built wealth and prestige under successive monarchs of Aragon. They and their Jewish ancestors had been financiers, ambassadors, astronomers, doctors, jurists and translators. As conversos they served the Church among the highest ranks of the clergy. They had raised money for the Reconquest wars and collected taxes for the king. Now they were under mortal attack as heretics, for being less than orthodox in their Christianity at a time when orthodoxy was the only measure of a life.

Suddenly García de Moros stood up. "It seems that we can do nothing more," he told his friends. "Our only chance is to kill one of the inquisitors, or two, or even three. Then others will be afraid to take the job and the Inquisition in Saragossa will be forced to close down."[9]

A shocked silence followed. Then Jaime de Montesa rose to his feet: "Praise God, what you say is right. If we do this other inquisitors will stay away. None of us will miss one or two hundred florins to pay someone to do it for us."

They all agreed, reluctantly, saying they had no choice. But there was much to think about, much to arrange. The victims they had in mind were Pedro de Arbués, Martín de la Raga, and Pedro Frances. Should they murder one, two, or all three? That would have to be decided. Juan de Pedro Sánchez agreed to take on the job of hiring an assassin because he was an experienced merchant who could negotiate a contract. Jaime de Montesa said he would help, and so did Guillén Sánchez and Luis de Santángel, both of whom were well known as swordsmen.

There was nothing more to say; the fateful meeting had come to an end. In the luxurious surroundings of Luis de Santángels's family palace, dressed in the rich velvets and brocades of their class, these dozen powerful, hunted men stood alone and swore each other to secrecy.

Over the next months the conspirators conferred often in various houses and in three of the major churches of Saragossa: the Temple, Santa Engracia and Nuestra Señora del Portillo. They met under the cover of night, but according to the *Libro Verde de Aragon* (The Green Book of Aragon), written in 1507, it was "public knowledge that they were plotting against the Inquisition and threatening the Inquisitors."[10] In a tiny community like late fifteenth century Saragossa, it would have been impossible to conceal the fact that something was going on, even if no one knew exactly what; in fact, the conspirators were observed in deep conversation by many people on many occasions.

Juan de Pero Sánchez made the necessary arrangements and hired a chief assassin—the tanner Juan Esperandeu. Esperandeu was not a professional murderer, nor was he especially interested in the money Pero Sánchez offered him. He only wanted to rescue his father, Salvador. Esperandeu also persuaded Juan de Labadía, a nobleman of converso background, to join the plot and in April 1485 they made their first attempt to murder an inquisitor. The plan was to throw Martín de la Raga into the Ebro River while he was taking his daily walk along the quay, but on the day in question Raga just happened to be strolling with two others and the plan had to be abandoned.

Since Gaspar Juglar had died a few months before, in January 1485 (it was whispered that he was dispatched by conversos who laced his favorite cupcakes with poison),[11] the conspirators decided to concentrate on Pedro de Arbués who was emerging as the most dangerous of the inquisitors—dangerous because he was a stickler for correctness and procedure. "He took strength in the exact observance of the rules . . . and was an example to all his colleagues. He divided his time between study and prayer . . . and mortified his body with harsh whips in order to strengthen his virtue," wrote a seventeenth-century hagiographer, an inquisitor named Diego García de Trasmiera. Arbués knew Saragossa and its inhabitants well, having been born in the nearby village of Epila to a family of the lesser nobility. According to García de Trasmiera, the family was "of noble blood, a prerequisite of estimation that adheres to gentiles, and that the Hebrews affected; for the best source of virtue is in the quality of lineage . . . [and] the gold of noble blood is conserved in the veins." Here was the snobbery of *hidalguía* and the undiluted racism of blood purity a full two hundred years later.

Once their victim had been picked, the conspirators ordered Juan Esperandeu to hire more men for the job. Esperandeu brought in Vidal Durango, his servant, Mateo Ram, a member of an established converso family, and Ram's servant, Tristanico Leonis. The fee for the assassination was set at one thousand gold florins.

Twice more the inept assassins tried to kill and failed. One night they went to Arbués's room, which was inside the cathedral of the Seo, and attempted to force the grating of the window; but they were surprised by an unexpected sound and ran away. Next they planned to kill him in the church as he prayed, but Arbués didn't show up on the appointed night. By this time Pedro de Arbués suspected there was a plot against his life. Everyone in Saragossa knew that he had taken to wearing coat-of-mail armor under his vestments and a steel cap.

It was now August 1485, and the conspirators were growing concerned about their bungling hirelings. The longer things dragged on, the more likely it was they'd be found out. That month they held two more secret meetings, one in the home of Jaime de Montesa and another in the home of Juan de Pero Sánchez "in the smallest study in the interior of the house."[12] Everyone was worried. They wanted the assassins told that unless the murder was carried out soon they were not going to get the money.

Juan de Pero Sánchez reassured the nervous men. He had a letter from his brother, Gabriel, the king's treasurer, he said. It was written in code.

Pero Sánchez read aloud: "I am amazed at the delay in this business of the deaths of *Maestre* Epila, *Maestre* Martín de la Raga and *Maestre* Pedro Frances. Given the power that conversos hold in court, what is the problem in carrying this out?"

Reassured, the conspirators set a date with the assassins. The night of September 14, 1485.

The Murder

Midnight on the appointed night. Juan Esperandeu arrives at the house of Juan de Labadía to find Labadía still in bed.

"What are you doing in bed?" he whispers from the street. "Get up. It's past the hour."

Labadía dresses, fastens his sword, and creeps stealthily out of the house.

The men make their way through the darkness to Esperandeu's house where Mateo Ram is waiting with "three others with masks so no one could know who they were." They nod a greeting, then move noiselessly along El Cosso street, the main thoroughfare of the city and the avenue that divides the Jewish quarter from the neighboring district where the conversos live. They leave the shops of the shoemakers, tanners, and boilermakers of the quarter behind. Soon they reach the palace of the governor, and at the end of El Cosso street they enter the empty square of the Seo cathedral.

The Seo square is the official center of the city. Just beyond the *Puente de Piedra,* the stone bridge that crosses the Ebro River, are the municipal offices and the House of Deputies, and next to them are several well-off shops selling select merchandise. The lawyers have their offices here, as does everyone having anything to do with the social life of the city. The Inquisition also has moved in; between the archbishop's palace and the Seo cathedral are several houses it recently appropriated.

This is where the terrifying auto de fe processions take place, the miserable penitents stumbling barefoot across the paved stones carrying candles, chanting prayers, and wearing the dreaded *sanbenito* that will stigmatize them and their families into an infinite future.

The brick naves of the Seo cathedral loom in the dim moonlight. Three centuries of gothic construction have just recently been completed over the ruins of what was first a Roman temple, then the central mosque of the city under the Moors. The sight of the church and the square and the memory of recent horror lend the assassins new resolve. They press into the shadows of the church wall and creep around to the back. The cathedral door is open for prayer.

Esperandeu, Mateo Ram, and Ram's servant, Tristanico, enter the church while the three unknown masked men remain outside to keep watch. Vidal Durango and Labadía continue around the building to the main entrance and enter stealthily. Music fills the richly decorated interior with its alabaster tombs, intricately carved wood ceiling, and polychrome altarpiece on which the religious works of Hans de Suabia, a contemporary artist, are displayed. The canons are in the choirstalls chanting prayers.

The men wait tensely for Inquisitor Arbués to arrive, wondering whether this will be another missed opportunity. But there he is, walking through the door that opens to the cloister. He is carrying a lantern—and a short lance in case he needs to defend himself.

Arbués walks to a place below the pulpit between the high altar and the choir, leans his lance against a pillar, and kneels to pray. The assassins huddle in the dark wall shadows. The outlines of the inquisitor's body are clear behind the leaping flame of his lantern.

Labadía and Durango creep behind the choir and the singing canons, then hesitate: Arbués is, after all, at prayer. It looks as though the moment may be lost. "Give it to him, he is a traitor!" Labadía whispers hoarsely to Durango.

Durango steals up behind Arbués and slashes his neck—the one spot where Arbués is not wearing armor. Arbués staggers to his feet and stumbles toward the choir. Labadía rushes after him, stabs him in the arm. Now Mateo Ram and Esperandeu are thrusting their swords through Arbués's body.

Arbués falls to the ground groaning final words: "Praised be Jesus Christ for I die for His holy faith."

The assassins flee as the terrified canons rush over from the choir stalls. Some of them carry Arbués into his bedroom while others tear through the darkened city to find "two famous surgeons," master Johan de Valmeseda and master Prisco Laurencio. The doctors run to the cathedral and they examine the inquisitor. "His wounds are mortal," they tell the shocked canons gathered around the bed.

It is two o'clock in the morning, but the city is wide awake as dozens of church bells ring with that distinctive, hollow, Spanish clang one can hear to this day. Hundreds of screaming people are running to the cathedral. "Conversos to the fire! They have murdered the inquisitor!" The townspeople rampage through the streets killing conversos, Moors and Jews, although Moors, and Jews have had nothing to do with this horror. In a frenzy of indiscriminate hatred, the enemy is the Other.

Fearing that dozens of illustrious conversos may be indiscriminately killed, Alonso de Aragon, archbishop of Saragossa (he is fourteen years old and the bastard son of King Ferdinand), rides through the streets on horseback promising that the Church and the civil government of Saragossa will find the perpetrators and punish them cruelly. He promises five hundred florins to anyone who turns in a fugitive, and threatens excommunication to anyone who offers protection.

"This was the most atrocious crime that had taken place (in Saragossa) since paganism was conquered, and there was great turbulation," recorded the chronicler Zurita for posterity.[13]

The archbishop and all the functionaries of the city, both ecclesiastic and civil, held an urgent meeting at the House of Deputies and decided to proceed against the culprits "without concern for the laws or customs of the kingdom."[14] This phrase, from the pen of the chronicler Zurita, indicates the death of the old ways in the face of a new reality. We will never know how well the fiercely autonomous, non-Church civilians in the room understood the implications of the agreement they signed at the urging of the inquisitors. In one pressure-filled meeting they effectively abandoned their historic constitutional claims to independence.

Three years earlier when the first Castilian tribunal began its investigations in Seville, the inquisitors had moved quickly to establish their power over the unruly nobility of Andalusia, who were so closely identified with conversos. Divide and conquer. Deliver your converso relatives or suffer the consequences. Now, in Aragon, the murder of a priest-inquisitor by panic-stricken conversos provided the Holy Office with a perfect opportunity to achieve the same result.

Inquisitor Pedro de Arbués, alias Epila, died between one and two o'clock on the morning on September 17, 1485, exactly forty-eight hours after he was attacked. The doctors agreed that the wound to his neck was mortal. Arbués was cut "from the nape to throat, [and] the organic veins and the jawbone were broken," they reported.

Eleven days later the Saragossa notables sent the following blunt letter to King Ferdinand:

> Very High and very Powerful King and Sir: Two weeks ago Wednesday at the time of matins, it happened that some disloyal and diabolical persons twice stabbed the reverend *Maestre* Pedro de Arbués, also known as Epila, inquisitor—once in the neck and once in the arm—and this took place in the cathedral, and although he was on his knees praying, he was murdered. It was such an unusual and serious event, so wicked and scandalous, and caused such a great disturbance in the city that at the same hour, while the bells were tolling, a great number of people armed themselves, and with the idea that this murder had been perpetrated by the conversos at whom the Inquisition is directed, all those people came armed, talking of killing and robbing the conversos, and the Jews and Moors as well, and it is certain that if the sacking had begun it would have included all the houses in which anything of value could be found, as commoners like thieving. . . .

They concluded by assuring Ferdinand that "it is the universal intention and will of all to pursue and punish the culprits rigorously."[15]

* * *

After the attack, the assassins ran from the cathedral to Jaime de Montesa's house, where the other conspirators were waiting for them in the study. They were concerned about the uproar, but everyone was elated and relieved. Juan de Pero Sánchez was so pleased with himself, and so sure they had halted the course of the Inquisition, that he had already been bragging openly to a few select friends. His friends were apparently less optimistic. The author of the *Libro Verde* tells us that they warned Pero Sánchez with prophetic words: "Your joy may turn to tears."

The conspirators were sustained by a tragic misinterpretation of reality. "We have nothing to worry about," Jaime de Montesa told his excited accomplices. "The king is really on our side and so are all the knights of Aragon. The magnates in court all support us. Only the queen is opposed to us and on the side of the prior of Santa Cruz [Torquemada] who is a satanist and a disciple of the Antichrist. With her excessiveness and pride, the Queen would like to use this event to strike against us in unjust retribution."[16]

They were genuinely convinced that the murder of Pedro de Arbués had the support of their powerful relatives at court: Gabriel Sánchez, Alfonso de la Caballería, and Luis de Santángel. These men had the ear of the king, they reassured each other, and the king would never betray his trusted advisors.

Their misplaced confidence was quickly shattered. Jaime de Montesa was arrested within days.

A hurried strategy meeting was held at the house of Juan de Pero Sánchez. Pero Sánchez's brother, Guillén, was present, along with Sancho de Paternoy, chief financial officer for the kingdom of Aragon. Paternoy's son, González, arrived with two friends who had not been involved in the plot; these offered to hide the conspirators. But bragging Juan de Pero Sánchez now seemed less sure; he was leaving Saragossa, he said, under the pretext of going to see the king, which he often did. Sancho de Paternoy proclaimed that he had not been directly involved, and had an alibi. He chose to stay in Saragossa.

Juan de Pero Sánchez and his wife; Gaspar de Santa Cruz and his wife; Martín de Santángel, García de Moros, and a father and son both called Pedro de Almazan all escaped to Tudela, a frontier city in the kingdom of Navarre. They were pursued relentlessly by both Ferdinand and the Inquisition, the former threatening war on the kingdom of Navarre if the heretics were not returned. (Navarre refused, but Ferdinand had no ready troops available as he and Isabella were putting down a rebellion of nobles elsewhere.) Several other conspirators also managed to escape along with innocent people who were related to, or acquainted with, the plotters.

Before long the Inquisition knew the entire story in astonishing detail. Vidal Durango was picked up in Lérida, about two hundred kilometers from Saragossa, and under torture he provided the inquisitors with information about the plot and the names of the conspirators. With every arrest that followed, more names were cited.

Far from stopping the Inquisition, the murder of Inquisitor Arbués was a made-to-order gift to King Ferdinand and Torquemada. There was no more opposition to the Inquisition in Saragossa, in the kingdom of Aragon, or anywhere else in Spain as public fury against conversos and Jews—they were no longer distinguished—reached gigantic proportions. The historical laws and liberties of Aragon were a thing of the past; peasants grasped the opportunity to revenge themselves on converso tax collectors and rid themselves of the crippling debts they owed. A popular revolution was underway effecting another shift in the transformation of society. Now anyone who dared defend the conversos was suspected of being an accomplice to murder, or a heretic.

Soon there were so many accused heretics that the receiver of confiscated property at Saragossa asked for permission to appoint deputies throughout the territory and for the right to move the Inquisition headquarters to larger premises. Ferdinand sent orders to all local officials in the realm commanding them to suppress any resistance to the confiscations, then moved the Tribunal from the Seo square to the palace of the Aljafería, a beautiful Moorish extravaganza that had been built in the eleventh century and was now the Saragossa residence of the Catholic Monarchs themselves. Ferdinand left no doubt about the relationship of this move to the murder of Inquisitor Arbués. According to the chronicler Zurita:

> By provision of the king and by order of the Inquisitor-General, the tribunal of the Holy Office was seated in the royal palace of the Aljafería as a sign of perpetual royal safeguard and public faith, under which sign the king and his successors were to protect this Holy Ministry which had been introduced into the kingdom with the blood and martyrdom of that unfortunate man.[17]

Today the inner courtyard of the Aljafería remains an oasis of flowers, sunshine and birdsong, just as it was five hundred years ago. An upper balcony encircles and overlooks the entire courtyard. Off this balcony are the state rooms and bed chambers of Ferdinand and Isabella.

The walls of their throne room are still red, and still sculpted with their joint escutcheons, her yoke and his bundled arrows, in the flamboyant style known as "Isabelline." (Ferdinand had borrowed his symbol of authority from the ancient Romans. Five hundred years later another authoritarian, Benito Mussolini, would readopt the bundled arrows [*fasces*] as his own.)[18]

The ceiling of the throne room is decorated with sculpted, three dimensional wood pine cones gilded, according to legend, with the first gold brought back from the Indies. Around the borders is a Latin inscription extolling the absolute power the Catholic monarchs coveted and eventually achieved: "In the year of salvation, 1492, Ferdinand, king of the Spains, Sicily, Sardinia, Corsica, the Balearics, the most noble, wise, vigorous, pious, constant, just king of princes, and his wife, Isabella, whose greatness of spirit surpasses that of other women."

Just yards from the palace, and connected by an underground tunnel, is the tower of the Aljafería, ten stories and about one hundred feet high. It is windowless, except for several vertical slits. The tribunal and torture chambers of the Inquisition were in the basement and on the main floor. A narrow, spiral staircase mounting one side of the structure climbs to what were the prisoners' cells.

In this tower, the murderers of Pedro de Arbués spent the last days of their lives.

*   *   *

The conspirators were hunted down relentlessly and almost all were caught. Between 1485 and 1488 there were sixty-four burnings in Saragossa, most of which were related to the assassination. Those who succeeded in escaping were burned in effigy; if they had died in the interim and their burial place was known, their bones were dug up and officially committed to the flames.

On June 30 1486, at noon, just nine months after the murder, a spectacular auto de fe was celebrated with "magnificent solemnity" in the public square outside the Seo cathedral.[19] Moments before the assassination the killers had been galvanized to action on this very spot by the remembered sight, imprinted in the mind's eye, of the two autos they had already witnessed here. Now, in terrible, predictable retribution, the first of them were about to be punished as part of a carefully orchestrated spectacle of sound and light designed to impress the agitated crowd with the might of the Inquisition. No one in Saragossa willingly missed this exciting event. Small wooden platforms were dotted around the square so that people might see better; some enthusiasts had been waiting since six o'clock in the morning.

A slow procession left the Seo. The priests in their dramatic robes, the penitents in *sanbenitos* of different colors, depending on the sentence they were to receive. The prisoners shuffled forwards, reciting their rosaries; they sobbed pathetically, their heads bent toward the ground. A trembling silence fell over the citizens of Saragossa.

Seated on a specially constructed platform at the main door of the Seo was Pedro de Arbués's replacement, the newly appointed inquisitor Juan de Colmenares, Abbot of Aguilar. He was flanked by several other inquisitors from Palencia and Barcelona. The priests wore the long white robes of the Dominican Order, the black cowls draped about their shoulders in velvet folds, and each man held before him an ornate gold cross encrusted with jewels.[20] Banners floated from high poles carrying the logo of the Inquisition (a cross, a sword, and an olive branch) and the kingdom, a symbol of the symbiosis of Church and State.

Two prisoners stood facing the inquisitors: Juan de Esperandeu and his servant, Vidal Durango, both of them barefoot and wearing the black *sanbenito* of death. Yet the first to be sentenced this day was Juan de Pero Sánchez, who was conspicuously absent. From Tudela he had succeeded in escaping to Toulouse, France.

The inquisitors now knew the most minute details of the assassination plot. The Abbot of Aquilar read aloud:

> Juan de Pero Sánchez, merchant, told Juan de Labadía that he would pay him five hundred florins of gold to kill Maestre Epila. Further, he told Gaspar de Santa Cruz and Mateo Ram, in the house of Juan de Esperandeu, that he would pay them well to kill the Inquisitor because he was treasurer of the money that they had collected to defend the Jews.

The abbot had even more information. "Juan de Pero Sánchez was heard to say that the religion of Moses was the true religion," he proclaimed to the hushed crowd. "And he cursed his father for having become a Christian." An effigy had been prepared of Juan de Pero Sánchez.

Now it was the turn of Juan de Esperandeu. He stepped forward to the dais where the inquisitor sat.

"Juan de Esperandeu, for the assassination of *Maestre* Epila, for stabbing him in the left arm, and for having attempted to kill him several months earlier with Vidal Durango and Mateo Ram, except that they were discovered."

The final moment had also arrived for Esperandeu's servant, Vidal Durango. It was from his confession under torture that the inquisitors had gleaned most of their information.

> Vidal Durango has confessed that he went many times to the houses of Gaspar de Santa Cruz and Juan de Pero Sánchez as they and Sancho de Paternoy planned the murder of *Maestre* Epila, and that Juan de Labadía took him

aside and told him to strike the inquisitor with a strong blow on the face, or the neck, because otherwise they would not kill him as he was wearing mail armor on his body and a steel cap on his head. Vidal Durango stabbed the inquisitor and opened his veins and he died of this blow.

The prisoners were "released to the secular arm."

Punishment was swift: Juan de Esperandeu was dragged alive through the streets behind a team of mules, then back to the Seo. There they cut off his hands and nailed them to the door of the House of Deputies before dragging him, still living, to the central market of the city. The crowd howled with pleasure as a hooded executioner cut off his head and chopped his body into four pieces. Then they scattered the body parts through the streets.

Vidal Durango received "merciful" treatment. He, too, was dragged through the streets and back to the cathedral, but because "he told all the truth" he was strangled before they cut off his hands. After he was dead they pulled his body to the market where they cut him into pieces which also were scattered in the streets. His severed hands were nailed to the door beside Esperandeu's.

The effect of this spectacle on the good citizens of Saragossa was overwhelming, as it was meant to be. Ten thousand people lived in the city and about two thousand had been able to squeeze into the plaza. Any uncertainty about the power of the Inquisition and the role it intended to play in Aragon was swept away in an afternoon.

Gaspar de Santa Cruz was burned in effigy two months later on July 28, 1486. He had died while in Toulouse and his son Jerónimo was forced to go there, dig up his father's bones, and bring them back for burning. Gaspar's wife, Violante Salvador, was also burned in effigy. Her servants had testified that there were more Jews than Christians in her house, that she ate before she went to Mass, and that she put bacon in the servants' plates and not in her own because she kept the Jewish religion.

Martín de Santángel was burned in effigy on July 28 (he also had escaped to Toulouse). Santángel was accused of contributing money to the conspiracy, and of concealing four Hebrew prayers in his *Book of Hours* prayer book.

Pedro de Moros was burned on November 29, 1486, for claiming the Jewish religion was best, and for saying that the king was making war against the Moors (in Granada) against the will of God. At the same auto de fe, the brothers Pedro and Luis de Almazan were banished from Saragossa for ten years because they were found to be circumcised.

Francisco de Santa Fe did not wait to be condemned and executed. On the morning of December 15, 1486, he threw himself out of the window of his cell in the tower of the Aljafería, "in his shirt." Later that day the tribunal formally sentenced him and read aloud his trial confession in which he admitted that he had participated in Jewish ceremonies and that a Jew came to his house to teach him the prayers. Did Jerónimo de Santa Fe turn in his grave as his grandson endured this shame at the hands of the church Jerónimo had converted to? Francisco had, it seemed, returned to the ancient religion.

Francisco's ancestry did not save him from infamy. They burned his body and tied his bones up in his shirt, then threw them into the Ebro River.

On January 21, 1487, the body of Juan de Labadía was carried out of prison to the auto de fe. Like Santa Fe, Labadía hadn't bothered waiting for the inevitable. The prospect of the death that awaited him must have seemed more horrible than the terrible suicide he chose, for he killed himself by breaking a lantern and swallowing the shattered pieces of glass. The executioners dragged his dead body around, cut off his hands, quartered him, and strewed the pieces around the streets.

On March 15, Mateo Ram was condemned for Jewish practices, and for his involvement in the murder. "While Esperandeu stabbed him in the arm, and Vidal stabbed him in the neck with a dagger, Mateo Ram ran a sword right through his body." Ram was a live victim. They dragged him through the city, cut off his hands which they nailed to the door of the House of Deputies, then burned him.

At the same auto de fe, García de Moros was condemned for Jewish practices, and for having hinted to a friend before the murder that "before many Sundays had passed he would see a major event take place." After the assassination Moros purportedly said to still another friend, "Do you not think this murder was well done, all the same?" They dragged his effigy through the streets then burned it.

Alonso Sánchez, another brother of the king's treasurer, Gabriel, was condemned for eating *hamin* (another word for *adefina*, the slow-cooking stew that could be put on the stove before the Sabbath) and "because he dressed up as a rabbi and read from the Torah to other false Christians; and "for scourging a crucifix and throwing it into the fire." Sánchez was also accused of going to the synagogue to pray with his "Jewish skull cap and prayer shawl," and for working "with all his strength plotting the murder of the Holy Inquisitor, for which he promised good pay." They dragged his effigy through the streets, then burned it.

On August 18, Luis de Santángel, the proud nobleman who had been knighted by King Juan II of Aragon in 1462, was condemned for reverting to the Jewish faith after his conversion to Christianity, for praying in Hebrew, and for keeping a Torah in his home. When his son was sick he purportedly told a priest who was saying mass that God would not cure the boy because he, Santángel, had abandoned Judaism. And he "scourged a crucifix and swore at it, and tied it up in a sack with mule heads." He had also held meetings in his house to plan the murder of *Maestre* Epila, or *Maestre* Martín de la Raga, or *Maestre* Pedro Frances, or all three.

Luis de Santángel's head was cut off and impaled on a stake in the marketplace, then his body was burned outside the city gates. His brother, Pedro, the prior of the monastery of Daroca, tried to save him by bribing one of the domestic servants of the Aljafería prison to testify before the inquisitors that Luis was a good Christian, and that he, the servant, had seen Luis mortify himself before a crucifix. Pedro was tried and penanced for his loyalty to his brother, but treated leniently; his punishment was to appear before the main altar of the Seo carrying a penitent's candle, "but they did not deprive him." Luis de Santángel was the father-in-law of the powerful court treasurer, Gabriel Sánchez. Significantly, and ominously, Sánchez was unable to rescue a family member, in spite of his intimate connection to the king and queen.

The Ordeal of Jaime de Montesa

The quick arrest of the elderly and distinguished jurist Jaime de Montesa was intended to send out an unmistakable message: Far from being intimidated by the murder of Pedro de Arbués, the inquisitors were firmly in control; and no one under suspicion would be spared, regardless of their station.

Jaime de Montesa languished in prison for two years in a cell measuring about twelve feet by eight. The space was unlit and unheated. A straw mattress lay on the floor. He was allowed a water jar and a pot for excreting that was emptied once a week.[21]

For two years Montesa saw no one except his jailer, but he could hear the groans of women and men in surrounding cells. Many were dying of disease and hopelessness. Some went mad during the years that elapsed between their arrest and their sentencing. Not one of them knew what he or she was accused of until they were brought before the inquisitors. (Legal counsel of sorts was provided, but lawyer and "client" never met and the lawyer had no more information about the charge than the prisoner. In any case, counsel dared not defend too vigorously since to support heresy was a mortal sin and he, too, might be arrested.)

On August 10, 1487, Jaime de Montesa was brought before the inquisitors Alfonso de Alarcón, canon of Palencia, and Miguel de Monterubio, the prior of the monastery of San Pedro de las Duyenas. Also present on that summer day were Martín García, the vicar general of the Holy Office, Rodrigo Sánchez de Cuaco, crown prosecutor for the Inquisition, and the notary-scribe, Johan Donper, whose precise records provide us with an account of what took place.[22]

A pulley and rope hung from the ceiling. The hooded, masked men who did double duty as torturers and public executioners waited quietly on the sidelines. At a sign from the inquisitors the hooded men stepped forward and undressed Montesa. Prisoners of the Inquisition were always tortured naked.

The scribe wrote:

> Señor Jaime de Montesa, prisoner, was questioned under torture in the presence of the above reverend inquisitors. The said Sr. Montesa was raised approximately six hands above the ground with the torture rope, and remained in the said torture for the time it would take to recite three credos very slowly. Then the aforementioned Sr. Montesa said that if they released him from the torture he would tell the whole truth about the plot to murder the inquisitor *Maestre* Epila. The reverend prior and inquisitor who was present asked if he would not tell it then and there, and Sr. Montesa replied and stated that if he were let down, upon his honour he would tell the whole truth. Then the reverend prior and inquisitor ordered that Sr. Montesa be let down from the rope. He was then lowered, and then he was dressed, and the said Sr. Montesa, before the reverend father inquisitors and the vicar general, and in the presence of myself, Johan Donper, notary-scribe of the Holy Office, prepared to make his confession.

The rope torture would have been unbearable for a man of Montesa's advanced age. His hands were tied behind him and heavy weights were attached to his feet; then his wrists, still tied behind him, were attached to a ceiling pulley which raised him slowly off the ground. Sometimes the victim was allowed to fall with a jerk before being raised again, although it seems this was not the case with Montesa. The result of such torture was often the dislocation of arms and legs, although the inquisitors usually tried not to break bones or mutilate.[23]

On August 20, 1487 Jaime de Montesa was led out to a "magnificent" auto de fe. His black *sanbenito* was decorated front and back with grinning devils.

The judgment was read aloud:

> In the name of Jesus Christ, we, Alfonso Sánchez de Alarcón, master of Holy Theology, canon of the church of Palencia, chaplain of our lords, the king and queen, and of their council; and friar Miguel Monterubio, graduate in Holy Theology, prior of the monastery of San Pedro de las Duyenas, [both]

inquisitors of heretical and apostate depravity in the kingdom of Aragon . . . , and Martín García, canon of the Seo in Saragossa, master of Holy Theology, vicar general for the inquiry into the aforementioned heresy and depraved apostasy. . . .

The present criminal trial was witnessed by us in hearings between the prosecutor of the Holy Inquisition against heretical and apostate depravity on one side, and on the other side, the prisoner, Sr. Jaime de Montesa, jurist and resident of the present city.[24]

There follows a six-thousand-word description of Montesa's crimes which included heresy as well as murder. Montesa's confession may have contained a few confabulatory details invented to fend off a renewal of torture—a little like throwing choice morsels of meat to the lions—but in the main his reconstruction of the plot and the assassination closely matched the accounts of the other conspirators.

Jaime de Montesa was "released to the secular arm," and the functionaries wasted no time. "They cut off his head in the market and impaled it on a stake; then they burned his body outside the city gates."

In a singularly cruel act, Montesa's daughter, Leonor, was condemned at the same auto de fe. Leonor Montesa was the wife of Juan de Santa Fe (from the same converso family as Jerónimo and the hapless Francisco). She lived in the city of Tarragona, but had been brought to Saragossa to be sentenced with her father. Leonor was convicted of "although being baptized, living as a Jewess and following the rites; of fasting on Yom Kippur for fifty years, and of making charitable donations to the synagogue to buy oil for the lamps." The original document describes her fate in chilling brevity. *Quemáronla*: "They burned her."[25]

The Ordeal of Sancho De Paternoy

On January 29, 1488, Sancho de Paternoy, chief financial officer for the entire kingdom of Aragon, was brought before the same inquisitors in the "lowest room of the main tower of the Aljafería." Because of his exceptional prestige two additional witnesses were present: Jaime de Monclus, a representative from the central body of the Inquisition (the *Suprema*), and Gil del Campilla, a paid informer who was an assistant to inquisitor Alarcón.[26]

It was night and the torches cast flickering shadows along the walls and across the stone floor of the dark, bottom-floor room in the Aljafería where inquisition and torture took place. Like Montesa before him Paternoy was attached to the ceiling pulley "with his hands tied behind him" and raised off the floor, the inquisitors questioning him with every turn of the rope. And thus "said and confessed the aforementioned Sancho de Paternoy before the Reverend Inquisitors."

When the pain became unbearable Paternoy begged the inquisitors to stop, crying, "I cannot think or remember." In growing distress he pleaded with them two or three more times saying that if they released him he would remember and tell them everything the next morning. He promised that if he did not tell the whole truth the next day the inquisitors might continue the torture. (According to the rules torture could be inflicted only once, so it was routinely described by all concerned as "continuing.")

It was midnight when they lowered the pulley and released Sancho de Paternoy from his agony. They took him from the room where he had been tortured to another place "much higher in the tower" and there he lay down on a bed they had prepared, still "dressed in his stockings and doublet." The inquisitor read him the testimony he had just given and asked him to swear that all he had said so far was the truth. "Sancho de Paternoy replied that all he had said and confessed was true, and he swore on the cross and by the Four Holy Gospels that he would think and remember better the next day, and he wanted the reverend inquisitors to leave the option of torture open in case he did not tell the whole truth."

Paternoy's confession closely resembled that of Montesa, except that he conspicuously absented himself from the events of the assassination whenever possible. He also maintained that the illustrious Gabriel Sánchez, treasurer to the king and queen, had approved of the murder of Arbués, and added that the conspiracy could not and would not have proceeded without the support of the treasurer, and that he had personally seen Gabriel's private, coded letter to his brother, Juan, urging the conspirators to go ahead with the murder. During the course of his confession, Jaime de Montesa also had incriminated Gabriel Sánchez, and it would have been impossible for both men to synchronize their stories while in prison. The inquisitors were delighted. There would be no better demonstration of their power and no faster way to destroy the converso-heretics than to bring Ferdinand's distinguished treasurer to trial.

The Session: February 3, 1488

"What did you know of the plot to kill the two inquisitors?"

"Nothing. I was never in any place where anyone was planning to kill or to harm the inquisitor, *Maestre* Epila, or Senor Martín de la Raga, or any officer of the Inquisition. I do not know who murdered the inquisitor, or on whose advice."

"You know nothing?"

Paternoy had to say something. "I only know that about three months before the murder I was talking one day with Juan de Pero Sánchez about inquisitor [Juan de] Anchias. We were talking about the Inquisition, and Pero Sánchez said malevolently, 'I will have to see about this.' "

"You never uttered a threatening word about *Maestre* Epila while he was still alive?"

Paternoy was under pressure. Not knowing how much his interrogators already knew, he had to weigh and gauge his words. "One day I was in the Seo with Gaspar de Santa Cruz—Juan de la Caballería was there, too—and *Maestre* Epila walked in front of us; he came out of the cloister of the church to get holy water at the pillar. I said *Maestre* Epila was a hypocrite, or words to that effect."

"Why did you say that?"

"I had heard that *Maestre* Epila was treating my friends badly. [preparing heresy cases against them]

"Who were your friends?"

"My friends were the Sánchez brothers and a few commoners such as Gaspar de Santa Cruz."

"Did you ever talk with one Labadía either before, or after the murder?"

"Yes, once. I was on my way to the hospital with my servant and I met Labadía. I talked to him about a grey nag I wanted to buy and I asked him the price." The inquisitors waited in silence for more. "Yes . . . after the murder I was in an upper room of the town hall with Domingo la Naja and he told me it was rumored that Labadía promised money to Mateo Ram to kill the inquisitor, but Domingo la Naja told me that the rumor wasn't true."

The inquisitor was not about to be distracted from his goal which was confirmation of Paternoy's own involvement, in word or deed. "Have you personally ever been angry at any officer of the Inquisition, or wanted to harm him?" he demanded.

"Yes . . . I was angry at [Juan de] Anchias because I heard he asked a Jewish tailor if I had a seat in the synagogue." Paternoy understood that what he had just confessed to might be interpreted as a motive for joining the conspiracy, and he immediately sought to ingratiate himself with the inquisitors. He begged them to punish him by lengthening the interrogation session. He even suggested the king might want to have a hand in disciplining him.

"Do you know whether the Treasurer, Gabriel Sánchez, and Juan de Pero Sánchez wrote each other in code?" they asked, moving on to an important subject.

"It is true. Pero Sánchez told me. I asked him if there were letters from the court, and he said, yes, there were letters. . . ."

"Do you remember anything else about this business?"

"No, I remember nothing else, but if I do I shall say it."

The session was over and they returned Sancho de Paternoy to his cell, but the inquisitors did not believe he had told them the whole truth as he had promised to do. Five days later they "continued" his torture—with "the rope, and stones on his feet." This time he told them what they wanted to hear.

Was there a meeting at the house of Juan de Pero Sánchez? Yes there was, and someone—it was Pero Sánchez—said that *Maestre* Epila was treating them all so badly that "if they did not do something, all was lost." Yes, they decided to kill *Maestre* Epila, and yes, they gave money to Mateo Ram to find people to do the job. Ram found Juan de Labadía and Esperandeu and they killed *Maestre* Epila, and yes, Juan de Pero Sánchez was very happy about their success.

But Paternoy had an alibi. He was not part of the conspiracy, he insisted. On the night of the murder he was in the company of a royal official.

Once again they carried him from the torture chamber back to his cell.

Two days later, on February 10, the inquisitors came to his cell with a written transcript of the confession. They read it to him word for word. Would he confirm that everything he had said was true? Sancho de Paternoy surprised them: "There's nothing true in it," he cried. "I said it because you were torturing me. The only true thing is what Juan de Pero Sánchez said about his brother, Gabriel. Otherwise I knew nothing of these events."

For unknown reasons—probably because he enjoyed the direct protection of the king—Sancho de Paternoy was absolved and released; in fact, he continued in his post as chief financial officer of the realm until his death in 1496 after which his son González took over the position.

Gabriel Sánchez also escaped prosecution. It is, of course, possible that he was innocent and that both Montesa and Paternoy had tried to save themselves by incriminating a more powerful man. The more likely truth is that Sánchez was profoundly involved, and that his approval for the assassination gave the Saragossa conversos a tragically false sense of confidence.

Sánchez, too, was protected. In spite of being informally indicted twice, his name was never mentioned publicly by the Inquisition—quite probably by direct order of King Ferdinand himself.

*   *   *

The Inquisition seized on the murder of Pedro de Arbués with an intimidating display of righteous wrath, but what stands out in the recorded convictions and sentences handed out to the culprits is that the crime of heresy clearly took precedence over the assassination. Jaime de Montesa was a case in point. For more than a decade he had openly flaunted his ongoing commitment to Judaism, becoming cautious about his practices only when the Church increased its surveillance. The charges brought against him by witnesses and other informers, even considering that some may have been manufactured for reasons of personal gain, retribution, or envy speak volumes about the strange double life led by many conversos who remained attached to Judaism, and to a familiar culture they were loathe to leave generations after their families were converted to Christianity.

Since the New Christians lived in close proximity to their Jewish relatives and friends, it was easy enough to maintain some religious ties. And the Jews were naturally more than willing to help the prodigals return to Judaism, for which they were accused of "aiding and abetting heresy."

As part of his sentence the Inquisition charged that "being a baptized Christian, [Jaime de Montesa] returned to the rites and ceremonies of Judaism, which he praised; and he said he was more devoted to the Jewish religion than to the Christian religion; and that the Inquisitor of the Faith [Torquemada] was a satanist and a disciple of the Antichrist." In sum, Montesa's actions and attitudes were typical of defiant men and women who were the offspring of coerced converts, or who were returning to the familiar comfort of Jewish culture in a time of crisis.

Jaime de Montesa seems to have been deeply attached to his Jewish origins, although probably not for religious reasons. Like most upper class conversos, he was an educated rationalist in the Aristotelian/Averroist tradition. Witnesses quoted him as often repeating the favorite saying of contemporary skeptics: "In this world you will not see me in trouble, and in the other you will not see me in pain."

Montesa's mother lived in the neighboring town of Calatayud, and when he visited her only kosher meat was served—by a "judaizing" converso. He and his mother ate food that was prepared by his mother's sister who was still a Jewess, and the dishes were carried over by a trusted Jewish servant girl. One Good Friday while Christians were in church, Montesa's relatives congregated at his mother's house and the family celebrated a secret Jewish wedding for Montesa's nephew. "May you have many sons and daughters!" Montesa toasted the new couple. Everyone danced, and when someone suggested it might be in poor taste to dance while Christians were weeping in church, Montesa purportedly cried, "Dance, dance, may God give us the art to dance with happiness. Next time *they* will be happy and *we* will cry."

But Montesa's brother was a pious monk who excoriated his mother and Jaime for being bad Christians and blind to the truth of the Gospels. "For this reason this brother always excused himself from eating in his mother's house and when he did eat there it was on condition that no Jew enter the house while he was there, and when he came to the door, he always called out, "Are there Jews in the house?' "

This was the tragedy of the conversos. In a society constructed on religious identity, some members of one family might be sincere Christians while others were unconverted Jews. Families were forced apart, trapped in a spiritual and social limbo. It is no surprise that hostility to Christianity ran high.

The Inquisition produced a litany of other revealing charges against Montesa. He had gone to the synagogue to listen to a sermon and pray, then had had the audacity to proclaim there was no sin in doing so. And there was a secret room in his house where the Sabbath table was laid with a clean, white cloth and candles were lit, and *hamin* was served, at which he held long conversations with Jews. The Inquisitors also suspected Montesa was circumcised, although they had not been able to properly verify this "by ocular inspection." They explained: "Persons skilled in the art of surgery confirmed that a good part of the circular prepuce was missing, but without a scar or any other sign that an accident might have occurred." In spite of the cardinal role he had played in the assassination of an inquisitor of the Holy Office, it was Montesa's "Jewishness" that was of interest.

All the same, with the murder of Inquisitor Pedro de Arbués the Holy Office had acquired a martyr and an excuse to rally massive popular support; in fact there is intriguing evidence that both Torquemada and King Ferdinand were aware that a plot was being hatched and deliberately allowed events to happen. On January 29, 1485—eight months before the assassination—Ferdinand wrote a letter to the governor of Aragon informing him that there was a conspiracy and that a large sum of money was being collected to be used against the Inquisition; and after several unsuccessful attempts on his life, none of which were secret, Pedro de Arbués took to wearing chain mail and a steel cap. Still, nothing was done to stop the inevitable. The Inquisition was new in Aragon. It was having problems handling the rebellious nobles with their insistence on old constitutional rights and hereditary laws. The death of Arbués was useful.[27]

To capitalize on the event, no time was lost in conferring heroic status on Pedro de Arbués. For days the inquisitor's body lay on a brocade-covered dais in the cathedral, dressed in crimson and surrounded by burning candles; and when it was time for the funeral ceremony, his coffin was paraded through the streets. Following behind the casket walked all the inquisitors of Aragon and Castile. Behind them were the nobles of Aragon, dressed in red, blue, and green brocade and velvet. Representatives of the municipality, the province, and the kingdom attended; so did city councilors, members of the trade guild associations, military knights, monks and ecclesiastics of all orders, and deputies from the religious institutes and brotherhoods. Silent crowds of ordinary people lined the streets to watch.

When the procession returned to the cathedral, the coffin was lowered into a grave at the very spot where Pedro de Arbués fell, and next to his body they placed a glass bottle containing a parchment that told the tale of his death. Bishop Bernardo Faber recited mass, and one of Arbués's canonical colleagues from the Seo delivered a eulogy so moving and "incendiary" that the emotion of the mourners "intensified until the moment when the inquisitor disappeared" in the earth. "And thus the hatred of the Jews [*sic*] for the inquisitor served precisely to ascertain his crown of glory before God and men," wrote a commentator confirming the political consequences of a desperate act.[28]

The king and queen commissioned a magnificent marble mausoleum, a statue of the deceased, and a bas-relief showing scenes from the assassination. On the monument was engraved: "As a sign of her exceptional piety, Queen Isabella has erected this monument to her confessor, the martyr Pedro de Arbués."[29] Arbués never was the queen's confessor; the Catholic monarchs had simply decided that the reputation of the murdered inquisitor ought to be enhanced.[30]

In Saragossa the swords of the four assassins were commemorated as holy relics and hung on a stone pillar in the Seo, where they remain to this day. And engraved on a tombstone on the floor of the church are the words: "Here he fell, his throat cut by Jews."

The miracles began happening at once. At the moment of the inquisitor's death a church bell was said to ring all by itself (it was immediately called the "Miracle Bell"). At Arbués's funeral, blood that had dried on the cathedral floor miraculously liquified, and the townsfolk had to be held back as they fought to dip pieces of cloth in it. Within a year of the murder, several people had been visited by the inquisitor's ghost dressed in crimson robes, and by 1490 his apparition was said to have cured innumerable sick people and to have protected Saragossa from a serious attack of the plague. By the mid-sixteenth century his image hung in many Saragossa houses as protector of the hearth.

Rome was dubious about the methods of the Spanish Inquisition, and for almost two hundred years the papacy refused to beatify Inquisitor Arbués. Pope Alexander VII finally conceded, in 1664, and when the announcement reached Spain a new funerary inscription was engraved on Arbués's tomb in the Seo.

It reads:

> Stop passer-by. On this spot fell the blessed Pedro de Arbués, of Epila, a canon of this church. The Holy See chose him as first inquisitor of the faith, [but] the zeal he showed made him hated by the Jews; and they killed him. He died here a martyr in the year 1485. Their serene highnesses, Ferdinand and Isabella, erected a marble mausoleum in his honor, and by his glory miracles happened. The sovereign pontiff Alexander VII beatified and placed his name among the holy martyrs, April 17, 1664.[31]

By 1664, no one remembered the despair that had motivated the most prominent citizens of Aragon to plot and carry out the terrible murder of a public man, or the struggle to retain ancient constitutional rights in Aragon, or any distinction between Jews and conversos.

The assassination of Pedro de Arbués reaped a lasting harvest. Between 1481 and 1520, most of the famous converso families of Aragon who had occupied the highest positions in the land and linked their blood with royalty were destroyed until, in the early sixteenth century, a zealous inquisitor was heard to complain that there were too few converso-heretics left to prosecute. Over succeeding centuries the Inquisition targeted new victims, progressing from conversos, to humanists and followers of Erasmus, to Lutherans, witches, fornicators, homosexuals, and freethinkers of all stripes. But after the murder of Pedro de Arbués in the Seo cathedral, no group ever again challenged the right of the Holy Office to operate in Aragon or elsewhere. In 1484 the indignant nobles of Teruel had lined up at the gates of the city to refuse the inquisitors entry; clans from all over the kingdom converged on Saragossa to plan their offensive. All this had changed and was forgotten, until it was said with utmost sincerity that "No nation surpasses the Aragonese in their veneration and respect for the Holy Office. All are honored to take glory in this."[32]

Notes

1. My main sources for this chapter are the following: Jerónimo Zurita y Castro, *Anales de la Corona de Aragón*, 20, ch. 55; Juan Antonio Llorente, *Histoire Critique de l'Inquisition*; Manuel Serrano y Sanz, *Orígenes de la Dominación Española en América*; author disputed, *El Libro Verde de Aragón* (early sixteenth century); anonymous, "Memoria de Diversos Autos de la

Inquisición Celebrados En Caragoca Desde El Ano 1484 Asta El De 1502," included in H. C. Lea, *A History of the Inquisition in Spain,* 1; Diego García de Trasmiera, *Epitome de la Santa Vida;* Angel Alcalá Galve, *Los Orígenes de la Inquisición en Aragón;* Conde de Castellan, *Un Complot Terrorista en el siglo XV;* H. Kamen, *The Spanish Inquisition,* and *Inquisition and Society in Spain.* The history of the *Libro Verde* is worth noting. The book traced the genealogies of the great converso families of Aragon and told the story of the murder of the inquisitor, Pedro de Arbués. When it was published there was such an uproar from people who wanted their "Jewish blood" hidden that by order of the king the book was confiscated. It disappeared into the archives of the Inquisition until it was rediscovered by José Amador de los Rios and published in his seminal book *Historia de los Judíos en España y Portugal.*

2. Lea, *History,* 1: 230.

3. We have already encountered earlier generations of this family including Benveniste, Oravida, Vidal, and Pedro de la Caballería.

4. Zurita, *Anales.*

5. December 10, 1484, cited in Lea, *History,* 1: 247.

6. Serrano y Sanz, *Orígenes,* 1: 161. See this book for details of the murder of Pedro de Arbués and the subsequent interrogations and *autos* of the conspirators, 152–70. See also *El Libro Verde de Aragon;* anonymous, "Memoria de Diversos Autos," included in Lea, *History,* 1; and Zurita, *Anales,* 20, ch. 55.

7. Serrano y Sanz, *Orígenes,* 519, appendix 4, note 1.

8. Ibid., 162.

9. *Libro Verde,* 70.

10. Ibid., 80.

11. "Memoria de Diversos Autos," in Lea, *History,* 1: 244.

12. Confession of Sancho Paternoy, *Libro Verde.*

13. Ibid., 20, 205.

14. Zurita, *Anales,* 20: 210–20.

15. Saragossa, September 26, 1485, Serrano y Sanz, *Orígenes,* 158.

16. Serrano y Sanz, *Orígenes,* appendix 4, 509. Confession and sentence of the Inquisition against Jaime de Montesa, August 1487.

17. Zurita, *Anales.* Lea notes that the Inquisition eventually began to encroach upon the royal apartments. In 1511 Ferdinand wrote a letter complaining of this, and in 1515 he ordered the inquisitors to rent premises elsewhere. Eventually, the Inquisition obtained permanent possession of the palace. Lea, *History,* 1: 255, note 5.

18. The *fasces* were a symbol of law and order in ancient Rome.

19. Details on this and subsequent autos de fe derive from "Memoria de Diversos Autos," in Lea, *History,* 1, and an interview with Saragossa historian Miguel Angel Motis Dolader, November 1994.

20. See also D. García de Trasmiera, *Epitome de la Santa Vida.*

21. Kamen, *The Spanish Inquisition,* 172, for an interesting discussion of the prison cells of the Spanish Inquisition.

22. Serrano y Sanz, *Orígenes,* 163ff.

23. The Spanish Inquisition used three kinds of torture: the rope torture with pulleys; the water torture, which consisted of pouring jars of water down the throat of the victim who was tied to a rack; and later on (after the sixteenth century) the *potro,* where the victim was bound to a rack with ropes that were tightened bit by bit until they cut into his or her body.

24. Serrano y Sanz, *Orígenes,* appendix 4, 509ff.

25. "Memoria de Diversos Autos," in Lea, *History,* 1.

26. The confession of Paternoy appeared in the *Libro Verde.*

27. This was not the first time an inquisition established itself by means of an assassination. In thirteenth-century Italy the papal Inquisition also was successful only after the murder of an inquisitor.

28. F. Izquierdo Trol, *San Pedro de Arbués, primer inquisidor de Aragón*, 66.

29. In 1989 this monument was still in the Seo in Saragossa.

30. Eventually all inquisitors were formally designated "confessors to the monarchs" as a sign of the esteem in which the sovereigns held the Inquisition.

31. Still to be seen in the Seo.

32. Diego José Dormer, *Anales de Aragón*, 118.

12

A Strategic Victory for Torquemada: The Holy Child of La Guardia Trial Leads to the Expulsion of the Jews

The 1480s were terror-filled for converso and Jew alike as dangerous myths took hold. Both groups were identified as "devils"—a useful dehumanizing fantasy that was invoked to justify rising levels of hostility and aggression. (The story of the priest who kept a devil in his shoe was a ludicrous example.)[1]

The intimidation strategies being played out by the Inquisition were unlike anything Spaniards had seen. Families were wrenched apart as individuals sought to save themselves by informing on one another. Converso parents recoiled from their own children in case innocent tongues betrayed them. Half-forgotten heresies were dug up from the past, just as bodies were dug up from their graves to face formal trial and punishment. A degraded society of spies had come into being—informants paid to peer into the lives of former friends and neighbors.

This Inquisition that had taken over Castile and Aragon—psychologically as well as politically—had the full support of the secular monarchy. Tomás de Torquemada had positioned himself as the most powerful man in the kingdom, next to the king and queen, and he, alone, set the tone for the Inquisition. Like his spiritual predecessor Alonso de Espina, the inquisitor-general had an intuitive understanding of propaganda as a social tool. He had commissioned writers to strengthen the connection between conversos and heretics in the popular mind, and the culpability of the Jews as cause of this heresy, and petitioned King Ferdinand and Queen Isabella to expel the Jews in 1486.

They refused, but Torquemada did not give up hope. If the Catholic Monarchs were unwilling to understand the logic of expelling the Jews from Spain to prevent the spread of heresy among conversos, Torquemada believed it was only a question of time until they changed their minds; or until changing public attitudes allowed, perhaps even *demanded*, an expulsion to cleanse the land, just as the purifying fires were ridding the nation of heretics. All the same, Torquemada needed something spectacular to make his point clear and the desired expulsion inevitable, something that would excite public wrath—the way the murder of Pedro de Arbués had invoked anger and consolidated the Inquisition.

In June 1490, the Inquisitor-General found what he needed in a promising looking upcoming trial entered into the roster of one of the Inquisition tribunals. Torquemada left no incriminating documents, to be sure, but surviving evidence strongly indicates that the notorious trial of the Holy Child of La Guardia—a story of blood libel, murder, and magic that incorporated the entire gamut of anti-Semitic mythology—was a fabrication from start to finish.

Six conversos and five Jews were accused of kidnapping and crucifying a Christian child in a cave in order to mock the agony of Jesus on the cross. But according to the Holy Office, what they *really* had in mind was much more ambitious. In the short term, they were reportedly determined to destroy the Inquisition and all Christians. Following this feat of magical omnipotence, they planned to replace Christianity with "the religion of Moses."

These accusations echoed the charges that had been brought against both Jews and conversos a generation earlier by Alonso de Espina in his *Fortalitium Fidei*, but they had an even longer history. Torquemada and Espina were merely dipping into an ancient stream that was available to anyone who could read.

The Blood Libel

Two pronouncements of the early Catholic Church had set the stage. According to the Gospel of John, Jews are not the children of God, but the children of the Devil,[2] a theme that was expanded in the fourth century C.E. by the influential Archbishop John Chrysostom, who called the Jews "demons devoted to idolatrous cults, assassins of Christ, and a criminal assembly." The important thing about demons is that they are not human. Demons are committed to doing evil, and they must be opposed by Christians who are (unlike Jews) the children of God.[3]

The theme of devils, devil cults, and criminals was the central core of the blood-libel myth as it evolved over the centuries. There were variations on the content, but the story usually followed familiar lines: the Jews require human blood to mix with their unleavened bread at Passover, and to get it they kidnap and sacrifice Christian children. The children in question are almost always male—that is, the most precious sex and there-fore most likely to touch off rage in the hearer. The alleged attack almost always occurs around Easter so the murderers can purportedly use the child to reenact the agony of Jesus Christ.

The blood libel contained all of the necessary ingredients for inciting hatred: the murder of an innocent child by cannibals who use human blood for their savage rites, combined with the most powerful, shared belief of all: the murder of Christ by the Jews.[4] When this explosive brew was fed to an insecure, suggestible population the result was predictable. A supposedly spontaneous pogrom exploded. A massacre. A "rightful" attack on the devil killers of innocent babes, the satanic destroyers of Christ.

Even a brief look at the history of the blood libel myth underlines its use over the centuries by religious or political interests, or a combination of both. The reason for reinventing the myth is always the desire to point a finger at the enemy Other.

The earliest recorded political use of blood libel occurred in the sec-ond century B.C.E when the Greek warrior Antiochus Epiphanes invaded the Temple in Jerusalem. According to myth, a Greek captive found in the Temple told Antiochus that the Jews ritualistically captured a Greek every seven years, fattened him up, killed him, and ate him while swearing undying enmity against the Greeks.[5] The story was part of war propa-ganda devised to whip up passion in the Greek population against the Jews who happened to be their political enemies. (This deliberate dehu-manizing of the other side continues in contemporary warfare so that oth-erwise decent folk will support the inevitable killing.)

A second charge surfaced in 415 C.E., again in Greece, but it seems to have disappeared without a trace and the accusation of Jewish ritual murder went underground until the late eleventh century when the medieval version was born. This was the era of the Crusades when reli-gious hatreds were reignited and many Jews along the Crusaders' path were massacred. Eyewitness accounts related that some Jewish parents killed themselves and their children as an act of martyrdom or self-sacri-fice in the wake of the rampages, and some scholars believe that the source of the legend may originate in the horror of Christians who wit-nessed this. As the story developed over years and decades, the martyred Jewish children were translated into Christians. The murder myth would also have coalesced with one of the central ideas of Christianity—the sac-rifice of the child Isaac—and the sacrifice of Jesus himself, the son of God.

The first fully documented charge that Jews had crucified a Christian child occurred in Norwich, England. In 1144, the body of William, a twelve-year-old skinner's apprentice, was found in a wooded area near the town. The cause of death was unknown, and the event attracted little attention, until five years later when a monk named Thomas of Monmouth arrived to take up a position in the cathedral. Thomas grew suspicious. He interviewed the peasant who had discovered the body, then published a book entitled *The Life and Miracles of Saint William of Norwich* in which he attempted to confer martyrdom on William, and to pursue sainthood for him as a Christ-figure, by accusing the Jews of kidnapping and crucifying the child on the second day of Passover in order to mock the Passion of Jesus. A new cult leaped immediately into being, and it spread like a virus.

The tale of young William is so embedded in anti-Semitic mythology that eight hundred years later the American scholar, Gavin I. Langmuir, published an examination of Brother Thomas's evidence, detailing the author's fabrications and distortions.[6] Brother Thomas had handily fabricated his desired conclusions, but who was to argue with an educated priest in an illiterate age? According to Professor Langmuir, Thomas of Monmouth is the first source of the "modern" blood-libel accusation against the Jews.

A frenzy of excitement seized the good citizens of Norwich and the Jews would have been murdered had they not been allowed to take refuge in a nearby castle. The story of the ritual murder of a child spread quickly. Another charge was brought forward in Gloucester in 1168. It was followed by massacres. More attacks took place in late 1189 and throughout 1190.

In 1171 the blood libel surfaced in Blois, France, accompanied, as usual, by massacres of the Jews. Now any time a child disappeared, or was found dead (a not uncommon occurrence in the twelfth century), it was because he, or occasionally she, had been killed by the Jews. Retaliation always followed.[7]

Soon a companion crime was invented to accompany the ritual murder accusation: the desecration of the consecrated host. Jews were accused of stealing the wafer, believed by Christians to be the body of Christ, in order to flog it, stab it, and commit otherwise unspeakable acts on Jesus himself. (An example of host desecration purportedly took place in France in the year 1290. A Jew tried to destroy a consecrated host, but his knife miraculously broke into three symbolic parts representing the Trinity. He tried to put the wafer in boiling water, but it turned into flesh and blood. Eventually he was caught and burned to death. The pious were content that good had come from this terrible event, and when the Jews heard about the attendant miracles many of them converted to Christianity.)[8]

The psychology of ritual murder and host desecration accusations was, and is, familiar. The enemy-other is a perpetual outsider and is therefore dangerous; in fact, the more alienated he is from the majority main-stream, the more fearful he becomes. In addition, ritual murder and host desecration accusations were built on uniquely Christian assumptions and could only have been dreamed up by propagandists who knew nothing of Judaism. The idea underlying ritual murder was, of course, the divinity of Christ, since it was believed that the Jews wanted to reenact the death of Jesus. The belief underlying host desecration was that Christ was present in the wafer. That Judaism subscribed to neither of these credos was of no interest to illiterate, suggestible populations.

An on-the-spot report comes to us from a fifteenth century Francis-can cleric with an ironic eye. In 1438, John of Winterthur noted that a fel-low priest of his acquaintance had taken to sprinkling wafers with animal blood, then dropping them in a square where Jews gathered. The wafers were picked up by Christians, brought to this man's church and wor-shiped; and the money deposited for such prayers enriched the parish. As it happened, the enterprising priest was betrayed by a colleague and thrown into prison, but not for harming the Jews. His crime was to have encouraged idolatry by tricking people into worshiping an unconsecrated host.[9]

From the middle of the thirteenth century, the Roman popes spoke out unambiguously against the ritual murder and host desecration calum-nies. The educated higher clergy knew that there was no authority in Jew-ish law or literature to permit such acts and that the Mosaic code actually forbade the consumption of any blood (let alone human blood) as the root of kosher practice.

In 1247 Pope Innocent IV did not mince words: The accusation against the Jews comes from those who "covet their [the Jews'] posses-sions or thirst for their blood . . . contrary to the clemency of the Catholic faith," he wrote.[10]

Although this message was repeated many times over the centuries as the official position of the Roman Catholic Church on the subject, suc-cessive popes were pitifully unsuccessful in stemming the popular tide. Ordinary people were not impressed with high-sounding rationalizations; far more importantly, the protestations of the popes stood in direct oppo-sition to writings within primary Church literature concerning the crimes of the perfidious Jews and accusations of devilry. The coarse parish priests of medieval Europe were sometimes less instructed than the peasants they preached to. They and their parishioners knew all about the Devil and the Jews.

* * *

Although the blood-libel accusation had circulated widely in northern Europe from the twelfth century on, Spain came late to the myth. The reason was simple. Until the fifteenth century Spaniards, with their history of pluralism, were not psychologically ready to believe it.[11] By 1490 this was no longer the case.

The trial of the Holy Child of La Guardia was a perfect tool for realizing one of the goals of the Inquisition, the expulsion of the Jews, and to achieve this end familiar charges of ritual murder and host desecration were adapted to fifteenth century Spanish realities. For example, not all the accused were Jews, as was the case elsewhere. In the Holy Child affair they were Jews *and* conversos, the contemporary Spanish amalgam for "Jews." The accusations were also atypical; no Christian child was reported missing and no body was ever found—or even looked for, as it happens. The details of the story also were slanted to reflect the social reality of late fifteenth-century Spain. It was charged that a seven-year-old boy had been kidnapped and crucified in a cave so that the conversos in the group could perform magic on his heart and protect themselves from the Inquisition. The link with the common version of the myth was that the deed was alleged to have taken place on Good Friday.

There was a consecrated host in this tale as well, but it was not used for the usual avowed purpose of torturing the body of Christ. Like the heart of the kidnapped child, this host was intended for magical incantations against the Inquisition, and to make the inquisitors die "crazed from rabies" if they dared to arrest the converso-conspirators. The accused were also charged with placing a hex on Christians so the latter would disappear from the face of the earth along with their religion, which would then be replaced by Judaism.

In 1887 the Spanish scholar Fidel Fita discovered and published the complete trial records for one of the defendants in the case.[12] The transcript concerns a young Jewish shoemaker from the village of Tembleque near Toledo named Yucé Franco, and his trial allows us to peer directly into the social, political, and psychological world of Castile at the beginning of the 1490s. More surprising still, it uncovers a bridge between the Inquisition and the expulsion of Jews from Spain, which took place just months after the end of the trial in early 1492.

Three of the eleven accused were dead when the drama opened in June 1490. The cast of living characters was as follows:

- Yucé Franco, the shoemaker, who is probably under the age of twenty;

- Yucé's eighty-year-old Jewish father, Isaac Franco;

- four converso brothers also called Franco: Alonso, García, Iohan, and Lope. (They are apparently in the transport business. They own a cart, or carts, and travel constantly between the town of La Guardia and Murcia.);

- Benito García, an itinerant wool-washer and baptized Jew from La Guardia. He is in his forties.

- the inquisitors: Juan López de Cigales, Pedro de Villada, and Fernando de Santo Domingo. (In 1488, Santo Domingo had written the preface to a book commissioned by Torquemada charging converso-heretics with obeying the laws of the Talmud.)

* * *

In June 1490, Benito García is arrested by the Inquisition in the city of Astorga and interrogated by Inquisitor Pedro de Villada. The charge against him seems to be fairly commonplace: practicing Judaism, although Benito says later that he was forced to confess to "more than he knew." Benito provides the inquisitors with the names of several people, including the Jewish Franco family from Tembleque who may have been teaching him about Judaism, and the converso brothers of the same name.[13]

On July 1 Yucé Franco is arrested by the Inquisition along with the rest. There is no written statement of any charge against him, although he has probably been detained as one of the Jewish Francos who corrupted Benito García. Yucé is the youngest and the most naive of the prisoners, making him the easiest to incriminate.

Yucé Franco is left alone in his cell for approximately three weeks after his arrest. He is frightened and he seems to have heard an alarming rumor about why he is being held. Since he is in solitary confinement, the rumor may actually have been insinuated by his jailer, whose job it is to make suggestions to prisoners regarding events the inquisitors wish to hear about during upcoming interrogations.

Yucé is feeling sick, perhaps as a result of what he has heard. A medical doctor named Antonio de Avila comes to his cell. Fearing the worst Yucé begs him to ask the inquisitors to send a rabbi "who might recite the things that are customarily said by Jews at the time of their death."

But the inquisitors do not send a rabbi. They send a priest disguised as a rabbi—one who knows Hebrew and is familiar with Judaism—someone almost certainly of converso origin. Yucé pleads with the imposter to contact Abraham Seneor, the chief rabbi of Spain on his behalf. He confides the terrible rumor he has heard: that he and the other men from La

Guardia and Tembleque are in jail "because of a 'boy' who was killed eleven years ago in the place of 'that man.' "

Thinking he is speaking to a rabbi, Yucé has whispered the words "boy" and "that man" in Hebrew. He knows a fellow Jew will instantly understand the import and the horror of the rumor. Yucé believes he is being accused of ritual murder.

Yucé Franco is in no position to gainsay the existence of such a crime, which is said to have occurred when he was a child of ten or less. He is appropriately terror-stricken at the implication that this is the true reason he has been arrested and begs that the most important Jew in all of Spain be informed of his predicament.

This conversation is reported to the Inquisition. The rumor Yucé confided to the priest he thought was a rabbi is converted by the inquisitors into a confession of guilt.

On August 27, 1490, Inquisitor-General Tomás de Torquemada signs an order transferring everyone involved in the case from Segovia to Ávila. He had planned to conduct the trial himself, he writes, but he has been called to the royal court of Ferdinand and Isabella in Andalusia (where the long war against Granada is winding down). Torquemada announces that he has appointed several of the most experienced inquisitors in the country in his stead, all of them close associates who share his zeal for the defense of the faith.

A question already arises for the reader of the trial records. Why would the inquisitor-general of the Holy Office of the Inquisition for all of Castile and Aragon have planned to preside over the trial of a group of inconsequential nobodies when there were hundreds of trials going on all over the territory? There is no obvious answer—unless something important was in the works. And it was.

Prisoners of the Inquisition were always isolated from one another, as we have seen, but in the prison in Avila (which was connected by a tunnel to Torquemada's monastery of Santo Tomás) a strange thing occurred. Yucé Franco and Benito García found that they could talk to each other "privately." Yucé's cell was directly above Benito's, and there just happened to be a hole in the floor between them.

Under threat of torture Yucé later confessed everything that was said between them. Their conversations were touching and revealing.

*   *   *

"Jew," says Benito to break the ice. "I am in the cell beneath you. Have you a needle you can give me?"

"Just a shoemaker's needle," replies Yucé.

Benito dives straight to the point. "Your father, Don Isaac Franco, is also in prison. . . . The inquisitors told me they would burn him little by little."

There is a silence. This is news to Yucé. "Who are you? Why are you here?" he asks.

Benito tells Yucé that he was tortured with two hundred lashes, the water torture "in his nostrils," and two thumbscrews by "that dog of a doctor" (the Inquisitor Pedro de Villada) until he made a damning confession "he would burn for."

"Are you a converso?" asks Yucé.

Benito replies that he was baptized by his father some forty years ago, but he has recently been trying to recover the Judaism he never knew. What has finally severed him from Christ, Benito confides, was being subjected to the water torture. "Include me in your [Jewish] prayers so the Creator will release me from this prison," he begs Yucé. This will not be easy, he acknowledges, because "under the torture I said more than I knew."

The following Sunday Benito hears Yucé reciting his prayers and asks him again to pray for him. "The inquisitors are devils," he says.

"Don't say that," whispers Yucé, frightened.

"I say they are worse than Antichrists," persists Benito. "And the prior of Santa Cruz [Torquemada] is the worst Antichrist." He shifts his tack. "The Antichrist is a Jew who became a Christian. My father cursed me like the bones of a snake, and the curse stayed with me because I left the good and held on to the evil. I have lived with the evil for forty years, so I know what it is. The only good thing I have ever done was to prevent a Jewish boy from converting. I said to him, 'You see how they are burning them, and you want to become a Christian?' After that I gave him some money and sent him to Ocaña so he wouldn't convert.[14] But now that I know what is good and what is evil, I just want to get out of here."

Benito believes that all his suffering is the result of having been converted to Christianity. The whipping he received from the inquisitor was payment for beating his own children so they would go to church, the water torture was a consequence of having put coins in the basin for holy water, and the fleas that torment him in his cell are punishment for the money he gave for souls in purgatory.

In his sorrow he tells Yucé that he would gladly suffer for all the prisoners who come from his region if they were freed. He says the Inquisition is false and unjust, and that all it wants is converso money. "For that they hold them prisoner and for no other reason." If he ever gets out of jail he says he will leave Castile and go to Judea.

Benito questions Yucé about Judaism. Why do Jews fast on "the great day"(Yom Kippur)? What is the meaning of the prayer Jews recite on Saturday night? Why do Jews wear phylacteries. What, he asks, is the meaning of Zion?

Finally he requests a knife with which to circumcise himself. Yucé refuses. "You might die," he protests.

"That way I will not be burned," replies Benito. "God once came to me and said, 'I shall take you to a place where you will know me,' and on that day I gave my soul to my Maker."

Yucé Franco repeated these intercell conversations to the inquisitors on April 9, 1491, and his detailed recollections were dutifully recorded by the scribe and preserved over hundreds of years. Ritual murder was not on the mind of poor Benito García. He was a simple, suffering man who wanted only to escape from the Inquisition and find his way "home," back to the idealized religion of his parents and grandparents.

Yucé's trial before the Inquisition opened on December 17, 1490. The official charges were: attempting to entice Christians back to Judaism, and being an accomplice to the crucifixion of a Christian child on Good Friday. There was no date attached to this heinous crime.

According to the inquisitors, the conspirators had cut out the murdered child's heart and stolen a consecrated host for their magical rites on Passover. They intended to infect the inquisitors and all Christians with rabies in order "to inherit their possessions," and so that "their [Jewish] seed should multiply throughout the land, and the seed of faithful Christians should be uprooted."

"That is the biggest lie in the world!" cried Yucé when the chief prosecutor finished reading the charge.

Although the inquisitors spent almost eighteen months constructing their case against the accused in the Holy Child affair, the source for their charges was close at hand. The entire sequence of accusations, including the part about rabies, had appeared in Alonso de Espina's *Fortalitium Fidei*. The frame-up was carefully constructed. Once Yucé Franco's "confession" to the priest who had masqueraded as a rabbi was established early on in the process, the inquisitors could start their interrogations of the other accused prisoners with what they "knew." The results were predictable: since the Inquisition promised clemency to people who informed on others, each of the prisoners tried to appease his tormentors, and save himself, by embroidering on the story to his own advantage. They accused each other, and denied or attenuated their own supposed involvement.

As the months passed, and fear grew, Yucé Franco supplied—or was said to have supplied—all the gruesome details the Inquisition needed to hear. He allegedly described the insults the murderers hurled at the child who was, Yucé agreed, a stand-in for Christ. The conspirators knew the crucified child was a representation of the person of Christ because "light shone out of his *culo* (anus)," Yucé told the inquisitors. (From our point of view it is difficult to interpret this rather extraordinary piece of reportage.)

Yet there were moments of hesitation when loyalty and love took precedence over self-preservation. Isaac Franco was given the water torture in spite of his eighty years, but he stopped short of incriminating his son, Yucé. Yucé, in turn, tried not to implicate his father, saying he "did not remember" whether Isaac Franco had said or done anything in particular. Benito García refused to name any names at all, even though he was eventually pinpointed as the person who stole the consecrated host and carried the heart of the child from place to place while awaiting a propitious moment to enact magic. (Encouraged by torture Benito did provide other details such as where the wood for the crucifixion cross came from.)

By July 1491 the tale of ritual murder had reached fabulous dimensions, but since the prisoners were interrogated individually and each was trying to disculpate himself, they naturally differed on details—crucial details such as the year in which this event had occurred, who among them was present at the awful moment, who was the chief sorcerer, and even where the crime had taken place. Parts of their testimony were materially impossible; the heart was apparently kept around for six months between hexing ceremonies, and a trip covering hundreds of kilometers would have to have been accomplished in an impossibly short time.[15] (The editor of the trial transcript was clearly aware of these problems for he explains that a second heart was involved without saying where it came from.) Most of these discrepancies were simply ignored and left out of the final summation at the auto de fe that marked the culmination of the Holy Child affair.

On November 14, 1491, the inquisitors brought the prisoners together for the first time to "confirm" and coordinate the ritual murder confession. The utterly incredible comment in the transcript is that the men spoke together comfortably and were happy to see one another. (*Se hablaron é holgaron en verse.*)

Auto de Fe

Two days later. Wednesday November 16, 1491. A cold autumn wind sweeps across the central market place of Avila, whipping the trees in front of the beautiful church of San Pedro with its lovely rose windows and perfect Romanesque door. A large scaffold stands on the square in front of the church. Seated there are a dozen of the most important ecclesiastics of Spain dressed in the cloaks of their orders, or according to their rank. The inquisitors Pedro de Villada, Fernando de Santo Domingo, and Juan López de Cigalles are all present, as well as "other judges in the case." This auto de fe is so important that Pedro Gonzáles de Mendoza, the archbishop of Toledo and cardinal of Spain, has come to Avila. Mendoza was once a moderate who wanted to teach conversos Christian dogma, not burn them to death. But fourteen years have passed since he gave up in the face of opposition and accompanied Alonso de Hojeda and Tomás de Torquemada to Cordoba to urge an Inquisition against heresy on the young queen.

Facing these august representatives of the Church of Spain from his own wooden scaffold is Yucé Franco. He has been marched up the steep hill that leads from the Inquisition prison in the monastery of Santo Tomás to the market square. He is wearing a black death *sanbenito* covered with flames and devils.

Hundreds of people pack the square, noisily jostling each other for position. Many have traveled for days so as not to miss the spectacle.

One of the inquisitors stands and unravels a scroll of paper. He looks at his audience, waiting for silence. A hush falls on the crowd.

> Yucé Franco, citizen and resident of Tembleque in the district of Toledo, seduced Christians into his religion by telling them that the Christian religion was false and that Judaism was the true religion. And he crucified a Christian child with other Jews and Christians in recollection of the Passion of our Redemptor, Jesus Christ, and cursed Him, denying His divinity. And he participated in magic rites with the heart of the said child and with a consecrated host so that the inquisitors and all Christians would die of rabies.

There was, however, a disagreeable catch to these proceedings, and according to the rules of the Inquisition it had to be made public. In spite of the story that had been woven together through many and separate interrogations, the inquisitors had not brought Yucé to admit his own complicity in the purported crime. Other people's, yes; but not his own.

"The said Yucé Franco, Jew, expressly denied the contents of this charge," continued the inquisitor. However, this was not a problem, he maintained reassuringly, since the inquisitors had already obtained Yucé's confession of guilt (from the "rabbi") and corroborative proof from their interrogations of the other accused.

The sentence was predictable: the loss and confiscation of all his goods and "release to the secular arm." In addition Yucé was formally "excommunicated from the Holy Mother Church," to which he had, of course, never belonged. Here was yet another instance of the convergence of converso and Jew.

Yucé, Benito García and all the Franco brothers died that day at the "bonfire of Dehesa," on the burning fields of Ávila.[16]

★   ★   ★

The trial of Yucé Franco, Benito García, and their codefendants was a corrupt exercise from start to finish, a deliberately instigated frame-up that entrenched the ritual murder accusation in Spain. The "investigation" into the purported crucifixion of a child was entirely internal, taking place within the walls of the prison of the Inquisition in Avila. No one outside was interviewed, no sites were sought out. What remains striking is that the inquisitors seemed indifferent as to whether or not a real child had ever been reported missing, let alone murdered. Parents were parents, then as now. A lost child would have been reported to friends and relatives.

It is equally striking that the Inquisition made no attempt to put a name to this child, and that conflicting details such as when and where the crime occurred were quietly left out of its summation. The only "fact" the prisoners apparently agreed on, following Yucé's lead, was that the alleged murder apparently took place somewhere "in a cave."

What *was* stressed was the "how" and the "why" of the murder, both of which were shaped to conform to the blood libel mythology of northern Europe with a twist to suit the circumstances of inquisitorial Spain. This meant creating a cabal composed not merely of Jews, as was usual, but of the twin enemies, Jews and conversos, who here conspired jointly against Christ *and* the Inquisition. They had committed a triple treason: against man, God, and the institution that stood for the religious integrity of a united Spain. "Jew" and "converso" were now proved, indisputably, to be one creature, the demon enemy of Christ and country.

Torquemada wasted no time. He ordered the story translated into Catalan and sent to the Inquisition of Barcelona, and to churches and cathedrals across Spain. Shock washed over the country as priests in local parishes informed their stunned congregations about the kidnapping and murder of an innocent child who embodied Christ and a conspiracy to kill all Christians. There were no open doubters, at least none who dared write or whisper an opinion that has endured. The consecrated host allegedly used by the conspirators was transported to Torquemada's monastery of Santo Tomás, where it is said to remain, miraculously preserved, to this day. (It is, however, not viewable, according to a resident monk.)[17]

Aftermath

The myth of the Holy Child of La Guardia entered the history of Spain where it helped keep anti-Semitism alive for centuries. Missing details of the Holy Child's name, age, birthplace, and place of murder were obligingly provided by willing contributors. Writers proffered explanations about the embarrassing lack of a corpse; one suggested that the Holy Child's body was never found because it was carried to heaven along with his soul.[18] Believers raised shrines, miracles happened, and the town of La Guardia inaugurated a solemn festival to the memory of the child. Paintings of his martyrdom hung in churches and cathedrals (some were later moved to public galleries as examples of Renaissance art). In the sixteenth century the dramatist Lope de Vega wrote a play entitled *El Niño Inocente* (The innocent child) in which all the accused are Jews and none are conversos.

The cult of the Holy Child was officially formalized in the eighteenth century in a book entitled, *La Historia Del Martiro De La Santo Niño De La Guardia* (The history of the martyrdom of the Holy Child of La Guardia) by Martiń Martinez Moreno, a priest of the church of La Guardia who was pleased to provide more uncorroborated details.[19] In his preface we learn that the child's parents were actually from Toledo, that he was baptized in the church of San Andrés in that city, and that he was three or four years old at the time of the murder. The author also knows precisely where in Toledo the child was born. It seems that in 1613 the archbishop of Toledo had written a letter identifying the house, so the author went there and noticed three crosses on the wall. Furthermore, the current owner of the house agreed with him that the child had certainly been born there.

Martinez Moreno added a more sinister twist to the Holy Child tale by creating a direct link between Spain's notorious ritual-murder trial and the earlier blood-libel legends of France. In his version of the story, Benito García crossed the border to escape from the Inquisition and encountered a group of French Jews who had made a pact with the devil to kill all Christians so they could destroy the religion of Jesus and become masters of the world. One of their rabbis had taught them that a consecrated host burned with the heart of a Christian child would produce a powder that could be thrown into wells and rivers to poison Christians.

By the end of the nineteenth century at least seven full-length narratives had been written, and in the twentieth century the story of the Holy Child of La Guardia entered the standard reference work of Spain: the seventy-volume encyclopedia *Espasa-Calpe*. The entry begins as follows:

The blessed child of La Guardia was sacrificed by the Jews in imitation of the passion of Christ. The Jews cut out his heart in order to mix it with a consecrated host supplied by the judaizer, Juan Gómez . . . who was under the impression that the Jews intended to work a spell that would destroy the power of the inquisitors.

The most significant twentieth-century contribution to the Holy Child legend was written in 1945.[20] The familiar story is embellished; now we learn that the child's name was Cristóbal. A preface by the Marqués De Lozoya describes the Holy Child affair as "the Jewish offensive during the last years of the [royal] house of Trastámara [that] preceded the decree of expulsion in 1492," and concludes with a crucial statement of exclusion as the necessary precondition of national unity: "[The story] is of singular importance in the history of the heroic and painful task carried out by royalty and the people in the last decades of the Middle Ages in order to bring into being a Spanish nationality capable of effecting . . . its providential mission," writes the marqués.[21]

This was the core ideology, emerging pristine and intact through the long centuries.[22] From November 16, 1491 (the day of the auto de fe in Avila), the ritual murder of the Holy Child of La Guardia was invoked as a cornerstone of a new, united Spain joined by Ferdinand and Isabella under the banner of Catholicism: the Spain that conquered the last outpost of Moors in Granada, the Spain that expelled the Jews and later the Moors, the Spain that dispatched Christopher Columbus across the sea. That Spain did not officially disintegrate until Generalissimo Francisco Franco died in 1975 and a king who was both a liberal and a democrat acceded to the throne. But in spite of radical political and social change, the Holy Child lives on. In a 1989 popular history of Spain being sold in department stores along with videotapes and stationary, the apparently undisputed fact of ritual murder was confirmed once again and invoked as a reason for the expulsion of the Jews.

*   *   *

Over five hundred years have passed since the sensational trial when I take the winding road from Toledo toward the sleepy village of La Guardia. The route is paved, in a manner of speaking, but there is little reason to doubt that this thin ribbon drawn over a vast plateau dotted with serrated table rocks and the ruins of fortress castles is any other than the cart and mule track of centuries ago.

In the central square of the village a few old men sun themselves on chairs around an ancient well. A lone woman sells carrots from a cart. All is still.

The church, on the other hand, shines in glorious tribute to the Holy Child, patron saint of La Guardia, whose feast day has just passed. A statue of the child graces an alcove, a Christ figure with a crown of thorns flanked by the Virgin Mary and Jesus, himself. Votive candles burn brightly at his feet. Near the altar another statue of the child stands on a decorated processional wagon lavishly smothered in fresh flowers.

A priest approaches, eager to talk about his church's claim to fame. The story appears to have gone through another metamorphosis. The child, I learn, was five years old and his name was Juan. His mother, who was blind, was begging in front of the cathedral in Toledo when he was kidnapped by the Jews, a few men from around this very village. The Jews renamed the Child Cristóbal, as in Christ, then murdered him to recreate the martyrdom of the savior. This act, says the priest, was the ultimate reason for the expulsion of the Jews from Spain. The cave where he was martyred is not far from here. I may see it if I wish, he says, smiling.

Standing here in this church I am thinking about a terrified, ignorant boy named Yucé, so desperate to live. I think about his eighty-year-old father undergoing torture, and about Benito García who alone had the strength not to implicate the others though he knew he was trapped. "Is the story true?" I ask the priest.

"Well," he replies slowly, "the Jews did admit to taking the child into the cave." He hesitates. The priest of La Guardia is an honest man, a modern man. On the other hand, the murder of the Holy Child has been enshrined in Spanish history and it is his church's claim to fame. "I suppose that is all we can know," he concludes ambivalently, turning his head away.

Notes

1. Unless otherwise noted, my main sources for this chapter are: Cecil Roth, ed., *The Ritual Murder Libel and the Jew: Cardinal Ganganelli's Report*; Fidel Fita, "La Inquisición y el Santo Niño de la Guardia," *BAM* 11 (1887); Isidore Loeb, "Le Saint Enfant de La Guardia," *REJ* 16 (1887); Baer, *A History of the Jews in Christian Spain*, 2: 398ff; Manuel Romero de Castilla, *Singular Suceso en el Reinado de los Reyes Católicos*.

2. John 8: 44, 47.

3. Ibid., 8.

4. This part of Christian liturgy was taught from the pulpit until the advent of Pope John XXIII and the Second Vatican Council in 1962.

5. Gavin I. Langmuir, "Thomas of Monmouth: Detector of Ritual Murder," in A. Dundes, ed., *The Blood Libel Legend: A Casebook in Anti-Semitic Folklore*, 7.

6. Langmuir, "Thomas," note 4.

7. Geoffrey Chaucer immortalized a case that emerged in England in 1255: little Hugh of Lincoln. The Prioress's Tale from *The Canterbury Tales* is a clear exposition of the ritual-murder accusation. A little boy allegedly angers the Jews by singing a prayer to Mary as he walks through the ghetto streets on his way to school.

First of our foes, the Serpent Satan shook
Those Jewish hearts that are his waspish nest,
Swelled up and said. "O Hebrew people look!
Is this not something that should be redressed?
Is such a boy to roam as he thinks best
Singing to you, canticles and saws
Against the reverence of your holy laws?"

From that time forward all these Jews conspired
To chase this innocent child from the earth's face
Down a dark alley-way they found and hired
A murderer who owned that secret place;
And as the boy passed at his happy pace
This cursed Jew grabbed him and held him, slit
His little throat and cast him in a pit.

Cast him, I say, into a privy-drain,
Where they were wont to void their excrement.
O cursed folk of Herod come again,
Of what avail your villainous intent?
Murder will out, and nothing can prevent
God's honour spreading, even from such seed;
The blood cries out upon your cursed deed . . .

O Hugh of Lincoln, likewise murdered so
By cursed Jews, as is notorious
(For it was but a little time ago),
Pray mercy on our faltering steps, that thus
Merciful God may multiply on us
His mercy, though we be unstable and vary,
In love and reverence of his mother, Mary.

8. 1290 was also the year the Jews were expelled from England.

9. Raynaldi, *Annal.*, 1338, nos. 19-21, cited in H. C. Lea, "El Santo Niño de la Guardia," *EHR* 4: 229ff.

10. Cited in Roth, *The Ritual Murder Libel*, 20. In July of 1247 Pope Innocent IV published his famous Encyclical, *Lachrymabilem Judaeorum Alemannie*, addressed to the clergy of Germany and France, in which he repeated his claim that ritual murder accusations came from people who were, above all, anxious to avoid paying their debts to the Jews. He added:

Nor shall anyone accuse them of using human blood in their religious rites, since in the Old Testament they are instructed not to use blood of any kind, let alone human blood. But since at Fulda and in several other places many Jews were killed on the ground of such a suspicion, we . . . strictly forbid that this should be repeated in future. If anyone knowing the tenor of this decree should, God forbid, dare to oppose it, he shall be punished by loss of his rank and office, or be placed under a sentence of excommunication, unless he makes proper amends for his presumption.

In 1272 another pope, Gregory X, wrote his own coda:

It sometimes happens that certain Christians lose their Christian children. The charge is then made against the Jews by their enemies that they have stolen and slain these children in secret, or other Christians who are envious of the Jews even hide their children in order to have a pretext to molest the Jews, and to extort money from them. . . . They assert, most falsely, that the Jews have taken away these children and slain them, and have sacrificed the heart and blood. Yet their law expressly forbids the Jews to sacrifice or to eat or drink blood: even though it be of animals which have the hoof cloven. . . . We accordingly have determined that no Christian shall be allowed to make any allegations against the Jews on such a pretext. We command, moreover, that the Jews imprisoned on this account shall be released from prison. . . .

11. There had been two other charges of ritual murder in Spain since the twelfth century, but they remained isolated cases. In 1250 a boy from Saragossa was said to have been crucified by the Jews when a "miraculous light" shone over his grave, but the accusation was considered anomalous and the Jewish community was protected by King Jaime I. The second occurred in 1468, shortly after the publication of the *Fortalitium Fidei.*

12. Fidel Fita, "La Inquisición y el Santo Niño de La Guardia," *BAH* 11. Unless otherwise indicated, Fita is my main source for this chapter.

13. The name Franco was so common among Spaniards of Jewish ancestry that General Francisco Franco was whispered to be of converso stock. Notions of pure and impure blood remained imbedded in consciousness well into the twentieth century.

14. Ocaña was then a large Jewish settlement.

15. Isidore Loeb, "Le Saint Enfant de la Guardia," *REJ* 16. Loeb determined the distances between places mentioned and the disparate time calculations the prisoners assigned to each voyage and concluded that these were materially impossible fabrications. Loeb was the first scholar to examine and dismiss the Holy Child case on the basis of available evidence. Henry C. Lea also dismissed the affair as an instrument of propaganda in *Chapters from the Religious History of Spain*, 203ff.

16. The notary who was present at the execution, one Antón Gonsález, purportedly wrote an appendix to the trial records stating that Yucé Franco confessed at the stake, that three of the victims were strangled after repenting, and three were burned alive "as good Jews." There has been no corroboration of this report, but many victims of the Inquisition did confess at the stake in order to die less painfully, just as many made up confessions during their interrogations to avoid or minimize torture. The notary added material about where he thought the Holy Child's birthplace was, and where the body was buried; and he expressed his hope that miracles would occur. The authenticity of this document has been disputed as the notary's speculations resemble additions incorporated into the story as facts at a later date.

17. The author put the question in early 1989.

18. Francisco de Quevedo, cited in Burke, *A History of Spain*, 153.

19. Published 1785.

20. Manuel Romero de Castilla, *Singular Suceso.*

21. Many Spanish Inquisition scholars have continued to believe in the Holy Child ritual murder in spite of internal inconsistencies and obvious fabrications. This appears to be integral to the ideological polemic that has characterized Inquisition studies. Fidel Fita, the discoverer of the trial records, also believed the guilty verdict. In his case it is well to remember that at the time of his discovery (1887) many ritual murder cases were being propagandized and brought to trial across Eastern Europe.

22. Claudio Sánchez Albornoz, a noted modern historian, wrote that the Inquisition was "a Satanic invention of the Hispanic Jews that reflects the sinister and mysterious processes of the Jewish courts"; cited in Sanford Shepard, "The Present State of the Ritual Crime in Spain," in Alan Dundes, ed., *The Blood Libel*, 170.

13

Full Circle: The Last King of the Moors

The noose was tightening. Conversos burned, the Jews were under siege, and the Moors of Granada—the last Arab kingdom—braced themselves as the armies of the Holy Reconquest prepared for final victory under the banner of *Santiago* and the king and queen of Spain.

Behind the royal couple, one figure was constant in these assaults: Tomás de Torquemada.

If the Holy Child trial was staged to revive the anti-Jewish passions that followed the assassination of Pedro de Arbués in Saragossa, it had also been timed to coincide with the end of the war in Granada, the final phase of the eight hundred-year Holy Reconquest. The armies of Ferdinand and Isabella had been at war with Boabdil, the last king of Granada, since 1481—in other words since the inauguration of the Inquisition when money to fight this last battle became available from confiscations. By 1491, final victory was imminent. Throughout this period the inquisitor-general was in close touch with Ferdinand and Isabella. With the Reconquest coming to an end, Torquemada knew better than anyone that the time to defeat heresy and false religion of every sort had arrived. The spectacular Holy Child auto de fe, in which both Jews and conversos were convicted of the ritual murder of "Christ," was arranged to take place on November 16, 1491, just nine days before King Boabdil formally surrendered to the Catholic monarchs, and the execution of the condemned men had been followed by a campaign of carefully orchestrated anti-Semitic propaganda. Before Ferdinand and Isabella signed the famous edict to expel the Jews from their kingdoms in March 1492, one other name had appeared on an earlier draft of the document: that of Tomás de Torquemada.

The Final Assault

On the day King Boabdil was born the royal astrologers recoiled in visible fear. "Allah Akbar! God is great," they cried prostrating themselves. The infant's horoscope had revealed that he would sit on the jeweled throne of Granada, but that the kingdom would be lost during his reign. From this day the prince was called *El Zogoybi,* or The Unlucky.[1]

Since 1236, the year the Christian armies retook neighboring Cordoba, the ancient seat of the caliphs, the last remaining Arab kingdom of Granada had reached remarkable heights of prosperity and artistic sophistication. The fertile plain surrounding the capital was planted with figs, lemons, pomegranates, oranges, and mulberry trees; and the surrounding snow-capped Sierra Nevada brought constant enjoyment to the city's pleasure-loving inhabitants. Water diverted from the mountains provided the entire kingdom with fountains and streams. The Moors called Granada paradise on earth, and with reason. Artistry had reached stunning levels, including the building of the Alhambra which was (and remains) one of the most magnificent structures on earth.

For centuries the Christian kings of the north had been content to collect tribute from the Arab kings of Granada and live in relative peace, but when Boabdil's father came to the throne in 1465 he refused to pay. Muley Aben Hassan was "a fierce and warlike Infidel," according to a Christian chronicler.[2] As a child he watched his father pay the tribute in Cordoba, feeling humiliated by the sneers of the Castilians. Subservience was not for him. Muley Aben Hassan even dared to insult the envoy of Ferdinand and Isabella who came calling in 1478 demanding payment. "Our mint coins only the blades of scimitars and the heads of lances," was his contemptuous reply to the ambassador.

These fighting words only delighted King Ferdinand. Now that Castile and Aragon had been united through his marriage to Isabella, the armies of Christian Spain were probably unbeatable in battle. The sultan's refusal to pay tribute looked like a delicious opportunity to conclude the Holy Reconquest and so to capture worldly fame, religious renown *and* the indescribable wealth of Granada. The latter benefit was never far from Ferdinand's mind.

As it happened, the pugnacious sultan struck first. In December 1481 his men scaled the walls of the Christian fortress of Zahara during a storm when the guards were unprepared. The Moors killed, raped, and pillaged in the style of contemporary warfare, and took captive slaves back to Granada.

Two months later Ferdinand retaliated. For four days his army of seven thousand men struggled through little-traveled mountain passes until they reached the Moorish border fortress of Alhama. Three hundred knights scaled the walls. After twelve hours of fighting, they took the city.

When the news reached Granada, the people of the city poured into the streets in mourning. A strategic post was lost; a dangerous indication of the enemy's strength. A lament entered the literature of Spain:

> Men, children, and women
> Lamented their terrible loss
> All the ladies in Granada wept,
> Alas, my Alhama.
> In the streets and in homes
> There was great mourning,
> And the king crying like a woman
> For the enormity of his loss.
> Alas, my Alhama.[3]

In the spring of 1486 the entire army of the Holy Reconquest assembled in Cordoba. Trumpets sounded as the scions of Castilian nobility entered the gates of the city dressed in gorgeous finery, their banners streaming and hundred of vassals in attendance. (Iñigo López de Mendoza had brought with him five hundred armed men and horses harnessed in gold and brocade cloth.) The warrior-priests of Spain also had come to wage what they hoped would be the last battle for Christ and Santiago. The clergy had kept the idea of the Holy Reconquest alive over the centuries.

A contingent of knights arrived from France, having doubtless heard tales about the magnificence of Granada and, one might guess, the pleasures of the harem. (The French were looked down on by the Castilians because they seemed unduly interested in women, but this changed to admiration when they proved brave in the field.) The English knight Lord Scales, Earl of Rivers, also appeared on the scene fresh from the battle of Bosworth Field where his brother-in-law, King Henry VII, had recently defeated Richard III. Lord Scales had brought along one hundred long-bow archers and two hundred foot soldiers, all carrying pikes and battle-axes, but it seems clear that not everyone appreciated their presence. A jaundiced chronicler described the English dryly:

> This cavalier was from the far island of England, and brought with him a train of his vassals, men who had been hardened in certain civil wars which raged in their country. They were a comely race of men, but too fair and fresh for warriors, not having the sunburned warlike hue of our old Castilian soldiery. They were huge feeders also, and deep carousers, and could not

accommodate themselves to the sober diet of our troops, but insisted on eating and drinking after the manner of their country. They were often noisy
and unruly . . . and their quarter of the camp was a scene of loud revel and
sudden brawl. . . . Though from a remote and somewhat barbarous island,
they believed themselves the most perfect men on earth.[4]

In May 1486 King Ferdinand rode from Cordoba at the head of an
army of twelve thousand cavalry and forty thousand foot soldiers accompanied by six thousand men whose job it was to level roads. Armor glittered, banners streamed, and plumed headdresses shivered in the breeze
as the Christian knights of Europe advanced slowly toward Granada. A
battle took place in the mountain city of Loxa and was won by the Christians, but not before Lord Scales lost his two front teeth. King Ferdinand
consoled the English earl by suggesting he might have lost his teeth anyway from natural decay, and the earl replied that it was a small thing to
lose two teeth in the service of God. "This was a speech full of courtly wit
and Christian piety," recorded the chronicler approvingly. "One only
marvels that it should have been made by a native of an island so far distant from Castile."[5]

In August 1487 Ferdinand took Malaga, where he found a community of four hundred and fifty Jews who spoke nothing but Arabic. (The
Jews of Castile ransomed them from slavery with twenty thousand gold
doblas and had them transferred to Castile in galley ships.) Never one to
miss an opportunity, Ferdinand also devised a scheme to extort money
from the wealthy Muslims of the city. Everything they owned was taken
as a down payment on their future release from captivity and they were
given eight months to pay the rest.

Every house in Malaga was numbered and the contents of each carefully noted using the methods of the Inquisition. After the residents had
brought their possessions to a central drop-off depot, they were arrested
and shipped off to Seville as servants until the eight months had passed.
But the captive Moors had no obvious way of raising more money. When
the allotted time elapsed their status was altered from servant to slave, and
Ferdinand got to keep everything they had left on deposit. Machiavelli
had good reason to admire King Ferdinand of Aragon.

The king found plenty of heretics inside the newly conquered cities:
conversos who had escaped from the Inquisition into Muslim territory
and become Jews again. The punishment varied. In Malaga they were
sometimes tortured to death with sharp pointed reeds, sometimes burned
by the Inquisition, sometimes held to ransom.[6] Occasionally they were
offered a choice of becoming Christians again, or exile, and if any vacil-
lated the inquisitors of the Holy Office were never far behind the battle

lines. Torquemada personally supervised the bonfires of the faith that were kindled all over the reconquered kingdom of Granada, as the Reconquest armies took town after town, and with every new battle more property was confiscated for both the Inquisition and the war coffers of the king and queen.

*   *   *

From the Alhambra's tower peaks, King Boabdil looked down on the level land surrounding the city of Granada at the army of the Catholic monarchs. The green plain was the breadbasket of Granada, but the Christian armies had deliberately scorched and destroyed it.

In autumn 1491 the capital city, Granada, was under siege, and a winter without food loomed ominously ahead. Every day two hundred thousand starving men, women, and children watched the supply caravans entering the Christian camp below. Dark whispers circulated through the streets about the cosmic curse that had settled on the head of their ruler and the end of the kingdom that was predicted the day he was born.

Boabdil held a meeting of his counselors in the Alhambra. Most agreed there could be no relief from any source. Sorrowfully the king decided to surrender.

The envoy Boabdil sent to Ferdinand returned with a promise of fair terms. Ferdinand and Isabella affirmed that the entire kingdom of Granada now belonged to them, and that every Granadian was now their subject. In the old style they also promised freedom of religion and the right to keep possessions.

In a Reconquest negotiation such as this, the rules that had once characterized a tolerant nation came automatically into play, but like the continuing employment of Jews in high places and the historical "protection" of minorities, such behavior was already an anachronism. In the era of the Inquisition and the Holy Child trial, the liberal terms offered to the Moors in Granada would soon be seen for what they were: a well-intentioned but now outdated gesture, a remembered formula from days past.

The capitulation of Granada was signed on November 25, 1491. The royal household grieved, and the city mourned. Boabdil's family left the Alhambra in the early predawn light, the last of the Moors to rule in Spain. From the plains below, Hernando de Talavera, Bishop of Ávila, rode toward the city to take possession of the Alhambra in the names of Ferdinand and Isabella as the Christian warrior-knights waited in silence below, watching his horse climb the mountain path, all anticipating the moment when the royal standard of the Catholic monarchs would fly from the tallest tower of the palace.

And there it was, the silver cross and the ensign of Santiago whose name their fathers, grandfathers, and their ancestors for centuries past had shouted as they rode into battle against the Moors. "Santiago, Santiago!" The roar of victory rose from the field below. "Castile! Castile! For King Ferdinand and Queen Isabella!" The king, the queen, and their entire army dropped to the ground in prayer. A resident choir sang the *Te Deum*.

*　*　*

King Boabdil stopped on a ridge high above the city and looked down at the famous fountains of Granada sparkling in the sunlight. The banners of Castile and Aragon already floated from the highest tower of the Alhambra. Boabdil cried, but his mother, Aicha, who had navigated him through years of internecine conflicts and intrigue until he was ensconced on the throne of Granada, did not offer comfort. "You weep like a woman for what you failed to defend like a man," she hissed at her son.

Boabdil the Unlucky turned his back on Granada. Later the ridge from which he last looked at his city was named *El Ultimo Suspiro del Moro*: The Last Sigh of the Moor.

On January 2, 1492, Ferdinand and Isabella entered Granada in triumphal procession. They stopped to pray in the main mosque which had already been converted into a church; then they climbed the hill to the Alhambra and entered the gates of the palace. They smiled with pleasure at the gold filigree that decorated walls and ceilings. In the perfect court-yards, sculpted fountains shot jets of cool water into the sky. The fabled kingdom was theirs; they had transformed the romance of the Holy Reconquest into reality.

So great was the import of this victory that in 1504 Ferdinand and Isabella commissioned a Royal Chapel in the cathedral of Granada where they might lie for eternity.

In the eighth century, in the wild Asturian hills of northern Hispania, Pelayo emerged as a fighting remnant of the defeated Christian Visigoths. Eons ago his name and his deeds had passed into legend, and now that myth was vindicated. The Visigoths and their powerful clergy were back, transformed into a new race of proud and would-be "pure" Christian Spaniards. That all of Spain was a mix of Roman, Celt, German-Goth, Moor, and Jew was of little interest. What mattered was that Pelayo and Santiago had held the nation in sway on the plains of Granada, and the last remnant of the Moors was uprooted. It was the end of a nation that had brought unimagined richness to a rude outpost on the Mediterranean and introduced a culture of religious pluralism that had set Spain apart for centuries. A different ethos had come into being, symbolized and presided over by the Catholic monarchs and their chief deputy for ideology, Tomás de Torquemada.

Notes

1. The dramatic tale of King Boabdil and the siege of Granada is wonderfully told by Washington Irving in *Tales of the Alhambra*.

2. Fray Antonio Agapida, cited in Washington Irving, *Tales of the Alhambra*, 10.

3. Cited in Anwar G. Chejne, *Islam and the West: The Moriscos, A Cultural and Social History*, 5 (translation by Erna Paris).

4. Ibid., 150ff.

5. Ibid., 166.

6. H. C. Lea, *The Moriscos of Spain: Their Conversion and Expulsion*.

14

The Expulsion of the Jews

They were caught by surprise. Things had been bad for years, but wasn't it just a matter of degree? Was there any reason to think the traditional roles many of them continued to occupy were any less valued, or less necessary? For in spite of prohibitions that had been advanced then ignored over the century, Jews still collected taxes and a few still operated "banks" by extending credit and loans to all sectors, including the royals. There seemed no obvious reason to believe traditional royal protection was any less secure, in spite of harassment from the Inquisition. As late as 1487 the Jews of Castile were calling Ferdinand their "just and loving sovereign," and there is no reason to dismiss this as mere formula.

The Jews were proud of their contribution to the decade-long war against Granada, for only they and the conversos had the experience to raise the necessary capital. There was never enough money, even though the Inquisition was appropriating property daily and directing the funds to the war coffers, even though Ferdinand had imposed a special tax on the Jews—the extraordinary sum of five hundred million maravedis.[1] Queen Isabella had sent letters demanding loans to every duke, count, and would-be *hidalgo* in Castile and to every municipality. She also supervised the provision of supplies, ordering merchants to ship wheat and cereals at a fixed price.[2] The Jews were responsible for supplying the Reconquest battalions which meant delivering food and arms by mule caravan over thousands of miles of wild, mountainous terrain where roads were nonexistent or practically inaccessible. Isaac Abravanel, financial advisor to the court and a scholar of the Torah and Talmud who was known throughout the Jewish diaspora, headed the operation. He was assisted by Rabbi Abraham Seneor, treasurer-in-chief of the *Hermandad* (the local police force set up by the queen), head of tax farming for

Castile, and the acknowledged leader of the Jews of Spain. Seneor was eighty years old and a long-time counselor to the queen (years earlier he had helped negotiate her marriage to Ferdinand). With his close, long-standing ties to the king and queen, what harm could possibly come to the Jews? The rabbi was so important he was attended by a retinue of thirty mules wherever he went.[3]

It is a particular irony of Isaac Abravanel's life (and a telling observation on the times) that he entered the service of the Catholic monarchs in 1483: the same year the *Suprema* of the Inquisition came into being and Torquemada, an anti-Semite, was appointed inquisitor-general. Royalty continued the old ways by appointing a Jew to a top position, while all around him an uncertain future was unfolding for his people. Conversos were being burned for being "Jews," and Jews were coming under increasing scrutiny and pressure from the Inquisition, but Ferdinand and Isabella still chose the best talent from both communities. For most of the 1480s Isaac Abravanel, Abraham Seneor, and powerful conversos such as Alfonso de la Caballería, Gabriel Sánchez, and Luis de Santángel sat in government council with Torquemada and others who shared the inquisitor-general's vision of a "pure" Spain—with people who wanted nothing less than their destruction.

In fact, the Catholic monarchs maintained a custodial relationship with the Jews until the very last moment. In 1485, in response to a petition from Abraham Seneor, they ordered officials in Segovia to intervene with a Dominican priest from Torquemada's monastery of Santa Cruz who was "exciting and provoking simple people" to attack the Jewish quarter;[4] and they reprimanded the city for refusing to give the Jews access to ovens where they could bake unleavened bread for Passover.[5] Ferdinand and Isabella reaffirmed their policy of protection in 1491 when the Holy Child trial provoked a new outburst of anti-Semitic attacks; and until the final hour they continued to employ court Jews as their personal physicians, counselors, and financiers. Most intriguing of all, they renewed four-year contracts with Jewish tax farmers in 1491 and signed others as late as the first months of 1492.

There were dozens of reasons to believe life would go on as usual, albeit in a more precarious environment, for if the good times didn't last forever, neither did the bad. No one imagined that a community with a history of close to one thousand and five hundred years, a community that had coexisted with the Romans in this distant corner of that ancient empire, might abruptly be thrust into perpetual exile.

On January 2, 1492, Ferdinand and Isabella marched triumphantly into Granada. On March 31, 1492, they proclaimed the Edict of Expulsion. What could have happened during those eighty-nine days?

One scans the timescape, searching for Torquemada. What was the inquisitor-general doing at this crucial juncture? One discovers him at the vortex of events, as usual, whenever decisions affecting religious-national policy were being weighed. Torquemada interpreted the defeat of Granada, meaning the end of the Holy Reconquest, as a sign that God approved of the Inquisition. There were connections: the Reconquest helped rid the country of the infidel and the Inquisition purified the faith against heresy. The two operated together like a well-oiled machine. But there remained one seemingly intractable obstacle to national unity—that is, the single entity of "One Church, One State" that Torquemada and the Catholic monarchs so fervently desired. That unity would never come about while there were Jews to seduce conversos into heresy, Torquemada argued. Were the records of the Holy Office not filled with testimony and confessions to prove this corruption? Did the holy fires of the Inquisition burning so vigorously all over the land not prove this corruption?

There were other equally compelling reasons for the Edict of Expulsion. Popular hatred, for one. Beyond the hurricane of emotion that had been whipped up over the breadth of the century and beyond by religious fanatics, culminating with Torquemada, there had also been a succession of natural disasters. In 1485 it rained for sixty days, flooding the crops; and in 1487 a devastating drought catapulted millions of peasants into extreme poverty, making it impossible for them to pay their taxes or their debts. Encouraged by their village priests, they prayed, confessed, took communion, and went on pilgrimages. And they swore to take revenge— not against the king and queen who insisted that they contribute to the war in Granada (that kind of rebellion was impossible)—but against the Jews and conversos who collected taxes in the name of royal and landed interests.

Something similar had taken place during the fourteenth century when floods, famine, and plague devastated all of Europe and it was collectively agreed that God was pointing an accusing finger at the Jews. Natural disaster was one reason for the wild, uncontrollable pogroms of 1391. Now, exactly a century later, the flame of popular anti-Semitism burned dangerously bright again. The Catholic monarchs were concerned. They had only just succeeded in reestablishing law and order after decades of anarchy, and from now on it would no longer be possible to initiate a rattling Reconquest war to divert popular passions if necessary. Ferdinand and Isabella had not brought the nobility into line and defeated King Boabdil of Granada only to see their country torn apart by class and religious conflict.

The Catholic monarchs knew that for hundreds of years the Jews had helped finance the Reconquest and settled the new border regions after each victory. They were aware that Jews had been the natural brokers between Christian and Arab Spain when there were kingdoms on both sides and opposing rulers, and that having lived under both regimes, the Jews reflected the two cultures, spoke several languages, traded internationally, and translated. While Christian Spain remained proudly illiterate, the Jews valued scholarship, and their learning had always been indispensable to those who governed.

But the Reconquest was over. There would be no more wars to finance and no more Arab rulers to deal with. The days of border settlement had long passed. Jewish erudition remained important, but whatever talents the Jews possessed lived on in their converso relatives. In any event, the Renaissance had finally taken hold in the peninsula and Queen Isabella was aggressively promoting learning. Living without the Jews would not be easy for the Catholic monarchs, but their loss would not be a total disaster either.

On the purely negative side of this ledger, volatility among the Jews was creating serious problems. Historically, the Jews had had the right to self-government, the right to collect their community taxes, and the right to run their own criminal courts; but internal wrangling and external pressure had weakened the communal framework. Rabbis and judges were sanctioning the executions of informers and lynchings went unpunished. Although Ferdinand had already tried to control this by removing the community's right to pronounce the death sentence, difficulties persisted.

Underlying all these considerations was a crucial, unspoken reality. The crown already had access to the fortunes of convicted conversos through the Inquisition, but Jewish wealth was only available through taxation. A general expulsion would appropriate entire fortunes in an instant. It would also cancel all outstanding debts, including those of the beleaguered and dangerously volatile lower classes.

Torquemada's unique access to the king and queen allowed him to argue each of these points over and over again during the critical days of early 1492. The chronicle of Cardinal Pedro González de Mendoza, archbishop of Seville, is illuminating. "They [Ferdinand and Isabella] considered that up to that period they had not derived so much fruit from the institution of the Holy Office as they had promised themselves upon the information of the inquisitor-general, by whose persuasion and constant advice they had determined to expel the Jews from all their kingdoms," he wrote revealingly.[6]

There would be much to lose by expelling the Jews, but possibly even more to gain, and it was this balancing of interests that set Ferdinand of Aragon apart as a distinctly "modern" king. Ferdinand's decision to expel the Jews (although Isabella ultimately laid the responsibility on God, as we shall see) was a perfect mirror of the way Machiavelli's astute Renaissance Prince saw the world.

* * *

The edict was signed in the Alhambra palace in Granada, the symbolic, captured heart of the defeated infidel. The Jews were commanded to leave Spain by the last day of July 1492 "by order of the King and Queen, our sovereigns, and of the Reverend Prior of Santa Cruz, Inquisitor-General in all the kingdoms and dominions of Their Majesties."[7] The measure of Torquemada's influence had finally entered the record of state.

But the edict was not pronounced publicly throughout Castile and Aragon until a full month later—it was held secret on pain of death—and there is no better explanation for this than that forwarded by Isaac Abravanel. When the news became known in court circles, a deadly struggle took place: influential Jews and their sympathizers rallied around Abravanel and Abraham Seneor to overturn the edict, while their enemies rallied around Torquemada. There is evidence that some prominent conversos, including Alfonso de la Caballería, joined Abravanel in his struggle to save the Jews,[8] but it is also true that anti-Semitism among the converso elite drove many of them to support the edict. Self-interest appears to have dictated this position. With the Jews out of the way, conversos would be less vulnerable to the Inquisition from informers who knew about their religious practices or were settling scores. And as long as old Christians thought the Jews were trying to entice conversos back to Judaism, the conversos, would be suspect.[9]

A dramatic though possibly apocryphal story has come down through the centuries. It is a tale that encapsulates the knife-edge indecision of final moments when Ferdinand and Isabella seemed, fleetingly, to hesitate before committing themselves to an extraordinary course of action.

Isaac Abravanel and Abraham Seneor have reached the climax of their struggle to save their people. Abravanel kneels before the Catholic monarchs in the fabulous throne room of the Alhambra which was (and is) profusely decorated with beautifully engraved Arabic poetry throughout. The king and queen are seated in front of an alabaster-latticed window. Similar lacings decorate the upper walls so the light in the room is scattered and diffuse. This design was a deliberate feature of the Moorish palace: when ambassadors and other envoys left the blinding sun of Granada and entered the presence of the king, they were temporarily blinded by the change in light, and thus all the more impressed and intimidated.

Isaac Abravanel is chief financial advisor to Ferdinand and Isabella, the man who fed and supplied the thousands of soldiers who recently brought the Reconquest to a final and glorious end, the man who advanced his own money to the cause, and the man who has just negotiated with one Christopher Columbus on their behalf. He is, in other words, their "friend" in so far as courtiers and royal servants can be the friends of kings. Kneeling beside him is eighty-year-old Rabbi Abraham Seneor, he who helped mediate the marriage of the royal couple who now sit stiffly before him on their jewelled thrones, he who loyally supported them during the dark days of civil war two decades before. Abraham Seneor, too, is a "friend."

The two men speak. They remind the king and queen of the long history of the Jewish people in Aragon and Castile, and of their unparalleled service through the centuries. They remind them that the Jews have fought in the Reconquest wars for hundreds of years. They pledge money in the usual way. Abravanel offers his personal fortune of thirty thousand gold ducats.

Ferdinand starts to waver at the prospect of this ransom, when suddenly a small side door into the throne room bursts open. Tomás de Torquemada has been listening there, and now he is standing in the magnificent hall, trembling visibly, waving a crucifix in his hand.

"Behold the crucified Christ whom Judas Iscariot sold for thirty pieces of silver!" he shouts. "Your Majesties are about to sell him again, for thirty thousand pieces of gold. You shall have to answer to God!" Torquemada places the crucifix on a table, turns, and leaves abruptly.

If Ferdinand and Isabella have been momentarily irresolute, this is the deciding instant—especially for the pious queen. For Torquemada is not merely the inquisitor-general of the Holy Inquisition against Depraved Heresy; he is her childhood confessor, the teacher of her youth, the man who shaped her own, very Catholic faith. If Torquemada has seen fit to challenge her personal commitment to Christ himself, there is no further question for Isabella. Or for Ferdinand, whose faith is certainly less, but whose understanding of politics is second to none.

The queen turns to Abravanel and Seneor. "Do you believe that this comes upon you from Us?" she asks. "The Lord has put this thing in the heart of the king."[10] It appears that God, and not man, has decided the fate of the Spanish Jews. There is nothing more to say.

"As the adder closes its ear with dust against the voice of the charmer, so the king hardened his heart against the entreaties of his supplicants and declared he would not revoke the edict," wrote Isaac Abravanel from his exile.[11]

The Expulsion

It is Sunday April 29, 1492, just after noon. Trumpets and drums sound in cities and towns across Castile and Aragon. The royal heralds have an important announcement.

In and around Saragossa, women in the midst of preparing the midday meal leave their ovens, men abandon their Sunday amusements, and excited children run to the central plaza in front of the Seo cathedral.[12] Worshipers leave their prayers, and priests leave their rites. The local nobility trots in astride their decked-out horses, and the sound of hundreds of horseshoes clip-clopping along pavement stones adds to the pitch of expectation. The nobles are dressed in their sumptuous red, blue and green velvets. Colored plumes wave from their hats.

The Jews flock to the plaza like the rest of the citizenry. No one has any idea of what is to come. There has been no reduction in any social or economic activity, and as we have seen the king and queen only recently renewed their agreements with the community.

The crowd presses in and the royal banners flutter overhead as the heralds raise their trumpets to sound a final call. "Hear ye, Hear ye!" A proclamation from their most royal Majesties, His Highness King Ferdinand of Aragon, and Her Highness, Queen Isabella of Castile.

Someone steps forward and unravels a parchment. The citizens of Saragossa fall silent as he reads the proclamation.

> Since we were informed that in these our kingdoms there were some bad Christians who judaized and apostasized from our Holy Catholic Faith, the chief cause of which was the communication of Jews with Christians, at the Cortes [which] we held in the city of Toledo in the year 1480 we ordered the said Jews in all the cities, towns and places in our kingdoms and dominions to separate into Jewries and places apart, where they should live and reside, [because we hoped] by their separation alone to remedy the evil. Furthermore we sought and gave orders that inquisition should be made in our said kingdoms . . . whereby many guilty persons have been discovered, as is notorious. And as we are informed by the inquisitors and many other religious, ecclesiastical, and secular persons that great injury has resulted, and does result . . . from the participation, society, and communication they held with Jews, who it appears always endeavor in every way to subvert our Holy Catholic Faith, and to make faithful Christians withdraw and separate themselves [from Christianity], and to attract and pervert them to their injurious opinions and belief, instructing them in the ceremonies and observances of their religion, holding meetings where they read and teach them what they are to believe and observe according to their religion; seeking to circumcise them and their children; giving them books from which they may read their prayers; and explaining to them the fasts they are to observe; assembling with

them to read and to teach them the histories of their law; notifying them of the festivals previous to their occurring, and instructing them what they are to do . . . ; carrying unleavened bread to them from their houses, and meat slaughtered with ceremonies; instructing them what they are to refrain from, in food and other matters, for the due observance of their religion . . . giving them to understand that there is no other law or truth [except the law of Moses], [all of which] is proved by many declarations and confessions of Jews themselves as well as those who have been perverted and deceived by them, which has greatly added to the injury, detriment and opprobrium of our Holy Catholic Faith.

Notwithstanding . . . we [believed] the certain remedy . . . was to separate the said Jews from communication with Christians, and to banish them from our kingdoms, yet we contented ourselves by ordering them to quit all the cities, towns, and places of Andalusia where . . . they had done the most mischief. . . .

But we are informed that neither that, nor the execution of some of the said Jews who have been guilty of the said crimes and offenses against our Holy Catholic Faith, has been sufficient to obviate and arrest so great a danger and offense to the Catholic faith and religion.

As it is found that the said Jews, wherever they live and congregate, daily increase their wicked and injurious purposes, [we must] afford them no further opportunity for insulting our Holy Catholic Faith, or [insulting] those who, until now, God has been pleased to preserve, or those who have fallen, but have amended and are brought back to our Holy Mother Church. [However] given the weakness of our human nature and the diabolical temptations that continually wage war with us, [backsliding] may occur unless the principal cause of it be removed, which is to banish the said Jews from our kingdoms.

When any serious and detestable crime is committed . . . it is right that those who disturb the welfare and proper living of cities and towns, [and] who by contagion may injure others, should be expelled therefrom. . . .

Therefore we, by and with the counsel and advice of some prelates and high noblemen of our kingdoms and other learned members of our council, having maturely deliberated thereon, resolve to order all the said Jews and Jewesses to quit our kingdoms, and never to return or come back to them. . . . Therefore we command . . . all Jews and Jewesses, of whatever age they may be, that live, reside, and dwell in our said kingdoms and dominions, natives as well as those who are not, who in any manner or for any cause may have come to dwell therein, that by the end of the month of July next, of the present year 1492, they depart from our said kingdoms and dominions with their sons, daughters, manservants, and Jewish attendants . . . and that they not presume to return to, nor reside therein . . . either as residents, travelers, or in any other manner whatever, [or] they shall incur the penalty of death, and confiscation of all their property to our treasury . . . without further trial, declaration, or sentence.

And we command and forbid any persons of our said kingdoms, whatsoever rank, station, or condition they may be, that they do not presume publicly or secretly to receive, shelter, or defend any Jew or Jewess after the end of July, in their lands or houses . . . henceforward for ever and ever, under pain of losing all their property, vassals, castles, and other possessions; and furthermore forfeit to our treasury any sums they have, or receive from us.[13]

It is immediately obvious that the text and wording of the Edict of Expulsion carry the stamp of the Inquisition; indeed, Professor Miguel Angel Motis Dolader of the University of Saragossa points out that if one compares the wording of the edict with contemporary inquisitorial documents, the language is identical.[14]

In 638, at the Sixth Council of Toledo, the Visigoth priests declared that "only Catholics can live in Spain." In 1413, during the Disputation of Tortosa, Jerónimo de Santa Fe said "Christians ought not to allow you to live among them." In the 1460s Alonso de Espina's powerful *Fortalitium Fidei* painted the devil with a Jewish face and disseminated the anti-Semitic myths of northern Europe throughout Spain with a brilliant sense of media.

It was left to Tomás de Torquemada to accomplish the rest—when the time was right. After long centuries in the cold the Spanish Church was back where it wanted to be. Catholicism and the political state were one and indivisible again: One state, one faith was the motto of the Catholic monarchs. As in the days of the Visigoths eight hundred years before, the very presence of the unconverted Other in a state defined as uniquely Christian was religiously and politically intolerable.

*   *   *

Shock coursed through the crowd in Saragossa and through hundreds of other communities where the Edict of Expulsion was read aloud at precisely the same time. In Saragossa, twelve hundred Jews were, until this moment, leading normal lives. They enjoyed excellent relations with the old Christian population and had only recently paid their taxes to the king and queen.

Four hundred and sixty municipal guards rushed immediately to the Jewish quarter to take up posts at the gates and at the doors of private homes. They warned the Jews not to try to dispose of their goods and furniture. The Inquisition had already issued its own proclamation making it a crime for any citizen "to receive any goods or property that belongs in any way to Jews or Jewesses," on pain of excommunication.[15]

One by one, every Jew in the city was brought before the chief inquisitor for the Holy Office in the city and made to swear on the Torah that he or she would not dispose of property without the prior authority of the Holy Office. Those who broke their oath would be punished like "relapsed heretics." In the jargon of the Inquisition this meant being burned at the stake.[16]

To ensure compliance, every Jewish home was inventoried by salaried "house evaluators" representing both the monarchy and the Inquisition; their lists, which have survived, provide an intimate look at the inside of a well-to-do family home in Saragossa. Among many other items the house of one Vidal Abnarrabi contained "a silver cup, gilded on the bottom, weighing nine ounces and ten *arientos*[17]; a gold ring with a ruby weighing one ounce and one *ariento*; a gold ring with a garnet stone weighing one *ariento* and a half; and a crimson Torah cover with fringes and a big button."[18] As for paper wealth, the "house evaluators" noted all outstanding debts and credits in a central registry. When it came to recording the details of about-to-be appropriated property, the Inquisition was highly motivated. Everyone's salary would issue directly from these holdings.

Ferdinand and Isabella had guaranteed royal protection so the Jews could wind up their business, but there was a stinging qualifier. Yes, the banished Jews were allowed to "take out their property," *except* for "gold, silver, coined gold, and other objects which fall under the general export prohibition."[19] This was an important caveat since the nation's wealth was held in precious metals and gemstones belonging both to the Crown and to individuals. The Catholic monarchs were willing enough to expel the bankers, but they were not to remove any of the reserves.

In a span of three short months, the Jews needed to translate their assets into property they were allowed to take with them, but since most of what they owned was on paper and largely unrecoverable, and the rest was in precious stones that they were forbidden to remove, this proved virtually impossible.[20] In defiance, many people simply gave their property away to Christian friends.

Thousands faced exile *and* personal ruin, and when the municipality of Saragossa demanded repayment of a debt of four million sueldos owed by community in addition to the tax the Jews still had to pay (ironically) for royal "protection," terror loomed.[21] A few notables were rich, but an estimated half of the community was not. Andrés Bernáldez wrote: "The Jews begged Christians to buy [their property] but found no purchasers; fine houses and estates were sold for trifles; a house was exchanged for an ass; and a vineyard given away for a little cloth or linen."[22]

People smuggled out what they could, and sympathetic Christian friends helped in spite of the risk, which was far from negligible. On May 13 a judge in Cáceres issued an order confiscating all property belonging to people caught smuggling *and* the property of anyone caught assisting them. Guards were posted across Spain to search the exiles as they made their final journey to the ports and frontiers. Some individuals swallowed their jewels. When this became known men, women, and children were assassinated and cut open by bandits.[23]

There was an immediate push for new conversions. In Teruel municipal councilors went from door to door, and more than one hundred people were baptized in a morning.[24] This drive could not have occurred without the express will of the king and queen, and it suggests that Ferdinand and Isabella may have expected the edict to propel the Jews into the arms of the Church. That way Spain would acquire more "Christians" (under constant inquisitorial scrutiny) and talented people would remain in the country.[25]

In the three months that elapsed between edict and expulsion thousands of Jews did convert although a sudden love of Christianity can hardly be thought to have motivated them. Many others sought refuge in a renewed surge of messianism, the Jews' habitual retreat from the real world of persecution. Mystics prayed "to restore to the world its original nature and properties, such as belonged to it in the beginning of Creation in the time before the first sin. For with the sin of the first man Nature was transmuted, but with the coming of the King Messiah it will revert to its archetype, for then the Divine plan will have arrived at its completion."[26] Unrelenting distress was undoubtedly easier to bear if one believed that redemption and the end of days was at hand. One writer tried to console himself and others with words every suffering Jew and converso would have understood:

> Whoever firmly resolves to devote himself to the honor of His name, come what may and befall him what may, the blows he receives shall cause him no pain. . . . And if such a man, being exposed to cruel tortures and sorely tormented . . . will but concentrate and put between his eyes the "awe-inspiring and great Name," and resolve to undergo martyrdom, his eyes will incline toward the Holy One of Israel. . . . Then he may be sure that he will withstand the test . . . [and] not feel any pain, blows, or torments.[27]

Before abandoning their homes, the Jews of Segovia spent three days and nights in the cemetery weeping inconsolably over the graves of their ancestors. Their sorrow moved even the hardest hearts, and "some religious and secular persons of the city who desired to save souls took the occasion to preach their conversion."[28] Many accepted baptism on the spot, and the site of the cemetery was subsequently named the "Holy Field."

The Jews of Vittoria tried to protect their family graves by making a gift of the cemetery to the city "in consideration of the good and neighborly treatment they had received," on condition it would remain a meadow that never would be "broken up or ploughed."[29] Their touching plea was ignored.

The bitterest news of these last, despairing days was the announcement that Rabbi Abraham Seneor, the leader of all Spanish Jewry, was preparing to convert to Christianity. Seneor's conversion was to be sponsored by Cardinal Mendoza and the papal nuncio, himself. On June 15, 1492, hundreds of guests climbed the road that still winds alongside a mountain stream flanked by olive trees to the magnificent, sand-colored fortress church of Guadaloupe, whose towers and battlements dominated the landscape. There, Ferdinand and Isabella of Spain personally, and publicly, celebrated Rabbi Seneor's conversion to Christianity with the greatest possible pomp.

The baptism of Abraham Seneor and that of his son-in-law, Meir Melamed, was an exceptionally important propaganda victory for the Catholic monarchs. It also ensured that the court would not lose one of its ablest men.

The condemned Jews looked to each other for comfort saying that Queen Isabella had warned Rabbi Seneor that if he refused to convert, she would destroy them all, without exception; therefore, he had allowed himself to be baptized to save their lives.[30] Abraham Seneor may well have been intimidated; it is now impossible to know, although it is unlikely the rumor the Jews spread was true. What seems more obvious is the universal and poignant desire to believe that a beloved leader had not betrayed his people.

They began to leave in the early days of July, gathering in small groups in the central plazas of their towns and cities, taking leave of Old Christian friends and New Christian family. Poor tradespeople who could not pay for the voyage were assisted by the rich as everyone prepared to face an unknown future in a world where large movements of populations were practically unheard of. Some one hundred and fifty thousand Jews took the road to exile. About fifty thousand very recent converts remained behind.[31]

Vidal Benveniste de la Caballería (of the famed Saragossa family) negotiated an agreement with King João II of Portugal allowing the Jews provisional entry upon payment of eight *cruzados* per head. An estimated ninety thousand of the exiles made their way there. Many were accompanied by noblemen hired by the Catholic monarchs or their municipalities to ensure their safety.[32]

In Saragossa the Jews gathered in the plaza of the Seo church on the banks of the Ebro river. The entire population of the city was there—converso relatives, old Christian friends, and all the priests of the city. These were neighbors, people whose ancestors were Jews, or had worked side-by-side with Jews in the central market place. They were in no way enemies. Friends called out; they begged the Jews to convert, to avoid exile.

Small boats waited on the Ebro to carry the young, the infirm, and those who could afford the fare to the Mediterranean coastal city of Tortosa from which they would leave the country. As the Jews stepped on to the ancient stone bridge of the city to embark, or to begin their journey by foot, they were followed by the priests holding crosses and bibles. The priests were determined; they followed the exiles all the way to Tortosa where they tried to convert them on the docks and the gangways to the ships.

Some women, children and people who were ill traveled by donkey, but most Spanish Jews took to the road by foot. Scholars, the sons and daughters of families who had served their monarchs from time immemorial, nobles of the court who had remained loyal to their religion, shoemakers, tanners, butchers, the old, the pregnant, the young, all stumbled in the crushing heat of July across parched and difficult terrain. Gryphon vultures and red kites circled watchfully above. Those headed toward Portugal looked ahead at the legendary, almost impenetrable mountain ranges of Extremadura and wondered how they would cross.

The most vivid eyewitness description comes from the normally hostile Andrés Bernáldez:

> In the first week of July they took the route for quitting their native land, great and small, old and young; on foot, on horses, on asses, and in carts; each continuing his journey to his destined port. They experienced great trouble and suffered indescribable misfortunes on the roads they traveled; some falling; others rising; some dying [and] others coming into the world; some fainting, others being attacked with illness; that there was not a Christian but what felt for them, and persuaded them to be baptized. Some from misery were converted, but they were very few. The rabbis encouraged them, and made the young people and the women sing, and play on pipes and tabors to enliven them and keep up their spirits.[33]

From Aragon the Jews made their way to the Mediterranean sea ports of Tortosa, Tarragona, Barcelona, and Valencia. From the south they left from Cadiz, Malaga and Cartagena. From the north they entered Navarre, or sailed from Laredo on the Cantabrian coast. There were frequent ambushes along the way, in spite of promises of safeconduct.[34] Near Zamorra, brigands hid in the hills and demanded a ransom for each person and cart (with a higher fee for pregnant women). In León, the

Jews' hired protector absconded with most of the thirty thousand maravedis he had been paid in order to protect them.

Some rabbis announced that as God had led the Jews out of Egypt
over the Red Sea, so would he help them now. Thousands listened with
their hearts, believing and hoping, and when they reached the sea ports
of Spain they stood in anticipation at the water's edge, waiting for the
waves to part.[35]

The king and members of the wealthy nobility had arranged for ships
to carry them away, but when the reality of exile struck home, one hundred and fifty people standing on the docks at Cartagena panicked and
begged to be baptized on the spot. In Malaga, four hundred more chose
instant conversion when they saw the fleet that was to carry them away
from Spain actually sail into the harbor.[36] The women proved more steadfast than their husbands. Men turned back at the last moment and families were separated forever.

Those who chose exile were, for the most part, the salt-of-the-earth
of Spanish Jewry: the artisans, the tradesmen, and the women—the historical carriers of religious tradition. Many among the educated elite
chose baptism, just as other members of their class had done after the
pogroms of 1391 exactly a century before.

Many years later Rabbi Joseph Ya'abetz wrote:

> Unto you, O men, I call from the Spanish exile, whither we were banished
> for our many, great sins. Nearly all those who took pride in their wisdom
> relinquished their glory [converted] on the bitter day, while women and
> humble folk surrendered their bodies and possessions for the sanctification
> of their Creator; . . . and this is mighty proof that had they not sought after
> wisdom, but remained among the simple, their simplicity would have saved
> them, for God preserveth the simple.[37]

Isaac Abravanel was an exception among the exiles. The pressure on
him to convert was heavy, including a failed attempt to kidnap and baptize his one-year-old grandson. But once the Catholic monarchs realized
that he would not succumb and would therefore have to leave the country, they privileged him with special treatment. In recognition of his service to the Crown, Ferdinand and Isabella allowed Abravanel and his son
each to take away two thousand gold ducats of their own money. In
return, Abravanel forgave the huge debt that was owed him.

On July 31, 1492, Isaac Abravanel and his family left Spain from the
port of Valencia. The man who pleaded hardest to save Spanish Jewry had
waited until the last day before submitting to his banishment.

Thousands sailed for North Africa, Italy (Pope Alexander asked all the

Italian States to receive them), Flanders, the Low Countries, the south of France, and the lands of the expanding Ottoman Empire. Ironically, "the Turk"—the would-be messiah whom mystical Jews had hoped would lead them back to the Promised Land—was the only power to extend an unqualified welcome to the exiles. Asked about the Catholic monarchs and the wisdom of the Expulsion, Sultan Bayezid II replied, "Can such a king be called wise and intelligent—one who impoverishes his country and enriches my kingdom?"[38]

But travel by sea was dangerous in 1492, and thirty years later Solomon ibn Verga wrote of things he "heard from the mouths of certain old men who [had] left Spain." Overloaded ships sank, and others caught fire. Several captains threw people overboard and stole their possessions, while others sold the Jews into slavery claiming they were prisoners of war. Plague broke out aboard one ship, and the frightened captain dropped his passengers on an island where there was no food or water. Plague was declared on another ship as well; it landed in Naples and twenty thousand Neapolitans died of the disease.[39]

One captain stole the Jews' clothes and left them on an unpopulated island where a number were purportedly attacked and killed by "wild animals." (The rest were picked up by the captain of another ship who dressed them in old sails and took them to Genoa.) In Fez the Jews died of hunger, or were murdered for the gold they were rumored to be carrying.[40]

So extreme was their suffering that many Jews returned to Spain "in rags, barefoot, and full of lice, dying of hunger and so unfortunate that it was painful to see them," wrote Bernáldez.[41] By law they were baptized on the spot where they landed. And they were watched like prey by the Inquisition.[42]

The memory of the Jews was effectively "erased" from Spain. Tombstones from ancient cemeteries were used as building blocks, or to pave roads. Some synagogues were destroyed while others were converted into churches. For a time one of the largest synagogues in Saragossa was used as a pigsty. Tomás de Torquemada received a personal prize. In a letter dated March 23, 1494, Queen Isabella and King Ferdinand bequeathed the Jewish cemetery of Avila to his monastery in that city "to do with what they wished."[43]

*   *   *

In many of the dispersed communities of exiles, the old internecine bitterness that had long troubled relations in Spain between "faithless" intellectuals and "faithful" believers did not diminish, but deepened with the despair of banishment. Some rabbis claimed that sin and conversion were responsible for God's anger against his people. In the *Book of Tradition,* composed in Fez, Rabbi Abraham ben Salomón wrote of the expulsion: "God was angry at His chosen people, but with less severity than they deserved [for having committed] such grave sins, and for having forgotten His law."[44] The rabbi expressed the anger of his generation when he wrote:

> Most of the Jews and their great men and their nobility and their magistrates remained in their homes and converted. . . . And chief among the multitude of heretics was the rabbi of the Spanish community, Don Abraham Seneor and his children; . . . And there were only a very few of the great men and leaders of Spain who resolved to submit to martyrdom, and the greatest of these was Rab Don Isaac Abravanel, may he rest in peace, who publicly sanctified the name of God before the king and his officials . . . he and the old scholar, Don Solomon Seneor, the brother of the said Rab.[45]

A later chronicler reflected on the expulsion from a more political perspective that did not hide his hatred for the queen of Castile or the terrible pressure to convert that had been inflicted on the Jews of Spain for the whole of the fifteenth century:

> The Lord delivered into my hands a copy of a certain manuscript which was found by one of our notables, R. Abraham Portal, in a ruined synagogue in the kingdom of Catalonia. Now this manuscript was written four, or five years before the Expulsion from Spain, which took place in 1492. . . . It says that in the two-hundred-and-thirty-fifth year of the sixth millennium [1475] a she-bear full of eyes would arise in Spain, and this refers to the wicked Queen Isabella. Furthermore, it says that the . . . *anusim* [conversos] would be [seduced away] to worship foreign gods, fulfilling the prophecy of Ezekiel. . . . It tells of decrees to be issued against the Holy People, which to relate would surpass all belief . . . ; and they shall know that these are the birth-pangs of the Messiah . . . and at the onset of this the Jews shall be expelled from their places of habitation into the wilderness.[46]

Just weeks after the banishment of the Jews, another voyage set sail from Spain in the opposite direction. The gold that was carried back from America to the court of Ferdinand and Isabella widened eyes and mesmerized the nation for the next century. There was ample time to forget the exiled Jews and more than a thousand years of communal life.

The year 1492 marked the end of their days in the Iberian peninsula, but for hundreds of years after, a memory of Spain clung to songs and fables crooned into the ears of the children from generation to generation. Wisps of words evoking a remarkable lost civilization where once, long ago, a king of Castile had proudly crowned himself Emperor of the Three Religions.[47]

A continuing clash of conflicting ideals had endured since the invasion of the Moors, and the defeat of the Visigoths, eight centuries before; but now the slow transformation of Spanish society was complete. The tolerance that had inspired kings, and the mix of religion and ethnicity that had underscored the richest of medieval European cultures, was finally and officially dead. A monolith ruled by inquisitorial terror and stifling conformity had grown in its place.

Notes

1. M. Kriegel, "La prise d'une décision: L'expulsion des juifs d'Espagne en 1492," *RH* 260 (1978): 60.

2. F. de Pulgar, cited in Adolfo de Castro, *Historia de los Judíos en España,* 132.

3. Anonymous contemporary chronicle in Alexander Marx, "The Expulsion of the Jews from Spain," *JQR* 20 (1908).

4. Antonio de la Peña's name comes up frequently as a particularly virulent anti-Semite. It is no surprise that he was a colleague of Torquemada.

5. Luis Suarez Fernandez, *Documentos,* 258. Letter dated April 15, 1485.

6. Cited in Adolfo de Castro y Rossi, *History of Religious Intolerance in Spain,* 24.

7. Y. F. Baer, *A History of the Jews in Christian Spain,* 2: 434.

8. Ibid.

9. Stephen H. Haliczer, "The Castilian Urban Patriciate and the Jewish Expulsions of 1480–92," *AHR* 78 (1973).

10. A. Marx, "The Expulsion of the Jews From Spain," *JQR* 20 (1908): 254.

11. E. H. Lindo, *The History of the Jews of Spain and Portugal,* 284.

12. Details of these events in Saragossa are in Serrano y Sanz, *Orígenes,* 56ff; José Cabezudo Astrain, "La Expulsión de los Judíos Zaragozanos," *Sefarad* 14 (1954), and Miguel Angel Motis Dolader, *La Expulsión de los Judíos de Aragón,* 1–2.

13. E. H. Lindo, *The History of the Jews of Spain and Portugal,* 277ff with some modernizations for clarity.

14. Interview, Saragossa, November 1994.

15. Lindo, *History of the Jews of Spain and Portugal,* 104.

16. M. Serrano y Sanz, *Orígenes,* 56.

17. An ancient measurement that has fallen out of use.

18. J. Cabezudo Astrain, *Inventario de Alhajas de Vidal Abnarrabi, notario Martín de la Catalayud,* Archives of Zaragoza, 116.

19. Valeriu Marcu, *The Expulsion of the Jews from Spain,* trans. by Moray Firth, 148.

20. This was largely in letters of exchange obtained from Genoese bankers.

21. *Actos de ayuntamiento de 14 mayo, 1492,* cited in M. Kayserling, "Notes sur l'Histoire des Juifs d'Espagne," *REJ* 28 (1894).

22. A. Bernáldez, *Memorias del reinado de los Reyes Católicos,* ed. Juan de Mata Carriazo.

23. Investigations into the smuggling of gold and silver out of the country lasted for years.

24. Baer, *A History of the Jews,* 2: 436.

25. It is not in the least evident that the Catholic monarchs were propelled by anti-Semitism, as suggested by B. Netanyahu. Ferdinand was, above all, a pragmatist and an opportunist.

Because he was aware of this, Torquemada made sure his main arguments to the king and queen were appropriately practical: the Jews were creating heretics within the Church and that was not good for the country.

26. Rabbi Meir ben Gabbai, *Avodaath ha-Kodesh,* Baer, *A History of the Jews,* 2: 427ff.

27. Rabbi Abraham ben Eliezer Halevi, cited in Baer, *A History of the Jews,* 2: 430.

28. Colmenares, *Historia de Segovia,* 9, cited in J. Amador de los Rios, *Historia de los Judíos en España y Portugal,* 3: 313.

29. Lindo, *History of the Jews of Spain and Portugal,* 282–83.

30. Baer, *A History of the Jews,* 2: 436.

31. Estimates of the number of Jewish exiles has varied wildly over the centuries. Today the generally accepted figures are based on census numbers for 1492.

32. A. Bernáldez, cited in L. Suárez Fernández, *Documentos,* 57.

33. A. Bernáldez, *Memorias del reinado de los Reyes Católicos,* ed. Juan de Mata Carriazo.

34. See Suárez Fernándaz, *Documentos,* 58ff. for a description of abuses.

35. A song about the crossing of the Red Sea was sung by the exiles and their descendants in Turkey for centuries afterwards.

> *Cuando el puevlo de Yisrael*
> *d'Ayifto salieron cantando*
> *con hijos y con mujeres*
> *sir sirim ivan cantando . . .*
>
> *Vido venir a Paró*
> *con un pendón colorado.*
> *—Ande mos truxites, Mosé*
> *a morir en estos campos;*
>
> *A morir sin suboltura*
> *o en la mar ahogados?*
> *—No vos espantéx. judios,*
> *ni seax despazenciados . . .*
>
> *Que miremos sus maravillas,*
> *aue mos haze el Dio de alto.*
> *El es uno y no sigundo;*
> *el es Patrón de todo el mundo.*
>
> When the people of Israel
> fled from Egypt singing,
> the women and the children
> left singing the Song of Songs . . .
>
> He [Moses] saw Pharaoh pursuing them
> waving a red flag.
> "Where have you brought us, Moses,
> To die in these sands
>
> To die with no graves
> or to be drowned in the sea?"
> "Do not be afraid, my people,
> do not despair . . ."
>
> Let us remember the miracles
> of God on high.
> He is one, there is no other,
> he is Master of all the world.

Judeo-Spanish song: *El paso del Mar Rojo.* Traditional ballad from the region of Marmara, Turkey.

36. Lindo, *History of the Jews of Spain and Portugal,* 288.

37. Ibid., 509, note 11.

38. Cited in Immanuel Aboab, *Nomologia,* seventeenth century. The Jews of Spain prospered in the Ottoman Empire and for hundreds of years many of the great names of Aragon and Castile, including the Benveniste and the Abravanel family, were found in places like Salonika, Istanbul, Cairo, and Damascus. The exiles brought manuscripts and Hebrew books with which they established schools and synagogues. Their education and brilliance overwhelmed indigenous Jewish communities. As in Spain the exiles and their descendants became physicians, lawyers, rabbis, writers, merchants, and diplomats. They also managed to retain elements of the language of Spain as it was spoken in the fifteenth century.

In Salonika and elsewhere the descendants of the transplanted Jews of Spain lived freely for 450 years, until they were deported to Auschwitz.

39. Solomon ibn Verga, *Shebet Yehuda.* This may be apocryphal.

40. Solomon ibn Verga, *Shebet Yehuda,* numbers 52–58.

41. Suárez Fernández, *Documentos,* 60.

42. One of the returnees was the personal physician of Cardinal Mendoza, Zag Abuazar. Interestingly, he was allowed to keep Hebrew and Arabic books as long as they did not concern religion. Suárez Fernández, *Documentos,* 59, note 22.

43. Pilar Leon Tello, *Judíos de Avila,* 101.

44. M. Gaspar y Remiro, *Las Cronistas Hispano-Judíos,* 35.

45. Baer, *A History of the Jews,* 2: 509, note 12.

46. Ibid., 500, note 66.

47. An example:

> *¿De quién eran estas armas*
> *que aqui las veo yo?*
> *Vuestras son, el mi señor rey,*
> *Vuestras son, mi señor,*
> *que os las trajo mi señor padre*
> *de las tierras de Aragón.*

> Whose are these arms
> That I see before me?
> They are yours, my noble king,
> They are yours, my lord,
> Brought to you by my noble father
> From the land of Aragon.

A. Danon, "Recueil de romances judéo-espagnoles," *REJ* 32.

15

Afterword

For centuries, ultraconservatism marked the Spanish church. The Inquisition was transplanted intact to the colonies in America, where no act of nonconformity escaped the watchful eyes of inspired investigators. Nor was there mercy. Hundreds of Catholic nuns and priests died, the purity of their faith found wanting. Outsiders were no safer than locals; shipwrecked English sailors found themselves tied to the stake as heretics of the *Protestant* persuasion.

Tomás de Torquemada died in 1498, after a fifteen-year term as inquisitor-general during which 8,800 men and women were burned at the stake, 6,500 were burned in effigy, and just over 90,000 were "reconciled" to lifelong imprisonment, or shame. None of the fifty-three chief inquisitors who succeeded Torquemada over the subsequent three hundred years of the Spanish Inquisition came close to approximating these numbers, although more than a few tried to match the first inquisitor-general's intransigence.[1]

There was little dissent in Spain or in the colonies, since to protest was to invite investigation, regardless of one's rank. Crushing real or potential resistance was a perennial priority for the Holy Office, and liberal, bold-looking individuals were quickly targeted. In 1506, Torquemada's successor, Inquisitor-General Diego Deza (a professor at the University of Salamanca and former tutor to Ferdinand and Isabella's only son, Prince Juan), arrested Hernando de Talavera, the outspoken archbishop of Granada who had once been confessor to Queen Isabella herself; in the world of the ecclesiastical elite, persecutors and their victims were united in a web of relationships. Talavera was arrested along with his entire extended family—including a sister, nieces, a nephew, and servants—and imprisoned, in spite of his eighty years. He was released in 1507. A day later he collapsed and died.

Diego also confiscated the papers of the humanist scholar Elio Antonio de Nebrija, charging that the philologist was planning to distort Holy Scripture. (Sixteenth century humanism was emerging as a serious threat to conservative Catholicism, for without denying most Christian beliefs, humanists dared to place people, not God, at the center of the universe.)

Unlike Archbishop Talavera before him, Nebrija had power enough to counteraccuse the inquisitor-general of trying to stop him from writing altogether, which was of course the case. "Must I reject as false what appears to me in every way as clear, true and evident as light and truth itself?" he asked, demonstrating considerable courage. "What does this sort of slavery mean? What unjust domination when one is prevented from saying what one thinks although to do so involves no slight or insult to religion. . . ?"[2]

This centuries-old plea for freedom of expression fell on deaf ears, for the very few who risked raising their voices were now no more than a remnant of old Spain, and their personal struggle against secrecy and oppression hardly mattered.[3] By the early sixteenth century, the vast majority of Spaniards had shifted their minds elsewhere—to gold and "Indians" in the New World.[4] More to the point, they *liked* their Inquisition. The Holy Office had been imposed, and accepted, as a solution to endemic social conflict, but even Ferdinand and Isabella might have been surprised to discover that the Inquisition they initiated in 1482 publicly burned victims until 1731 and was not officially abolished until 1834. (The last to be executed was an old woman accused of "conducting carnal converse with the Devil, after which she laid eggs with prophecies written on them.")

In 1497, King Manuel of Portugal ordered the forced conversion of all Jews in his country, including those who had arrived just five years earlier at the time of the Spanish Expulsion. Soon, as in Spain, there was a need to "purify the faith." When Portugal introduced its own inquisition in 1536, thousands of converts escaped to neighboring France where they returned to Judaism (in Bayonne, their descendants are still called *les juifs portugais* [the Portuguese Jews] although they have been French for four centuries). Others took their religious practices underground. Four hundred years later in a village called Belmonte (population 2,500), in the province of Beira, a few kilometers from the Spanish border, live one hundred and twenty descendants of the secret Jews of Portugal, still practicing Judaism in a vague, "secret" way. They are officially Christian, baptized, married by the local priest, and buried with the last sacraments of the Catholic Church. But in the intimacy of their families they celebrate the Sabbath, Yom Kippur, Passover, and Purim with half-remembered rituals. Their prayers are spoken in Portuguese, with one sustaining Hebrew word: Adonai, the name of God. In the village they are known as "Jews."

They are esteemed. Yet still they hide, often conducting their rites in the woods outside the village.[5] In Toronto, Canada, and elsewhere, there are Portuguese immigrant women who still light candles in their basements on Friday nights. These women are devoutly Catholic. They do not know why they light candles except, as one of them recently explained, "my mother and grandmother did it, so I do it, too."

During the sixteenth century, gold and silver from the colonies flooded Spain; but since most of it was used for decorating churches and royal throne rooms, and almost none was invested, the country remained poor over the long term. The expulsion of the Jews and the harassment of the conversos had eliminated a pool of financial expertise that would surely have helped, but ideology had overtaken need. The bubble of Spanish prosperity burst definitively in 1588. The arrogantly named Invincible Armada was humiliated and destroyed; and nothing dramatized Spain's loss more spectacularly in the eyes of Europe than the sight of the once proud fleet drifting helplessly off the Bay of Biscay.

After an explosive, but brief cultural flowering that included Miguel de Cervantes (*Don Quixote*), Fernando de Rojas (*La Celestina*), and artists who believed in making literature accessible to greater numbers of people by translating it into vernacular languages (among other Renaissance values), the country that had once rediscovered, translated, and disseminated the lost learning of the ancient world shrank to an intellectual backwater where ignorance and censorship ruled. It is intriguing to learn that Cervantes, Fernando de Rojas, and many other luminaries of the "Golden Age" are now known to have been conversos. Their sense of marginality and their extreme watchfulness in the face of blood purity obsessions sharpened a razor edge of imagination and perception and forced them to veil social commentary in the same way that dissident writers in the Soviet orbit, centuries later, would sometimes hide their judgments in subtext and allegory.[6]

The roster of famous victims grew to include Fray Luis de León, a monk, professor at the University of Salamanca, lyric poet, and one of the most lucid prose writers of the sixteenth century. Luis de León's translations from Greek, Latin, Hebrew, and Italian into the vernacular included the Old Testament Book of Job and the Song of Songs, a populist gesture that angered the Dominican clergy who controlled the Inquisition (Fray Luis was a Franciscan). Luis de León's most serious offense, according to the inquisitors, was to criticize the Vulgate, the authorized Latin version of the Bible prepared by St. Jerome at the end of the fourth century. They counterattacked by initiating a movement to forbid the study of Greek, since all right-thinking people knew the true Bible of St. Jerome was written in Latin.

Fray Luis was arrested for heresy one afternoon as he lectured to hundreds of students seated before him on benches in a large stone-arched classroom. The genealogy experts had discovered a Jewish great-grandmother. From 1572 to 1576 León was isolated from the world in an Inquisition prison cell. The day he returned to his class, the gothic-arched room was filled to capacity. Physically weakened, Fray Luis climbed laboriously to the lectern, then opened his notebook to the page he had been lecturing from those many years before. He looked up at his students, paused, and spoke: "As I was saying . . ."

When Luis de León was arrested by the Inquisition the church Index of banned books already included Dante, the collected works of Peter Abelard, Thomas More's *Utopia*, Machiavelli, Rabelais, William of Ockham—the list covered the entire range of Europe's literary production, including Virgil and Ovid. (One hundred years later a professor in Logroño was removed from his post and jailed for four years for merely mentioning a prohibited book.) With its stern insistence on propriety and intellectual correctness, Spain had symbolically revived the era of the Visigoths. They, too, had condemned Virgil, Tacitus, and Livy as pagan atheists.

Monasteries, municipalities, and other institutions enacted legal statutes to exclude conversos as racism in the guise of blood purity poisoned society. The anonymously authored *El Libro Verde de Aragón* (The Green Book of Aragon) circulated clandestinely. It was a literary bomb detailing the genealogies of hundreds of aristocratic families in Saragossa whose "tainted blood" had been hitherto hidden from view. The passions induced by *El Libro* were so violent and endured for so long that a century later, in 1623, King Phillip IV ordered all extant copies seized and sequestered. *El Libro* lay hidden (though not forgotten) for another century until a copy was discovered by the historian José Amador de los Rios. It is from this text that the details of the assassination of Inquisitor Pedro de Arbués came to light.

By the 1520s the Inquisition had thoroughly investigated everyone who looked in the least suspicious, and there were few, if any, secret Jews left in Spain. Living conversos had been scrutinized and absolved. Either they were sincere Christians, or they were privately—*very* privately—indifferent. It is ironic and telling that now, when there *were* no Jewish heretics to speak of, pure blood was a condition for every post of merit. The most critical shift in this direction came in 1547 with a statute that excluded all conversos and their descendants from the Cathedral Chapter House of Toledo in which the canons conducted church business. Toledo was the center of Spanish Christianity, as it had once been the center of Spanish Jewry. The new law was taken as a model, and when it was later validated by both the pope and the king, *limpieza* became official, legitimate policy at every level.

Many Spanish Christians only learned about their converso heritage when they applied for a position and a genealogical investigation was carried out. Since there were neither Jews nor heretic conversos to fasten on, only blood and racism remained valid reasons for exclusion. By 1673, a "Jew" was being described as someone with as little as twenty-one degrees of blood relationship, or—and here the poisoned flower bloomed—an old Christian who had been suckled by a wet nurse of "infected blood." The word Jew was stripped of all content; like "pure" and "impure" it was a multipurpose, abstract trigger word for class hatred, rejection, and otherness.

Can we really understand the experience of those stigmatized generations that followed a convicted heretic parent, or the brutalizing, constantly terrifying sight of flaming pyres, or the social and psychological aftermath of centuries of genealogy fixation? The "stain" of Jewishness in a family barred children from universities and careers. Not surprisingly, corruption followed. A dual industry of genealogy forgers operated in league with legions of well-bribed functionaries to validate the revisions.

While Spaniards struggled in a web of fear, accusation, and lies, others looked on in puzzled amusement. In 1652 the Spanish ambassador to Rome complained: "In Spain it is held in great horror to be descended from a heretic or a Jew, but here they laugh at such matters, and at us, because we concern ourselves with them."[7] All the same, the "horror" of which he spoke held strong in Spain with the sturdy grip of a deeply held grudge. So it was that in 1989, more than three centuries after the ambassador to Rome blurted out his frustration, a Spanish acquaintance in Toronto, Canada, could still explain with a smile that members of a certain prominent Spanish family we were discussing were not of converso lineage, but *puros*.

* * *

The persecution of Spanish minorities did not stop with the Jews and the conversos. After a rebellion in 1502, Muslims were faced with the same uncompromising choice: conversion or exile.[8] Most converted, but in 1519 a controversy erupted over whether baptism *could* turn Muslims into Christians. Significantly, it was argued on racist grounds that it could not. The medieval belief that conversion to Christianity was sufficient was dying.

Like the conversos before them, newly baptized Moriscos became instant, suspect heretics, new fodder for the Inquisition. Before long they, too, were being hauled before the tribunals by the thousands and charged with the familiar litany of crimes: practicing the Muslim religion, having Arabic names, showing contempt for Christian sacraments, refusing to eat pork and drink wine (recall that the consumption of pork and wine was the outward sign of a true Christian), and practicing circumcision. (Some prisoners defended themselves against the last charge imaginatively: in 1587 a bishop complained that Moriscos being questioned about their circumcised children insisted they had been born that way.)[9]

Eventually, Moriscos no longer knew Arabic and were ridiculed for speaking a hybrid dialect. They were barred from schools and universities, then contemptuously dismissed as ignorant fig peddlers (the opposite of conversos who were attacked for being educated). Because Moriscos were industrious, they were accused of competitiveness; old Christians whispered they were a fifth column agitating in collusion with the (Ottoman) Turks.[10]

The inevitable expulsion order came in 1609. Following the exile of the Jews and the rise of the Inquisition, this last decree was promulgated as a final solution, "so that all the kingdoms of Spain will remain pure and clean from this people," as the Duke of Lerma phrased it.[11] It was ethnic cleansing, but this time of a baptized population. By 1614, approximately half a million Moriscos had left Spain, with the exception of an estimated thirty-five thousand who went into hiding. One hundred and seventeen thousand were expelled from the region of Valencia alone, representing over half the local population. Like the expulsion of the Jews more than a century before, banishing the Moors was an ideological victory and an economic idiocy. The Moors-Moriscos were brilliant agriculturalists. Their departure set the stage for quick rural decay.[12]

The reality of Spanish "blood" was diametrically opposed to the myth; it was more mixed than any in Europe. That this was undeniable, and known in the deepest recesses of the heart, may help explain the fanatic rejection of truth that animated the newly united nation. The Spain born of Ferdinand, Isabella, and Torquemada was built on a false foundation that ignored fact in order to pursue an impossible fiction of purity.

Notes

1. Inquisitor Gaspar de Quiroga (1573–1593) managed to burn 2,816 people.

2. J. A. Llorente, *Histoire Critique de l'Inquisition d'Espagne,* 1: 343–45.

3. Of particular note are Pulgar, whose objections we have encountered, Hernando de Talavera, archbishop of Granada and confessor to Queen Isabella, and Fray Joseph Siguenza (sixteenth century).

4. Columbus initially thought he had discovered India.

5. For further reading and interesting photographs see Frederic Brenner and Yosef Hayim Yerushalmi, *Marranes.*

6. Research into the converso origin of many of Spain's most illustrious men and women was initiated by Manuel Serrano y Sanz in 1918, but not pursued with any seriousness until the publication of Américo Castro's seminal book *España en su historia*, 1948 (*The Structure of Spanish History*, 1954).

7. Kamen, *The Spanish Inquisition*, 289.

8. For the fate of the Moors see H. C. Lea, *The Moriscos*; A. G. Chejne, *Islam and the West*; F. Dánvila, *Expulsión*.

9. Chejne, *Islam*, 12.

10. They did ask the Turks for help in 1501.

11. Ibid., 13.

12. One hundred years later two-thirds of the families in the village of Gandia owned no mules or other plough animals.

Part Two

Epilogue

16

Europe Then and Later

The violence that swept Castile and Aragon in 1391 marked a turning point in the history of a country that had practiced cultural pluralism for almost eight hundred years. It was both instigated *and* spontaneous; it exposed fault lines that had been widening for a century. But what has any of this to do with us? Nothing, if one is attempting to match the world of five hundred years ago with ours in any literal way; but what we *can* hear, perhaps, if we listen, is the remarkably familiar echo of historical transformation, the recurrence of certain reactions under stress, and the early appearance of racism as a populist tool for nation-building.

Although the crude baptisms-on-the-spot in the *juderías* of Spain may strike a disturbing note, the stated reasons for the forced conversions were entirely coherent with contemporary thinking: first, it was believed the baptism of all the Jews would bring about the Second Coming of Christ, when the world would move to a better, happier plane. On a more practical level (since even the most enthusiastic millennarians agreed that the Apocalypse might still be sometime in the future), it was hoped that forced baptisms might resolve the conflicts and social ills of the age, most of which had resulted from the multiple horrors of the fourteenth century. But beneath the surface of these beliefs, religious conversion—either forced or voluntary—was as "modern" as today. Put simply, it was a policy of assimilation, albeit in its bluntest form, a dream of universal conformity.

Unfortunately, the dream evaporated; the policy of assimilation-by-conversion not only failed to solve old problems, it actually created new ones. An entirely new social class came into being, and the conversos profoundly confused fifteenth-century Spaniards. Social identity was traditionally defined by religion only. Who then *were* these so-called New

Christians? They and their parents had been baptized, but were they *Christian?*

This was the crucial question, and the answer that emerged over the course of the fifteenth century was a resounding no. When it was recognized that conversion had failed to create a homogeneous, religiously pure society, and that fifty years of attempted assimilation had barely altered the cultural and economic patterns of Jewish life that had incited resentment, new criteria of exclusion were invented to set apart authentic Christians. The push to dissolve one cultural group forcibly into another had apparently crashed in massive failure. The new solution was racism. Now conversos were the excluded Other. Conversos were . . . Jews.

The eighteenth-century French writer Montesquieu correctly observed that the Spanish Inquisition merely reinvented the anti-Jewish legislative code of the Visigoths: in both societies religious conformity was a condition of membership in the polity, exclusion a reason of state, and minority outsiders the enemy of God and king. Without imposing too tidy a pattern on the past, the shift from intolerance under the Visigoths, to pluralism under the Moors, then back to intolerance transparently prefigures more recent political transformations: The absolutist, centralized government of religious-national unity set in place by Ferdinand and Isabella through their various reforms stands out squarely as a precursor of the modern authoritarian state in which the idea of nationhood is built upon a defining orthodoxy and totalitarianism is characterized by the pursuit and exercise of raw power.

*   *   *

Secular totalitarianism was the defining failure of politics in the twentieth century, whether one casts an eye on Nazi Germany on the Right, or the Soviet Union and Pol Pot on the Left, to name just three regimes. Totalitarian states have much in common, regardless of when they lived and died: nationalism, absolutism, and a narrow yardstick for measuring the right of citizens to belong.

But a voyage through time with thoughts of fifteenth-century Spain in mind brings the traveler to a halt before the looming presence of the Nazi monolith. For it was the consequence of a remarkably similar metamorphosis.[1]

In retrospect, the signposts along the way to tyranny in both Spain and Germany are easy to pinpoint: pogroms, proposed assimilation, the racial exclusion of Jews, or presumed Jews, then a "final solution." In the case of Spain it was two solutions: an inquisition for the converted and an expulsion for the unconverted. What do we make of this when we learn there is no evidence Hitler knew anything about the history of medieval Spain? Something important, perhaps, for what this hints at is the existence of underlying patterns of culture and behavior under stress that may be worth adverting to. In spite of cultural differences spanning hundreds of years and seemingly unrelated concerns, the transformation of German society during the late eighteenth and nineteenth centuries mirrors, at least in part, the structural changes and inner forms of an earlier world of which it knew nothing.

In both societies, the push to assimilate minorities was central to the transforming process. In late fourteenth-century Spain the most important implication of massive baptisms was that after suffering arrogant rulers and relative marginalization for centuries, the Catholic church had finally amassed sufficient power to impose its ancient agenda: One nation under the banner of Christ. In Germany, the assimilation of the Jewish minority happened for different reasons, but the results were the same.

* * *

The French Revolution exploded in the midst of feudal Europe. A new order was born to serve a utopian dream. Devout believers were convinced that history had come to an end and was beginning anew, starting with a new calendar marked Year 1. Wipe the slate clean with a dead king and a guillotine that works overtime. Declare the most radical shift ever: the inalienable rights of universal humankind.

Purging winds blast across the Continent bearing unheard-of ideas into stagnant backwaters; but in Germany the dream of liberalism and equality takes a different turn. The German "revolution" is less overtly political and more "spiritual." German Idealism is a potent mix of mysticism and displaced religion, as its language makes clear. The goal is self-perfection and "redemption" in the name of all humanity.

All the same the revolution is not *entirely* devoid of politics. The philosopher Georg Friedrich Wilhelm Hegel elaborates an idea of all-embracing mind or spirit that is, in fact, identical with the political state. This "spirit" requires the growth of a community that will fully express and embody reason, says Hegel. To follow reason means that individuals must involve themselves in the larger life of the state.[2]

Hegel's abstractions in the name of reason had obvious political implications, but they were light years from the French reality of tumbrels stuffed with dukes and duchesses en route to the guillotine. Where the French rushed into the streets to execute their royals and thousands of sycophants in the name of universal rights, German philosophy glorified the archetypal, benevolent despot whose job it was to prepare the way for a new Golden Age of humankind. There was, however, an underlying, shared idea. The new ideals of universal humanity included *all* humanity. The concept of religious tolerance had been born, and that meant the legal emancipation of the Jewish minority with civil rights and citizenship.

Such legalities were important; most people could agree on that, but distrust of Jews was so deeply embedded in the historic fabric of German society that it would take more than new ideas and a violent revolution in someone else's country to change things. Centuries earlier some of the worst massacres of "well-poisoners" had taken place in this community; on an icy February day in 1349, nine hundred people had been hurled into bonfires in the city of Strasbourg alone. The blood libel had long before calcified into "truth" everywhere in northern Europe, but Germany was especially volatile, and indelible images of "murderous Jews" cleaved to memory and folklore. Back in the sixteenth century, after a failed attempt to convert the Jews, Martin Luther had dipped into this ready pool, alluding to the evil, unalterable Other.[3] Luther's accusations were an uncanny echo of Alonso de Espina:

> The Jews are lords of the world and all the gentiles flock to them . . . while the Jews curse, spit on and malign the Germans. . . . They say that God [will] kill and exterminate all of us Germans through their messiah, so that they can lay claim on the land, the goods, and the government of the whole world. . . .
>
> We are at fault in not avenging all this innocent blood of our Lord . . . and the blood of the children which they have shed since then, and which still shines forth from their Jewish eyes and skin. We are at fault in not slaying them.[4]

In the light of Germany's twentieth-century holocaust against the Jews, one cannot, in conscience, ignore Martin Luther's call to murder at the end of this passage. The point is this: Given Germany's long history of anti-Jewish hatred, it is not surprising that the expression of would-be universal humanism in German Enlightenment philosophy was flexible enough to allow the eventual exclusion of some Germans from humanity. "Redemption"—a key word with overtly religious overtones—finally came to mean the redemption of Germans *from* the Other.

In her classic study *The Origins of Totalitarianism*, social philosopher Hannah Arendt emphasized that "the breakdown of the feudal order [gave] rise to the new revolutionary concept of equality, according to which a 'nation within a nation' could no longer be tolerated."[5] This was the heart of the new emancipatory thinking. Liberalism promoted equality and assimilation, but darker forces in the tradition of Martin Luther coexisted with the new revolutionary thinking from the start. Well before the end of the eighteenth century, the philosopher Johann Gottlieb Fichte (often called the father of German nationalism *and* the father of modern German anti-Semitism) was accusing the Jewish minority of being "a state within a state." As Arendt makes clear, this accusation carried special poison; it undermined support for equality.

Simmering anti-Semitism assumed mainstream prominence in the 1870s with nationalism, anticapitalism, and a perception of Jewish influence at its core. At the beginning, emancipated Jews were useful, even necessary. As the business of the state diversified, capital and financial expertise were in demand. Given their business expertise, a tiny minority of privileged Jews were useful in an expanding nineteenth-century economy built on commercial relations between new nation-states, just as a similar elite had been useful in Spain after each Reconquest victory when recovered territories needed settlement and development, and international merchant trade increased. The great banking dynasties represented by court Jews who had once handled the financial affairs of the feudal aristocracy became the financial support of government, just as they had been in Spain centuries earlier. These courtiers were privileged, wealthy, and the recipients of noble titles even before emancipation, just as in Spain. In both countries such Jews were dependent on and identified with the state making them diversionary scapegoats for the disgruntled. The French Revolution, exploding industrialism, radical social change and the emergence of modern capitalism represented a frightening rupture from the tranquil certainties of feudalism. And capitalism—loans, guarantees, interest payments, and the rest—was as distrusted in Christian Germany as it had been in Christian Spain.

The elusive notion of *Volk* came into being around the middle of the nineteenth century—a mysterious, ineffable, transcendent essence of "Germanness" deemed to characterize those privileged to partake. Ordinary folk who might be having trouble understanding the ineffable, à la Hegel, could happily rejoice in the superior status conferred on them by their sanctioned membership. *Volk* was myth-making at its most potent, and the retrieval of Teutonic folklore from the mists of time (by the composer Richard Wagner in particular) only enhanced its legitimacy. As a nation-building tool, larger-than-life storytelling was, of course, hardly new. Back in the eighth century, the Visigoth survivors of Tariq the Moor had fashioned comparable myths with their creation, Pelayo, who was later joined by Santiago and a fictionalized version of El Cid.

Early on, Fichte had glorified Germany and "Germanness":

> Among all modern peoples it is you in whom the seed of human perfection most decidedly lies, and you who are charged with progress in human devel-

opment. If you perish in this your essential nature, then there perishes together with you every hope of the whole human race for salvation from the depths of its miseries.[6]

As George L. Mosse has written, "Racism defended utopia against its enemies."[7]

Germany was now a divided train careening along separate tracks: the belief in liberal, universal humanity leading to the emancipation of the Jews on one side and the exclusiveness of *Volk* on the other.

German Jews identify with the first track, leap at the "invitation" to join society, to speak German as a mother tongue, to adopt the culture of the larger community. They enter the larger world as proud new citizens, succeeding brilliantly in the liberal professions just as they had in Spain, centuries before. And for precisely the same reasons: A rigorous religious education has trained men's minds well (women have notoriously been denied the privilege) and is easily translatable into law, science, medicine, journalism, finance, and literature. Although German Jews move steadily into the urban middle class over the course of the nineteenth century, they are less influential as a group than their enemies claim. In 1895, almost 85 percent are in commerce, business, crafts, or industry, none of which are policy-making occupations.[8] Jewish members of the intelligentsia are largely excluded from pivotal civil service occupations, from powerful judgeships, and from high prestige university teaching posts. Somewhat less than two percent are prominent in high-profile banking.[9]

High acculturation and a tendency to abandon orthodox religion continue to characterize the emancipated Jews until these attributes are seen as "an essential part of [German-Jewish] identity,"[10] until it is a cliché to speak of being "a Jew at home and a German in the street." German Jews embrace the new religion of statehood, yearn to belong, to dissolve into the nation. And the majority culture anticipates nothing less. Eventually, a not illogical expectation emerges, among Jews as well as gentiles: "the . . . disappearance of the Jew, as Jew, if necessary by conversion."[11]

But an inescapable ambivalence over identity persists. Some Jews convert to Lutheranism, the majority religion, many more intermarry; still, perhaps in spite of themselves, they continue to be "different." Some of this perceived difference is imposed upon them by anti-Semites, but much of it is real insofar as distinctive values and attitudes have been forged over centuries. For this they are criticized. Many strive harder to rid themselves of the hated traits.

Substitute Catholicism for the religion of statehood and one is staring at the mirror image of a process. The Spanish conversos also yearned to belong, to dissolve into the (Christian) nation. And the majority culture also anticipated nothing less than the disappearance of the Jew, as Jew. Although German emancipation claimed to tolerate religious differences as long as religion did not conflict with the more important allegiance to the nation-state, the subtext (as with baptism) was the assimilation of the individual into the majority culture at the expense of the myriad allegiances and attitudes that had characterized Jewish life for more than five thousand years. This proved to be as difficult in the nineteenth century as it was in the fifteenth.

By the middle of the nineteenth century, *Volk* and a superior "Germanness" that excludes the Jewish minority from national "redemption" is overtaking the universal humanism that was supposed to include everyone; and by 1848, when new revolutions sweep Europe, the romance of the German nation is transformed and transfigured. In 1849, Richard Wagner proclaims with ecstatic enthusiasm: "I am Revolution, I am the ever-fashioning Life, I am the only God. . . . The millions, the embodied Revolution, the God become Man . . . proclaim to all the world the new Gospel of Happiness."[12]

Wagner's transport comes closer to the mystical fervor of John of the Cross than to the revolution across the Rhine River. One year later the composer published *The Jews in Music,* the first major work of a secular, entirely racist mode.[13] Here Wagner clearly articulates the transformation of all-encompassing universalism into racism.

> Our liberalism was not a very lucid mental sport. . . . We went for the freedom of that nation . . . with a dislike of any real contact with it. So our eagerness to level up the rights of the Jews was rather much more stimulated by a general idea, rather than any real sympathy; for with all our speaking and writing in favor of the Jews' emancipation, we always felt instinctively repelled by any actual, operative contact with them. . . . Even today we only purposely fool ourselves when we think it necessary to hold immoral and taboo all open proclamation of a natural repugnance against the Jewish nature. Only in quite the most recent times do we seem to have reached an insight that it is more rational to rid ourselves of that strenuous self-deception. . . .
>
> If emancipation from the yoke of Judaism appears to us the greatest of necessities, we must hold it crucial above all to assemble our forces for this war of liberation. . . . Then we can rout the demon from the field . . . where he has sheltered under a twilit darkness . . . which we good-natured humanists have conferred upon him.[14]

Wagner aside, there are still two tracks in the new Germany. More than twenty years after the famous composer writes these prescient words, the rocky process of political *inclusion* not only continues, but expands. In 1871, Bismarck promulgates a final declaration of Jewish legal equality. This leads to anti-Semitic attacks on "The German Empire of the Jewish Nation" and on Bismarck's "parody of a Reich," but the Jews cling to their official status, striving collectively and individually to internalize ineffable "Germanness." Early on, Moses Mendelssohn, a scholar, critic and translator who is famous enough to be called "The German Socrates" during his lifetime, is held up as a model by liberal Christians who admire what they see as his attempt to help his fellow Jews "Germanize" and assimilate. But Mendelssohn rejects the idea of full assimilation. Jews will never melt entirely into German, Christian culture, he claims, and furthermore the entire issue is irrelevant. What matters is that men and women of good will and ethical inclination agree to live with reason as their yardstick of the good life, regardless of their religion. Difference is not an issue when it comes to civil rights.

But the liberal pluralism Mendelssohn had in mind does not develop and in 1771, after a searing dispute with Johann Lavater, a theologian who has challenged him to convert to Christianity, he suffers a nervous breakdown. Mendelssohn's despair seems to reflect a general ambivalence over what emancipation is supposed to mean. For Mendelssohn, equality must include the right of the minority to remain itself, and *in theory* this is so: there is no forced baptism in Enlightenment Germany. But the true intent of emancipation is absorption at every level, as Lavater's challenge to Mendelssohn revealed. What Lavater has implied is that even the great Moses Mendelssohn will never be a "real" German as long as he remains a Jew. Fichte's vision of an alien "nation within the nation" prevails. To be nonconforming or distinct is to invite exclusion.

Because he thoroughly understood this, the writer Heinrich Heine agreed to accept baptism a half century later in 1825. Much later Heine resentfully asserted he was "no Christian" and that he had converted to obtain "an entry ticket to European civilization . . . ; I make no secret of my Judaism to which I have not returned because I have never left it," he asserted toward the end of his life.[15]

Heinrich Heine comes as close to the troubled, still-"Jewish" conversos of fifteenth century Spain as can possibly be imagined over a gap of four hundred years. In Germany, as in Spain, the price of acceptance was too high. Simply stated, human beings are unable to shed their historical and emotional selves like a snake discarding its skin.

* * *

German Jews continued to walk a tightrope of ambiguity until the Nazi movement rendered their concerns irrelevant. In 1926, on the occasion of his seventieth birthday, Sigmund Freud wrote a letter to the B'nai B'rith Lodge of Vienna in which he attempted to sort out the psychological complexities of assimilation and ethnicity:

> I am a Jew myself, and it has always appeared to me not only undignified, but outright foolish to deny it. What tied me to Jewry was—I have to admit it—not faith, not even national pride, for I was always an unbeliever, having been brought up without religion, but not without respect for the so-called "ethical" demands of human civilization. Whenever I have experienced feelings of national exaltation, I have tried to suppress them as disastrous and unfair, frightened by the warning example of those nations among which we Jews live. But there remained enough to make the attraction of Judaism and the Jews irresistible, many dark emotional powers, all the stronger the less they could be expressed in words, as well as the clear consciousness of an inner identity, the familiarity of the same psychological structure, and before long there followed the realization that it was only to my Jewish nature that I owed the two qualities that have become indispensable to me throughout my difficult life. Because I was a Jew, I found myself free of many of the prejudices that restrict others in the use of the intellect: as a Jew I was prepared to be in the opposition and to renounce agreement with the "compact majority."[16]

In a paragraph Freud explained why, after more than a century of trying, assimilation in the sense of complete cultural absorption into the majority Christian culture was as impossible for the Jews of twentieth-century Germany as it had been for the conversos of fifteenth-century Spain. When assimilation did not—*could* not—succeed entirely, when conversos and then emancipationists continued to reflect specific cultural differences and occupational patterns, and when they experienced inner conflicts brought about by the abandonment of "self" and, in Spain, secretly returned "home" to old practices, an identical crucible of racial "otherness" was invented.

So it is nonsensical to read, as one often does, that the brief regnum of Adolf Hitler (1933–1945) was an anomaly, an incomprehensible demonic bleep in a long pattern of German good will toward Jews. The truth is a lot less mysterious. For more than a century preceding the election of the Führer, a society in unsettled transition struggled with emancipation and equality on the one hand, and the growth of radical, anti-Semitic nationalism on the other. Equality was interpreted to mean homogeneity, and when homogeneity proved impossible, disillusionment led to rejection.

It is worth digressing to recall that during the era of the early Moorish caliphs there was no overt drive to assimilation. The Muslim rulers did not make demands that minorities could not humanly meet and were certain to fail at if they tried. No one during this period was forced to convert to Islam (although they were encouraged to do so), nor was the acceptance of religious minorities premised upon their abandoning their communities or their collective sense of self.

Since there was no coercion, ethno-religious groups could not "fail" at an impossible task; since there was no "failure," there was nothing to punish. Cultural and religious differences were sufficiently respected. When, eventually, they were not, blood reddened the streets of Spain.

*   *   *

Adolf Hitler completed the long transformation of German society by using *Volk* and "Germanness" to exclude the minority Jews from humanity itself, and with his ascent to power the two-track conflict between universal humanism and nationalist anti-Semitism was resolved. Since Nazi propagandists could demonstrate that those who were marked for death lived outside the human sphere, it was theoretically possible to be a humanist *and* to commit genocide.[17]

Hitler successfully dissolved the in-group exclusions of *Volk* and the anti-Semitic politics of "The Jewish Question" into a single defining orthodoxy that he identified as the ideological grounding of the nation state. For centuries there had been sporadic calls to violence in Germany interspersed with long periods of calm. Adolf Hitler was merely the most recent caller in a long tradition.

A similar transformation of "The Jewish Question" (meaning "the minority question") had occurred in medieval Spain. There, too, final solutions did not emerge genielike from a bottle. In the early fourteenth century, the convert Alfonso de Valladolid had called for a massacre of the Jews to spur the survivors to baptism. One hundred years later Jerónimo de Santa Fe told Jews gathered at the Disputation of Tortosa, "You must be continually offending God with forms of idolatry, murder and execrable adulteries. . . . The earth ought to swallow you and Christians ought not to allow you to live among them." Two generations later, Alonso de Espina described Jews as diabolical, semimagical creatures whose goal was the destruction of Christians and Christianity; he called for an inquisition against "the ravening wolves." Allowing for differences in content, these progressive calls (all of which were echoed by less prominent figures) positioned the Jews as enemies of the (Christian) nation and set the stage for political change.

Finally, in both medieval Spain and twentieth-century Germany, relentless hate propaganda played a crucial role in conditioning minds. In Nazi Germany careful instructions to the media echoed the equally brilliant, anti-Jewish campaign of Alonso de Espina:

> Stress: In the case of the Jews there are not merely a few criminals (as in every other people), but all of Jewry arose from criminal roots, and in its very nature it is criminal. The Jews are no people like other people, but a pseudo-people welded together by hereditary criminality. . . . The annihilation of Jewry is no loss to humanity, but just as useful as capital punishment or protective custody against other criminals.[18]

In Spain, the Holy Child trial was a direct outcome of Espina's carefully put-together almanac of Jewish devilry and the event that enabled Torquemada to convince the Catholic monarchs to expel the Jews for the sake of the nation. "[The story of the Holy Child] is of singular importance in the history of the heroic and painful task carried out by royalty and the people in the last decades of the Middle Ages in order to bring into being a Spanish nationality capable of effecting . . . its providential mission," the Marqués de Lozoya wrote (perhaps not so astonishingly) in 1945, during the Nazi era.[19] The "Spanish nationality" was Christian and pure; indeed, Hitler might have spoken these very words with minimal change. Pure blood, pure religion, pure nationhood.

Mind-Sets and Other Recipes for Tyranny

When does intolerance trigger tyranny and final solutions? Was there anything more than coincidentally similar in the conditions that prevailed in medieval Spain and modern Germany before racism choked off other options?

In his landmark study of the Nazi Holocaust, Raul Hilberg published a revealing chart comparing canonical, anti-Jewish measures with those adopted by the Nazis.[20] In essence, the Nazis abstracted the older, regulatory laws of the Church and stripped them of their religious content. In a society that had been Christian for more than a millennium (Nazi irreligion was an overlay that never penetrated deeply), propagandists had only to dip into a collective pool of premodern, anti-Semitic memory to revive old demons. Hatred of Jews did not spring into being without familiar referents and antecedents, Luther being a prime example.

Although he formally expunged traditional religion from the one thousand-year-reich-to-be, Adolf Hitler expressed himself in openly Christian language that made Aryanism, the new national "faith," appear familiar and comfortable. "I believe I am acting in accordance with the will of the Almighty Creator; by defending myself against the Jew, I am fighting for the work of the Lord," he wrote in *Mein Kampf.* If Fray Alonso de Espina had accused the Jews of wanting to kill Christians and destroy Christianity, Hitler accused them of wanting to obliterate *his* religion, the mystical Aryan Reich. Both the religious and the secular versions of this accusation allow the accuser to expel the evil enemy from the universe of "goodness" personified by himself and his group.

If one is planning a persecution-to-come, the progressive devaluation of a minority is the place to start, paying careful attention to blur the features of the individuals within. Once fifteenth-century Spaniards had concluded that human traits were inborn and that something called "pure blood" was the unique indicator of worth, all considerations of merit, capability, good citizenship, loyalty, propriety, and even social usefulness counted for nothing. The Nazis constructed an identical bulwark against the Jews.

Once the targeted minority has been stripped of value, anything becomes possible. Enemy-heretics can die at the stake for the sake of the greater good—in this case the purity of Christian Spain. Enemy-Jews can be expelled after a millennium of successful cohabitation for the same reason. And at the far reaches of the spectrum, the enemy can be massacred virtually without guilt. In the absence of remorse, his wealth can be appropriated without shame—*especially* if it is to be used for a "higher good."

In Spain and Germany, violence was triggered by a long period of exceptional stress. Medieval Spaniards were crushed by famine, plague, war, and death—the Four Horsemen of the Apocalypse. Their despair was thickened by corrosive religious malaise, previously unquestioned expectations were undermined: stability, predictable comfort, and the prospects of temporal and eternal safety. In this volatile environment an elite that was a virtual arm of government excited anger and envy. That this elite came largely from a minority made rejection easy and even righteous, an escape valve for rising tensions and a consolation.

During the civil strife that followed the reigns of Juan II of Castile and his son Enrique IV (culminating in the astonishing public "dethroning" of Enrique), warring factions found common cause in blaming conversos who were fighting on both sides. Conversos had characteristics in common: everyone knew this, but because they were at least nominally Christian there was no basis, or language, for repudiation. Once blood purity was proffered as a solution, formal oppression was quick to emerge. The Inquisition became an instrument for quelling disorder *and* a tool of national unity.

In Germany, simmering *völkisch* nationalism also exploded into violence after decades of strain. The chaos that ravaged Germany following World War I has been well documented and need not be repeated here, except to note, for example, that 1,783 printing presses ran twenty-four hours a day in 1923 to create enough banknotes to keep pace with inflation, and an estimated 24 percent of schoolchildren were seriously undernourished. The connection between this misery and minority scapegoating should not be underestimated. As proof, anti-Semitism reached its pre-Hitler peak between 1918 and 1923 after which the German mark was finally stabilized.[21]

The dream of a distressed nation is grounded in stability, law and order, and the nostalgic "memory" of a fantasy world that once unfolded calmly and comprehensibly, day by day. But the educated Jewish/converso minority seemed to live on the cusp of a frightening "modernity." The Jewish aristocrats of Spain did not react to social and political upheavals with recourse to the Bible, or mysticism, or by preparing for the imminent arrival of a savior-messiah. They were firmly rooted in this world, where they advised kings, represented their country, interpreted among peoples, and advanced scholarship. Educated conversos maintained the pattern, and when the tolerant traditions that held all this in place collapsed, they bore the brunt of the failure. Similarly, Hitler's anger at the elite status of Jewish professionals has been widely documented. Scientists, doctors, teachers, writers, painters—everything forward looking in culture, science, and the arts—was tarred as "Jewish," a code word for modern, decadent, and "un-German." Deeply conservative values animated both societies as they struggled to recover from anarchy and confusion. To many people the avant-garde—in large part educated Jews or conversos—represented a threat to a fragile stability.

*   *   *

The most elusive question about tyranny is this: How are ordinary people persuaded to comply passively with injustice, or to take the next step and actively turn on neighbors with whom they may have lived in peace for decades, or even centuries?[22] Fear of attracting attention in an authoritarian state is a practical reason for passivity. But is this explanation sufficient?

A devalued, marginalized minority seems to be the key, for exposed to a continuum of propaganda, decent human beings are transformed and desensitized. (This will not come as news to army personnel wherever they are. Young recruits are trained to kill by devaluing the enemy.)

Antiminority propaganda labors to give birth to one and only one offspring: a population that is psychologically conditioned to accept the abuse of the excluded group. In the twelfth century, the rhetoric of the Crusades awakened dormant anti-Jewish rivalry, sharpening "us" and "them" divisions. Before long the non-Christian was described as an eater of Christian hearts, an incarnation of the devil, and a would-be destroyer of God's true religion. These myths were legitimized by the lower clergy (as in the case of Thomas of Monmouth, who first committed the blood libel to manuscript) resulting in the massacres of thousands in the name of righteousness. In the fourteenth century, terror spawned by a plague that killed peasant and monarch alike seeded fantasies of poisoned wells that culminated in mass murder. In the late fourteenth century, a ceaseless barrage of anti-Jewish fulminations tipped the lid in Spain, a country that had been relatively immune to northern European hostilities. By formally introducing the entire compendium of northern, anti-Semitic myth at the same time as the newly invented printing press was expanding literacy, Alonso de Espina accelerated the social reconditioning process and laid the groundwork for legal oppression.

Such propaganda is not subtle; frequently it includes an attempt to depict the enemy as a blood-sucking, disease-infected, reeking metamorphosis of a despised animal or insect—in other words, as inhuman. These pointed, deliberate metaphors permit decent people to reject the pariah from the community; they enable persecutors and passive onlookers to accept the unacceptable on grounds that the victim does not deserve or even need their compassion. Conditioning Germans to the idea that Jewish fellow citizens were less than human was central to Hitler's mission. To this end the newspaper *Der Stürmer*[23] revived the blood libel in a special issue devoted entirely to the subject (the cover showed a group of Jews in medieval dress cutting the heart out of a Christlike child).

In spite of implausible crudenesses, the dehumanization of the designated Other is often wildly successful. A contemporary commentator has noted:

> The most general condition for guilt-free massacre is the denial of humanity to the victim. You call the victims names like gooks, dinks, niggers, pinkos, and japs. The more you can get high officials in government to use these names and others . . . the more your success. In addition, you allow no human contact . . . so that men cannot confront other men. . . . Or if it cannot be prevented, you indicate that the talk is not between equals.[24]

So one is not surprised to observe that the language of dehumanizing propaganda is, in reality, interchangeable. In 1981 *The New Republic* published a piece in which the following passage written by Leo Wine of the Oregon Moral Majority was quoted. Here the enemy is the secular humanist.

> Why are the humanists promoting sexual perversion? . . . Because they want to create such an obsession with sex among our young people that they will have no time or interest for spiritual pursuits. . . . So what do we have? Humanist obsessions: sex, pornography, marijuana, drugs, self-indulgence, rights without responsibility.
>
> Humanists control America. America is supposed to be a free country, but are we really free? . . . Now the humanist organizations—ACLU, AHA (American Humanist Association)—control the television, the radio, the newspapers, the Hollywood movies, magazines, porn magazines, the unions, the Ford Foundation, Rockefeller Foundation. . . . They, 275,000 humanists, have infiltrated until every department of our country is controlled by the humanists.
>
> Humanists will continue leading us towards the chaos of the French Revolution. After all, it is the same philosophy that destroyed France and paved the way for the dictator Napoleon Bonaparte. This time the humanists hope to name their own dictator who will create out of the ashes of our pro-moral republic a humanist utopia, an atheistic, socialistic, amoral humanist society for America and the rest of the world. In fact, their goal is to accomplish that takeover before the year 2000.[25]

Compare this stock speech (only the enemy has changed) to the following company song of a French collaborationist organization during the Nazi occupation of that country, noting the themes of occupation (the country is not "free"), stink, and sickness.

> SOL, make France pure,
> Bolsheviks, Freemasons, Israel, all rotting manure,
> All will be vomited, you'll soon see,
> Only then will France be free.[26]

Although there are hundreds of examples of such propapanda in the many tomes that have appeared on Nazi Germany, I have chosen this little French ditty to raise a question: Germany had had a long history of dour national superiority, but how had this happened in *France* itself, the very birthplace of equality?

The answer is psychological reconditioning—propaganda. And as in Spain and Germany, the change did not occur overnight. For fifty years before the German army marched into Paris on June 14, 1940, and began a gallant *pas de deux* with its collaborationist partner, Marshal Philippe Pétain, the walls of French streets had been pasted with anti-Semitic posters and the population bombarded with printed leaflets.

Although French anti-Semitism had been building slowly for decades, it erupted in earnest in the last decade of the nineteenth century with the Dreyfus affair, a slanderous fabrication that divided France at its dinner tables and is still talked about today. The *Affaire* quickly gobbled up and disgorged poor Alfred Dreyfus, becoming a battle for and against the Jews and everything they were presumed to stand for: capitalism, liberalism, rapacity, secularism, otherness, progress, modernity. The list was a long one in an era of fast industrialization and, to some, incomprehensible social change. In essence the Dreyfus affair symbolized a standing division in French society between those who welcomed post-Revolutionary France, and those who did not, and since the Jews were thought to be the main beneficiaries of the Revolution, having been emancipated and made citizens of the Republic, conservatives saw them as embodying the "revolutionary" characteristics they most feared and hated.

Between 1918 and 1940, right-wing nationalism attracted some of the brightest minds in France. The abstracted word *Jew* came to mean "enemy"—as it had in Spain, as it had in Germany. So it was that when German soldiers entered Paris in 1940, they were eagerly welcomed by some while millions more remained passive. By 1940 anti-Semitism was, quite simply, as commonplace as a whiff of freshly baked baguette.[27]

This is not to deny that millions of French men and women maintained liberal values, but rather to emphasize that long exposure to propaganda had diminished reactions. A half-century of persistent anti-Semitic argument and propaganda had effectively prepared the terrain for pro-Nazi sentiment in the cradle of human rights.

*   *   *

When attacks on the vulnerable go unpunished, a progressive desensitization occurs. After the king of Castile was unable to protect "his" Jews in Seville, pogroms erupted all over the country. When Enrique IV callously ignored crime at every level, including sexual violence against his royal mother-in-law, he encouraged rapaciousness. When civil anarchy destroyed respect for government, people drafted their own self-serving laws, such as the statutes of blood purity. Similarly in post World War I Germany, unpunished attacks against Jews and communists fostered ever bolder acts. Eventually street violence was sanctioned and legal.

A progressive continuum of group devaluation and individual desensitization will likely produce a nucleus of active perpetrators, but millions more onlookers are simultaneously conditioned to neither "see," react to, nor feel personally connected to the degradation of the Other.

This inability to "see" may also affect the oppressed groups themselves. One suspects that the "blindness" that afflicted so many assimilated German Jews and made them reluctant to leave the country in spite of the indignities visited upon them during the 1930s can best be understood through the prism of their perceived "Germanness" and their determination that they belonged. Were they not at the heart of German *Kultur*, the soul-siblings of Goethe, Heine, and Schiller? In German-Jewish writings one finds hundreds of examples of this point of view: in the confusion and disbelief of people whose forebears had long ago abandoned orthodox religion for the new faith, the nation-state; of people who were entirely secularized, or whose families had converted to Christianity generations before. To "see" the implications of what was happening would have required them to abandon the central identity of their lives, their Germanness, leaving nothing to fill the void.

In *The Drowned and the Saved*, Primo Levi recounts the story of Hans Meyer (later known as Jean Améry), a philosopher and survivor of Auschwitz. Meyer was born into an assimilated Viennese family in 1912 and did not consider himself a Jew. "Although nobody had converted to Christianity with the due formalities, Christmas was celebrated in his house around a tree adorned with shiny objects; on the occasion of small domestic accidents, his mother invoked Jesus, Joseph, and Mary, and the souvenir photograph of his father, who died at the front in World War I, showed not a wise, bearded Jew, but an officer in the uniform of the Tyrolean Kaiserjäger."[28] Levi tells us that Hans was nineteen before he heard about the existence of the Yiddish language; he did not know Hebrew or Hebrew culture; and he was not interested in Zionism. Nor did he believe in God. His religion was German culture.

When Ayranism became the unique measure of dignity and citizenship, Hans Meyer was deprived of the integrating factor of his life. He was degraded, his new Jewish identity defined by the obscenities of *Der Stürmer*, in other words he was now, according to Levi, "a hairy parasite, fat, with crooked legs, a beaked nose, flapping ears, good only at harming others. German he is not, by axiom."[29] His opinions matter not at all; his individual person matters less. Meyer is tortured, then interned in Auschwitz. Like Levi he survives, but the demons of the heart will not let him forget. Like Levi, he will commit suicide many years after the war.

A similarly poignant invocation of "blindness" then despair at being abandoned by the "parent" nation derives from France, the birthplace of European emancipation. On October 2, 1940, when he read that the Vichy government was preparing tough new anti-Jewish laws, Raymond-Raoul Lambert, head of the French Jewish Council in the southern zone wrote in his diary:

> It is possible that within a few days I shall be diminished as a citizen, and that my sons, who are French by birth, by culture, and by faith will be cruelly cast outside the French community. . . . Is this possible? I can't believe it. France is no longer France. . . . Last night I cried like a man who has suddenly been abandoned by the woman he has loved throughout life, by the unique tutor of his thoughts, and by the commander of his actions.[30]

Lambert and his family were deported to Auschwitz in 1943.

When the Spanish Inquisition first held its victims in death's embrace, they too had difficulty understanding reality. Like the assimilated Jews of Germany, the conversos were *Spanish*, some of them were of the nobility, many were men and women of substance. Tragically, fancifully, a handful thought their connections at court—in other words, their status—would or could stop the Inquisition machine if they attempted a judicious assassination. The autos de fe that followed this debacle finally opened their eyes. A decade later, when they learned of the imminent expulsion of the Jews, Isaac Abravanel and Abraham Seneor, two of the brightest men of their age, were similarly unable to register the meaning of an edict that would expel the Jewish people from their homeland of fifteen hundred years. They reminded Ferdinand and Isabella of the long centuries of Jewish service to the crown, as if that mattered anymore. A transformation had occurred, times had changed. Like Hans Meyer, Raymond-Raoul Lambert, and the prominent conspirators in the murder of Pedro de Arbués who believed their behind-the-scenes connections at court would save them, Isaac Abravanel and Abraham Seneor might have claimed that "Spain was no longer Spain." What they failed to "see" was that there was now only one criterion for belonging and it excluded them.

* * *

Desensitizing, distancing, and the inability to "see" are enhanced by various tricks—euphemism, for example. The Spanish Inquisition takes painstaking care not to kill directly. The Holy Office is a religious institution, not a murder factory; victims are condemned at the auto de fe, then "released to the secular arm" to be dispatched offstage by the state. In Germany the lie of euphemism is elevated to an art form. People about to take a last train ride to a death camp are being "resettled" in "the East." Gas chambers are "bath houses"; crematoria are "special buildings." Euphemism throws up a screen that deflects reality and reduces the likelihood of resistance. During the construction of the crematoria, one official ordered future buildings to be placed away from the gaze of "all kinds of people." Later a deceptive "green belt" of trees was planted.[31]

Desensitization must penetrate to the very heart of the totalitarian society so that decent human beings will not revolt. The Nazi machine was organized by a complex, highly structured bureaucracy where workers with limited jobs could punch in at nine and leave at five. What could be more routine? Few had an overview, although as historians have demonstrated many people "knew" something awful was happening in the camps.[32] Perhaps the devaluation of Jews had been so thorough that it was easy to turn one's thoughts to other things. Such individuals were probably less vicious than indifferent. On the other hand, in certain more knowledgeable quarters the gassing of Jews was a joke; in the General Directorate of the Eastern Railway officials in charge of transport trains regularly cackled to one another that another batch of soap was in the offing.[33]

In occupations where a degree of understanding was unavoidable, duty to the laws of the state came first in the minds of responsible individuals, and just how they distanced themselves from reality is instructive. In 1993, Gerald Fleming, emeritus professor at the University of Surrey, published just available, archival transcripts of a 1946 Soviet interrogation of four, senior German engineers.[34] The men were employees of the German firm, Topf und Söhne, whose name was stamped on cremation furnaces at five Nazi death camps.

These conscientious engineers had specific jobs: they designed and built the crematoria, paying special attention to ventilation systems, conveyor belts, and the rest. (Conveyor belts were constructed so that corpses would serve as additional fuel for the furnaces.)

Asked what he saw in Auschwitz in spring 1943, one engineer replied, "I witnessed the incineration of six corpses and came to the conclusion that the furnaces were functioning well." Yes, he acknowledged, he knew that innocent human beings were being liquidated.

"What motivated you to continue?" asked the interrogator.

"I had my contract with the Topf firm and I was aware of the fact that my work was of great importance for the National Socialist state." He added that he thought he would be liquidated by the Gestapo if he refused.

Asked the same question a second engineer replied, "I was a German engineer and a key member of the Topf works and I saw it as my duty to apply my specialist knowledge in this way in order to help Germany win the war, just as an aircraft-construction engineer builds airplanes in wartime, which are also connected with the destruction of human beings."[35]

A third man said, "I am a German and supported the government in Germany and the laws of our government. Whoever opposes our laws is an enemy of the state."[36]

*   *   *

Desensitization by means of a faceless bureaucracy was a feature of the Spanish Inquisition as well, astonishing as this may seem at a time when monarchs were still conducting hands-on government, including hearing personal appeals from ordinary people who thought they'd been wronged at lower levels, a time when the commonest of folk still had individual faces. Of the thousands of people employed by the Inquisition, few would have fathomed the entirety of the enterprise. What they knew was what the Topf und Söhne engineers knew: that they were part of something important and that they were serving the national good. Every spy, informer, prison guard, notary, property evaluator, torturer, executioner, and inquisitor was a cog in the wheel of a huge machine he or she could not fully grasp. At the top of the pyramid sat the grand inquisitor, but even he was responsible to superiors, namely the king and the queen.

The fifteenth century understood the uses of secrecy as well as the twentieth, and intuited its handmaiden relationship to terror. Secrecy and fear were—and are—the advance shock troops of anxiety—all-pervasive and unpredictable. A woman (or man) is awakened by banging at the door. She is no longer safe. Someone, somewhere, has identified her as a heretic. In an atmosphere bordering on hysteria, conversos confess to deeds they may, or may *not*, have committed years or even decades before.

Where terror rules, compassion is always subversive, for empathy weakens propaganda and can move the most unlikely hearts. During the spectacle of the expulsion, Andrés Bernáldez wrote, "There was not a Christian but what felt for them." Bernáldez was one of Castile's most virulent anti-Semites, but one presumes he was also speaking for himself.

Nazi ideology struggled against compassion by stressing hardness of body and mind. One troubled officer at Auschwitz hung a sign over his desk that read, "Sympathy is Weakness"—presumably to remind himself.[37] Rudolf Höss, who became chief commandant of the notorious death camp, recalled that he "went hot and cold all over" the first time he saw a beating, let alone a gassing; however, by the time he witnessed his first execution several years later, he was, he reported cheerfully, "much less bothered."[38]

The fear is, of course, that if the emotional distance is bridged and the "enemy" is somehow reassembled into a suffering human being, compassion may conceivably have enough power to bring the totalitarian machinery to a halt. In his book, *Ordinary Men,* Christopher Browning cites an intriguing event. In 1942, reserve soldiers who were ordered to shoot Jews in Poland on a face-to-face basis suffered severe emotional reactions if they were allowed to converse with their victims, or—worse still—if they recognized them as deported Germans, some of whom they knew from home.[39] (Outside the fatherland, all Germans, including German Jews, had metamorphosed into "Us.") The dehumanized enemy must remain faceless lest he (or she) is revealed to be father, mother, friend, neighbor, or someone's beloved child.

When the most powerful propaganda fails to dissolve moral barriers in strongly principled individuals, the latter may subject themselves to personal risk in order to help people whose faces they recognize to be as human as their own.[40] Like the Dane who explained fifty years later why he and his parents had helped rescue thousands of Jews. "We did not look upon the Jews as Jews," he said. "They were Danes—our fellow countrymen."[41] In other words, they were not abstractions, but human beings. In Spain, in spite of a century-long, anti-Semitic propaganda war enveloping the whole of the fifteenth century, public sympathy for the expelled Jews ran so high that a judge in Caceres was forced to issue an order appropriating the property of Christians who were assisting them. To help during the Nazi era was infinitely more dangerous, but in 1492 and in 1943, five centuries later, those who risked their goods or their person were the same kind of individual: principled, nonconforming and angry at injustice. It is impossible to know at this distance what proportion of the Spanish population attempted to assist the Jews, although the record suggests that large numbers of friends, neighbors, and converso members of Jewish families tried to prevent the expulsion by encouraging last-minute conversions. With regard to the Nazi period, approximately six thousand men and women of exceptional courage have been honored at the Yad Vashem Holocaust memorial in Jerusalem to date.

Here and Now

When I began to research this book in early 1989, happy fantasies of human progress had recaptured the imagination of pundits and politicians in the West for the first time since the debacle of 1914–1918 damaged optimism and altered the way we view the world. The Cold War between titan ideologies had ended after almost half a century of nuclear fear and balance-of-terror trapeze acts. My own generation grew to maturity during this era. When we were very young we debated the problems of life in a bomb shelter; later on we wondered—occasionally aloud, but more often in the quiet recesses of imagination—whether we would live out our allotted life span.

So when televised pictures of children and their parents hacking down the infamous wall in Berlin scattered across the world in November 1989, a collective euphoria exploded: triumphant Cold Warriors claimed victory, the victory of democratic liberalism (an ideology descended in a less-than-straight line from the eighteenth-century Enlightenment) over the newer religion of Marxism, which had committed the fatal error of insisting that the root of our complex being is determined by abstractions of economics and social class. One American luminary wrote an astonishing essay informing the world that history had reached a definitive end, as though "history" was invented in 1945 when hot war froze into cold.[42] Humanity had suffered trials and tribulations, but we on the winning side of the moral divide could stand proud on the spur of the twenty-first century. God was in his heaven, which was located in the West; and He had already booked a return engagement to the former empire of evil atheists in the East.

A divine New World Order of freedom, riches, and spiritual renewal was in the making, each evocative noun a resonant clue to a complex belief system. "Freedom" was the catch-word of American democracy; "riches" would flow from unregulated market economies. "Spiritual renewal" spoke for itself in America where millions of people still attend church every Sunday and religious considerations are a component of political life.

But if these touchstones of democracy had an ongoing basis in reality in the United States—and there were plenty to argue that in an increasingly unequal society plagued by violence and racial distrust they did not—it was because people knew, more or less, what the magic words meant or were supposed to mean. On the other hand there was nothing to suggest that the citizens of formerly Communist countries would be in tune with the content of Western liberal ideology, beyond the fact that they were sure to be dazzled by televised images of impossibly rich people and seduced by a promise of imminent wealth. Could they have known that millions of Americans also live outside this paradigm of the good life? Hardly. During this orgy of self-congratulation, I recalled that in wealthy, Western, tuned-in France of all places, a sociology professor of remote acquaintance told me she had been teaching American culture by screening videotapes of the television program "Dallas" for her students. Marshall McLuhan's medium was carrying a ludicrously distorted message.

Few appeared to notice that the shibboleths of the global market economy faithfully mirrored the ideological certitudes of an earlier era—those pronounced by one Karl Marx, for example. He, too, had promised global salvation through economics. Measures that might have eased former communist states into a more comfortable transition were swept aside in the euphoria, political parties such as the New Forum in East Germany, which proposed more gradual change. In the former Warsaw Pact countries there *was* no history of democracy to remember or reinstate, let alone any precedent remotely resembling the free-fall capitalism of a global economy. No one had previously thought of the workers of the world as international bond traders.

More importantly, generations that had grown to maturity in societies built on lies and maintained by terror were maimed; and nothing exposed this tragedy more transparently than revelations out of the former East Germany disclosing that for decades an astonishing network of spies had been spying on other spies, who were in turn spying on them, until no one was safe from anyone else including husbands from wives or wives from husbands. Perhaps the ultimate in upside-down reality was the discovery that East Germany's most famous *dissident* poet, Sasha Anderson, had been spying on his friends since 1972.[43]

Perhaps it was the sheer pervasiveness of betrayal that shocked and overwhelmed people when six million Stasi* documents were opened to the public in early 1992; although given the dimension of the collaboration, some declarations of surprise had to be more staged than spontaneous. One writer and filmmaker spoke about *Mitlaüfer* (people who take part in whatever is going on). "The GDR [East German or German Democratic Republic] system was a system of participation," he said. "They [the secret police] really gave hundreds of thousands of people the opportunity to participate, to feel important. This was a very smart system. And the same happened during the Nazi time, but you have to admit it was executed with more perfection during the GDR time."[44]

Yes, it happened during the Nazi time. And it had also happened during the Spanish time. *Mitlaüfer*: collaboration, participation, identifying with the powerful, and a willingness to shift moral ground. Thinking about *Mitlaüfer* one begins to ask questions about guilt itself. What *is* "guilt" when everyone is guilty—either of the crime they are charged with, or of lies, distortion and betrayal? What is "crime" when torture and murder are sanctioned for ordinary behavior? Hannah Arendt was the first to identify the horrifying banality of Nazi evil, but the same held true during the Spanish Inquisition when a man or woman might be accused of heresy for wearing clean clothes or for an allegedly misplaced smile.

The triteness of "heretical" behavior in the GDR was no less astonishing. The man assigned to examine the history of the Stasi was, he allowed, "repulsed by the level of human vulgarity." There was, he recalled, the case of the man who wanted to divorce his wife and marry his girlfriend, to whom he confided his desires. Week after week the girlfriend reported her lover's sexual longings to the secret police in graphic detail. "I thought the Stasi would interrupt and say we just don't care

---

*The East German secret police

about this, all we want to know is what kind of politics is he involved in?" reported the reader. "But they never did."[45]

A "heretic" is someone who is deemed "outside," according to whatever criteria of belonging has been established, and the lines may be drawn so narrowly, so crazily, that everyone is suspect. In the GDR the memory of the Holocaust was instantly erased from the history books (only *West* Germans were responsible) so that even the remotest degree of understanding became impossible. The totalitarian mind-set persisted intact. The cunning and the callous survived best, those with the ability to live a double life behind an alert Janus face. In the German Democratic Republic the heretic-enemy was everyone.

*   *   *

In 1989, at the start of this book, I thought the story of Christian attacks on Jews and Muslims in the fifteenth century might trigger new insight into the most carefully orchestrated, far-reaching attack on a minority population in history: the Nazi program to exterminate the Jews. But before a year had passed the fifteenth-century paradigm was as timely as the daily news. Within months of the symbolic destruction of the Berlin Wall, the dry stuff of childhood school texts had sprung to life again. Ethnos emerged intact from Pandora's box, ready to resume. New/old countries were reborn: Bosnia, Herzegovina, Croatia, Serbia. Ancient hatreds reawakened, Rip Van Winkle-like, seizing neighbors and destroying families that had intermarried years before. What had happened? Perhaps a partial answer is that Marshall Tito's Federal People's Republic of Yugoslavia had summarily interred the memory of bloody ethnic war. After the debacle of the Second World War, no official mourning soothed national wounds. Personal grief was left unresolved. Truth was suppressed. The glue of the Party sealed tongues, but it did not heal hearts.

A mindless time warp reinvented brutality. In the late 1980s a group of Serbian artists and writers in Belgrade asked Canadian author Myrna Kostash whether she was aware that Croats tore the hearts out of their Serbian neighbors, drank their blood, and ripped their children to pieces. And did she know that newborn Serbian infants were being strangled and starved in their cribs by Albanian hospital staff in Kosovo?[46] Within this fantasy of killing innocent babes (the genetic future of the "race"), drinking blood, and tearing out hearts lived the enduring, primitive myth of "otherness," purposely designed to dehumanize: the blood libel against the Jews cleaned up for new service.

Tribalism and xenophobia reemerge—in Eastern countries torn too suddenly from their moorings where people now are "free" to starve after generations of cradle-to-grave security; in Western countries where recession eroded economies and where Third World immigration has introduced unfamiliar cultures; in post-Soviet Russia, where the price of bread rose 700 percent in one day, where men can now expect to die by age fifty-eight, where people have been reduced to bribing doctors and nurses for adequate care, and nostalgic imperialists, nationalists, religious traditionalists, and anti-Semites have risen from a seventy-year grave.

These are times when rescuing saviors arise. Ferdinand and Isabella salvaged a Castile that was fragmenting in civil war and brigandry by uniting the Christian tribe behind a banner of fiscal reform and religious purity. Hitler united his Aryan tribe against civil strife and the perceived humiliation of the Treaty of Versailles behind a banner of *Volk* and national purity.

At this writing forty-eight different tribal and religious wars rage in Europe, the Middle East, North Africa, sub-Saharan Africa, Asia, and Latin America.[47] Islamic fundamentalism is on the rise in the occupied territories of Israel, in Algeria, and in Egypt. Novelist Salman Rushdie remains condemned to death by an ayatollah for heresy, militant Hindu fundamentalism is escalating in India, secular and religious right-wing movements gain ground in the United States, and religious-national ideologues threaten to disrupt the government of Israel. That Jews have so often been the object of other peoples' ire has not prevented some among them from nurturing their own versions of exclusivity, to the surprise of rationalists who think people who have been persecuted should know better. On the contrary, rejection of the Other is a human trait bred in the primitive places of the psyche. The retreat into the tribe is easy and visceral, and satisfying. For what is more comforting than to attribute the best to oneself (in the company of splendid, like-minded fellows) and the worst to the Other?

Was it an unwillingness to accept this ugly truth that skewed our response to the explosion of horror in the former Yugoslavia, and left us unprepared for news of starvation, death camps, sadistic guards, rape, and the indiscriminate massacre of both old and young, as though none of this had happened before? Had we come to believe that only the isolated madman was capable of degrading us in this way? Had the artificial calm of the Cold War lulled us into rationalizing the atrocities of the twentieth century as an aberration and not endemic to our nature?

A half-century ago, George Orwell forced himself to confront the issue: "It is possible that man's major problems will *never* be resolved," he wrote in an essay about Arthur Koestler during the dark days of 1944. But Orwell was a utopian, like many of his generation, and he chose not to tolerate the implications of his words. "It's unthinkable!" he added immediately. "Who is there who dares to look at the world today and say to himself, 'It will always be like this, even in a million years. . . ?' "[48]

The thought that major social problems may never be resolved is impossibly depressing for utopians who believe people and societies are perfectible. Orwell struggled with this. "Perhaps the choice before man is always a choice of evils," he mused. "Perhaps even the aim of Socialism is not to make the world perfect, but to make it better."[49]

The tidy solution is comforting and perennially tempting. After the pogroms of 1391, assimilation by baptism was put forward as the answer to Spain's woes. In Enlightenment Germany, conversion to the religion of nationhood was seen as the rational choice—an ideology that has prevailed in the West ever since. In both of these countries, and in France, to name only those places I have alluded to, the "solution" led inevitably to blood. One reason seems clear: the presence in each case of *coercive* assimilation, either direct or indirect. In all three societies the proffered cure-all left too little room for the historical/ethnic/religious self to survive.

We continue to live in ahistorical times. Memory dies from neglect, or is deliberately destroyed by totalitarian regimes. A fantasy of each era as a sealed time capsule bearing little relation to a before, or an after, prevails. But history neither begins, nor ends; it is an endless loop, a broad continuum of experience where the past never "dies," nor is the future "born." One thousand years ago there were signs in Arab Spain of the rational, quasisecular perspective that eventually flowered during the eighteenth century Enlightenment and has been with us ever since. Conversely, the mind-set of the Middle Ages is with us still, as a casual perusal of almost any newspaper on any day will underline, sometimes amusingly, sometimes horrifyingly.[50]

Can the recognition that we live on an endless loop of past and present and not in carved-off, unrelated time capsules help make sense of tribal barbarism when it climbs out of Pandora's Box under the right conditions? Is it useful to acknowledge that the urge to distinguish ourselves—to discriminate, in other words—on behalf of the self, the family, the tribe, the religion, or the nation is a human characteristic that cannot be wished away with liberal good will?

To acknowledge what may be true, psychologically, is not to condone violence; it is, rather, to stop pretending that the behavior we abhor is less than human. To deny that ethnic and cultural differences will always exist in varying degrees in mixed societies seems far more certain to invite danger. The Jews of medieval Spain did not become the cultural inheritors of Pelayo the day after they were summarily baptized into Christianity, and neither did the Moors, but both minority groups suffered from being forcibly amputated from a way of life that was their legacy, even if they were no longer believers in Judaism or Islam. The majority culture that oppressed them was brutalized as well. Similarly, the Jews of nineteenth-century Germany did not become instant inheritors of Teutonic myth when they were emancipated into the larger society. Had open pluralism and not a drive to assimilation been the ethos of the day, tragedy might have been averted. On the other hand pluralism can also fragment into tribalism. Success calls for continuous vigilance.

*   *   *

Multireligious, multiethnic society is already a reality everywhere in the West. And in a shrinking world of free trade and universal communications where little children from remote African tribes have been pictured, wide-eyed, watching American sit-coms, it is certainly the future. Artificial distinctions between refugees (are they economic or political?) will surely become increasingly harder to determine as television bombards poverty-stricken, war-torn Third Worlders living in postcolonial disarray with daily images of previously unimaginable wealth. Nervous governments will invent policies to rationalize immigration. But the facts are unlikely to change: multicultural society has been with us a long time and is the way of the future. It has had some remarkable successes, but its inherent faultline—the delicate high-wire act needed for balance—requires constant monitoring.

Where the balance falters, danger lurks. Not long ago an Arab taxi driver in Paris told me about his ambitions for his daughter. He had lived in France for thirty years, he said, since he was a small child at the end of the Algerian war. After three decades he barely spoke Arabic anymore, and he was certainly not religious. French was his tongue, French culture was his culture, less from conscious choice than from absorption, osmosis, and, yes, the expectation that he would be "French" one day. Instead, he is insulted daily in the streets of Paris, and told to "go home." But France *is* his home, his only home.

He drove a taxi, but he had hoped his daughter would do better. She was only ten. For two years he tried to place her in one of the better schools in the city. Finally, the headmistress spoke to him bluntly. "You must put her where there are children who look like her. She won't fit in, she'll feel badly." My driver thought about approaching the French Human Rights League, but humiliation and bitterness overwhelmed him. Now his daughter is studying Arabic and Islam. She will attend a school where there are no white "French" children, and when she reaches the right age, he says, she will cover her head with the *chador*.

I thought about Hans Meyer as described by Primo Levi, and about Raymond-Raoul Lambert. They and millions like them also believed that they belonged. This was, and is, the promise of the secular, pluralist, national state—and its ongoing challenge.

The United States and Canada

Pluralism in its North American incarnation has an uncanny resemblance to ancient Andalusia under the early Moors. Then and now, multicultural society evolved from the incorporation of different peoples and not from anything so rational, or idealistic, as choice. The incentive was purely practical: vast tracts of land were sparsely populated and needed developing; and in all three places (though separated by a millennium), mixed populations produced an unparalleled explosion of raw energy and inventiveness.

The American ideology of a "melting pot" of peoples has had a long and successful run. On the surface "the pot" promises equal membership in the sacred church of the nation state. What is required in return is a common declaration of faith in an idealized dream of America whose visible sacraments are a flag, a national anthem, and a quasireligious pledge of allegiance.

Yet to me (whose detached view derives from the northern side of the forty-ninth parallel), the "melting pot" looks like a fiction—a *fortuitous* fiction—a multipurpose myth that is, or may have been, the saving feature of American pluralism. I suspect it would not occur to a majority of Americans to deny, less still to decry, cultural distinctiveness even as they hold their hands over their hearts in collective, patriotic ardor. There are seventy-five neighborhoods in the city of Chicago alone, each vaguely or overtly identified with a different ethnic population; New York was/is "Jewish"; the Midwest was/is "Scandinavian" and "German"; Boston was/is "Irish." Americans of all origins and persuasions espouse the fiction of melting-pot homogeneity while simultaneously tolerating difference generation after generation. They "imagine" America while inhabiting a world of myriad variation.

This imagined America strikes me as a strength. All nation-states are more or less "imagined" on the basis of shared myth, and there is built-in danger in this; however, unlike societies in which the push to assimilate minorities is real and not symbolic—where the promise of acceptance is conditional on a virtual abandonment of culture or religion—the American melting pot ideology has actively supported diversity under an umbrella of shared national identity. Had the United States taken its own unifying myths more literally, quite a different history might have resulted.

I am reminded of a revealing conversation that took place during a trip to Israel in the mid-1980s when I interviewed a proudly American rabbi who was happy to provide a personal, if startling, interpretation of the flow between ethnic particularity and national identity that characterizes his country. Every Fourth of July this rabbi's father gathered his family around him on the front porch of their home in Denver, Colorado and read aloud from the American Declaration of Independence and the Constitution. "We read it as a religious document, the way we read from a text on Passover," explained the son. These seminal, political works were "Jewish," he said, "because all human beings are created in the image of God and have a right to life, liberty, and the pursuit of happiness. I would like to see tolerance and pluralism as contributions that America will make to Israel, because they are also Jewish values."[51] This was religious messianism translated to the secular state, the minority adapting and interpreting values to match the overarching ethos of the nation. It was not unlike the acculturation that minority Christians and Jews experienced in eighth, ninth, and tenth century Moorish Spain, an adaptation that permitted the retention of cultural difference and religious identity.

The symbolic power of this all-embracing, expansive ideal of America is poignantly transparent in the recent history of black civil rights. Although race-related inequality is blatantly obvious in the land of "The Dream," the stirring rhetoric of equal promise inspires renewed belief in the future in a way that non-Americans, particularly Europeans, find naive. Martin Luther King, Jr., did not look at the history of slavery and bred-in-the-bone racism and conclude, as citizens of other nations might have, that bigotry was ingrained and ineradicable. That would have been heresy. In American ideology there *are* no permanently dispossessed people, only the temporarily disadvantaged. Only the future matters. It is *always* possible that tomorrow will wipe today's slate clean, even if it never does.

In his famous Washington speech in which the touchstone phrase "I have a dream" was both theme and flashpoint of unrequited longing, King demonstrated that he and millions of black Americans believed fervently in the promise of equal, melting pot America, in spite of their evident exclusion; and in 1963 liberal, white America resonated to King's words, the ideal of a common identity subsuming difference inspiring them to work ever harder. To be American required of them that they try again and again, and that they never abandon hope.

Until now, the acceptance of ethno-cultural difference married to a fiction of equal access to the benefits of "The Dream" has sustained a fragile interdependence of race, religion, and ethnicity in America. But there are signs of disturbing change.

*   *   *

On October 14, 1904, Prime Minister Sir Wilfrid Laurier announced to his proud compatriots that "the twentieth century will be the century of

Canada and Canadian development." Immigration was humming along at high speed and a raw-resources economy was booming. If the industrialized nineteenth century had "belonged" to the United States, the new one would be Canada's.

According to most standard measurements of power and influence, this did not happen: Canada remains hampered by a small population huddled along its (warmest) southern border; by "the broken patterns of its geography," as the late George Woodcock put it in his book *The Canadians*, by internecine jurisdictional squabbles between federal and provincial governments; by intractable constitutional debates between French and non-French citizens (which Laurier himself entered politics to try to resolve); and by an unavoidable mouse-to-elephant relationship with the most powerful nation in the world.

Yet Canada is considered one of the most successful multicultural societies on earth. Today, more than 40 percent of the population of the city of Toronto was born outside the country and 30 percent of Canadians point to a language other than English or French as their ancestral tongue. When the Iron Curtain fell in 1989, delegations from eastern and western Europe descended on Ottawa to find out how this country had managed to integrate millions of new citizens over the decades.

Until the last war, Canada's cultural umbrella was Britain—and (usually) polite racism was the rule. Genteel argument frequently concluded that non-British migrants were "unassimilable." "We cannot assimilate the yellow, black, or brown races . . . any race that cannot blend satisfactorily is a menace," wrote a professor in a respected academic journal.[52] A colleague worried pointedly about "the high fertility of certain foreign stocks."[53]

There have been recurring strains over the decades as Canadians have confronted unfamiliar cultures, but in recent, post-war decades few people publicly questioned the desirability of immigration. These were boom years, as at the time of Laurier—jobs, growing industrialization.

Canadians never adopted the American fiction of a "melting pot"; instead, they devised their own fiction to facilitate needed immigration. In the early 1970s, capital "M" multiculturalism was adopted as official government policy, ostensibly to help preserve the distinctive cultural identity of new Canadians within a pluralist nation. Underlying reasons for establishing a formal multicultural policy may have been more political than idealistic, but unlike the United States with its stress on individualism, Canada has always recognized the idea of collective rights (the rights of English and French, Catholics and Protestants), so the concept of a multicultural mosaic of peoples had a natural precedent. Sir Wilfrid Laurier had articulated these attitudes as early as 1900: "As long as I live . . . I shall repel the idea of changing the nature of [Canada's] different elements. . . . I want the granite to remain the granite; I want the oak to remain the oak. I want the sturdy Scotchman to remain the Scotchman; I want the brainy Englishman to remain the Englishman; I want the warm-hearted Irishman to remain the Irishman."[54]

Turn-of-the-century stereotypes aside, official Multiculturalism was an elaboration of this uniquely Canadian mind-set. If America had successfully entrenched a plural reality by quietly ignoring its own proassimilation ideals, Canada succeeded by supporting ethnic and religious multiculturalism without any pretense to the contrary, knowing from experience that within a generation children educated together in the public schools would emerge as integrated citizens. In any event, American Dream patriotism makes most Canadians squirm with discomfort. Canadians do not hold their hands over their hearts when they sing their national anthem; many do not even know the words to the national anthem. An American-style bill to make destroying the flag a crime was roundly defeated in Parliament. Flag worship is embarrassing.

But without corny symbolism and an ideological superstructure where everyone is presumed to have melted into a common pot, even if they clearly have not, it has been harder to create an umbrella identity. If anything, Canadians have traditionally defined themselves in opposition to their gigantic neighbor, as a more tolerant nation with more humane, universally accessible social programs, as a "peaceable, caring people who do not put their economic self-interest ahead of caring for the disadvantaged, and who will not countenance injustice within their borders."[55] Americans have their mythologies; this has been ours. But here, too, there are signs of change.

If self-conscious cosmopolitanism is the most workable and least dangerous social structure in a resource-hungry, fragmented, unequal world of universal communications where people are increasingly on the move, the United States and Canada are each in a strong position since both countries have successfully absorbed immigrants and capitalized on their presence. But Canada and the United States are simultaneously undergoing cultural transformations that threaten to undermine the very belief systems that have historically sustained the balance.

If any truth has emerged during the course of my research, it is that the expectation of ideological or political stasis is the most dangerous naiveté of all. Spanish society altered very slowly, almost invisibly, until an ethos that had prevailed for almost eight hundred years was undermined—or, more to the point, was finally *seen* to have been undermined. Those who found themselves excluded in this seemingly sudden shift were unprepared; they had not seen. In Germany, a social transformation that was in process for more than a century realized its apotheosis with

Adolf Hitler, but there are still those who claim the Führer was an aberration. In France, the pendulum set swinging by the 1789 Revolution careened to the nationalist right a century later during the Dreyfus Affair, after which four decades of unrelenting anti-Semitic, antidemocratic propaganda prepared people for an easy acceptance of the collaborationist Pétain government in 1940—in the very land where minority emancipation had been born.

In both Canada and the United States, a public consensus that has emphasized *in*clusiveness is being replaced by an ideology of exclusiveness (although those responsible for this increasing fragmentation often claim to be struggling in the name of the former, not the latter). In the 1980s, President Ronald Reagan and his coterie of neoconservative true believers handed the wealthy a useful rationale for ignoring the plight of the poor. The self-serving sophistry of trickle-down economics condoned rapaciousness, undermined the general commitment to community welfare, and divided America along jagged race and class lines. Yes, class lines—a most un-American conceit. "Political correctness," which was born of a noble desire to right long-standing wrongs, has increased minority self-consciousness and special-interest activism, but the fallout has been a reduced interest in the welfare of society as greater than the sum of its parts. An aggressive ethos of Us versus Them exclusivity is on the rise.

The shift to the right in American political culture is reflected in the proliferation of foul-mouthed talk-show hosts who daily spew hatred and antigovernment paranoia over the airways. When a government building was bombed in Oklahoma City in April 1995, killing scores, the spotlight rightly fell on these public haters and the cumulative, desensitizing effect of their harangues. Just as the French were conditioned by continuous propaganda to accept anti-Semitism following the Dreyfus Affair, and were therefore psychologically "prepared" for Nazi anti-Jewish hatred, so many Americans are being conditioned to find extreme and irrational ideas ordinary and "true."

As usual, the social shift is abetted by economic failure. Entire sections of cities look virtually abandoned. Walk the downtown streets of Detroit or Flint, Michigan. There are no corner grocery stores because there are no residents. Entire blocks resemble war zones; grafitti is scrawled over broken walls; wild grasses push stalks through wind-strewn, rotting garbage. Privately funded Yale University, with its own armed police force, is a bastion of privilege surrounded by the slums of once prosperous New Haven, Connecticut, and the university administration warns incoming students not to walk alone after dark, not to get out of a car in certain neighborhoods, or even to open the window. In Atlanta, Georgia, the police department warns visitors with a long checklist of dos and don'ts, including a warning to resist if you are being forced into a car at gunpoint. (Apparently the hapless guest in the city is more likely to survive that way.) The poor grow poorer, fathers disappear, mothers are overwhelmed, and the next generation of children is destroyed. The United States has the highest incidence of crime in the world with a murder rate per 100,000 males that is more than five times that of Canada.[56] In the first ten months of 1993 there were 270 gang-related killings in Los Angeles; in 1991 hispanic gang violence registered a 95 percent increase; and more than 70 percent of gang members use drugs regularly.[57] The incarceration rate in California is six times that of Canada (were that state a country, this would represent the highest rate in the world). The United States Congress has turned its back on head-start education and funding: Jail 'em or kill 'em is the new mentality as state after state reintroduces the death penalty.

As middle class society, once so supportive, closes ranks, chronically dispossessed visible minorities seem finally to be losing hope in Martin Luther King's dream of integration. Some black groups are lobbying for a return to racially separate "black-focus" schools while, on the other side of the race divide, a grass-roots citizens group in California mounts an attack against affirmative action legislation—the most important recent symbol of American Dream optimism. White enclaves build walls around their towns and hire guards to patrol the ramparts, as in the Middle Ages. De facto apartheid is already in place: a two-tiered society based on race and class.

"American society is schizophrenic on the subject [of race], proclaiming on the one hand the virtues of a color-blind society and the illusive melting pot of immigration, and on the other doing everything possible to be conscious about race and racial matters," wrote the editors of the Columbia University Media Studies Center *Journal* in 1994.[58] There is probably nothing new about this dichotomy. What does seem new is an attitudinal shift in favor of the second part of the equation: increased racialization. In February 1995, long before evidence was completed in the O. J. Simpson trial, a nationwide Harris poll found that 61 percent of white Americans believed the defendant was guilty and 68 percent of black Americans believed he was not.

Underlying this self-conscious racialization is the apparent disintegration of older, buttressing myths of integration. A question emerges: If these myths are lost, and the sustaining dream of communality and the possibility of equality is eroded, what will stand in the way of escalating civil strife? If the central American faith in redemptive change is undermined, will there still be an ideological buffer against interethnic violence?

*   *   *

Canada is also undergoing a major ideological shift. For decades we have imagined that our lack of fake "Dream" references and the absence of noisy patriotism were a bonus in our lives, and that "mosaic" multiculturalism was our strength. We congratulated ourselves on being tolerant, kind, and just, and claimed that these characteristics defined us as a nation. Then we were put to the test. In the 1980s recession seriously eroded income. Economic restructuring following free trade with the United States undercut manufacturing, definitively killing thousands of jobs. In the same decade, nonwhite immigration to urban areas increased significantly, introducing a (relatively) new racial dimension. (I say "relatively" because Canadian racism toward native peoples and others has been present, but less visible.) Especially disturbing is new evidence that in the African-Canadian community, which is largely of Carribean origin, many second generation children are actually more alienated from the mainstream than their immigrant parents.[59] (Following new cultural patterns in the United States, the focus of Afro-Caribbean identity seems to be shifting away from integration and toward racialization, toward an emphasis on color and perceived powerlessness.) This deviation from the usual pattern of immigrant acculturation fuels anxiety about the viability of our vaunted Canadian multiculturalism, since the assumption has always been that integrated, second-generation Canadians are created naturally in the neighborhood school yard.

A 1989 poll reported that 63 percent of Canadians continued to favor multiculturalism as a national policy,[60] but by the end of 1993 support had dropped to 28 percent. Seventy-two percent of respondents claimed to prefer the American-style melting pot, saying they were "increasingly intolerant" of demands made by ethnic groups and frustrated by the "lack of conformity" in Canadian society.[61] In the past, every Canadian would have laughed with recognition at the quintessential national joke: "Why did the Canadian chicken cross the road? To get to the middle." Canada is an unlikely geography that has held together with the glue of compromise, but compromise for the sake of the collective interest is currently out of fashion.

The failure to project a clear and visible "Canadianness" to which new immigrants from vastly dissimilar cultures can aspire creates confusion as the new "rights culture" infiltrates the older ethos of multiculturalism with no balancing emphasis on explaining Canada. For example, some Vietnamese have tried to argue that wife beating is not wife abuse because it is part of indigenous Vietnamese culture, and since Canada is officially multicultural the law must accommodate this difference. Two organizations have tried (unsuccessfully) to have provincial governments recognize Islamic law in Canada. During the summer of 1993, a Muslim women's group succeeded in closing a public swimming pool one day a week so they could bathe unobserved. And the Ontario Human Rights Commission, of all unlikely institutions, published a paper stating that "the legal presumption of innocence is inappropriate at the investigatory stages of race discrimination complaints ... [because] racism is in fact the norm rather than the exception."[62] If Canadians are unwilling to draw lines that protect law, democratic institutions, and secular universality (and by so doing help new arrivals adjust), the future of majority-minority relations looks bleaker than it has in decades.

Multiculturalism is Canada's greatest success, but the compass needle needs resetting. For one thing, the word itself. Originally used to describe a program and a philosophy of integration through an acceptance of cultural diversity, the term "multiculturalism" has become a tool for underscoring demands that sometimes contradict secular and democratic values. The result is a lessening of public attachment to the best idea ever to come out of this country—the basis for the very tolerance Canadians think characterizes them as a people.

Multiculturalism was, and is, a humane ideal in an ethnically diverse society—a model for an increasingly heterogeneous world. Canadians are right to be proud. But Multiculturalism as a program and a philosophy did not go far enough. Our treasured differences were just one half of the picture. We have neglected the other half by assuming the natural integration of the second generation, and by failing to weave a canopy of Canada over our multiple cultures with the same energy we dedicate to a celebration of our differences.

Professor Mary Ann Glendon of Harvard Law School put it this way regarding a similar splintering in America: "By indulging in excessively simple forms of rights talk in a pluralistic society, we needlessly multiply occasions for civil discord. We make it difficult for persons and groups with conflicting interests and views to build coalitions and achieve compromise, or even to acquire that minimal degree of mutual forbearance and understanding that promotes peaceful coexistence and keeps the door open to further communication."[63]

If social fragmentation and a breakdown of hope are undermining the dream of a culturally and racially inclusive America, so similar (though lesser) splintering threatens to disrupt an already fragile sense of Canadian identity and diminish traditional ideals of tolerance. As I hope this book has helped to demonstrate, the most dynamic communities are inherently as vulnerable as the rest.

* * *

One returns to the endless loop of time, to the endemic problem of majorities and minorities, to common identity and disparate otherness, to the human propensity to create categories of "Us" and "Them," then to close ranks and exclude, and to the potential for tragedy that all this contains. One returns to Orwell's despairing thought, "It is possible that the major problems of humanity will never be resolved," followed quickly by a disbelieving, "It's unthinkable!" A half-century later, in a still violent (though now anti-utopian) age, it is perhaps easier to accept that Orwell was probably right the first time, and to ponder the implications.

The first implication is that given endemic wars, economic need, and easy travel, the developed world will become increasingly cosmopolitan. Canada, the United States, Australia, Argentina, Chile, and many other countries, including medieval Spain under the Moors, have demonstrated the rich creativity of such diversity—provided there is a nurturing climate.

The second implication is that we will always have our primitive, rejecting selves to contend with. "The most terrible human capacity is that of profoundly devaluing others who are merely different," psychologist Ervin Staub has written.[64] It is daunting to think that this tendency is probably endemic. It means we cannot, by definition, ever take peace for granted. And it forces us to ask questions: Are we prepared, or able, to teach our children to protect themselves, and by extension their societies, by monitoring public policy as well as their personal reactions to others? Outside the family, what kind of education will ensure this? And as we enter the twenty-first century, are we prepared for the prospect of increasingly diverse, multi-ethnic societies that will include the inevitable fault-line of majority-minority accommodation?

Although I suspect the answer is still a daunting "no," I am convinced that the most important protection is the education of the young. The communications revolution that sends distorted images of the First World to the Third, and fosters migration north, also transmits distorted images in the other direction. The stand-up reporter in Somalia takes a long stride to Croatia, then wings his way to Chechen until the next catastrophe calls him elsewhere. Ensconced in our living rooms we learn little. There is not enough time between commercials. What sells soap, and keeps ratings high, is emotion: crying women and children, abandoned babies, grief-stricken men shovelling dirt in a far-away graveyard. Their suffering is cheapened because the wider moral issues elude us.

Television curtails reflection; and since it is an axiom of democratic capitalism that everything must sell a product to the largest numbers of consumers, and other peoples' sorrow is a proven winner, programming is unlikely to get better.

One antidote to the coarsened sensitivity this must inevitably induce

is an educational curriculum that stresses history, for context, and literature—to convey what is universal to the human spirit. Children also need
to learn "critical thinking," the study of elementary logic, to help them
pick their way through the onslaught of information and recognize when
they are being fed propaganda. (Some school jurisdictions in the United
States, Canada, and Europe already offer such courses.)

Judging from the kind of civil conflict that has erupted since the end
of the Cold War, it may become more difficult to sustain pluralist, tolerant societies. Transcontinental migrations and uneasy cohabitation are
already creating cultural strains. Although critical thinking represents only
one response to a complex future, it is possible to hope that people who
are trained from childhood to understand politics contextually through
the study of history, as well as to view "information" skeptically and independently, will be less vulnerable to demagoguery, and more vigilant:
vigilant with regard to emerging changes in the general consensus that
governs society, and vigilant with regard to the darkness within, the universal human urge to hive off and reject the Other.

Disconcerting as the future may appear at the turn of the third millennium, it is reassuring to remember that the Moors of Andalusia were
dealing with similar issues back in the ninth century C.E. The early Muslim caliphs fought among themselves and were incapable of sustaining
political autonomy, but their greatness lay elsewhere. The world of ancient
Andalusia was far from perfect, and it held the usual mix of tensions. But
the decision to reject coercive assimilation, to embrace tolerance, and to
respect difference under an umbrella of shared language and integrated
culture diminished conflict. Beneath a common canopy, the "three religions" of Muslim Spain maintained their uniqueness and generally lived
in peace, cross-fertilizing one of the most dynamic civilizations the West
has seen. When a ninth-century Christian, Pablo Alvaro, dared to insult
Muhammad, the caliph tried not to respond with the sort of blunt retal-
iatory force that would have resulted in hatred and suggested, diplomat-
ically, that Alvaro might have made a mistake. Compare this to the crude
fatwah against the life of Salman Rushdie, a missive from twentieth-century Islam in its newer, more radical incarnation. When the tenth-century
caliph Abdur Rahman III made the Jew Hasdai his chief advisor, he sent
a message to all of Europe that Andalusia was a strange, open society
where talent mattered. Compare this to the eventual expulsion of the Jews
from Spain, although they had served their royal governments with loyalty for centuries. At the dawn of the last millennium, Arab Spain had
developed a dual structure of common identity based on language and
culture, with protected ethnicities folded within. This early success shines
through the centuries like a brilliant star.

New Faces

The good news is the Catholic Church which has repudiated those parts of its ancient liturgy that encouraged hatred of Jews and Judaism, including the enduring designation of "perfidious Jew" and the notion of collective Jewish guilt for the death of Jesus Christ. The Second Vatican Council of 1962 to 1965 under Pope John XXIII opened an era of reconciliation: since the end of the Second World War many Catholic theologians have led the struggle for ecumenical understanding, and for a greater appreciation of the role traditional Christianity has played in the rejection and demonization of the Other.

In the final days of 1993, the Vatican confirmed its new thinking by signing a fundamental agreement with Israel, in which the Holy See deplored attacks on Jews and Judaism and committed itself, with the Jewish state, to combat anti-Semitism, racism, and religious intolerance.[65] Finally, in November 1994, Pope John Paul II issued a remarkable statement in anticipation of the forthcoming two-thousand-year anniversary of Christianity. The Catholic Church, he wrote, has an obligation to express "profound regret for the weaknesses of her sons and daughters who sullied her face over the centuries." Members of the Church, he went on to say, have practiced "intolerance and even the use of violence in the service of truth."

Theologically, the papal announcement was revolutionary; it opposed the position taken by the Catholic Church (not least during the Spanish Inquisition) that the individual rights of human beings on Earth matter less—Earth being but a temporary abode—than the status of a person's immortal soul. During the Inquisition, the end—salvation—justified the chosen means, which included death by fire.

Had Pope John Paul II visited the Prado museum in Madrid? If so, perhaps he chanced upon a masterpiece of fifteenth-century Spanish art hanging in one of the galleries—a canvass entitled *Auto-da-Fé* by Pedro Berruguete. The painting was commissioned by Tomás de Torquemada for the altar of his monastery in Ávila (where the Holy Child prisoners were held), and it ostensibly depicts the earlier papal Inquisition that was established in the thirteenth century to root out the Albigensian heresy.

The painting's contemporary meaning would have been perfectly clear to Torquemada and his fellow Dominicans. The presiding inquisitors sit on a raised platform; their figures are large and imposing and they are in sumptuous dress. They are also deeply bored. One of them is asleep. Beneath them, in the lower right corner of the canvass, two men are shackled to the stake. Flames lick at their ankles; but unlike the inquisitors, these are stick figures without importance; the loss of their insignificant lives is clearly irrelevant to the somnolent men seated above.

Berruguete has depicted the essence of tyranny: the desensitization of the perpetrator and the diminished human status of the victim, a message that a late twentieth-century pope of the Roman Catholic Church has apparently come to understand.

* * *

The other good news is Spain itself. Although the Holy Inquisition came to a formal end in 1834, the inquisitorial worldview remained in place for another century and a half (with the exception of several short, liberalized periods) until the death of Francisco Franco in 1975. Over the centuries the Holy Office attacked conversos, Jews, Moors, the Illuminati (reforming Catholics), Protestants, Jesuits, homosexuals, and women who were accused of witchcraft. Conformity had produced sterility and decay. But the advent of a democratic king to the ancient throne of his very Catholic ancestors, Ferdinand and Isabella, propelled the enduring land of contradictions—of avant-garde tolerance and avant-garde tyranny—into the orbit of modern Europe.[66]

A man named Sam Toledano came to Spain from Morocco in the 1950s, when that country, too, had made its minorities unwelcome. Franco, of all people, was encouraging the immigration of Jews back "home." (Legally they were already able to return: in 1860 the first constitution of Spain recognized freedom of religion and made it possible for Jews to live in Spain, but few wanted to do so.) Franco's interest in the Jews was probably economic since, to put it kindly, he was not a known lover of minorities. During and after the Spanish Civil War (1936–1939), right-wing Francist writing ranted obsessively about a so-called Jewish-communist threat to Spain—proof (if such were needed) that "the enemy Other" can be guilty of treason even when absent.

When Sam Toledano, his brother, and his sister-in-law first considered immigrating to Spain, they deliberately told Spanish acquaintances they were Jews in order to gauge their reaction. "I found no sense of social prejudice in terms of possible restrictions on this or that, but quite a few were genuinely curious, and many people held medieval, anti-Semitic ideas," he recalled one day in 1989 when we met in Madrid. "I soon realized where the medieval ideas came from. When my son started school in 1960, his texts were full of stories of Jews poisoning wells and using the blood of Christians to bake unleavened bread for Passover. The standard illustration was the Jews opening the gates of Toledo to the Moors."[67]

Toledano and a few other Jewish families raised the issue with school authorities and the Church, both of which were happy to make changes; but the textbook publishers didn't want to spend the money. Eventually the references were removed, but Toledano says the rich history of the Jews and the Moors in Spain is still not being taught to school children as part of their heritage.

This too may change as a new generation of Spanish historians begins to comb municipal archives for local histories of the Inquisition and the expulsion of both the Jews and the Moors. In Saragossa the municipal government recently published a two-volume history of the expulsion of the Jews from that city by Miguel Angel Motis Dolader. In 1992, Professor Motis personally hosted a small group of rabbis from New York and Israel. Together, they held the first Jewish Sabbath service in Saragossa in five hundred years, in the same building which was, until 1492, the major synagogue of the city.

In December 1992, the Madrid daily *El País* published an article entitled "Citizens of the World," in which the editors took stock of Spain's recent transition to democracy.[68] "The civil war and Franco marked the end of a long, historical cycle characterized by an aversion for the Other, self-satisfied, jingoist patriotism, and the general impoverishment of our society . . . a society marked by rigidity, a phobia with regard to foreigners, and a disregard for any idea that went beyond the lines of so-called national-Catholicism," wrote Juan Luis Cebrián. "[Spain's] full integration into the European Community assumes the end of a period of almost five centuries marked by Spanish isolationism, intolerance, and self-absorption," he added in a burst of liberal optimism.

There are still those who dream nostalgically of law, order and fascism, the modern legacy of Ferdinand and Isabella. In 1989 large, idealized portraits of Franco, Hitler, and Mussolini were being offered for sale on the streets of crusty, upper-class Madrid. These were tended by frail old men with rheumy eyes and memory etched into their faces.

But the new face of Spain was visible on March 31, 1992, exactly five hundred years after the expulsion edict was signed by the Catholic Monarchs. On that day their direct descendant, King Juan Carlos, stood before the ark of the Torah in Madrid's only synagogue wearing a traditional skullcap on his head. Flanking him were his wife, Queen Sofia, and Chaim Herzog, the president of Israel. The Beth Yacov synagogue was crowded with foreign observers and as many of Spain's sixteen thousand Jews as had managed to squeeze a place for themselves.

King Juan Carlos spoke: "May hate and intolerance never again cause desolation and exile," he said. "Let us be capable of building a prosperous and peaceful Spain based on concord and mutual respect." Then he added: "What is important is not an accounting of our errors or successes, but the willingness to think about and analyze the past in terms of our future, [and] the willingness to work together to pursue a noble goal."

The king had stopped short of apologizing for the expulsion of the Jews, something many had hoped for: this, it seems, he could not do. For five centuries Ferdinand and Isabella have been venerated as the parents of national unity, the vanquishers of Islamic Granada, the sponsors of Christopher Columbus. To formally, publicly, and officially apologize for their legislation was not something Juan Carlos would undertake, regardless of his personal inclinations.

It wasn't perfect, but with this symbolic reconciliation between the Jews of Spain and the kingdom that rejected them so long ago, a balm soothed old wounds. And when the synagogue filled with the sounds of Kaddish, the Jewish prayer for the dead, the ghosts of generations past wept to be remembered.

Notes

1. On the subject of the rise of anti-Semitism in Germany see George L. Mosse, *Toward the Final Solution*; Paul Lawrence Rose, *Revolutionary Antisemitism in Germany from Kant to Wagner*; and Peter Pulzer, *Jews and the German State: The Political History of a Minority, 1848–1933*.

2. Charles Taylor, *Hegel*, 389–90.

3. For an excellent discussion of Luther's role in the evolution of German anti-Semitism see Paul Rose, *Revolutionary Antisemitism*, ch. 1.

4. Ibid., 6–7.

5. Arendt, *The Origins of Totalitarianism*, 1 ("Antisemitism"), 11. My references are to the 1968 paperback edition.

6. *Reden an die Deutsche Nation*, Berlin (1808), 488, cited in Lucy S. Dawidowicz, *The War against the Jews: 1933–1945*, 34.

7. Mosse, *Toward the Final Solution*, 26.

8. For an overview of Jews in Germany, see Monika Richarz, *Jewish Life in Germany*, trans. by Stella P. Rosenfeld and Sidney Rosenfeld, introduction.

9. Ibid.

10. Pulzer, *Jews and the German State*, 3.

11. Ibid. Conversions increased toward the end of the nineteenth century.

12. *Richard Wagner's Prose Works*, 1892–99, trans. by W. A. Ellis, cited in Rose, *Revolutionary Antisemitism*, 360.

13. Ibid., 362.

14. Ibid., 364–65.

15. Geoffrey Wigoder, ed., *Encyclopedic Dictionary of Judaica*, 249.

16. Letter to the B'nai Brith lodge of Vienna, 1926, in Ernst L. Freud, ed., *Letters of Sigmund Freud, 1879–1939*, 367–68; cited in Pulzer, *Jews*, 12.

17. Harold E. Pagliaro, ed., *The Philosophical Basis of Racism, Studies in Eighteenth Century Culture*, 3: 248. Richard H. Popkin points out that sixteenth-century arguments for the enslavement of New World Indians were also based on a rationale of lesser humanity, i.e., a supposed incapacity for reasoning.

18. Raul Hilberg, *The Destruction of the European Jews*, 286.

19. Romero de Castilla, *Singular Suceso en el Reinado de los Reyes Católicos*, ch. 12.

20. Hilberg, *Destruction*, 10–11.

21. Pulzer, *Jews*, 344.

22. A number of recent books treat this subject interestingly. Raul Hilberg's *Perpetrators, Victims, Bystanders: The Jewish Catastrophe, 1933–45* contains relevant material, as do *Ordinary Men: Reserve Police Battalion 101 and the Final Solution in Poland* by Christopher Browning; *The Holocaust in History* by Michael Marrus; and Ervin Staub's enlightening cultural-psychological study *The Roots of Evil, Origins of Genocide and Other Group Violence*.

23. The reference is to a stormtrooper, or assault-trooper in battle.

24. T. Duster, *Conditions for Guilt-free Massacre*, cited in Ervin Staub, *Roots*, 61.

25. The *New Republic* article citing this attack was written by Charles Krauthammer and appeared under the title "The Humanist Phantom," July 25, 1981. Quoted in Staub, *Roots*, 61–62.

26. Translation by Erna Paris. SOL (Service de l'Ordre Légionnaire) was the forerunner of the French Milice.

27. See Erna Paris, *Unhealed Wounds: France and the Klaus Barbie Affair*, ch. 3.

28. Primo Levi, *The Drowned and the Saved*, trans. by Raymond Rosenthal, 127.

29. Ibid.

30. Raymond-Raoul Lambert, *Carnet d'un témoin*, ed. by Richard Cohen, 83–85.

31. Hilberg, *Destruction*, 234.

32. See Walter Laqueur, *The Terrible Secret: An Investigation into the Suppression of Information about Hitler's Final Solution.*

33. Hilberg, *Destruction,* 243. The rumor that Jews were turned into soap persisted long after the war. According to Hilberg the origin of the story is unknown.

34. *New York Times,* reprinted in *The Globe and Mail,* July 24, 1993.

35. Ibid.

36. Ibid.

37. Andrew Mollo, *To the Death's Head True: The Story of the SS,* 36.

38. Ibid., 35–36.

39. Christopher R. Browning, *Ordinary Men,* 67ff.

40. On the psychology of resistance see Staub, *Roots.*

41. Christian Algreen-Peterson and his parents helped ferry seven thousand Jews to neutral Sweden in September 1943. Interview, "As It Happens," Canadian Broadcasting Corporation, October 11, 1993.

42. Francis Fukuyama, *National Interest* 16 (Summer 1989): 3–18.

43. Jane Kramer's *Letter from Europe* on this subject is the most brilliant depiction of "maimed psyche" I have read anywhere. *New Yorker,* May 25, 1992.

44. Henryk Broder, cited in "Stasi," "Sunday Morning," Canadian Broadcasting Corporation, March 8, 1992.

45. Hans Jorg Geiger, in "Stasi."

46. Myrna Kostash, *Bloodlines: A Journey into Eastern Europe,* 82, 93.

47. *New York Times,* reprinted in *The Globe and Mail,* February 20, 1993.

48. September, 1944. *The Collected Essays, Journalism and Letters of George Orwell,* 3: 234ff.

49. Ibid.

50. The 1993 tragedy at Waco, Texas, where a megalomaniac named David Koresh called himself God and led a flock of followers to their violent death may be the most flamboyant instance of the medieval religious mind-set to emerge in recent years, but there will always be new contenders. One pundit has predicted that the Elvis-is-alive delusion is showing signs of becoming a full-blown religious cult. The Spanish inquisitors of yore would have attacked *this* heresy with alacrity.

51. Paul Laderman, cited in Erna Paris, *The Garden and the Gun,* 256–57.

52. W. A. Carrothers, "The Immigration Problem in Canada," *Queen's Quarterly* (Summer 1929).

53. W. Burton Hurd, "The Case for a Quota," *Queen's Quarterly* (Winter 1929).

54. August 15, 1900, cited in *Dictionary of Canadian Quotations.*

55. *Report of the Citizen's Forum on Canada's Future,* headed by Keith Spicer, 1991.

56. 1990 statistics, *The Economist,* reprinted in *The Globe and Mail,* January 1, 1994.

57. Report by L.A. County District Attorney Ira Reiner, *The Globe and Mail,* October 15, 1993.

58. *Freedom Forum* (Media Studies Center, Columbia University) 8, no.3 (1994).

59. Frances Henry, *The Carribean Diaspora in Toronto,* ch. 6, 9

60. Environics Research Group, cited in Seymour Martin Lipset, *Continental Divide,* 188.

61. Decima Research, *The Globe and Mail,* December 14, 1993.

62. Authored by Donna Young, July, 1993.

63. *Rights Talk,* cited in Jeffrey Simpson, *Faultlines: Struggling for a Canadian Vision,* 95.

64. Staub, *Roots.*

65. Agreement signed December 29, 1993.

66. Ironically King Juan Carlos I was hand-picked by the *Generalissimo* himself.

67. Interview, autumn 1989.

68. December 21, 1992.

Further Reading

The following English-language books from the bibliography may be of interest to the general reader. Some are the classic texts in the field, others are more recent.

Part I—The Story

Abrahams, I. *Jewish Life in the Middle Ages.* 1896.

Ashtor, E. *The Jews of Moslem Spain.* 2 vols. 1973–1984.

Bachrach, Bernard S. *Early Medieval Jewish Policy in Europe.* 1977.

Baer, Y. F. *A History of the Jews in Christian Spain.* 2 vols. 1961.

Baron, S. W. *Social and Religious History of the Jews.* 1965–67.

Beinart, H. *Trujillo: A Jewish Community in Extremadura on the Eve of the Expulsion from Spain.* 1980.

Burke, U. R. *A History of Spain from the Earliest Times to the Death of Ferdinand the Catholic.* 2 vols. 1895.

Castro, Américo. *The Structure of Spanish History.* 1954.

Castro y Rossi, Adolfo de. *History of Religious Intolerance in Spain.* Trans. by T. Parker, 1853.

Chejne, Anwar G. *Islam and the West: The Moriscos, A Cultural and Social History.* 1983.

Creighton, M. *History of the Papacy, 1882–1884.* 1919 ed.

Dundes, A., ed. *The Blood Libel Legend: A Casebook In Anti-Semitic Folklore.* 1991.

Edwards, John. *The Jews in Christian Europe, 1400–1700.* 1988.

Elliott, J. A. *Imperial Spain, 1469–1716.* 1964.

Gerber, Jane, S. *The Jews of Spain: A History of the Sephardic Experience.* 1992.

Gilman, Stephen. *The Spain of Fernando de Rojas: The Intellectual and Social Landscape of La Celestina.* 1972.

Glick, T. F. *Islamic and Christian Spain in the Early Middle Ages.* 1979.

Graetz, H. *History of the Jews.* 8 vols. 1891.

Grayzel, S. *The Church and the Jews in the 13th Century.* 1966.

Hauben, Paul J., ed. *The Spanish Inquisition.* 1969.

Hay, Denys. *Europe in the 14th and 15th Centuries.* 1966.

Hillgarth, J. N. *The Spanish Kingdoms.* 2 vols. 1978.

H'sia, R. Po-chia. *The Myth of Ritual Murder: Jews and Magic in Reformation Germany.* 1988.

Hughes, P. *A History of the Church.* 3 vols. 1949.

Irving, Washington. *Tales of the Alhambra.* 1835.

Kamen, H. *The Spanish Inquisition.* 1965.

———. *Inquisition and Society in Spain.* 1985.

Katz, Jacob. *Exclusiveness and Tolerance: Studies in Jewish-Gentile Relations in Medieval and Modern Times.* 1961.

Lane-Poole, Stanley. *The Moors in Spain.* 1888.

Lea, H. C. *A History of the Inquisition of the Middle Ages.* 3 vols. 1888.

———. *Chapters from the Religious History of Spain.* 1890.

———. *The Moriscos of Spain: Their Conversion and Expulsion.* 1901.

———. *A History of the Inquisition of Spain.* 4 vols. 1905.

Lecky, W. E. M. *History of the Rise of Rationalism in Europe.* 1865.

Lindo, E. H. *The History of the Jews of Spain and Portugal.* 1848.

Longhurst, J. E. *The Age of Torquemada.* 1964.

Marcu, V. *The Expulsion of the Jews from Spain.* Trans. by M. Firth. 1935.

Mariana, Juan de. *The General History of Spain.* 1699.

Merriman, R. B. *The Rise of the Spanish Empire.* 4 vols. 1918–1932.

Netanyahu, B. *The Marranos of Spain from the Late Fourteenth to the Early Sixteenth Century.* 1966.

———. *The Marranos of Spain.* 1973.

Neuman, A. E. *The Jews in Spain.* 1969.

O'Callaghan, Joseph F. *History of Medieval Spain.* 1975.

Poliakov, Léon. *The History of Anti-Semitism: From the Time of Christ to the Court Jews.* 1965.

Popkin, Richard H., and Gordon M. Weiner, eds. *Jewish Christians and Christian Jews: From the Renaissance to the Enlightenment.* 1994.

Prescott, W. H. *History of the Reign of Ferdinand and Isabella the Catholic.* 1837.

Roth, Cecil. *A History of the Marranos.* 1932.

———, ed. *The Ritual Murder Libel and the Jew: Cardinal Ganganelli's Report.* 1935.

Scheindlin, Raymond P. *Wine, Women and Death.* 1986.

Stillman, Norman. *The Jews of Arab Lands: A History and Source Book.* 1979.

Tuchman, Barbara. *A Distant Mirror.* 1978.

Vicens Vives, J. *Approaches to the History of Spain.* Trans. by Joan Connelly Ullman. 1967.

Part II—Epilogue

Arendt, Hannah. *The Origins of Totalitarianism.* 1951, 1968.

Browning, Christopher. *Ordinary Men: Reserve Police Battalion 101 and the Final Solution in Poland.* 1992.

Dawidowicz, Lucy S. *The War against the Jews: 1933–1945.* 1975.

Hilberg, Raul. *The Destruction of the European Jews.* 1985.

———. *Perpetrators, Victims, Bystanders: The Jewish Catastrophe, 1933–45.* 1992.

Laqueur, Walter. *The Terrible Secret: An Investigation into the Suppression of Information about Hitler's Final Solution.* 1980.

Lipset, Seymour Martin. *Continental Divide.* 1990.

Macartney, C. A. *National States and National Minorities.* 1934.

Marrus, Michael. *The Holocaust in History.* 1987.

Mosse, George L. *Toward the Final Solution: A History of Racism.* 1978, 1985.

Paris, Erna. *Unhealed Wounds: France and the Klaus Barbie Affair.* 1985, 1986.

Poliakov, Léon. *The History of Anti-Semitism: From the Time of Christ to the Court Jews.* 1965.

Pulzer, P. *Jews and the German State: The Political History of a Minority.* 1992.

Rappaport, Ernest, A. *Anti-Judaism: A Psychohistory.* 1975.

Richarz, Monika. *Jewish Life in Germany.* Trans. by Stella P. Rosenfeld and Sidney Rosenfeld. 1991.

Rose, Paul Lawrence. *Revolutionary Antisemitism in Germany from Kant to Wagner.* 1990.

Jeffrey Simpson. *Faultlines: Struggling for a Canadian Vision.* 1993.

Staub, Ervin. *The Roots of Evil, Origins of Genocide and Other Group Violence.* 1989.

Stern Strom, Margaret, and William S. Parsons. *Facing History and Ourselves: Holocaust and Human Behaviour.* 1982.

Selected Bibliography

Abrahams, I. *Jewish Life in the Middle Ages.* 1896.

Alcalá Galve, Angel, ed. *Inquisición Española y Mentalidad Inquisitorial.* 1994.

———. *Los Orígenes de la Inquisición en Aragón: S. Pedro Arbués, Martir de la Autonomía Aragonesa.* 1994.

Amador de los Rios, José. *Historia de los Judíos en España y Portugal.* 3 vols. 1875–1876.

Arendt, Hannah. *The Origins of Totalitarianism.* 1951, 1968.

Ashtor, E. *The Jews of Moslem Spain.* 2 vols. 1973–1984.

Ayala, Pero López de. "Crónicas de Pedro I, Enrique II, Juan I y Enrique III de Castile." Ed. by C. Rosell. *BAE* 66, 68.

Azcona, Trasicio de. *Isabel la Católica.* 1964.

Bachrach, Bernard S. *Early Medieval Jewish Policy in Europe.* 1977.

Baer, Y. F. *A History of the Jews in Christian Spain.* 2 vols. 1961.

Ballester y Castell, Rafael. *Las Fuentes narrativas de la historia de España durante la edad media, 1417–1474.* 1927.

Ballesteros Rodriquez, Juan. *La Peste en Córdoba, estudios Cordobeses.* 1982.

Baron, S. W. *Social and Religious History of the Jews.* 1965–1967.

Beinart, H. "The Judaizing Movement in the Order of San Jerónimo." *Studies in History, Scripta Hierosolymita* 7 (1961).

———. "The Converso Community in 16th and 17th Century Spain." *The Sephardi Heritage* 1 (1971). Ed. by R. D. Barnett.

———. "Judíos en las Cortes Reales de España." *Congreso Judío-Latinamericano* (1975).

———. *Trujillo: A Jewish Community in Extremadura on the Eve of the Expulsion from Spain.* 1980.

Benito, Ruano, E. "El Memorial contra los Conversos del Bachiller Marcos García de Mora." *Sefarad* 17 (1957).

———. *Del Problema Judío al Problema Converso.* 1972.

Bernáldez, Andrés. *Memorias del Reinado de los Reyes Católicos.* Ed. by Juan de Mata Carriazo. 1962.

Biraben, Jean-Noël. *Les hommes et la peste en France et dans les pays européens et méditerranés.* Vol. 1. 1975.

315

Bofarull y Sans, F. *Los Judíos en el Territorio de Barcelona.* 1910.

Borchsenius, Poul. *The Three Rings: The History of the Spanish Jews* (trans.). 1963.

Brenner, Frederic, and Yosef Hayim Yerushalmi. *Marranes.* 1992.

Browning, Christopher. *Ordinary Men: Reserve Police Battalion 101 and the Final Solution in Poland.* 1992.

Burke, U. R. *A History of Spain from the Earliest Times to the Death of Ferdinand the Catholic.* 2 vols. 1895.

Caballería, Alfonso de la; Felipe de la; Isabel Vidal de la; Luis de la; Jaime de la; Juan de la. See Fonds espagnols.

Cabezudo Astrain, J. *Inventario de Alhajas de Vidal Abnarrabi, Notario Martín de la Catalayud.* Archives of Zaragoza.

———. "La Expulsión de los Judíos Zaragonzanos." *Sefarad* 14 (1954).

———. "La Expulsión de los Judíos Zaragonazos." *Sefarad* 15 (1955).

———. "Testamentos de Judíos Aragoneses." *Sefarad* 16 (1956).

———. "Los Conversos Aragoneses Segun los Procesos de la Inquisición." *Sefarad* 18 (1958).

Cagigas, Isidro de, ed. *Libro Verde de Aragón.* 1929.

Canellas-Lopez, A. "La Judería Zaragozana." Conference on the Jewish Quarter of Saragossa, Saragossa. 1974.

Cantera Burgos, F. "Fernando de Pulgar y los Conversos." *Sefarad* 4 (1944).

———. *Alvar Garcia de Santa María y Su Familia de Conversos.* 1952.

Caro Baroja, J. *Los Judíos en la España Moderna y Contemporánea.* 3 vols. 1961.

Carpentier, Elisabeth. *Une ville devant la peste: Orvieto et la peste noire de 1348.* 1972.

Carrerras, Panchon. *La peste y los Médicos en la España del Renacimiento.* 1976.

Carriazo, J de Mata, ed. *Crónica de Alvaro de Luna.* 1940.

———. *Crónica del Halconero de Juan II.* 1946.

Carrothers, W. A. "The Immigration Problem in Canada." *Queen's Quarterly* (Summer 1929).

Castro, Américo. *The Structure of Spanish History.* 1954.

Castro y Rossi, Adolfo de. *History of Religious Intolerance in Spain.* Trans. by T. Parker. 1853.

———. *Historia de los Judíos en España.* 1847.

Catalogue des manuscrits espagnols et portugais. Ed. by Alfred Morel-Fatio. Bibliothèque Nationale, Paris. 1892.

Chabás, R. "Estudio sobre los Sermones Valencianos de San Vicente Ferrer." *RABM* (1903).

Chejne, Anwar G. *Islam and the West: The Moriscos, A Cultural and Social History.* 1983.

The Chronicle of Jean de Venette, 1340–1368. Trans. by Jean Birdsell. 1953.

Clemencin, Diego. *Memorias de la Real Academia de la Historia.* 1821.

Conde de Castellan. *Un Complot Terrorista en el Siglo XV.*

Creighton, M. *History of the Papacy.* 1882–1884. 1919 ed.

de la Pinte Llorente, M. *La Inquisición Española y los Problemas de la Cultura y de la Intolerancia.* 1943.

Danon, A. "Recueil de romances judeo-espanoles." *REJ* 32 (1903).

Dante Alighieri. *Divina Commedia.* Italian manuscript, Codex 74, fol. iv, reproduced in the *Horizon Book of the Middle Ages,* 1968, 286.

Dánvila, F. "El robo de la Judería en Valencia en 1391." *BAH* 7 (1886).

Dawidowicz, Lucy S. *The War against the Jews: 1933–1945*. 1975.

Diaz-Mas, Paloma. *Sephardim: The Jews from Spain*. Trans. by George K.. Zuker. 1992.

Dominguez Ortiz, A. *Los Conversos de Orígen Judío despues de la Expulsión*. 1955.

———. *Los Judeoconversos en España y America*. 1978.

Dormer, Diego José. *Anales de Aragón*. 1697.

Dozy, R. *Recherches sur l'histoire de la littérature de l'Espagne pendant le moyen age*. 3 vols. 1965.

Dundes, A., ed. *The Blood Libel Legend: A Casebook in Anti-Semitic Folklore*. 1991.

Edwards, John. *The Jews in Christian Europe, 1400–1700*. 1988.

———. "Race and Religion in 15th and 16th Century Spain: The 'Purity of Blood' Laws Revisited." *International World Congress of Jewish Studies* 2 (1990).

Elliott, J. A. *Imperial Spain, 1469–1716*. 1964.

Espina, Alonso de. *Fortalitium Fidei*. 1511.

Fages, H. *Histoire de Saint Vincent Ferrier*. 1892–1894.

Falcón Pérez, Maria Isabel. "Notas sobre los Corredores de Comercio de Zaragoza en el Siglo XV." *Aragón en la Edad Media, Estudios de Economía y Sociedad*. 1984.

Fita, Fidel. "La Inquisición y el Santo Niño de la Guardia." *BAH* 11 (1887).

———. "El Proceso y Quema de Jucé Franco." *BAH* 11 (1887).

———. *La España Hebrea*. 2 vols. 1889–1898.

Floriano, A. *El Tribunal del Santo Oficio en Aragón*. 1925.

Fonds espagnols. Bibliothèque Nationale, Paris. Source material on Alfonso de la Caballería, Juan de Pero Sánchez, Luis de la Caballería, Juan de la Caballería, . Isabel Vidal de la Caballería, Jaime de la Caballería, Jaime Sánchez, Felipe de la Caballería.

Freedom Forum (Media Studies Center, Columbia University) 8, no. 3 (1994).

Froissart, Jean. *Chroniques, 1392–1396*. 1871 ed.

Fukuyama, Francis. "The End of History." *National Interest* 16 (Summer 1989).

Garcia Carcel, R. *Orígenes de la Inquisición Española: El Tribunal de Valencia 1478–1530*. 1976.

Garcia de Trasmiera, D. *Epitome de la Santa Vida*. 1664.

Gaspar y Remiro, M. *Los Cronistas Hispano-Judíos*. 1920.

Gerber, Jane, S. *The Jews of Spain: A History of the Sephardic Experience*. 1992.

Gilman, Stephen. *The Spain of Fernando de Rojas: The Intellectual and Social Landscape of La Celestina*. 1972.

Glick, T. F. *Islamic and Christian Spain in the Early Middle Ages*. 1979.

Gonzalez Davilá, Gil. *Historia de Enrique III*. 1405.

Gracia Boix, Rafael. *Autos de Fe y Causas de la Inquisición de Cordoba*. 1983.

Graetz, H. *History of the Jews*. 8 vols. 1891.

Grayzel, S. *The Church and the Jews in the 13th Century*. 1966.

Haliczer, S. "The Castilian Urban Patriciate and the Jewish Expulsions of 1480–92." *AHR* 78 (1973).

Hauben, Paul J., ed. *The Spanish Inquisition*. 1969.

Hay, Denys. *Europe in the 14th and 15th Centuries*. 1966.

Henry, Frances. *The Carribean Diaspora in Toronto*. 1994.

Hilberg, Raul. *The Destruction of the European Jews*. 1985.

Hilberg, Raul. *Perpetrators, Victims, Bystanders: The Jewish Catastrophe, 1933–45.* 1992.

Hillgarth, J. N. *The Spanish Kingdoms.* 2 vols. 1978.

H'sia, R. Po-chia. *The Myth of Ritual Murder: Jews and Magic in Reformation Germany.* 1988.

Hughes, P. *A History of the Church.* Vol. 3. 1949.

Hurd, W. Burton. "The Case for a Quota." *Queen's Quarterly* (Winter 1929).

Irving, Washington. *Tales of the Alhambra.* 1835.

Izquierdo Trol, F. *San Pedro de Arbués, Primer Inquisidor de Aragón.* 1941.

"Jews and Conversos: Studies in Society and the Inquisition." *Eighth World Congress of Jewish Studies.* Ed. by Y. Kaplan. 1985.

Kamen, H. *The Spanish Inquisition.* 1965.

———. *Inquisition and Society in Spain.* 1985.

Katz, Jacob. *Exclusiveness and Tolerance: Studies in Jewish-Gentile Relations in Medieval and Modern Times.* 1961.

Kayserling, M. "Notes sur l'Histoire des Juifs d'Espagne." *REJ* 28 (1894).

Kostash, Myrna. *Bloodlines: A Journey into Eastern Europe.* 1993.

Kriegel, M. "Un trait de psychologie sociale dans les pays méditerranés du bas moyen-age: le juif comme intouchable." *Annales ESC* (March–April 1976).

———. "La prise d'une décision: l'expulsion des juifs d'Espagne en 1492." *RH* 260 (1978).

Ladera Quesada, M. A. *Notas sobre la Política Confesional de los Reyes Católicos.* 1966.

———. "Un Empresitito de los Judíos de Avila y Segovia para la Guerra de Granada." *Sefarad* 35 (1975).

Lafuente, M. *Historia General de España.* Vols. 5 and 6. 1889.

Lambert, Raymond-Raoul. *Carnet d'un témoin.* Ed. by Richard Cohen. 1985

Lane-Poole, Stanley. *The Moors in Spain.* 1888.

Laqueur, Walter. *The Terrible Secret: An Investigation into the Suppression of Information about Hitler's Final Solution.* 1980.

Lea, H. C. *A History of the Inquisition of the Middle Ages.* 3 vols. 1888.

———. "El Santo Niño de La Guardia." *EHR* 4 (1889).

———. *Chapters from the Religious History of Spain.* 1890.

———. "Ferrand Martinez and the Massacre of 1391." *AHR* 1 (1896).

———. *The Moriscos of Spain: Their Conversion and Expulsion.* 1901

———. *A History of the Inquisition of Spain.* 4 vols. 1905.

Lecky, W. E. M. *History of the Rise of Rationalism in Europe.* 1865.

Leon Tello, Pilar. *Judíos de Avila.* 1963.

Levi, Primo. *The Drowned and the Saved.* Trans. by Raymond Rosenthal. 1988.

Lévi-Provençal, E. "España Musulmana, 711–1031." In *Historia de España.* Ed. by R. Menéndez Pidal. Vol. 4. 1950.

Levi, Yehuda ha-. *Antología Poética.* Trans. by Rosa Castillo. 1983.

Lindo, E. H. *The History of the Jews of Spain and Portugal.* 1848.

Lipset, Seymour Martin. *Continental Divide.* 1990.

Llorca, Bernardino. "San Vicente y el Problema de las Conversiones de los Judíos." *IV Congreso de la Historia de la Corona de Aragón* 1 (1955).

———. "San Vicente Ferrer y Su Labor en la Conversion de los Judíos." *Razón y Fe* 152 (1955).

Llorca, Bernardino. "La Inquisición Española y Los Conversos Judíos o 'Marranos.' " *Sefarad* 2 (1942).

Llorente, Juan Antonio. *Histoire Critique de l'Inquisition d'Espagne.* 1817.

Loeb, Isidore. "Le Saint Enfant de La Guardia." *REJ* 16 (1887).

———. *Joseph Hacohen et les croniqeurs juifs.* 1888.

———. "Le Livre Alboraique." *REJ* 18 (1889).

———. "Polémicistes chrétiens et juifs en France et en Espagne." *REJ* 18 (1889).

———. "Le Sac des Juiveries de Valence et de Madrid en 1391." *REJ* 19 (1890).

Longhurst, J. E. *The Age of Torquemada.* 1964.

Macartney, C. A. *National States and National Minorities.* 1934.

Mackay, A. "Popular Movements and Pogroms in Fifteenth Century Castile." *Past and Present* 55 (1972).

Maravell, J. A. *El Pensamiento Político de Fernando El Católico.* 1956.

Marcu, Valeria. *The Expulsion of the Jews from Spain.* Trans. by Moray Firth. 1935.

Mariana, Juan de. *The General History of Spain.* 1699.

Marin Padilla, E. "Relación Judeoconversa durante la Segunda Mitad del Siglo XV en Aragón." *Sefarad* 42 (1982).

Marrus, Michael. *The Holocaust in History.* 1987.

Martinez Millan, José. *La Hacienda de la Inquisición, 1478–1700.* 1984.

Martinez Moreno, M. *Historia del Martirio del Santo Niño de La Guardia.* 1785.

Marx, A. "The Expulsion of the Jews from Spain." *JQR* 20 (1908).

Menédez y Pelayo, M. *Historia de los Heterodoxes Españoles.* Ed. by E. Sánchez Reyes. Vol. 1. 1952.

Menéndez Pidal, R., ed. *Historia de España.* 1947–.

Merriman, R. B. *The Rise of the Spanish Empire.* 4 vols. 1918–1932.

Mezan, S. *De Gabirol à Abravanel: Juifs espagnols, promoteurs de la Renaissance.* 1936.

Millás Vallicrosa, J. M. "San Vicente Ferrer y el Antisemitismo." *Sefarad* 10 (1950).

———. "Un Tratado Anónimo de Polemica. . . ." *Sefarad* 16 (1953).

Mollo, Andrew. *To the Death's Head True: The Story of the SS.* 1982.

Monsalvo Antón, José M. *Un Conflicto Social: El Antisemitismo en la Corona de Castilla en la Baja Edad Media.* 1985.

Motis Dolader, Miguel Angel. *La Expulsión de los Judíos de Aragón.* 2 vols. 1990.

Mosse, George L. *Toward the Final Solution: A History of Racism.* 1978.

Netanyahu, B. *The Marranos of Spain from the Late Fourteenth to the Early Sixteenth Century.* 1966.

———. *The Marranos of Spain.* 1973.

Neubauer, A. *Medieval Jewish Chronicles.* 1895.

Neuman, A. E. *The Jews in Spain.* 1969.

O'Callaghan, Joseph F. *History of Medieval Spain.* 1975.

Orwell, George. *The Collected Essays, Journalism and Letters of George Orwell.* Vol. 3. 1968.

Ortiz de Zuñiga, Diego. *Anales de Sevilla.* 1795.

Pacios López, A. *La Disputa de Tortosa.* 2 vols. 1957.

Pagliaro, Harold E., ed. *The Philosophical Basis of Racism.* Vol. 3 of *Studies in Eighteenth Century Culture.* 1973.

Palencia, Alfonso de. *Crónica de Enrique IV.* Ed. by A. Paz y Mélia. 4 vols. 1904–1908.

———. *Crónica de D. Alvaro de Luna.* Ed. by Juan de Mata Carriazo. 1940.

Palencia, Alfonso de. *Crónica de D. Juan II.* Ed. by Juan de Mata Carriazo. 1946.

———. *Notas Biograficas.* Ed. by Juan de Mata Carriazo.

Paris, Erna. *Unhealed Wounds: France and the Klaus Barbie Affair.* 1985, 1986.

———. *The Garden and the Gun.* 1988, 1991.

Paz y Mélia, A. *El Cronista Alfonso de Palencia.* 1914.

Pérez de Guzmán, Ferán. *Generaciónes y Semblanzas.* Ed. by J. Dominguez Bordona. 1954.

———. *Crónica del Señor Rey Don Juan.* 1779 ed.

Pelaum, H. "Une ancienne satire espagnole contre les Marranes." *REJ* 86 (1927).

Pero Sánchez, Juan de. See Fonds espagnols.

Pinto Llorente, M. *La Inquisición Española.* 1948.

Poliakov, Léon, *The History of Anti-Semitism: From the Time of Christ to the Court Jews.* 1965.

Popkin, Richard H., and Gordon M. Weiner, eds. *Jewish Christians and Christian Jews: From the Renaissance to the Enlightenment.* 1994.

Posnanski, A. D. "Le Colloque de Tortose et de San Mateo." *REJ* 74, 75 (1922, 1923).

Prager, Dennis, and Joseph Telushkin. *Why the Jews?* 1983.

Prescott, W. H. *History of the Reign of Ferdinand and Isabella the Catholic.* 1837.

Pulgar, Fernando de. *Crónica de los Reyes Católicos.* Ed. by Juan de Mata Carriazo. 1943.

———. *Claros Varones de Castilla.* Ed. by J. Domínguez Bordona. 1954.

Pulzer, P. *Jews and the German State: The Political History of a Minority.* 1992.

Rappaport, Ernest A. *Anti-Judaism: A Psychohistory.* 1975.

Regné, Jean. *A History of the Jews in Aragon, Regesta and Documents, 1213–1327.* Ed. by Yom Tov Assis. 1978.

Renan, E. *Averroes et Averroisme.* 1861.

Resnick, S. "The Jew as Portrayed in Early Spanish Literature." *Hispania* 34 (1951).

Richarz, Monika. *Jewish Life in Germany.* Trans. by Stella P. Rosenfeld and Sidney Rosenfeld. 1991.

Romero de Castilla, M. *Singular Suceso en el Reinado de los Reyes Católicos.* 1945.

Rose, Paul Lawrence. *Revolutionary Antisemitism in Germany from Kant to Wagner.* 1990.

Roth, Cecil. *A History of the Marranos.* 1932.

———, ed. *The Ritual Murder Libel and the Jew: Cardinal Ganganelli's Report.* 1935.

Roth, Norman. "The Jews and the Moslem Conquest of Spain." *JST* 37 (1976).

———. *Maimonides: Essays and Texts. 850th Anniversary.* Hispanic seminar of medieval studies. 1985.

Ruiz, Juan. *The Book of Good Love, 1343.* Trans. R. Mignani and M. Dicesare. 1970.

Sánchez, Jaime. See Fonds espagnols.

Scheindlin, Raymond P. *Wine, Women and Death.* 1986.

Scholberg, K. R. *Sátira y Invectiva en la España Medieval.* 1971.

Serrano, Luciano. *Los Conversos D. Pablo de Santa María y D. Alfonso de Cartagena.* 1942.

Serrano y Sanz, Manuel. *Orígenes de la dominación Española en América.* 1918.

Shepard, Sanford. "Crypto-Jews in Spanish Literature." *Judaism* 19 (1970).

Sicroff, A. A. *Les Controverses des Statuts de Pureté de Sang en Espagne du XVe au XVIIe siecle.* 1960.

Simpson, Jeffrey. *Faultlines: Struggling for a Canadian Vision.* 1993.

Singerman, Robert. *Spanish and Portuguese Jewry: A Classified Bibliography.* 1993.

Sola-Solé, J., and S. E. Rose. "Judíos y Conversos en la Poesía Cortesana del Siglo XV: El Estilo Poligloto de Fray Diego de Valencia." *Hispanic Review* 44 (1976).

Staub, Ervin. *The Roots of Evil, Origins of Genocide and Other Group Violence.* 1989.

Stern Strom, Margaret, and William S. Parsons. *Facing History and Ourselves: Holocaust and Human Behaviour.* 1982.

Stillman, Norman. "Aspects of Jewish Life in Islamic Spain." In *Aspects of Jewish Life in Islamic Spain.* Ed. by Paul E. Szarmach. 1979.

———. *The Jews of Arab Lands: A History and Source Book.* 1979.

Suárez Fernández, L. *Documentos Acerca de la Expulsión de los Judíos.* 1964.

Taylor, Charles. *Hegel.* 1975.

Torquemada, Juan de. *Tractatus contra Madianitas et Ismaelitas.* Ed. by N. López Martinez and V. Proaño Gil. 1957.

Tuchman, Barbara. *A Distant Mirror.* 1978.

Valera, Diego de. *Memorial de Diversas Hazañas, Crónica de Enrique IV.* Ed. by Juan de Mata Carriazo. 1941.

Valois, Noel. *La France et le grand schisme de l'occident.* 4 vols. 1896–1902.

Vendrell, F. "Aportaciones Documentales para el Estudio de la Familia Caballería." *Sefarad* 3 (1943).

———. "La Política Proselitista del Rey D. Fernando I." *Sefarad* 10 (1950).

———. "La actividad proselitista de San Vicente Ferrer durante el reinado de Fernando I de Aragón." *Sefarad* 13 (1953).

———. "En Torno a la Confirmación Real, en Aragón, de la Pragmatica de Benedicto XIII." *Sefarad* 20 (1960).

Verga, Solomon ibn. *Shebet Yehuda.* Ed. and trans. by Francisco Cantero-Burgos. 1927.

Verlinden, C. "La grande peste de 1348 en Espagne." *Revue Belge de Philologie et d'Histoire* 17 (1938).

Vicens Vives, J. *Approaches to the History of Spain.* Trans. by Joan Connelly Ullman. 1967.

Walsh, W. *Isabella of Spain.* 1939.

Wigoder, Geoffrey, ed. *Encyclopedic Dictionary of Judaica.* 1974.

Wolff, Philippe. "The 1391 Pogrom in Spain: Social Crisis or Not?" *Past and Present* 50 (February 1971).

Yerushalmi, Yosef Hayim. "Assimilation and Racial Anti-Semitism: The Iberian and the German Models." Leo Baeck Memorial Lecture. 1982.

Zurita y Castro, Jerónimo de. *Anales de la Corona de Aragón.* 1610.

Index